MW01046687

UNFINISHED DREAMS:

COMMUNITY HEALING AND THE REALITY OF ABORIGINAL SELF-GOVERNMENT

Most writing on Aboriginal self-determination focuses on the constitutional or structural aspects of self-government or related philosophical issues. In this book, Wayne Warry argues that self-government can be realized only when individuals are secure in their cultural identity and can contribute to the transformation of their communities.

Warry draws on his research among Nishnawbe communities, as well as on the reports and recommendations of the Royal Commission on Aboriginal Peoples. Case studies are used to illustrate the processes of community development and cultural revitalization that are essential precursors to self-government. Warry's notion of 'community healing' involves efforts to rebuild the human foundations for self-governing Aboriginal societies.

The book analyses key areas such as health care and the judicial and political systems where Aboriginal peoples are engaged in practical everyday struggles to improve their communities. Central to these Aboriginal approaches to change is the need for holistic solutions to complex social problems. The search for these solutions is set against the broader political environment, which includes Euro-Canadian assumptions, government, policy, and post-colonial practices. The book also addresses the nature of applied social scientific research in Aboriginal communities and the need for collaborative, culturally appropriate research methods.

WAYNE WARRY is Associate Professor in the Department of Anthropology at McMaster University.

WAYNE WARRY

Unfinished Dreams: Community Healing and the Reality of Aboriginal Self-Government

UNIVERSITY OF TORONTO PRESS INCORPORATED
Toronto Buffalo London

Toronto Buffalo London
Printed in Canada

ISBN 0-8020-0954-9 (cloth)
ISBN 0-8020-7917-2 (paper)

Printed on acid-free paper

Canadian Cataloguing in Publication Data

Warry, Wayne
Unfinished dreams: community healing and the reality of Aboriginal self-government

Includes biographical references and index.
ISBN 0-8020-0954-9 (bound)   ISBN 0-8020-7917-2 (pbk.)

1. Native peoples – Canada – Politics and government.*   2. Native peoples – Government relations.*   I. Title.

E92.W37 1998   323.1'197071   C98-930077-3

This book has been published with the help of a grant from the Humanities and Social Sciences Federation of Canada, using funds provided by the Social Sciences and Humanities Research Council of Canada.

University of Toronto Press acknowledges the financial assistance to its publishing program of the Canada Council for the Arts and the Ontario Arts Council.

Contents

Acknowledgments

The research on which this book is based has been funded by many organizations, foundations, and agencies. I would like to acknowledge the assistance of the Social Science and Humanities Research Council, the Ontario Mental Health Association, the Laidlaw Foundation, the Ontario Child, Family and Policy Research Centre, the Ontario Solicitor-General, the Union of Ontario Indians, Medical Services Branch, Health and Welfare Canada; and Mamaweswen, the North Shore Tribal Council. Much of my recent work has been conducted in the Mamaweswen, North Shore Tribal Council area in Ontario. Royalties from the sale of this book are going to Mamaweswen's Anishnabek Health Board in support of traditional medicine initiatives.

My understanding of Aboriginal issues was first formulated while I was working at the Ontario Native Council on Justice. There I met many dedicated people who helped me to understand the complex issues that Aboriginal people confront on a daily basis. I would like to thank Carol Montagnes, Carrie Hayward, Sylvia Maracle, Alex Skead, Art Solomon, and Bob Watts for their guidance during my early entrée into Aboriginal affairs. Many individuals have given graciously of their time to speak with me about issues of self-government and community healing during the past several years. I wish especially to acknowledge the time and assistance given to me by Anna Marie Abitong, Steve Beaupré, Chief Alfred Bisaillon, Ernest Bisaillon, Darrell Boissoneau, Marlene Brant Castellano, Lindy Chiblow, Chief Earl Commanda, Ian Cowie, Gloria Daybutch, Arnelda Jacobs, Kienna Jones, Peter Marks, Lisa Meawasige, Chief Jeanne Naponse, Carolyn Noochtai, Marlene Nose, Gloria Pelletier, Rosana Pellizzari, Brenda Rivers, Carol Schwana, Doug Sider, Chief Angus Toulous, Nelson Toulous, Carol Trudeau, and Harvey Trudeau.

Mike Evans, Heather Young-Leslie, Patricia Seymour, and Christopher Justice let me talk about my ideas and helped me think about the shape and structure of the book. A special thanks to Christopher Justice for his comments on an earlier draft and for the many hours he spent discussing issues of community healing. Many people gave generously of their time to read early drafts and to provide comments that have been instrumental in revising particular arguments and discussions. My thanks to Chief Earl Commanda, Caroline Francis, Carrie Hayward, Don Jaffray, Carol LaPrairie, Carol Montagnes, Marlene Nose, Richard Preston, Jennifer Ranford, Rupert Ross, Carol Trudeau, and Dennis Willms for their time and comments. My thanks also to Virgil Duff, editor at the University of Toronto Press, to Darlene Money for her careful copy-editing of the manuscript, and to the two anonymous readers who provided comments on the draft.

My thanks also to the many students whose work has informed my own: Kathy Buddle, Judy Clarke, Jennifer Dawson, Marcia Hoyle, Ed Koenig, Marion Marr, Teresa McCarthy, Gwen Reimer, and Wendy Russell. To the staff and faculty in the Department of Anthropology at McMaster University I wish to extend my sincere thanks for their ongoing support and collegiality. I consider myself to be blessed to be able to work, day in and out, in a friendly and intellectually invigorating environment.

My parents, Dorothy and Bill, have blessed me with a lifetime of encouragement. My special thanks to family and friends, particularly the Old Crows, for their ongoing interest in Aboriginal issues – it was their questions and concerns that provided the stimulus for me to write this book. Finally, to Marion, thank you for reminding me that there is more to life than a book, but little more to life than love and friendship.

Abbreviations

AFHJSC	Aboriginal Family Healing Joint Steering Committee
AFN	Assembly of First Nations
AHA	Aboriginal Health Authority
AHAC	Aboriginal Health Access Centre
AHWS	Aboriginal Healing and Wellness Strategy
AIAI	Association of Iroquois and Allied Indians
CHR	Community health representative
CIT	Crisis intervention team
DIAND	Department of Indian Affairs and Northern Development
GWA	General Welfare Assistance
HPC	Health planning circle
MFN	Mississauga First Nation
MSB	Medical Services Branch, Health and Welfare Canada
NAN	Nishnawbe-Aski Nation
NIHB	Non-insured health benefits
NNADAP	National Native Alcohol and Drug Abuse Program
NSTC	North Shore Tribal Council (Mamaweswen)
ONCJ	Ontario Native Council on Justice
ONWA	Ontario Native Women's Association
OPP	Ontario Provincial Police
PAR	Participatory-action research
PTO	Political/tribal organization
RCAP	Royal Commission on Aboriginal Peoples
RCMP	Royal Canadian Mounted Police
TEK	Traditional environmental knowledge
UOI	Union of Ontario Indians (Anishnabek Nation)

UNFINISHED DREAMS:

COMMUNITY HEALING AND THE REALITY OF ABORIGINAL SELF-GOVERNMENT

We are confident that, given adequate financial resources, we have the human resources and strength to heal our community. That is our dream.

Roy Christopher, Canim Lake Band, Canim Lake BC

Our passion for anthropological knowledge is paradoxically xenophobic. Therefore, our many studies of world cultures are soulless, replacing the common bonding of humanity and its shared wisdom with bits of information that have no way of getting to us deeply, of nourishing and transforming our sense of ourselves.

Thomas Moore, *Care of the Soul*

Hope is a dangerous thing.

Frank Darabont, *The Shawshank Redemption*

[Change is] like cleaning a caribou. You've got to do it slowly.

Elder Charlotte Rich, Davis Inlet NF

Introduction: Dreams, Visions, and Plans

This book examines the rhetoric and the reality of Aboriginal self-government. It is concerned with the *process* of community healing and self-determination. I attempt to move beyond a discussion of Aboriginal rights, constitutional issues, or current socioeconomic conditions to an examination of the pragmatic struggles Aboriginal communities are engaged in as they go about the business of becoming self-governing. I have often been disappointed in portrayals of the self-government 'question' in the media. Much of the rhetoric about self-government seems to be out of sync with the thoughts and aspirations of Aboriginal community members. Confusion about the cost and meaning of self-government among mainstream Canadians is readily apparent. This confusion is also found in Aboriginal communities where 'public opinion' includes suspicion and confusion about government agendas for self-government, fears that basic rights will be lost, and concern that a long-standing trust relationship with the federal government will be jeopardized.

I examine self-government from a community-based perspective. The notion of self-government is ultimately linked to emotional, legal, and philosophical arguments concerning the inherent rights of Aboriginal people. However, the pragmatic foundation of self-government rests on First Nations' capacity for independence and self-reliance in a variety of fields. I describe how Aboriginal people are confronting 'on the ground' the many obstacles to self-government, so as to impress upon the reader that self-government is inevitable. My objective, then, is simple: I hope that by the end of this book the reader will recognize that it will be years, perhaps decades, before self-government truly arrives. Yet Aboriginal people are already managing their own affairs in many jurisdictions. They are in the process of healing their communities, and of building community capacity for self-government. Self-government, in the sense of self-actualization and self-reliance, has already arrived for many Aboriginal people. This process of self-determination exists regardless of constitutional negotiations. While constitutional recognition of the inherent right to self-government may be important symbolically, it is no more significant than the actual process of self-determination that already exists.

For me, the reality of self-government is unthreatening yet exceedingly complex. I argue that self-government is inevitable; indeed I suggest that it already exists in its incipient form. If we regard self-determination as a process that arbitrarily began with Aboriginal reactions to the 1969 White Paper, then we are able to observe a slow change in Aboriginal communities that continues today in the form of increasing self-reliance, self-definition, and self-sufficiency. Self-government can be viewed as the end result of this process. Given the inherently conservative nature of both the federal government and Aboriginal communities, the process of self-government is gradual, cumulative, and incremental. Self-government entails no revolutionary change, even though the distant end-point – political autonomy in a broad range of jurisdictions – is a radical departure from the status quo.

The disjuncture between the rhetoric and reality of self-government is well recognized by Aboriginal people who fear self-government on the grounds that 'they are not ready,' who criticize Aboriginal leadership as incompetent, or who argue that their communities must heal before they can become self-governing. The reality is that the vast majority of Aboriginal communities have yet to catch up to the rhetoric of many politicians – they wish to go slowly and are as confused about self-government as mainstream Canadians. This book attempts to answer concerns about what self-government actually entails – questions about how it will work, what it will cost, and what the parameters of Aboriginal power will be – by demonstrating the approaches that Aboriginal communities are developing to solve complex social problems. The solutions to these problems are both culturally appropriate and cost efficient.

Community development, capacity building, and healing are the major foci of the book. I examine these processes by analysing three interrelated areas that are grouped under the rubric of community healing. These topics are health care, mental health, and justice. This focus derives naturally from my work as an applied anthropologist during the past decade, work primarily concerned with understanding the development of health and social services both on and off reserve. But my emphasis on social development also stems from the assumption that the human resource capacity in Aboriginal communities must be increased in order for self-government to become a reality.

Two recurring themes run through the book. The first concerns the meaning of 'cultural revitalization,' a process that is central to community healing. I analyse the way culture, custom, and tradition are spoken about, and debated, in Aboriginal communities. This discussion is difficult because in generalizing about how people speak of revitalizing traditions it is possible to mask the degree of cultural diversity that exists among First Nations. The second theme is more elusive. It concerns the lessons mainstream Canadians can learn from Aboriginal approaches to healing. Aboriginal approaches to family and community health, mental health, and justice can provide Canadians with important insights into the nature of mainstream institutions and organizations. Central to these Aboriginal approaches is the need for holistic solutions to complex social problems.

This book, then, examines the problems and obstacles that confront Aboriginal people as they attempt to seize control of their institutions from the obstinate tentacles of the state. Along the way, I hope to obliterate many of the stereotypes that, to my mind, only confuse and confound our attempts to understand Aboriginal people. I show how arguments made concerning Aboriginal rights, the evils of colonialism, or the nature of Aboriginal culture and spirituality are often simplistic, and sometimes irrelevant, when measured against the actual complexities of Aboriginal community life.

Chapter 1 reviews the social and political environment facing Aboriginal people. I speak briefly about public attitudes to Aboriginal issues, examine notions of Aboriginal rights, and detail two critical issues related to self-government – the need for a resolution to land claims, and the development of regional political organizations. I argue that we must elevate the quality of public education and public debate in order to improve the political climate in which the project of self-government is taking place. This discussion speaks to issues that are beyond the focus of the book, but that none the less are critical to the self-government process. Chapter 2 examines the 'ill-health' of Aboriginal communities, and documents the current social, economic, and health status of Aboriginal people. The statistics in this chapter are dismal, and anyone who is concerned with Aboriginal affairs will already be aware of the fundamental discrepancies in standards of living that exist between Native and mainstream Canadians. My intent in this chapter is to point out the basic linkages between sociopolitical, cultural, and economic behaviours so as to emphasize the need for holistic and culturally appropriate community development. Chapters 3, 4, and 5 address issues specific to three aspects of community healing – health care, mental health, and justice services. These chapters examine the complex and painstaking work – including research and planning – that communities are engaged in as they attempt to wrest control over services and institutions from the government in order to better address the problems facing their communities. Chapter 6 revisits many of the processes outlined in the three previous chapters by analysing the relationship between individual and community healing. But this analysis is overlain with new discussion about the nature of Aboriginal community life, and the need for structural change within First Nations. The conclusion addresses the role of social science research, examines government reactions to the recommendations of the Royal Commission on Aboriginal Peoples, and summarizes the relationship between community healing and self-government.

There is, of course, great cultural and political diversity among Aboriginal communities in Canada. This essential truth means that there can be no single form or pattern to self-government. It is important, then, to acknowledge that my experience is primarily with Nishnawbe (Ojibwa) communities. During the past six years I have been fortunate to develop a good working relationship with several communities belonging to Mamaweswen, the North Shore Tribal Council (NSTC). Mamaweswen is a group of seven First Nations linked by road from Sudbury to Sault Ste Marie in north-central Ontario. Most of my examples and case studies are drawn from my experience working for these communities, specifically for the Anishnabek Health Board.

North Shore First Nations, as characterized by community members themselves, are 'less traditional' than those located in the remote north. In other words, they are communities that through historical circumstance and geographic location have experienced the full force of the government's assimilationist policies. As a result, the contemporary portrait of community life that emerges here may contrast dramatically with the reader's more traditional images of Native communities. These images include, for example, portraits of hunters and trappers who continue traditional lifestyles in the bush, and pictures of Native people emersed in the traditional practice of Aboriginal spirituality. The reader should understand, for example, that authentic Ojibwa political and spiritual practice may involve asking an elder to begin a band council meeting or retreat with a prayer – the Lord's Prayer, delivered in English. I present a picture of contemporary spiritual practice where many Native people are confused about, or even fearful of, traditional practices such as the sweat lodge or shaking tent. Along the North Shore, hunting is a recreational activity and arguments about fishing rights involve access to commercial enterprises on a scale previously unknown in Aboriginal communities. North Shore First Nations are inherently complex, and sometimes deeply divided, communities. I hope that this understanding gives rise to a portrait of First Nations that, rather than stressing culture loss or decay, emphasizes the reality of a contemporary and vibrant Aboriginal culture.

I ask the reader to indulge me by reading a brief summary of my background, so that my own bias, anthropological interests, and areas of expertise can be made explicit. When I was an undergraduate student at McMaster University in the early 1970s, I was oblivious to many important issues involving Aboriginal people. This was a time of great political activity for Aboriginal people, when, for example, an armed protest occurred at Anishnabe Park near Kenora, foreshadowing the events of Oka some sixteen years later (see Hedican 1995: 206). The American Indian Movement and National Indian Brotherhood (the precursor to the Assembly of First Nations) was active in Canada. It was a time when the concept of Aboriginal rights was first being articulated. Raised only thirty-five kilometres from Six Nations reserve, I had no direct experience with Native people, and met no Native students at university. This was a time when anthropologists were making important contributions to Aboriginal affairs, for example, through the program in the Anthropology of Development at McGill University (ibid: 18–19). And although there were professors at McMaster, like Richard Preston, who were active in applied anthropology, I took away from my classes a very traditional view of Aboriginal life – so much so that when I completed my bachelor's degree I remained largely ignorant of the abysmal conditions facing Aboriginal people on reserve.

As a Ph.D. student at the Australian National University, I pursued graduate fieldwork in the Papua New Guinea Highlands. I focused on the study of sociopolitical change and contemporary issues in a culture that, despite its geographic isolation, had been heavily influenced by Christianity, commercialism, and Western culture (Warry 1987a). The experience was instrumental in shaping my ideas about the fluid and synthetic nature of culture. Aboriginal issues, advocacy, and applied anthropology lay beyond my field of view until I returned to Canada in 1983. Unable to secure a university position, I began applying for non-academic jobs. I obtained a job as a contract researcher with the Ontario Native Council on Justice (ONCJ), an organization concerned with Native people who were in conflict with the law. My primary task at the ONCJ was to assist Aboriginal people in designing and implementing a substance abuse program for inmates. But in the end, the program that was implemented dealt only tangentially with alcohol or other drugs; instead it focused on cultural esteem and spiritual understanding (Warry 1986a, 1986b, 1987b). It was in this organization that my education in Aboriginal issues truly began. I began reading about the diverse work of applied and practising anthropologists who conduct research with the aim of directly intervening in a variety of settings to improve the lives of their 'clients.' In the two years I spent at the ONCJ I was fortunate to meet many Native people – chiefs, elders, front-line workers, and inmates, who began to introduce me to the 'Red Road' and who gently, and not so gently, informed me of the proper etiquette, ethics, and values that are intrinsic to Native ways. I was privileged to work with many non-Native public servants who were dedicated to improving the lives of Native people both on and off reserve. I attended meetings involving Aboriginal leaders and government bureaucrats. These meetings were sometimes frustrating; more often than not I came away feeling stymied by the intransigence and conservatism of government policies that entrapped and handcuffed the well-intentioned individuals who wanted to change the system.

From the ONCJ, I moved to the Department of Native Studies at Trent University, where I learned firsthand of the hopes and aspirations of Native students. I was fortunate to meet Professors Don McCaskill and Marlene Brant Castellano, both of whom were instrumental in furthering my understanding of government policy and of the history of Native-white relations that continues to leave its imprint on Aboriginal communities. After leaving Trent, I worked as a consultant doing curriculum development and program evaluation before joining the Department of Anthropology at McMaster University. Since that time I have continued to work with Aboriginal communities in research, policy development, program implementation, and training.

During the past decade I have had the opportunity to visit more than fifty reserves in Ontario, and many others across Canada. I have visited Friendship Centres and Aboriginal organizations in many cities, and attended conferences that have brought me in touch with a host of Native professionals. These visits have been short for the purpose of interviews, consultations, and small group meetings – a few days here, a week or two there – and all too often I have felt distanced from the communities in which I have worked. I regret that I have not had the chance to conduct the type of intensive fieldwork that I conducted in Papua New Guinea as a student and that is the hallmark of traditional anthropological research.

But it is precisely because my interaction with Aboriginal communities is temporary, intensive, and *focused* on programmatic, policy, and institutional issues that I believe I have a unique perspective to offer. As an applied anthropologist I work, often under contract, as a consultant for Aboriginal communities and organizations. My work has involved the evaluation of criminal justice programs, the development of health and mental health programs, and the assessment of federal and provincial policies. At one level, this book provides me with a platform to write about the relationship between research and planning. In each chapter I describe different styles of applied work and comment on the roles that applied anthropologists assume when working for various Aboriginal or government clients.

As will become evident in the pages that follow, I believe research should be conducted with specific objectives in mind – with the aim of promoting Native control over programs and institutions. Increasingly, of course, Aboriginal people are assuming primary responsibility for the research and program planning that needs to be done in their communities. The role of outsiders in Aboriginal research, and related questions concerning how to best 'represent' another culture or community are central to anthropology. Any non-Native person who has worked in Native communities has been challenged by individuals who question the role of outsiders or consultants in 'studying' Aboriginal people. Because of the factionalism that exists on reserve, researchers inevitably face suspicion by at least some part of the community – it is virtually impossible to win community-wide trust or support, even where researchers live in communities for extended periods. When applied work is episodic or short-term in nature, it is difficult to establish a good working relationship with all but a handful of key individuals. The consultant remains a stranger, in a very real sense, to most of the community.

As an outsider, I sometimes become the target of community criticism. Indeed, one of the key roles a consultant can play is in deflecting criticism that might otherwise be directed at another community member who is directly responsible for projects, proposals, or studies. Non-Native researchers and consultants continue to be in demand simply because there are many skills that are lacking in communities – skills associated with policy analysis, research methodology, or program planning. But unlike some Aboriginal people who believe that one day Aboriginal researchers and consultants will make non-Native consultants obsolete, I believe that the role of 'outsiders' will always remain important in research and evaluation of First Nations organizations. Social science consultants can identify processes that are taken for granted and so remain invisible to community members. In much the same way a third party brings a unique perspective to relationships, an outside observer can provide important insight that is critical to the analysis of cultural patterns.

Those readers who are knowledgeable about current developments in the social sciences will know that the above comments can be read against current critiques concerning the crisis in 'representation' or 'ethnographic authority.' Legitimate critiques by Aboriginal writers about who can best analyse, write about, or be considered experts of, Aboriginal cultures have led to an almost paralysing concern within the social sciences about the question of who should (or is able) to speak about 'the Other' (that is, members of other cultures or the non-dominant society). Increasingly, the right to render analysis, or even to conduct research, is challenged by members of Aboriginal communities. This criticism is partially based on the issue of authority; that is, on the expertise or experience (or lack of it) writers have had with Native people. The issue is also political in that it is coloured by whether portrayals of Aboriginal people can be considered unflattering or can undermine the images that Aboriginal people themselves desire to bring forward in representing their way of life. Efforts to save the 'ghost ship of anthropology' (Taussig 1993) include many different experiments in writing in an attempt to better represent an authentic reality lived by 'the Other' or to incorporate Aboriginal peoples' own perspectives and life stories (see, for example, Riddington 1988; Cruickshank 1991).

I am aware of the potential for distorting Aboriginal values or experiences during the writing process. I hope my 'representation' of Aboriginal communities is such that it leads to greater understanding of the cause of self-government among non-Native readers. I have shown parts of the draft text, and in some instances the entire book, to a small number of individuals – both Native and non-Native – who I believe represent a reasonable cross-section of interested and informed critics. I assume responsibility for any major error in fact or interpretation.

For me, the hornets' nest of representation is an inexorable and unresolvable debate, but one that is inherently academic in orientation, with little or no relevance to the more pressing and pragmatic issues confronting Native communities on a daily basis. This is not to suggest that Aboriginal people do not have concerns about the behaviour of non-Natives in their communities or that they are not concerned with how their communities are described in a book such as this. On the contrary, these are critical issues because they impact on the nature of Aboriginal peoples' relationship with mainstream Canadians. But what the debate on 'representation' tends to ignore is the personal trust relationships that develop between researchers and various individuals, if not Aboriginal communities in general (see Preston 1995). This relationship rests on the free and open exchange of information and on implicit understanding that knowledge given to outsiders will be used responsibly. In my own work there is also the explicit, and often contractual, understanding about the ownership of data or copyright over reports.

These issues are also important because they speak in some small way to the statement by Thomas Moore (on page 2). There is little doubt that many anthropological accounts of Aboriginal people have failed to resonate with Aboriginal readers – this despite the fact that Aboriginal people today sometimes turn to ethnographies written in the early part of this century as one way of relearning and revitalizing their traditions. Anthropologists, despite (or because of) much rational analysis, have often failed to convey an understanding of Aboriginal culture that either expresses the essence of Aboriginal spirituality or promotes a spirit of reconciliation and understanding between Natives and non-Natives. This, perhaps, is asking too much of any single work, but should be a goal of anthropology.

A more important crisis in social science than the nature of representation or ethnographic authority is the relevance of anthropology or other social scientific work. If anthropology is to become a ghost ship, it will be because access to Native communities is denied as a result of our failure to contribute to the objectives and priorities that communities have set. Increasingly, Aboriginal people argue that much of the study anthropologists have been involved in is largely irrelevant to the needs of communities. There is a need for research that directly bears on the needs of Aboriginal people (Warry 1990; cf. Becker 1971). Students of anthropology are consumed with questions of how to most appropriately continue to study Native issues, while assisting communities in their attempt to achieve self-government. As a result, they are conducting their research after consulting with Aboriginal communities, training researchers to assist them in their work, and conducting applied research that is of direct benefit to communities while attempting to meet a different set of academic requirements to obtain their degrees. Students are increasingly aware that their relationship to Aboriginal communities must be based on an open dialogue about the means and ends of research and that their research must be relevant to community needs.

In my experience virtually all bureaucrats, Native leaders, or service providers desire research that goes beyond 'study' to actually doing something that will benefit communities. Occasionally, there is recognition that there is still a great deal we do not know about Aboriginal communities, and that needs to be known, if self-government is to be successful. Thus, an important question is how social scientists can conduct research that has immediate utility and can be used to stimulate local initiatives that are in keeping with the aim of self-government. It has been my experience that Aboriginal people are prepared to participate in any research project, however sensitive the subject matter, if it provides the analytic context for the development of community-based initiatives.

Anthropology has a special perspective to offer Aboriginal communities. With that in mind, I examine the sociopolitical, rhetorical, interpersonal, and symbolic contexts of community healing. In the process, I touch upon a number of subjects that have been of traditional interest to students of anthropology – the meaning of communities, the importance of culture and identity, and the nature of organizations – essential understandings that inform policy making, promote program development, and foster institution building.

This book might also be considered an example of 'advocacy anthropology' (see Hedican 1995, 64–7; Ervin 1990, 24–7). Like Ervin, I assume that those who contend that anthropologists should not, or cannot, assume an advocacy role often seem to exhibit a superficial understanding of the nature of applied anthropology (ibid). There are political assumptions, and long-term agendas, embedded in research whether it is funded by an Aboriginal organization or by more traditional agencies such as the Social Science and Humanities Research Council. In both instances the independence of empirical enquiry is sustainable. Following Price (1990) I believe that informed advocacy should rest on the objective, though not value-free, assessment of sociocultural process. The distinction between 'objective' and 'value free' research is important, and one not easily understood by many people. All research is shaped by values, and these values are as intrinsic to questions that are asked, as they are to answers that are given. Objectivity, however, speaks to careful methodology and the honest assessment of all data that is gathered. All research is political in nature, but only *value explicit* research is ethical (Warry 1992). My values, which shape this analysis, include a respect for Aboriginal ways, a critical awareness that, as with any culture, not all aspects of Native life promote justice, and a belief that Aboriginal people have the responsibility to control and create institutions that are in keeping with their inherent right to self-government.

Reality is pieced together. Knowledge, particularly in an enterprise such as this, is assembled. This book is based on several sources of information and on the knowledge and expertise of a great many people. Many observations are drawn from the literature. Some of this literature comprises academic and journalistic accounts of Native people; a second major source of information draws on government reports, program evaluations, and policy documents that are not normally a part of academic writing. My own research and, as appropriate, students' and collaborators' research comprises a second source of understanding. My applied work has continued even as I have written this book; for example, chapter 6 outlines a number of findings from a major consultation conducted in 1995. Some of the text is drawn with revision from previously unpublished 'grey' literature, for example, from public information and policy writing that I have done for the Ontario provincial government, the Royal Commission on Aboriginal Peoples, and various Aboriginal organizations. My analysis has also been enhanced by a review of people's testimony and presentations before the Royal Commission on Aboriginal Peoples (RCAP). This database, some 70,000 pages, is available on CD-ROM, and has been invaluable to me in providing an Aboriginal perspective and framing the analysis in areas where I lack direct research experience. The book was written before the release of the RCAP final reports. I have, however, revised the text in light of some of the RCAP findings. In the conclusion I address the political and press reaction to the commission's final reports.

This book is written for a general audience – for anyone who eschews simple answers in favour of a complex understanding of Aboriginal issues. It is written for my friends and family, as well as for undergraduate and graduate students who are in search of a contemporary analysis of Aboriginal life. A secondary audience is the policy makers, front-line workers and leaders, both Aboriginal and non-Aboriginal, whose responsibility it is to devise and implement the many programs and initiatives that are in keeping with the project of self-government. In order to make the writing as accessible as possible I have used the traditional form of academic citation only where absolutely necessary in order to recognize the words and works of other authors. Additional references that draw on media reports, academic sources, and grey literature, including testimony from the RCAP, are listed in endnotes.

Finally, a brief note on the title of the book. I first used the phrase 'unfinished dreams' in a paper prepared for the RCAP concerning suicide among Aboriginal youth (Warry 1993; see chapter 4). In that paper I used the phrase to connote several themes. The notion of 'dreaming' conjures up for me obvious references to the idealism and long-term vision that are necessary parts of social reform movements; perhaps most notably, the idea of dreams is associated with Martin Luther King's famous 'I have a dream' speech. This is a common Aboriginal usage; testimony before the RCAP, for example, contains numerous references to the dreams and visions associated with self-government, and some of these quotations are included in the text. But for Aboriginal people there is a more tangible and visceral meaning to dreaming. Unlike Euro-Canadians, many Aboriginal people do not draw a sharp distinction between conscious waking and dream states. Hunters dream about animals, and on waking, know where to hunt. Dreams can also be essential components in healing and provide clues to recovery from spiritual illness. Aboriginal youth who have tried to commit suicide often say that they have heard voices of deceased relatives or friends calling to them in their dreams. Dreams often are entrance points to the spiritual world; people speak of their dreams in tangible ways, as containing messages or lessons that are to be acted upon or that give guidance to everyday life. For this reason the notion of unfinished dreams speaks to me of long-term aspirations and of a tangible reality already glimpsed by Aboriginal people, yet improperly understood by non-Natives.

Visions, experienced by individuals through fasting or other spiritual quests, were also an important part of traditional Aboriginal life, and they remain for some people an integral part of contemporary spiritual activity. Visioning is also a common exercise among various political and human service organizations. People come together by way of retreats or other meetings to rethink and re-vision the goals and objectives of their organization or community. In this contemporary setting, visioning is a contemporary practice that speaks to the need for leadership, foresight, and commitment to change; yet it is a pragmatic practice that also resonates with traditional Aboriginal spiritual practices. Much of my work is related to this type of community visioning exercise, though it is more concerned with the mundane and operational process of program planning and design. This is not to suggest that my own work is spiritual in nature. Although I have learned much about Aboriginal spiritual beliefs during the past decade, I do not profess any special insight in this area. But I do believe that there is an inherently spiritual component in the struggle of Aboriginal people for self-determination – a fact that is in no way contradicted by the divisions that exist in communities between Christian and traditional beliefs. And there is, in the manner in which Aboriginal leaders and front-line workers go about the business of improving their communities, a fundamental integration between spiritual and secular practice.

The bulk of my recent research can be characterized by the phrase 'community consultation and planning.' It is, in a very real sense, work that is aimed at developing concrete plans based on people's dreams and visions for their community. The actual practice of research consists of speaking to key consultants, summarizing their 'gifts' of knowledge, and using focus groups to further discuss and elaborate key issues and themes arising from these interviews. It is a natural process that often allows people to 're-frame' how they have been thinking about their jobs, organizations, or communities. And, when all goes well, the process leads to discussions based on a common foundation of (often new) information that allows people to develop strategies or programs or to see their communities in a new light.

The title of this book, then, is meant to elicit a sense of both the idealism and pragmatic effort that exist in Aboriginal communities as people strive to make self-government a reality. The dream of self-government is unfinished. The project is a long-term one that will only be accomplished through the combined efforts of Natives and non-Natives over many decades. Central to the project of self-government is the healing of individuals and communities. In the aftermath of the 1995 referendum, Canadians will perhaps understand references to the need for healing to occur before political reform can take place. In Aboriginal communities, however, the emphasis on healing is at once metaphorical and tangible. There is often the symbolic appeal to a spirit of cooperation and reconciliation between members of different families or communities, as well as between First Nations and the Canadian state. But there also exists the tangible need for individuals, many of whom have experienced personal tragedies or are struggling with issues of personal and cultural identity, to heal themselves in order that they might contribute to their community.

Charlotte Rich, an Innu elder, has remarked on the positive changes – most notably a rapid decline in alcohol abuse – in Davis Inlet following the tragic deaths of six children in a fire. 'Things are looking better and there's changes in the community,' she states. 'We have people who are sober. You can't rush it. We'll get our tragedies. It's like cleaning a caribou – you've got to do it slowly' (*Spectator* A10, 1995). At the risk of overgeneralizing, I would suggest that two qualities of Aboriginal personality are remarkable patience and perseverance. Invariably Aboriginal people speak of centuries of oppression, and of how their current labours are for the benefit of future generations. Elders' speak of prophecies transcending seven generations and of a future glimpsed or dreamed of where Aboriginal culture will be respected rather than denigrated, and where

Aboriginal people will assume complete control over their political affairs. Many young people believe that they are living in the seventh generation. They sense that self-government can be gained in their lifetime. This book speaks to the complexity of that journey, and to its inevitable conclusion.

WAYNE WARRY
HAMILTON, ONTARIO

1

Self-Government: The Political Environment

Chief Thunderchild was the last of the Plains Cree chiefs to sign Treaty 6; he did so in 1879. As he contemplated that decision, he spoke the following words: 'I had a dream – but I did not believe this dream – that there would be white men everywhere, overwhelming this land. Today I see it. I love this land greatly, and what is still the Indian's I am resolved to hold fast.'

Chief Thunderchild believed that treaties would allow Indians to hold fast to what was theirs. But that has not been the case. Today, Aboriginal Peoples are still struggling to hold on to what is theirs. More importantly, they are reclaiming what was theirs before the treaties were signed. Despite the greatest of odds, over the past century Aboriginal Peoples have survived policies of paternalism, suppression, evasion and indifference. These policies have created an enormous gap between Aboriginal and non-Aboriginal people in this country; a gap that must be bridged by both groups, working together. [These hearings] will contribute to the reconciliation of Aboriginal and non-Aboriginal People; a reconciliation that must occur if Canadians are to build a new relationship between First Peoples and those who have joined them in this land. A relationship based on partnership, trust, sensitivity and respect; one that will form the basis for a stronger, brighter and more honourable future for the Aboriginal Peoples and for all Canadians. (Winnipeg MB. 92-04-21 6. George Erasmus, Co-Chair, Royal Commission on Aboriginal Peoples (RCAP). PG 30–1)[1]

Introduction

By 1850, gold and other precious minerals had been discovered in what is now the Robinson Huron and Robinson Superior Treaty areas in Northern Ontario. W.B. Robinson, an Indian commissioner, was sent to 'make treaty' with Ojibwa leaders for surrender of title to their land. A copy of this treaty hangs on the wall of a boardroom on the second floor of a modern office building in Blind River, Ontario, a town of 3,000 situated equidistant from Sudbury and Sault Ste Marie. On the walls of the boardroom is some Native artwork, on loan from nearby galleries. Drawings of the 'Seven Grandfathers,' representations of important Ojibwa values – such as honesty, trust – line one wall. In the middle of the board table, perched on a stone ashtray, is a leather pouch filled with tobacco, which is smudged on important occasions.[2] It is in this contemporary setting, centred on spiritual images, and tinged with reminders of the historic past, that chiefs from the seven First Nations comprising Mamaweswen, the North Shore Tribal Council(NSTC), come together to discuss the business of self-government.[3]

The treaty hangs in recognition of the nation to nation relationship that exists between First Nations and the government of Canada. As elsewhere in the country, in return for their agreement to the treaty, the signatories received annuities, roughly five dollars for status Indians, as much as fifteen dollars for chiefs. Each year Aboriginal people all across the country celebrate Treaty Days. Band members line up to receive their annuity and, in so doing, affirm the fundamental nature of treaty agreements and their Indian status.[4]

In 1991 Mamaweswen, along with a handful of other communities in Ontario, entered into formal self-government negotiations with the federal government (Canada 1991a; NSTC 1991). The aim of these negotiations is no less than to map out, by way of formal agreement, the broad range of jurisdictions that the tribal council will have authority over – from policing and courts to fisheries and natural resources. These potential Aboriginal jurisdictions are outlined in a complex draft document that, for most people along the North Shore, remains a mystery.

The principal technical/legal adviser to Mamaweswen, Ian Cowie, has described the self-government process as a contemporary treaty-making process – one that expands and renovates the concepts of treaties as signed in the previous century (personal communication). Chiefs and councillors speak of frustrating self-government negotiations with federal representatives. They recognize that the federal government lacks a vision of what self-government means. And they express doubt that all the First Nations belonging to the tribal council will move forward together to sign an agreement. Many leaders feel that the process allowed the tribal council to do important preparatory work that might lead to an agreement in future years. But after several years, they are also aware that there remain significant misunderstanding and confusion about the meaning of self-government within their communities.

Since 1991 the political environment has changed greatly. In 1991 Canadians were enmeshed in constitutional negotiations. Aboriginal issues were a critical part of these discussions. The government had just committed itself to a Royal Commission on Aboriginal Peoples, and there was considerable hope that this, too, would enhance the cause of Aboriginal rights. In Ontario, the New Democratic Party, on the heels of the Supreme Court's *Sparrow* decision, recognized the right to self-government. The *Sparrow* decision, which ordered a new trial for Ronald Sparrow, a B.C. Musqueam fisherman, stated that while Aboriginal people were not exempt from government regulation, federal and provincial government legislation should take into account Aboriginal rights; that is, there should be a 'generous, liberal interpretation' of the notion of Aboriginal rights (D. Smith 1993: 128–30). As Smith notes, the NDP's actions were regarded with considerable suspicion by some Aboriginal leaders. Bentley Cheechoo, deputy grand chief of Nishnawbe-Aski Nation challenged Premier Bob Rae about the value of provincial recognition, noting that it was unable to 'provide the kind of community-wide healing programs' that were needed. Smith also states that Darrell Boissoneau, then chief of Garden River, a Mamaweswen First Nation, suggested to Rae that racism, bigotry, and discrimination within the bureaucracy would thwart government plans for improved relationships with First Nations (ibid).

Today those two views seem well placed. In the aftermath of Meech Lake and Charlottetown, Aboriginal rights are once again on the back burner.[5] The Royal Commission – the most extensive and expensive in Canadian history – was criticized as an expensive and irrelevant exercise during its tenure (*Toronto Star*, 1 October 1995, A16). It released its five-volume final reports in November 1996, and the government quickly distanced itself from its recommendations, seeming interested in recognizing only the most limited form of self-government (see chapter 7). Mike Harris, Ontario's Conservative premier, has already cut Aboriginal programs and, with links to non-Native sport hunters and fishermen, seems intent on undermining the Aboriginal rights that *Sparrow* aimed to protect. And in the aftermath of the Quebec referendum there is little hope or optimism that the Aboriginal right to self-government might be carefully revisited in constitutional negotiations.

And yet, important changes are continuing in all the North Shore communities. During the past five years a number of new agreements have been signed – for example, in health care and policing. The quality of many services has improved. There are constant, physical reminders of these improvements – new health-care centres, day-care centres, improvements to band offices. And there remains visible evidence of just how far these communities have to go – poor or nonexistent recreational facilities, housing that is in disrepair or short supply.

Incredibly complex work must be done, and is being done, in Aboriginal communities to obtain self-government. This work occurs within a much broader regional, provincial, and national political environment. As George Erasmus notes, the reconciliation of Natives and non-Natives is necessary if a 'nation to nation' relationship is to be re-established. The ability of First Nations to achieve self-government is related to mainstream Canadians' understanding of, and respect for, Aboriginal culture. Public understanding of Aboriginal communities must be enhanced.

In this chapter I assess some common arguments, assumptions, and attitudes associated with Aboriginal issues. Many of these concerns are tangential to my central analysis. But taken together, they form a general backdrop against which First Nations' actions and aspirations must be set.

Stereotypes and Attitudes

Aboriginal cultures are unique. Like people everywhere, Aboriginal people vary greatly in the interests and values they hold. And yet overlying this individual diversity is a cultural unity to which Aboriginal people from diverse communities will attest. To write about this uniqueness without resorting to stereotypes or underestimating the variation within and between individual Native communities is extremely difficult. The uniqueness of Aboriginal culture, for example, is often emphasized through an appeal to simplistic comparisons. Aboriginal cultures are characterized as 'shame' oriented, European culture as 'guilt' oriented.[6] Europeans have a linear conception of time, Aboriginal people a nonlinear, or cyclical conception. Aboriginal people are in harmony with nature; whites dominate nature. Native people are thought of as inherently 'spiritual,' whites as somehow less spiritual, more 'rational.' Entire dichotomies are drawn contrasting non-Native and Native ways (see, for example, Dumont 1993: 47). In the end, analysts extrapolate from these comparisons to create differences in 'world-view' or ideology. But care must be taken not to rely on simple contrasts. For example, Native healing beliefs are certainly different from those commonly associated with Western bio-medicine. But this is not to deny that many physicians fully understand there is a close relationship between physical health and spiritual or mental well-being. Likewise, the fact that Aboriginal languages do not contain a word for 'guilt' does not mean Aboriginal people lack concepts that connote transgression, wrongdoing, or personal responsibility (see R. Ross 1992).

Even well-accepted generalizations prove to be complex in everyday behaviour. To illustrate: Depew observes that the notion of 'sharing,' which is often hailed as a core Native value, is often viewed 'in ideal terms, applying equally across all situations and as a timeless principle of all Aboriginal life' (Depew 1994b: 33, citing Hamilton and Sinclair 1991: 32–3; Monture-Okanee 1993; and Turpel 1993b). He notes that this idea is not supported by the ethnographic record, where situational limits on sharing were observed. As important, he suggests that notions of reciprocity have undoubtedly changed dramatically with the shift to modern reserve settlements and a decline in land-based hunting activities.

I cannot explain the importance of sharing as a core value to Aboriginal people. Aboriginal consultants stress the importance of this value even while acknowledging that there is less concern for collective supports (generalized reciprocity) than in the past. Some people blame welfare for the decline in sharing or community support. People no longer feel they need to share among those who are less fortunate – the government has made this unnecessary. People acknowledge that jealousy sometimes emerges around material possessions – snowmobiles, trucks, houses – and the differences in wealth undermine the sense of equality, egalitarianism, and sharing that once existed. In many instances an ethic of sharing, or sense of generalized reciprocity, continues within extended families on reserve. This ethic is evident, for example, in ideas about adoption and child care, as well as the sharing of game. There is also a spirit of cooperation that emerges in times of community crisis and that is related to a profound sense of community membership. And this sharing is evident in normal activities – at bingos, at feasts and powwows. Clearly, family and broader kinship ties remain important organizing principles on reserve (see chapter 6).

Simplistic generalizations, which fail to account for variation between individuals or communities, can lead to dangerous stereotypes. Stereotypes of Aboriginal people, positive and negative, abound. As Berkhofer (1979) has demonstrated, these stereotypes have changed significantly over time, in accordance with different colonial objectives, so as to best situate Native people for the ideological onslaught that is the necessary precursor to colonial action (the enemy has to be created before they are defeated – or converted). One of the most popular and enduring images of Aboriginal people is that they are 'natural' environmentalists, people born and raised in the bush, hunters and trappers, knowledgeable about the land, protectors of Mother Earth. As Grinde and Johanson (1995: 1–28) note, despite modern critiques that would undermine the image of Aboriginal people as 'the first ecologists,' there is considerable evidence to suggest that Native American ideology has always reflected an important relationship to the land (see also Gill 1990; Kehoe 1990). Particularly in remote northern communities, this characterization is well placed and meaningful. Anthropologists have long documented the continued importance of bush life for Aboriginal communities (see, for example, Brody 1981; George et al 1992; Berkes et al 1994). 'Country' food continues to be important to local economies, and traditional activities, such as hunting and trapping, continue to sustain the spiritual and emotional needs of many people. There is also deep respect for the environment and a renewed interest in documenting traditional environmental knowledge (TEK) for sustainable development (M. Johnson 1992; Potts 1992). But the reality is also that in each community there is a divergence of values and behaviours. Even in the far North, for example, a significant percentage of men do not hunt or hunt only occasionally. Among the Cree of Moose Factory, for example, these men comprise 11.6% and 28.7% respectively (George et al 1992: 8–9).

There are also obvious differences between cultures – for example, between Iroquois, Ojibwa, Cree, and Dene. These differences are critical to the search for culturally specific, community-based solutions to the problems found on reserve. Variation between First Nations also results from the relative size of their land base, their geographic location, and the vagaries of local history. Along the North Shore, for example, people recognize that their communities are 'less traditional' than those in the far North. And even within these seven communities there are clear differences in the degree to that the Ojibwa language has been sustained, and variation in Aboriginal spiritual practices. These communities are also internally divided by religious beliefs, adherence to traditional values, economic status, and political allegiances (see chapter 6).

The apparent contradictions of Aboriginal life are very real (see, for example, Brody 1987: 171–3). And contradictions can be used in dangerous ways. I have heard non-Natives challenge the image of Aboriginal people as environmentalists by remarking on the refuse, litter, and waste found on any reserve. But such an observation ignores the fact that there are few recycling programs on reserve – not because there is no interest, but because the costs of these programs in small communities are much greater than in urban centres. Similarly, in the NSTC area, non-Natives challenge land claims by arguing that Aboriginal people no longer need to actively hunt and fish to survive. This view ignores not only the social and recreational significance of hunting, but the spiritual relationship Aboriginal people continue to have to the land.

An Aboriginal colleague once remarked that there are Aboriginal people who have lived in remote northern communities 'and the only thing they have killed in the bush is a case of two-four.' This struck me as a harsh characterization, but it illustrates the contradictions of Native communities by inverting the environmentalist image and pointing to a second stereotype. It is the myth of the drunken Indian, the welfare bum. Many Northern communities are racked with unemployment and welfare dependency – in some communities as much as eighty or ninety per cent of the population may be on some form of social assistance. Concomitant problems of alcohol and solvent abuse, and more rarely, drug abuse, abound in many communities. This harsh reality does not fit easily with another, more palatable, image of communities that are in recovery. Even where alcoholism is of deep concern, there is invariably a large sector of the community that totally abstains from alcohol (see Warry 1986a). And in every community that I am aware of, there are leaders, some of whom have recovered from alcoholism, who are promoting the revitalization of traditional spiritual practices.

Natives and non-Natives alike must be cognizant of how our images of hunters and trappers living 'in tune' with the environment serve to sustain a picture of 'traditional' rather than contemporary Aboriginal lifestyles. Likewise, we might consider how images of welfare dependency and alcoholism serve to sustain our belief that Native people are incapable of acting on their own behalf, in need of a *pater*, the state. We must be aware of how stereotypes either romanticize or infantilize Aboriginal people. Both these processes of projection undermine our ability to see Aboriginal people as contemporary equals.

If public awareness of Aboriginal issues is to be enhanced, we need to move beyond stereotypes to the complexity of Aboriginal life. Academic and media portrayals must offer up to Canadians the complete range of Aboriginal lifestyles. Social scientists can enhance this understanding by emphasizing small business development, as well as traditional economies, or by studying Native Christian beliefs and other contemporary aspects of reserve life (see Treat 1996).

Our current images of Aboriginal people, as evident in media reports, seem to me to be built around two opposed themes. One of these presents a picture of health, vibrancy, and potential, which is heavily laden with spiritualism. It presents Aboriginal people as fundamentally spiritual people, as healers, and as people who can provide something to whites which is missing from our society (see Churchill 1994). On the surface there seems to be a great deal of public interest in Aboriginal culture. Kashtin albums go double platinum; non-Native audiences continue to turn out in significant numbers for Aboriginal theatre; Aboriginal arts in general seem to attract increased attention. Dream catchers and medicine wheels are everywhere. Medical students are enthralled with the potential of Native healing; New-Agers are engaged by the re-emergence of Aboriginal spirituality. Native people, we are told, are uniquely placed to teach mainstream society about the environment, about the meaning of Canada; perhaps, if we are prepared to listen, to return to us the collective soul that seems so lacking in our national identity.

Native scholars like Ward Churchill (1994: 273–89) remind us that there is a potential danger in these enthusiastic and exuberant responses to Aboriginal culture, in part because the attraction to Aboriginal ideas can be based on a romanticized version of Indian culture. 'Wanabes,' as Aboriginal people sometimes call them, are viewed with ridicule, concern, and scepticism. Wanabes include New-Agers who are interested in Native spirituality but seem unprepared to invest the time and energy required to learn from elders. 'Plastic medicine men' who, in the extreme, 'borrow' Native spiritual practices such as shamanism and the sweat lodge are viewed as exploiters of Aboriginal culture (*Spectator*, 13 July 1995; see also Kehoe 1990). Native people speak of their concerns about the 'appropriation' of Native cultural practices: 'First you take our land,' they say, 'and now you want to take our spirituality.' There is little doubt that in the rush to New-Age spirituality, the fundamental messages of Aboriginal spiritual belief and practice are compromised. But here again, opinions are divided. Many (though not all) elders see the interest of whites in Native culture as part and parcel of the loss of faith in mainstream religion and of a search for spirituality that could, at least potentially, lead to reconciliation between non-Natives and Natives. And they point to their own prophecies, which suggest that a time will come when there is teaching of sacred lessons to non-Natives.

The second major portrait that emerges contains darker images, images of danger and desperation. The popular press profiles the 'plight' of Native people, including the common problems of suicide and solvent abuse. Here community dysfunction ('desperation') is overlain with the potential for violence. Articles on land claims, fishing and hunting rights seem always to refer to the potential use of force or to confrontation (see, for example, *Globe and Mail*, 29 July 1995, A4; 26 Sept. 1995, A10). Canadians have experienced the nightmare of Oka and Ipperwash and they realize the potential costs of such violence. Despair and violence are linked in our minds. George Erasmus, the former leader of the Assembly of First Nations (AFN) and co-chair of the Royal Commission on Aboriginal Peoples, has suggested that the internalized oppression that communities have experienced could be turned outward in anger and violence directed toward mainstream society (see Simpson 1994: 184–5). This idea, that internalized violence against oneself or one's community can be rechannelled against the oppressor, was popularized by Franz Fanon (1988). But as Dyck notes, the history of Indian resistance in Canada has for the most part been non-violent (1991: 87; see also chapter 3).

Both these portraits are extreme and must be tempered by an understanding of First Nations diversity. The first image, with its emphasis on spirituality and cultural revitalization, is particularly appealing to academics, to students, and to those sympathetic to Aboriginal calls for self-government. It is certainly the case that there is a renewed interest in 'tradition.' But the extent to which this renewed interest has, or has not, captured the imagination of the majority of Aboriginal people remains uncertain. Although many people profess that a return to 'culture' must be at the heart of community revitalization, this focus is alienating to many others who live on reserve. It is important to assess critically, then, the extent to which the self-government movement is reliant on, or synonymous with, a renewed sense of traditional culture and spirituality.

The second portrait, too, needs careful qualification. Aboriginal leaders increasingly seem willing to turn to blockades and other forms of direct, nonviolent action to convey messages about Aboriginal needs and rights. And as community expectations about self-government increase, there is some potential that widespread frustration over government inaction, particularly among youth, will grow. Hope is a dangerous thing. But in my experience, the majority of Native people believe that Oka and Ipperwash are anomalies caused by misunderstanding, government intransigence, and police overreaction. They believe that this type of confrontation, quite simply, is not the Indian Way. There is danger in overemphasizing the relationship between the desperation, that is so real for many Aboriginal people, and the potential for violence or societal upheaval. We would also be mistaken to suggest that despair is universal, or that it is so entrenched in communities that people feel incapable of self-reliance and social development. It is important that the wider public understand that in every community there are Aboriginal people who are working very hard to ensure that social problems are overcome. The reality, then, seems to lie somewhere in the grey area, with communities that remain deeply troubled, and in some instances dysfunctional, but that contain a small core of committed people – some of whom adhere to traditional values, others to a more contemporary outlook – who are trying to enhance their community's capacity for self-government.

What, then, of mainstream attitudes to self-government? On the surface, polls and surveys seem to indicate that the majority of Canadians favour self-government for 'our' Aboriginal people. Simpson (1994: 221) notes that polls and surveys taken throughout the 1980s consistently indicated that the majority of Canadians supported a broad range of Aboriginal positions. Following the Oka crisis in 1990, support for Aboriginal positions increased – for example, 51% of people surveyed believed Aboriginal land claims were valid; 61% percent believed Aboriginal people were citizens of nations that had made treaties with the government; and 62% believed they should maintain their way of life, rather than be assimilated into mainstream society. Yet on the key issue of self-government, the country remains divided: 47% in favour, 46% opposed, with support strongest in Ontario and Atlantic Canada, lowest in Quebec, the Prairie Provinces and British Columbia.[7] Significantly, the 'pattern of polling data also revealed continuing confusion in Canadians' minds about the nature of Aboriginals' demands and a skepticism about them *that grew as these demands became more precise*' (ibid; emphasis mine). This suggests that support for self-government is weaker than at first glance. That is, public support declines in response to the range and explicitness of Aboriginal demands. Public support is also strongest for the *least* radical of self-government options – 46% of people favoured Aboriginal governments that would exercise powers similar to a municipality. Only 15% favoured a form of self-government that would enable Aboriginal communities to exercise the powers of provinces (for example, control over health, education, and natural resources). Only 11% favoured truly sovereign governments with powers equal to those of the federal government.

Simpson also reports that people who have little direct contact with Aboriginal people are more likely to support Aboriginal causes than residents living in close proximity to Aboriginal communities.[8] As important, as pollster Alan Reid noted, 'when discussion turned to how to operationalize self-government, acceptable definitions are *very* conservative' and ultimately seemed to stress the cultural integration of Aboriginal people (Simpson 1994: 224). Thus, for example, focus-group studies suggest that Canadians favour land claims, to be followed by removal of tax-exempt status of reserve-based Indians (see below). And, contrary to the Aboriginal position, focus-group participants favour extinguishment of Aboriginal rights following the settlement of land claims. A significant minority of the population opposes self-government, and the majority support weakens as specific objectives of self-government emerge. There is a veneer of public support that can be lifted to reveal deeper and uglier attitudes, based, I would argue, irrationally, on the potentially destructive potential of self-government for mainstream interests.

But how valuable are these polls if people's attitudes to self-government are based on incomplete understanding of Aboriginal people? These results may be influenced by many false assumptions. As public understanding of Aboriginal communities grows, support for the notion of self-government may also increase. In conversations with students, friends, and acquaintances I am often struck by how people talk of self-government as if it promises an instant omnibus cure for the problems of Aboriginal communities. Many also seem to believe that self-government is a state of affairs that appears instantaneously if, for example, the principle is entrenched in the constitution. And many seem to suggest that self-government implies huge additional costs to the Canadian taxpayer (see below). From a simplistic 'expenditure' perspective, they are right. The Royal Commission on Aboriginal Peoples (RCAP), for example, placed its recommendations within a fiscal framework calling for between $1 and $2 billion a year in new monies for the next fifteen years (1996f). But the RCAP considers such expenditures as an *investment* in Canada's future, which would eventually pay dividends as welfare and health-care costs are reduced (see also chapter 7). A poll following the release of the RCAP reports showed that while 60% of Canadians supported the RCAP recommendations (we must assume people had formed their opinions on the basis of media reports), most – 54% – 'balk' at spending the monies to implement these recommendations (*Globe and Mail*, 15 Jan. 1997, A4)!

What public attitudes indicate, I believe, is a fear of rapid and expensive change. If this is so, then a deeper understanding of how Aboriginal communities are pursuing a deliberate and cautious approach to change may influence public attitudes to self-government. A case can be made, therefore, for the necessity of demonstrating how the process of self-government strengthens, rather than threatens, the social and economic fabric of Canadian society.

It is here that Native and non-Native leaders can influence the public discussion of Aboriginal rights. In Ontario, Conservative premier Mike

Harris played off public fears of land claims during the 1995 election campaign in order to obtain votes. He is reported as remarking, for example, that Natives 'spend all their time' on land claims and 'stay at home and do nothing' (*Spectator*, 1 Nov. 1994, A14). It is difficult to assess the impact of such remarks, but it is clear that changes in government can certainly influence the climate for change and negotiation at both federal and provincial levels. Harris' well-known affiliation with recreational hunters and anglers, for example, has led to a general cooling-off of positive relationships established during the Rae NDP government (*Spectator*, 25 June 1994, B4).[9]

Recent experience in British Columbia, where the New Democratic Party was re-elected, demonstrates government's inability to address Aboriginal issues when faced with opposition from lobby groups, including business, hunters and trappers, and tourist interests (see Howard, *Globe and Mail*, 11 Feb. 1995, A1). Similarly, Prime Minister Chrétien, intent on going to the polls in 1997, quickly distanced the federal liberal government from the RCAP recommendations so as to prevent Aboriginal affairs from becoming an election issue. In short, as Boissoneau (above, 19) notes, we must be aware of how negative stereotypes and attitudes are found not simply within the general public, but within political parties and government bureaucracies, and how these attitudes fuel racism and discrimination that thwart the creation of a new political relationship with First Nations.

Racism and Paternalism

As the polls cited above indicate, Canadian attitudes to self-government are deeply divided. There are certainly many individuals who agree with and support Aboriginal goals. But many Canadians continue to deny the validity of Aboriginal culture and challenge any suggestion that Aboriginal people should have a special status within Canada. I need only begin to explain to people that I work in Aboriginal communities to elicit remarks rooted in racism or simple intolerance – remarks about 'free rides,' tax exemptions, and land claims that will 'kill the country' (see also Hedican 1995: 204–5).[10]

Press reports continue to remind us that racism emerges when self-interest is threatened. Aboriginal land claims threaten to upset the bucolic lifestyle of cottagers and undermine the nature of other non-Native communities. Occasionally these attitudes coalesce, are sanitized, and are given substance in direct attacks on the idea of Aboriginal rights. Diane

Francis, for example, writing in *Maclean's* under the title 'Time to Get Tough with the Natives' draws on the recent self-published book, tellingly entitled *Our Home or Native Land,* by M.H. Smith, a columnist, former lawyer, and public servant. Smith has expressed 'concern' about 'the special privileges awarded to this country's Aboriginals, such as tax free status, questionable land-claim awards and special exemptions from the rule of law, as well as massive cash settlements' (*Maclean's,* 10 July 1995: 11; M.H. Smith 1995). Francis continues: 'Smith maintains that the Aboriginals have received an enormous and unfair giveaway for several reasons, including guilt about past misdeeds, ministerial ignorance, bureaucratic indifference to long-term consequences of land-claim settlements and appeasement by politicians for political gain' (1995: 11).

This statement may reflect widely held attitudes. But it is difficult to comprehend the attractiveness of such an argument, which is naïve and simplistic in its assessment of historical and contemporary reality. Such a position completely ignores the litany of social, economic, and health indicators that prove that Aboriginal people continue to experience poorer-than-average lifestyles and life opportunities than mainstream Canadians (see chapter 2). This propaganda also clearly overestimates (through omission and inappropriate analogy) the scope and extent of land claims and financial compensation to First Nations. For instance, Francis notes that the 2,370 Indian reserves comprise more than 10,000 square miles, which she says is about 'half the size of Nova Scotia,' for 314,843 status Indians on reserve (1.1% of the country's population).[11] She neglects to note that this land comprises only a tiny percentage of the country (less than .05% of Canadian territory) and a fraction of that land originally agreed to by treaty[12] (see also p. 41). This attack on Aboriginal rights is founded on alleged conspiracy – by bureaucrats and politicians – who 'have given away the proverbial store to buy votes or purchase peace from potentially troublesome Aboriginals' (ibid). Francis and Smith descend to fearmongering by suggesting that politicians are responding to an Aboriginal threat. The reality is that Aboriginal-white relations in Canada have been relatively devoid of violence and have been characterized by extreme patience and political diplomacy on the part of Aboriginal leaders. In so heavily relying on negative reasoning, therefore, what these attitudes reveal is a total lack of recognition that there may be sound, rational reasons for recognizing Aboriginal rights.

These attitudes, unfortunately, are found in every sector of society. They filter into bureaucratic decision-making, into academia, and into law. Remarks by judges in two recent court cases – one in British Columbia concerning the Gitksan land claim, the other in Alberta concerning the rights of First Nations to determine their band membership in lieu of the federal government's Bill C-31 – have clearly demonstrated a gross misunderstanding of Aboriginal people and culture (see Waldrum et al 1992). Such remarks, whether racist or simply paternalistic, suggest that Europeans, by virtue of their status as colonizers, have a continuing right to determine Aboriginal politics, and to deny the validity of Aboriginal history and culture. Both cases also re-emphasize the inherent conservatism of the judicial system and the dangers of attempting to challenge the state or define Aboriginal rights by way of European courts.

Evidence of racism and paternalism is rarely so publicly acknowledged. Systemic racism continues to exist in Canada. Aboriginal people feel this racism in many ways – when searching for a job, when in school, through subtle images in texts or television. The royal commission testimonies are full of references to and accounts of how racism continues to restrict individual and collective achievement. These statements make it clear that individual instances of racism, however intolerable, are much less insidious and dangerous than systemic forms of racism, which, as R. Leah notes, are 'embedded in western culture and European colonization' (Lethbridge AB. 93-05-24. PG11.)[13] Louise Chippeway, referring to the experience of Aboriginal employees, states: 'Implicit in the responses of Aboriginal employees surveyed is that racism is manifested in many ways. It is unconscious, direct, individual, systemic and institutional. Racism is prevalent in the employment system where the values underlying the corporate culture are different from the values of Aboriginal people ... [V]alues produce a self-protective attitude among the mainstream. Racism and discrimination are manifested when there is an unjust exclusion of individuals and groups who are different from the dominant values within the system' (Roseau River MN. 92-12-08 95. PG 56).

Racism is an attitude; discrimination is an action that results in marginalization. Racism, whether resting on self-interest or a belief in the superiority of European culture, continues to promote assimilation ('why can't they just be like the rest of Canadians?'). Systemic racism is 'built in' to institutions and organizations. It is an aspect of corporate culture that, for example, results in higher incarceration rates for Aboriginal people. The Manitoba Aboriginal Justice Inquiry found numerous instances of racist behaviour among criminal justice personnel (Hamilton and Sinclair 1991; RCAP 1993c: 15–42). Systemic racism results in inappropriate school curriculum, for example, in the use of texts that contain negative images of Indians. For Aboriginal students, racism can colour educational experiences and lead to low self- and cultural esteem. Systemic racism is also easily denied, though the passage of time throws a harsh light on past practice and reminds us of the possibility of contemporary racism. Current prejudice against Aboriginal people needs to be set against the backdrop of the many historic reminders of legislated discrimination: for example, the fact that only after 1985 were status Indian women who had married non-Natives allowed to reclaim their Indian status.

The effects of systemic racism and discrimination are often subtle, and for many Canadians easily deniable. Racism prevents understanding of the viability and integrity of Aboriginal cultural ways and inhibits governments' ability to respond reasonably and justly to First Nation initiatives. Belief in the superiority of Western ways is revealed when government fails to recognize the pragmatic wisdom of Native people or fails to understand Native political processes that are intrinsic to community control over services. Adherence to belief in the superiority of Western institutions exists even in the face of evidence that the impact of these institutions has been destructive, or that other, potentially more viable and culturally appropriate alternatives would better service communities.

This is a diacritical point. Aboriginal ways hold unique solutions to community problems. Aboriginal approaches also reveal important lessons that might assist mainstream society in renovating its social, political, medical, and legal systems. Anthropology has long been based on the principle that cross-cultural comparison and understanding can shed light on our own society. My experience has been that government researchers and policy makers concerned with improving the lifestyles of Native people often come to realize that there is an inherent genius in Aboriginal ways of knowing and experiencing the world that is highly instructive (see, for example, R. Ross 1992; 1996). But these same individuals are often caught in systems that are structurally designed to maintain the status quo. As I show in following chapters, the ability of Aboriginal communities to develop innovative solutions to their problems – even when based on extensive research – is often denied by governments that see alternative ways of knowing and acting as a threat to the integrity of existing institutional ways.

The Notion of Aboriginal Rights

During the writing of this book, the question of Indian taxation became a media story when, on 15 December 1994, members of the Toronto Aboriginal community occupied a Revenue Canada office to protest the federal government's plan to tax incomes for those Native people working for Indian organizations off reserve. The creation of 'Revenue Rez' for more than three weeks during the holiday season served to highlight status Indians' fight for freedom from taxation. Status Indians see this exemption – whether for work conducted on or off reserve – as a fundamental right. Many Canadians, of course, see this as a special and unwarranted reward for Indians (*Toronto Star*, 26 Dec. 1994, A4). The protest arose when new federal guidelines were developed to prevent Natives from avoiding the payment of tax by using employment agencies located on reserves, which acted as the 'official' employer while contracting jobs off reserve. Under the new guidelines, Indians would pay tax if they have no 'significant' link to the reserve (there is an exemption for those directly employed by Native bands or political organizations even if their office is located off reserve). The government estimated that only three thousand Indians would be affected. This number is undoubtedly low, but even if it is accepted, the new guidelines affect a 'new generation' of Indians, who will work for Aboriginally controlled institutions in urban settings. The guidelines, then, have the potential to influence the type of candidates who would apply for these positions.

These issues were not treated with great clarity in the press. Given the complexity of this issue, it is not surprising that press coverage only exacerbated the image of Aboriginal peoples as possessing special privileges. The protesters placed a full-page advertisement in the *Globe and Mail;* it stressed that Indians were not 'furniture,' they were human beings whose on-reserve rights were transportable off reserve (*Globe and Mail*, 30 Dec. 1994, A3). The reality is that Aboriginal people who live off reserve and work for corporations such as Stelco or Inco, located off reserve, have *always* paid tax. At that time I was involved in several conversations with people who assumed all Indians did not pay income tax. It became apparent to me that, in concentrating on taxation, people were failing to grasp the real issue: the notion that status rights are transportable. If status Indians have rights, these are, presumably political and personal rights that can be carried with them wherever they go. But the government, through a number of measures in the Indian Act as well as other legislation, ties status rights to the reserve. That is, the government does not regard special Indian status as a human right, but rather as a political right tied to territory. The subtleties of this debate were not understood by the general public. All that seemed to register with people was that Indians again were complaining and threatening violence over special rights that no other Canadian was granted.

Occasionally the words of the common people emerge through editorials or other public statements. Witness this remark in response to the taxation issue by J.E. Somerville of Hamilton in a letter to the editor of the *Spectator* (28 Dec. 1994, A10):

> The act of *insurrection* in the federal tax offices in Toronto by members of *our* Native population suggests to me that a review of ill-conceived treaties signed by poorly-advised politicians hundreds of years ago is sorely overdue. The blatant unfairness of a tax-free status for thousands of people is making slaves of the willing worker. *If there was any injustice done, surely it has been compensated for by now.* After all, every social service, all the welfare, health care and freedom has been available to everyone regardless of their station and must be worth something. Has anyone bothered to put a dollar and cents value on that? It is unreasonable to accept that a conquered Nation should be allowed to hold a country ransom forever. (emphasis mine)

One only needs to travel to the nearest pub to understand that when Aboriginal issues are discussed, the conversation rapidly deteriorates into a discussion of the 'special privileges' that are inaccessible to the ordinary Canadian. Many people are concerned about the 'tax free' status of Native people. Others seem to be jealous or envious that, collectively, Aboriginal people have access to huge (by comparison to non-Native Canadians) tracts of land, and, perhaps more important, that despite the signing of treaties, Aboriginal people *continue* to claim huge amounts of land. These examples concern the unique status of Aboriginal people. A solid understanding of the notion of Aboriginal rights is necessary to provide a foundation for rational discussion of the idea of self-government. The development of Aboriginal jurisdiction inevitably rests on the recognition of fundamental political rights, that distinguish Aboriginal First Nations or urban Aboriginal communities from mainstream communities.[14]

There are several common arguments against the idea of unique status. There is, for example, the often stated belief that Aboriginal people are no different from other minorities or ethnic groups. Similarly, two arguments are often put forward to suggest that Aboriginal people should not be treated differently than other Canadians. One argument suggests 'that we are all immigrants' – whether European, Asian, or Aboriginal. This line of thought often appeals to archaeological evidence concerning the Bering Strait migration, to suggest that Indians arrived in North America earlier than Europeans, but that, none the less, their claims to land or other rights can be ignored in light of subsequent migrations by settlers, including those involving forced conquest. This 'fact' is contested by Aboriginal peoples, who insist that they originated on the North American continent or who appeal to creation stories and legends to question the validity of Western scientific arguments (Churchill 1994; Sioui 1994). But even those who accept the anthropological evidence must acknowledge many thousands of years of Aboriginal history and occupancy. Failure to do so trivializes the profound relationship that Aboriginal people have developed with the land that is now called Canada, a relationship that is fundamental to Aboriginal culture and spirituality.

A more brutal version of this 'equal immigrant' position simply acknowledges the 'conqueror's' power, and suggests history is rewritten by migrants, including the definition of borders and frontiers. This argument accepts the special status of Aboriginal people as a founding people, but questions their right to land on the basis that their culture was inferior to that of the conqueror. This position has been used by the state in numerous court cases, including the Gitksan case mentioned above. In certain cases, claims for compensation or land are rejected unless Aboriginal people can prove they have inhabited a given territory 'since time immemorial' – that is, prior to contact. As a result, Aboriginal people are forced to demonstrate, through archaeological and ethnohistorical research, that they traditionally used a specific area of land. This position ignores a fundamental characteristic of most Aboriginal communities – that they were organized into small bands that occupied huge territories and that in the post-contact period many communities were forced off their traditional homeland.

Another more insidious argument seeks to undermine the notion of Aboriginal rights by suggesting that, whatever the status of Indian communities at contact, Aboriginal communities have subsequently changed, have lost their language and much of their culture, and have become like other Canadians. This argument, often put forward as commonsensical and pragmatic, acknowledges that the treatment of Aboriginal peoples may have been unjust, but suggests that we must face 'reality' and recognize that Aboriginal people are no different from other Canadians. It is reasonable, the argument goes, that people should respect the *remnants* of Native culture – including language, religious customs, and reserves – but it is unreasonable to suggest that Aboriginal people should have special status, because their culture and lifestyle is indistinguishable from that of mainstream society.

I have encountered many, often subtle, versions of this belief in my experience with various public servants. The idea that Aboriginal culture (and therefore rights) has been eroded over time undermines many attempts by Aboriginal people to develop initiatives that in any way diverge from mainstream programs. If Aboriginal people are essentially the same as other Canadians, then they should have access to services similar to mainstream Canadians. This argument is fallacious because it rests on a fundamental misunderstanding about the nature of culture. Specific ceremonies, or even traditions, may be lost, but culture is something that is enduring, while constantly transforming and changing. It is no more reasonable to expect Aboriginal people to be constantly behaving in a traditional fashion than it is to expect that whites should be using horses and buggies, or employing children to work in factories. If contemporary European, Asian, or Western culture exists – so, too, does a contemporary Aboriginal culture. Many Canadians believe that any rights Aboriginal people once possessed have been given up. If it can be argued that, by nature of culture loss, rights – for example, those to hunt and fish – have been eroded or lost, then any special status that is extended to Aboriginal people is extended only as an act of goodwill or charity. And this goodwill can, therefore, be withheld, withdrawn, or rescinded. This attitude underlies much of government history and current government practice.

Finally, there is the suggestion that even if Aboriginal rights have not been naturally eroded, they may have been relinquished by treaty or other government practice. Aboriginal people maintain that their rights have been consistently ignored in law, or violated through government policy. They do *not* suggest that these rights have been abandoned or relinquished in practice. There has never been a treaty or a legal agreement involving Native communities and the state, for example, that stated that Aboriginal people relinquished their right to hunt and fish, nor one to suggest that Indians ever abandoned their right to govern themselves. There is, however, historical information and oral tradition to suggest that Native people have never seen themselves as subjects of the Crown. Borrows demonstrates how recognition of Aboriginal oral history and the history of interaction between First Nations and the government can 'infuse legal and political discourse with different alternatives and grant to First Nations people the liberty that they desire to pursue their aspirations according to their collective goals' (1992: 291).

There is a substantial literature on the idea of Aboriginal rights, including the right to self-government and the legal basis for sovereignty.[15] And there are countless ways, some philosophical, some legal, some commonsensical, of approaching the issue of Aboriginal rights. A number of international organizations, such as the United Nations and the Organization of American States (1995), have recognized the validity of the concept of indigenous rights. These rights include, among others, the right to self-determination, the right to compensation for land seized, the right to traditional medicine and pharmacology, intellectual property rights, control of cultural resources, the right to participate in natural resource management, and the right to practice traditional systems of law.[16] But despite the clarity of international discourse on indigenous human rights, the practice of individual governments, including Canada, is such that complex legal and historical arguments are made to mitigate, obviate, and obfuscate the recognition of indigenous rights in practice.

As noted by the royal commission (1996b: 199–200) the Constitution Act of 1982 explicitly recognized the special status and rights of Aboriginal peoples. 'Section 35 of the *Constitution Act, 1982*, as amended in 1983, provides that existing Aboriginal and treaty rights of the Aboriginal peoples of Canada are recognized and affirmed.' The RCAP suggested that 'the adoption of section 35 (1) marked a watershed in relations between Aboriginal peoples and the Canadian state.' The recognition of Aboriginal rights has since been affirmed in Supreme Court of Canada decisions such as *R. vs Sparrow* where the court suggested that a 'generous, liberal interpretation of the words' was required (ibid). But despite state recognition of these rights, the notion of Aboriginal rights in general, and of the inherent Aboriginal right to self-government in particular, remains extremely muddled in common discourse. People remain concerned about the 'limits' of contemporary Aboriginal rights (how special is special status?) and about how, if at all, these rights are derived from historic treaties and/or contemporary agreements.

The general idea of Aboriginal rights, including the right to self-government, is accepted by many academics and constitutional lawyers. Without claiming to fully understand all the legal and constitutional arguments concerning Aboriginal rights, I am convinced from my own reading of the literature that beginning in 1763 with the Royal Proclamation (aka the Indian Bill of Rights), a long history of documents and treaties has laid a moral foundation for the notion that Aboriginal people have a unique *political* status in law and history, a status derived from their prior occupancy of the country, from their cooperation as allies, as well as from their recognition, by previous Canadian governments, as political entities – that is, nations (see Berger 1991; Cassidy 1991). A paper trail exists and can be interpreted as a legal and historical record that offers many guarantees to Aboriginal people. But, more pragmatically, I am convinced by centuries of actions – both individual and collective – by Aboriginal people who have consistently resisted the incorporation and assimilation of their communities and cultures into the Canadian state.

In anthropology, *resistance* is a concept (some would say a theory) that has emerged to explain the cultural survival and revitalization of indigenous peoples worldwide in the face of horrendous colonial and assimilationist forces. Work by Comaroff (1985) and Scott (1985; 1990) has done much to demonstrate how cultural integrity can be sustained, not by acts of revolution and rebellion, but rather by 'everyday acts' of resistance that are often hidden from the purview of the state, or so subtle in their symbolic content as to be misunderstood by outside observers.[17] In Canada the persistence of traditional medicine and ceremonies, the maintenance of indigenous languages, the survival of traditional political systems – these and many other examples speak to processes of resistance that have occurred throughout the country.

The failure of judges and government policy makers to understand the continued viability and integrity of Aboriginal culture over time rests as much on their misunderstanding of the nature of culture and the subtle nature of resistance as it does on a pragmatic and strategic desire to limit Aboriginal claims (see Waldrum et al 1992). The fundamental debate about the legitimacy of Aboriginal rights has been resolved, though limits or implications of specific rights have yet to be determined. The debate began vigorously with Aboriginal reactions to the Liberal government's 1969 White Paper, that sought to treat Native people as equal to other Canadians. Aboriginal advocates criticized the White Paper for its assimilationist agenda and put forward their claim to special status – the idea that Indians were 'Citizens Plus' (Indian Chiefs of Alberta 1970). The notion that Aboriginal people have all of the rights of Canadian citizens, *plus* additional rights related to their status as the original and founding First Nations, might be contested by the average citizen. But since the 1970s through numerous court cases, legal arguments, and government policy, this unique status has been affirmed (Berger 1991; Morse 1985; Slattery 1992; Pratt 1993). Most recently, the RCAP has argued that 'Aboriginal peoples in Canada possess the right to self-determination. This right is grounded in *emerging* norms of international law and basic principles of public morality' (1996b: 169; emphasis mine). The RCAP also acknowledges that Canada has played an important role in articulating international human-rights standards (ibid). But Canada has, as yet, refused to sign the International Labour Organization Convention No. 169 on Indigenous Peoples (1991), an important international agreement that outlines indigenous rights in many areas, including rights to land, educational systems, and traditional law.

Basic indigenous rights include the right to a land base, the right to hunt and trap on Crown land, the right to medical care and education, and the right to practice legal and spiritual traditions. What has not been clearly determined are the parameters of these rights. The government asserts that the right to medical care, for example, is a matter of government policy, rather than treaty obligation. Aboriginal sovereignty, or the *inherent* right to self-government, has yet to be entrenched in the Canadian constitution, and some Aboriginal advocates suggest that without this provision, the Charter of Rights and Freedoms may be used to limit collective or traditional forms of governance such as hereditary leadership (RCAP 1996c; 1996f: 120–1).

What is critical to understand, then, is that the very notion of Aboriginal rights is subject to change and renovation over time. As Ponting states: 'There is no concrete entity to which we can point and say 'This is Aboriginal rights.' Instead, rights are socio-political-legal constructions with a foundation in the moral order of a society. Furthermore, societal conceptions of morality change over time' (1986: 228). The implications of recognizing Aboriginal rights in law continue to be the subject of great contention. *Sparrow* confirmed 'that the regulation of an Aboriginal right to fish did not result in its extinguishment. Moreover, the burden of justifying legislation that has some negative effect on Aboriginal rights rested with the federal and provincial governments' (RCAP 1996a: 212). An Aboriginal right to hunt and fish on Crown land for individual consumption has been re-established, but there are currently cases where the right to commercial fishing is being challenged in the courts. The rights of Aboriginal people to commercial fishing in Lake Huron and Georgian Bay have recently been upheld by a Provincial Court decision that affirmed their priority right to the fisheries based on earlier treaty agreements. But this decision, pursued by Aboriginal people in courts, has resulted in great animosity among sport fishermen and the tourism industry in general. The issue has served to 'surface' racist beliefs and divide the communities of the Saugeen. During the summer of 1995, this issue became heated, with the burning and sinking of a Native fishing boat (Koenig 1995).

The government currently recognizes, through policy, a number of rights that are not formally acknowledged in law. We might say that, in many areas, the notion of Aboriginal rights is accepted as philosophy, but not yet legislatively encoded. Certainly, many decisions are made in government on the assumption that there is a recognition of Aboriginal rights through time. The federal government commitment to Aboriginal health care, for example, has never been linked to treaty rights.

The debate about the formal recognition of Aboriginal rights is a political one that, from the perspective of First Nations, aims to entrench existing rights in law so as to build a foundation for future institutions. For this reason the constitutional recognition of the inherent right to self-government has great potential symbolic value. But even where a specific Aboriginal right is recognized, the implementation or administration of that right can occur in different ways, across different jurisdictions. Thus, just as there is variation between provinces with regard to health or education, so too the right to control certain jurisdictions results in varying practices among Aboriginal nations. Recognition of an Aboriginal right to maintain peace and good order on reserve (that is, to control justice services), for example, will result in a myriad of different courts and policing arrangements. Aboriginal rights serve as the legal or philosophical foundation for action, whether by government through policy, or by Aboriginal groups who wish to establish their authority in a variety of jurisdictions.

This view of Aboriginal rights as organic and flexible, of rights that are amenable to the changing circumstances of contemporary life, is not in contradiction of the notion of inherency. Even though interpretations of Aboriginal rights change over time, these rights are still derived from a person's status as a descendant of the original inhabitants of the territory now called Canada. Aboriginal rights derive from an original status – a status as cultural and political equals to the European immigrants to the continent, and as Nations that held a territory sufficient for obtaining a standard of living in keeping with their collective practices. If we accept that at the time of contact, Aboriginal cultures were distinct, different, and in no way inferior to the European, then the way is paved to accept the 'nation to nation' argument. The relationship of equals (or allies) was recognized by representatives of the Crown, and later by the Canadian state. And it was symbolized by many ritual activities, including the exchange of gifts, the two-row wampum, and pipe ceremonies, as well as through written treaty. But the spiritual aspect of treaties has always been poorly understood – or simply ignored by governments (RCAP 1996a: 129).

From an Aboriginal Treaty perspective, European rights in the Americas – to the use of lands and resources, for example – did not derive legitimately from international law precepts such as the doctrine of discovery or from European political and legal traditions. Rather the historical basis of rights came about through treaties made with Aboriginal nations. In this view, the terms of the treaties define the rights and responsibilities for both parties. It is a result of the treaties that Canadians have, over time, inherited the wealth generated by Aboriginal lands and resources that Aboriginal nations shared so generously with them. (RCAP 1996a: 128)

We might hope that such a liberal interpretation of treaties would inform contemporary agreements concerning Aboriginal rights. Aboriginal rights, then, are inherent and changing. Over time, the political status and rights of Aboriginal peoples have been obviated by colonial practice. Recognizing Aboriginal rights does not entail 'going back' to an original or traditional status. It is about moving ahead to reforge the relationship of equality that was destroyed through colonialism. Arguments for the 'right' to self-government are about ensuring that the political integrity of First Nations is once again respected.

This perspective is best expressed through the idea of treaty renovation, which suggests that treaties be reinterpreted in light of contemporary circumstances (see RCAP 1996a: 178–9).[18] Upgrading and updating treaties signed in the last century can make them contemporaneous with modern ideals of social welfare and human justice. Perhaps the most obvious example of this philosophy is the recognition that original terms of treaties that called for the provision of a medicine chest, or the right to maintain 'peace and good order' can be translated, in the context of the 1990s, into the right to adequate medical care and to the development of Aboriginal police and court systems. 'In the past, governments and courts in Canada have often considered these treaties instruments of surrender rather than compacts of co-existence and mutual benefit ... It is time to return to the spirit of the treaties and to set a new course to correct the legalistic and adversarial attitudes and actions that have contributed to the badly deteriorated treaty relationships that exist between Aboriginal nations and Canada today' (RCAP 1996a: 178–9). The federal government, despite such pleas, has yet to recognize the concept of treaty renovation, and has gone further in formally denying that many aspects of federal policy, such as the provision of justice services, rests on treaty or other Aboriginal rights.

At the same time, as noted above by Ian Cowie, the federal government is engaged in a modern 'treaty making' enterprise, through its negotiations concerning self-government. These negotiations aim to map out the broad range of jurisdictions that constitute self-government for specific First Nations (Cowie 1993). A question that concerns Aboriginal people engaged in this process is the extent to which these paper agreements, like those of the previous century, will prove to be meaningful.

Land Use, Land Claims

It can be argued that constitutional entrenchment of the inherent right to self-government will prove meaningless without the development of self-sustaining Aboriginal economies. The question of land claims and financial compensation to First Nations, therefore, is central to the enterprise of self-government.

I have a large map of Ontario on my office wall. The map is speckled with tiny red splotches, irregular rectangles that take up a tiny fragment of the province. When students look at this map, they are invariably surprised, and sometimes outraged, by how little land is actually 'reserved' as First Nations territory. There are a small number of reserves in Canada, like Six Nations near Brantford, Ontario, or the Blood reserve near Lethbridge, Alberta, that are quite large in population or territory. In general, however, reserves are small in land base and population. In the North Shore Tribal Council area, for example, reserves range in size from 2.333 acres (on/off reserve population: 61/177) to 43,854 acres (population 225/275). In every community, half the population or more lives off reserve (NSTC 1992a: 1–3). As the RCAP analysis states: 'Except in the far north (including northern Quebec), where comprehensive claims settlements since 1975 have improved the situation, the present land base of Aboriginal communities is inadequate. Lands acknowledged as Aboriginal south of the sixtieth parallel (mainly reserves) make up less than one-half of one per cent of the Canadian land mass. Much of this land is of marginal value. In the United States (excluding Alaska) – where Aboriginal people are a much smaller percentage of the total population – the comparable figure is three percent' (RCAP 1996c: 422–33). Reserves are commonly situated on some of the poorest land in the country. In some instances, for example in Northern Ontario, Aboriginal people have limited access to fish and hunt game beyond their reserve borders. But as yet their commercial fishing rights have not been established. The vast majority of communities do not have access to mineral or timber rights beyond the reserve. Aboriginal people live on small parcels of land surrounded by huge tracts of Crown land that are licensed to international mining and logging companies.

It is a mistake to assume that First Nations have access to large territories, and that they are somehow advantaged compared to Canadians. The total reserve land in Canada is .05%, well below the Aboriginal population, which the RCAP estimated at between about 2.7% of the population at large. Aboriginal people in certain parts of the country – for example, Northern Quebec or the Northwest Territories – have access to sufficient land and resources to offer the prospect of sustainable economies. But Aboriginal people living in the rest of Canada have only limited control over a meagre land base (see RCAP 1996a).[19]

As previously noted, some Canadians are concerned that Aboriginal people will acquire huge tracts of land and that this will somehow jeopardize Canadian interests (including the interests of big business). This assumption is fuelled, perhaps, by press reports of recent comprehensive settlements in the Northwest Territories, which do indeed cover vast tracts of land and will, for example, give birth to the new Arctic province of Nunavut. But such comprehensive claims are atypical. This public perception is also reinforced by unsettled land claims that inflate the potential value of territories. During the writing of this book, I was asked by acquaintances, time and again, whether it seemed strange (unfair?) that British Columbia First Nations were claiming land in Vancouver and more land than actually existed in the entire province! The implication was that Aboriginal demands were somehow unrealistic or outrageous. However, land claims are an adversarial and political process – many claims are overlapping, and all First Nations expect that they will receive financial compensation in lieu of specific lands. For example, the Saugeen and Cape Croker First Nations are currently before the courts to seek control over land in the Saugeen (Bruce) Peninsula. Their claim, which includes prime real estate in cottage country, seeks compensation for the economic value of land loss since the last century, as well as new territory currently under Crown control. The total claim was initially evaluated, by First Nations' advocates, at $80 billion.

Under the federal government's policy there are two types of claims: comprehensive and specific. At the time of writing there were thirty-five comprehensive claims, and well over three hundred specific claims that remained unresolved in the country. Comprehensive claims arise in situations, like the Nisga'a claim in British Columbia, where land is unsurrendered; that is, where land has never been subject to treaty. Specific claims, like Ipperwash, concern any breach of federal responsibility, including survey errors, improper seizure, and so forth. Thus, even where treaties were signed much land is under claim because the treaty-making process has been questioned as illegal or unfair, or because subsequent, illegal encroachments on Indian land have drastically reduced the original size of reserves. The treaty-making process was also subject to much contention, and the surveying of reserve boundaries was often in error. Consequently, most First Nations have recourse through the courts or other forums to contest the boundaries of their reserves. Many succeed in expanding their territory and re-establish the terms agreed to in original treaties.

The land issue is complex, because it entails our conception of public and private land use, as well as the various constructions of collective versus individual rights. Mainstream Canadians are concerned that Aboriginal claims will undermine their own interests – for example, that cottagers will lose their homes, that businesses will be displaced. These claims also suggest for some that the 'cost' of self-government may be too great for the taxpayer to bear given current financial restraints. Placed in perspective, however, the final negotiated settlements do not seem outlandish. The Nisga'a, a six-thousand-member nation in British Columbia, has been pursuing a claim for more than twenty years. Their 1973 Supreme Court case, that ended in a split decision, resulted in the federal government's implementation of the comprehensive land claims negotiation process as a way to avoid court battles (*Globe and Mail*, 15 July 1995, A4). The Nisga'a case has been mired in federal and provincial politics and, more specifically, bogged down by provincial fears that the case may have negative impact on the financial cost of forty-three other claims in the province. The Nisga'a, however, initially sought land in addition to $2 billion in compensation. The 1996 agreement-in-principle includes a 1,930-square-kilometre territory, fishing and timber rights, limited self-government for four villages (including an independent court system), and financial compensation of $190 million.

As noted earlier, there is an expectation on the part of many Canadians polled that land claims and compensation might be positively regarded if they entailed the possibility of extinguishing Aboriginal title to further land, or if they created self- sufficient communities. The idea of extinguishment means, quite simply, that rights associated with Aboriginal title to land – including mineral and other resource rights – are abandoned forever, in return for a specific land base and access to various categories of surrounding lands – for example, the right to cut timber in certain lands, or to hunt and trap in land beyond the reserve. According to the Assembly of First Nations, 'the federal government's primary goal has always been to extinguish the "burden" of Aboriginal rights and minimize its legal obligations' (1991: 232). Polls seem to suggest that people accept the possibility that Aboriginal people might have the right to land, or to large financial compensation packages, but fully expect that if these settlements are agreed to there should then be a price attached, or that Aboriginal people should then be expected to 'give up' other rights. Public opinion, then, seems to indicate a desire for a final resolution to the question of Aboriginal status, a resolution not dissimilar to English Canadians' hope for an end to the Quebec question. But given the sheer number of claims before the federal government, this public wish is unrealistic in the foreseeable future. More to the point, the notion of extinguishment is in direct opposition to the idea that the interpretation of Aboriginal rights changes through time.

The federal government's policy to land claims can clearly be seen as a carefully constructed approach to appease the public, while minimizing the financial burden of potential land claims to the taxpayer. Under current policy, claims can routinely take fifteen to twenty years to settle. The reality of the past thirty years seems to point to an incremental and highly strategic approach by the federal government to consciously delay individual claims, and limit the number of claims heard at any one time, so as to decrease federal costs. Louis Lamothe notes, for example, that the Archives of Canada have 12,500 boxes of classified and non-accessible archival material related to Aboriginal land claims – and this control over information is designed to assist the government in delaying the land claims process (Ottawa ON. 93-07-07 128. PG 424). The potential power that lies buried in such documents was recently demonstrated in the Ipperwash crisis when, only after the shooting death of Dudley George, the federal government revealed correspondence that acknowledged, for the first time, the existence of a burial site in the Ipperwash Provincial Park, thereby confirming Aboriginal claims (Gulewitsch 1995). From an Aboriginal perspective, the federal government's comprehensive claim policy protects the Crown's rights concerning land and resources (AFN 1991: 236–8). The policy allows only six comprehensive claims per year; at the current rate of 'progress' some bands could wait thirty years or more for a settlement to be reached. The failure of land claims process has forced many bands in southern Ontario to consider the outright purchase of land in surrounding areas in order to provide a sufficient land base for economic development (*Spectator*, 23 July 1994, B5).

Treaty renovation and the settlement of land claims are intrinsic to the process of self government. Will Canadians continue to see land claims as a 'cost' of self-government? Or can they begin to think of claims as an investment in a new political relationship with First Nations? The real focus, I believe, should be on how best to provide land and compensation so as to ensure a sufficient resource base for sustainable development. In the following chapters the 'cost' versus 'investment' argument is played out in many areas. It is clear that the current federal policy simply attempts to defer claims over many years. The process is such that the sum of money spent on bureaucracy, travel, and legal fees over many years of negotiations can approach the amount of financial settlements. As a recent report by the Indian Commission of Ontario noted, much can be done to improve the negotiation process – which currently costs taxpayers millions of dollars per year with few tangible settlements to date (*Spectator*, 30 Jan. 1995).

Federal policy makes no linkage between self-government and land claims, and continues to try to sustain an antiquated view of Aboriginal rights that allows Aboriginal title to be 'superseded in law' in order to deny the basis for a claim. Perhaps the most obvious and explicit example of the government's arbitrariness, intransigence, and unashamed manipulation of historical claims in light of pressure from the national and international resource industry is the case of the Lubicon of Northern Alberta, a 'band without a land base.' This case is considered by many to have left a deep scar in Canada's international reputation (Richardson 1989: 229–64; Goddard 1991; Hill 1995).

Public opinion, however, does seem to support the idea that land claims should provide for self-sufficient and self-sustaining communities. According to one post-RCAP poll, 48% of Canadians believe that 'some' government-owned lands and resources should be transferred to Aboriginal communities to make them self-sufficient (*Globe and Mail*, 15 Jan. 1997, A4). The issue of economic self-sufficiency is critical to the ideals and aspirations of Aboriginal people. Land claims are essential if poverty and associated social problems are to be overcome (RCAP 1993f). There is, of course, considerable concern from local municipalities that land claims will have a negative impact on local economies in a variety of ways (see, for example, *Spectator*, 30 Jan. 1995b). Land claims are pursued in an atmosphere that can exacerbate pre-existing tensions between Native and non-Native communities. Non-Native entrepreneurs often see the development of reserve economies as a direct threat to their own small businesses, while failing to recognize that the long-term economic development of reserves cannot help but increase the viability of regional economics, while decreasing Aboriginal reliance on government assistance.

As James Gosnell, a Nisga'a leader, has stated, 'exclusive ownership' over land is not necessarily the end point of negotiations; rather, Aboriginal people seek agreements that recognize Aboriginal laws and systems of government (cited in D. Smith 1993: 86). Compensation packages can include cash settlements as well as political arrangements – for example, co-management regimes that allow First Nations a role in decision making about resource development. Land, financial compensation for land lost, or political authority over resource development can all be critical to the development of sustainable Aboriginal economies. Whether through purchase or expansion of existing boundaries, First Nations must have access to land that has resource potential. And they must receive compensation – based on recent history, in the area of roughly $7 to $15 million per reserve – investment capital to enable community members to develop business opportunities. Land claims can potentially re-energize communities that are mired in an environment of chronic unemployment and welfare dependency.

The power of land claims to transform a community cannot be underestimated. Mississauga First Nation (MFN), located outside Blind River, Ontario, has a population of 364 (another 313 people live off reserve). The reserve, which comprises roughly 4,887 acres, was established in 1850 under the Robinson Huron Treaty, but the northern boundary was incorrectly defined by the original surveyors. Almost 150 years later, after over a decade of land-claims research and extensive negotiations, the Mississauga First Nation signed an agreement that restored its northern border to a point originally agreed upon by the signatories to the treaty. In the process the Mississauga territory expanded tenfold, by approximately 40,000 acres. The band now possesses land with considerable recreational and resource potential (MFN 1994: 3). In addition to the land settlement, the band was awarded seven million dollars, and has created a trust fund that will be used to finance long-term economic development projects.

The land-claims process placed enormous pressure on members of Mississauga First Nation. The public consultation process 'sparked unexpected, heated and hostile public protests; threats; demonstrations and petitions against the claim, its Aboriginal peoples and governments in general' (MFN 1994:1–2). Band members were subject to 'tense, external, public scrutiny' during the final phase of negotiation, a time that coincided with the sudden deaths of twelve community members during a year-and-a-half period. Many community members believe that the stress caused by deteriorating relationships with non-Native communities may have indirectly contributed to these deaths; a band report suggests that five of the deaths were stress related (Daybutch 1994: 1). Several front-line workers believe that the stress of the land-claims process had a direct and negative impact on the mental health of band members. In addition, growing tension with the white cottagers and business owners of the Blind River community, who felt threatened by the land claims, created stress among community members, who felt as if they were under a microscope when they ventured off reserve.

The potential, long-term impact of this settlement, of course, is difficult to gauge. In many ways, Mississauga is a typical Ontario First Nation. The unemployment rate fluctuates between 51 and 63%; only 60 of 203 adults are employed full time; 45 of these are band employees. Eighty-two people are on some form of social assistance (disability, UIC, or GWA). The land claim holds enormous promise for long-term socio-economic development. The band has already started to develop a small business loan program, and trustees are examining other long-term business and economic development projects, including the development of recreational facilities and tourist lodges.

The aftermath of this claim is still being felt. Resentment among non-Native people about this 'give-away' remains. Band members suggest that the general atmosphere of the town has been poisoned against Natives. There is also considerable pressure on the part of band employees, chief and council, and trustees to ensure that the settlement becomes the foundation for long-term growth. One of the consequences of the rhetoric of self-government is rising expectations, which often place unreasonable demands on a small circle of First Nations leaders and employees (see chapter 6). But despite all of these difficulties, Mississauga band members feel a strong sense of justice and affirmation that their rights to land have been recognized. And they feel an enormous optimism and hope that this settlement will act as the catalyst for the development of a sustainable economic base, and eventually, for self-government.

Self-Government: An Iterative Process

The Assembly of First Nations (AFN) argues that the right to self-government is inherent, and has fought unsuccessfully that this be recognized in the Canadian constitution. The position of the AFN seems to be that because the right to self-government is inherent, Aboriginal people have the right to assume control over *any* power or jurisdiction that is legitimately defined as following their Aboriginal status. That is, it is up to First Nations, and not the federal government, to determine the legitimate parameters of self-government. As recently as July 1995, the AFN chiefs rejected as 'too restrictive' Indian Affairs Minister Ron Irwin's proposal to give First Nations some powers held by provinces and municipalities, in return for the AFN's assurance that the Charter of Rights and Freedoms would apply to First Nations (*Toronto Star*, 20 July 1995, A13).

Much of the rhetoric of self-government concerns a 'philosophical' position, which stems from the ideas of lawyers, academics, constitutional experts, and small elites of chiefs. It is concerned with the legal and philosophical foundation of Aboriginal rights in law and in the constitution. Public confusion about the meaning of self-government arises from the complexity of legal and constitutional arguments, that remain unfathomable to non-specialists. As early as 1984, Sally Weaver noted that the concept of self- government remained at the level of a 'value-notion.' Self-government, she argued, was a concept 'in need of a definition.' Despite a great deal of progress, the concept of self-government remains elusive. There remains confusion surrounding the practical implications of constitutional change; confusion about what self-government will mean 'on the ground.' And this confusion exists not simply within academia and government bureaucracy, and among the Canadian public, but within Aboriginal communities themselves, where self-government is misunderstood, and in many instances rejected, not only by average community members but by many political leaders.

This confusion is natural given the relationship between constitutional reform, legal precedent, and actual practice. The implications of legislative or constitutional decisions cannot always be anticipated, as can be seen in recent revisions to the Charter of Rights and Freedoms several years after its adoption, in which some interpretations by the Supreme Court are 'out of sync' with public opinion. The defence of extreme drunkenness in criminal cases, the outcry against homosexual rights in the area of family adoption or spousal benefits, and more relevant here, the reaction against the right of Aboriginal people to hunt and fish on Crown land, are all examples of how the constitutional protection of rights can run afoul of the values of mainstream Canadians – or the attitudes of a vocal minority.

It is precisely such instances that conjure up uncertainty and discomfort when people are faced with the rhetoric of self-government. Many Aboriginal people, for example, express concern that self-government agreements will result in an instantaneous removal of rights long protected by the Indian Act.[20] Mainstream Canadians do not realize that many Aboriginal people believe they may actually *lose* ground under self-government arrangements. Status Indians living on reserve are concerned that they will have to pay income tax, that they will no longer receive medical benefits or access to housing, and significantly, that their band councils will abuse new powers or frivolously appropriate new financial resources for their own use.

In contrast, many Euro-Canadians see self-government as potentially 'giving away the store,' and as an inappropriate response to the collective guilt trip whites experience when revisiting the legacy of colonial history. Mainstream fears of self-government also stem from the perception that Aboriginal people are not yet ready for political control. This suggestion, of course, is merely an extension of the paternalism that for years underlay colonial attitudes – it suggests that, like 'children,' Aboriginal people are incapable of looking after their own affairs. There are fears also that the costs of self-government are too great, that Aboriginal control will somehow result in a greater tax burden for the average citizen or that self-government will result in separate standards of law or rights; that is, that Native people will somehow be privileged over ordinary citizens. Many of these fears have some foundation in reality. Others are totally unfounded and based on a racist misunderstanding of reserve life. But all are based on anticipated consequences of self-government, that is, on people's speculation, rather than on any understanding of the process through which Aboriginal people are assuming political control.

To allay these fears, we must remember that self-government is an emergent, iterative process – its meaning and validity become clearer with its practice. Important social concepts emerge slowly; systems change gradually. This is especially true in a country like Canada, whose national character hinges on such qualities as compromise and caution and where concern for social justice and equality has been a paramount political concern. As an illustration of this politics of incrementalism we need only look at the twenty- to thirty-year-debate concerning gay and lesbian rights that is taking place amid an ongoing reformation of our concept of family. There has been a gradual movement to redefine, in law and social policy, the concept of 'family' to include same-sex spouses, and the children of these spouses. But there has been considerable mainstream, often religious, opposition to this re-creation of family; for example, to formal church recognition of gay marriages, to pensions and other spousal benefits for gay partners, and to the adoption of children by lesbians and gays. This issue pits basic social justice or fairness, that the majority of the population wants, against the violation of what is perceived to constitute a normal family (or parent, or spouse). Social reforms, then, rest on the long-term renovation of people's ideas about a specific minority, as well as their redefinition of concepts that are considered inviolable because of their 'natural' status. In terms of gay rights and family, long-term changes in policy are achieved by the actions of the minority, which demonstrates, over the long term, that the changing status of the family does not threaten essential characteristics of social life (for example, the sanctity of heterosexual marriage or the provision of a positive home environment for children). In this way a political environment is created where legislation can be supported, or court cases won.

The project of self-government, too, has a long history. It is clear that much public education about Aboriginal issues has occurred, and that much greater understanding of Aboriginal culture is needed. A pragmatic view of self-government affords Aboriginal people the opportunity to demonstrate, over time, how increased political control in different jurisdictions provides for more effective and culturally appropriate solutions to community problems. The reality of self-government concerns political authority at the local level. It is what happens 'on the ground,' when individuals and communities are recognized as having the right, and the ability, to conduct their own affairs. It is about increasingly self-sufficiency and the process of capacity-building whereby communities can identify their needs, exercise their ability to address these needs, and evaluate approaches so as to ensure that human and financial resources are allocated effectively and efficiently. Self-government is about whether children are properly educated and protected as they grow to adulthood and about whether offenders against public order are appropriately identified, helped, or punished. It is about the right to create institutions that are culturally appropriate and responsive to local conditions. It is about whether people feel they can contribute to political processes, and whether their duly elected representatives proceed in a manner that is in keeping with their expectations.

This pragmatic view of self-government has recently gained popularity among many Aboriginal leaders. Many chiefs note that there is an essential contradiction in calling for entrenchment of self-government in the constitution: if an inherent right to self-government exists, it can only be recognized in law by the colonizer. For this reason, some Aboriginal leaders reject constitutional reform, preferring instead to stress that self-government does not need to be recognized. Rather, they argue, inherent rights can only by enacted through the actions of individual First Nations. In the aftermath of the failure of Meech Lake, this position became increasingly recognized by chiefs across the country, who now speak of self-government that already exists, and that only needs to be demonstrated. Thus, for example, numerous statements made at the 1994 Assembly of Chiefs of Ontario stressed the need for First Nations to act independently in diverse fields to set precedents that demonstrate that they are self-governing and do not need constitutional recognition to exercise authority in any jurisdiction. One First Nation may challenge Ministry of Natural Resources policy by commercial fishing – recently, for example, Chief Richard Kahgee, of the Saugeen First Nation, through the Duluth Declaration, unilaterally claimed sovereignty over a significant portion of Great Lakes waters around the Saugeen Peninsula (*Globe and Mail*, 26 Sept. 1995, A10). Another First Nation may concentrate its efforts on removing provincial police from the reserve or creating its own justice system. First Nations can determine these priority areas on the basis of individual interest, community history, or, more strategically, to complement the actions of other nations. In this way, the government comes under assault, not through any constitutional movement, but through community action that aims to set precedent or challenge existing practice. In the long term, then, the realization of self-government comes through the collective and cumulative efforts of diverse First Nations. Some of these actions have the potential to lead to confrontation; many others involve non-threatening changes to the relationship between Aboriginal communities and the state. Much of the process of self-government, therefore, is composed of painstakingly cautious changes and negotiations to map out new areas of Aboriginal authority.

The rhetoric and reality of self-government is clearly illustrated in reactions to the call for a parallel system of Aboriginal courts. Virtually every discussion of this initiative results in major criticism in the media (see chapter 5). Editorial writers quickly appeal to the Charter of Rights and Freedoms, suggesting that there can be only one law in the country. There is an almost universal intolerance of the idea that Native people might be allowed to control their own justice system, or render punishments that somehow might be divergent from the application of law in mainstream society. But Aboriginal justice systems are slowly emerging across the country. Many First Nations already have their own police forces, and Aboriginal elders sit, along with judges, to help determine culturally appropriate sentences. These developments, the first step in a long process toward the creation of Aboriginal justice systems, are a pragmatic response to current patterns of interpersonal violence on reserve, and to Aboriginal conflict with state law. Thus, if we view self-government as an emergent and iterative experiment in social policy and practice, we can begin to understand how it offers mainstream Canadians many innovative solutions to problems in health, social welfare, and justice.

First Nations, Other Nations

What should be the operational political unit for self-government? At present there are 605 Indian bands in Canada with an average of 915 members (Depew 1994c: 13). The average size of on-reserve bands is about 500 people; in Ontario 69% of reserves have populations of less than 500 (Stenning 1992: 11). Aboriginal communities are small in comparison to municipalities, yet they seek, as First Nations, to control jurisdictions normally associated with provincial governments.

This situation may account for some of the general public's confusion about the nature of self-government. Fifty-two per cent of Canadians feel Aboriginal communities should have constitutional status similar to that of provinces (*Globe and Mail*, 15 Jan. 1997, A4). The RCAP clearly recognized the danger in First Nations' claims for autonomy.[21] The commission, while not being prescriptive, attempted to identity a range of possible or potential units of self-government, units that are large enough to exercise federal and provincial powers. It suggests as a 'rough baseline,' the potential for eighty nations, while noting that there were between fifty and sixty nations before contact. Under the above criterion, an Aboriginal nation might include a single large First Nation – for example, the members of Six Nations reserve near Brantford; groups of First Nations that have a shared history, treaty, or political relationship might also be identified. For the communities of the North Shore, for example, provincial-like powers might be assumed by a single tribal council, or larger groupings of communities, while federal powers or jurisdictions might be exercised by an existing political or tribal organization such as the Anishnabek Nation (Union of Ontario Indians) or by another regional grouping of Ojibwa nations. In all of the RCAP's analysis, there is a high degree of optimism concerning the emergence of potential nations over the next decades, and the recognition that there is a need to identify politically and economically viable units for self-government that share a sense of identity, history, and culture.

Numerous levels of Indian political organization have a role in shaping the process of self-government. Here I speak briefly of four of these levels: First Nations, tribal councils, political or tribal organizations (PTOs), and provincial or national organizations such as the Assembly of First Nations (AFN). First Nations are very diverse in their geographic, cultural, and economic characteristics. As Depew notes, there are important theoretical and practical questions 'concerning the role that community diversity plays in institutional development' (1994c: 17). Little work has been done on community classification since Gerber's 1979 typology of Indian reserves, that developed a basic comparison of bands according to degrees of 'institutional completeness'; that is, the degree to which various communities retained traditional language use, or resisted the influence of mainstream society. As Depew notes, Gerber's typology drew attention to many factors, including distance from urban centres, degree of personal resource management, and employment, that influence attitudes toward, and capacity for, self-government.

The size of reserves and their kin-based structure present special obstacles to self-government. At first glance it would seem that the small size of reserves makes the potential for community mobilization and revitalization great. There are certainly instances, such as in Alkali Lake, where dramatic transformations in communities have occurred within the span of a decade (see York 1992). But we must be cautious in over-generalizing about the cohesiveness of reserves. As Depew points out, forms of social organization have changed rapidly over many decades. He notes family and clan ties have been carried into contemporary settlements that are very different from those of the past (1994a: 33; Asch 1988). The shift to permanent settlements, which occurred in many parts of the country in the 1950s and 1960s, not only transformed traditional spatial arrangements, but radically transformed traditional patterns of kinship, band political structures, and clan systems. These changes have important implications for current patterns of social and political cooperation and for conflict resolution (see chapter 6; also Depew 1994a: 33; McDonnell 1992a: 60–2). All too often internal divisions stymie even the best-intentioned initiatives. And as with any form of political organization, we must remember that First Nations leadership may or may not be representative of the community at large. McDonnell notes: 'those who would administer and lead at the local and regional level have, in their education and through their experience, acquired a set of priorities and concerns that are far from representative' (1993: 19; cited in Depew 1994c: 35). Boldt (1993: 120–9) notes that there has evolved a two-tier structure involving kinship, class, and power, between those who have access to political office (and all its economic benefits) and those who are shut out of band administrations. Education is also increasingly an important criterion for success in First Nations politics. The conservatism of many community members often seems at odds with the liberal aspirations of a small, relatively young and well educated, administrative and human service staff who hold progressive beliefs and who see self-government as an important objective.

Conservative attitudes are common on reserve. Even the strongest advocate of self-government often professes a go-slow approach to community change. Some Aboriginal people have suggested that this conservatism may be bred of years of government dependency, and of a reliance on government services. There is, of course, a comfort that comes with an understanding of 'how life is,' which makes the idea of change unpalatable to many people – and self-government conjures up images of radical change. There is fear that self-government will result in a greater economic burden on reserve – that people will be taxed to support government institutions. There is concern that many safeguards entailed in the government's long-standing trust relationship to Aboriginal people will be eroded or lost. And there is cynicism; some people suggest that self-government negotiations, like treaty making of the past, will result in paper agreements that will be simply ignored by governments.

There is also a very legitimate concern that many communities are simply not ready to assume control over a range of services. Many communities lack human resources – people with professional, administrative, or management skills. For instance, there are only about fifty Aboriginal physicians in Canada, and even fewer people trained in health management (see RCAP 1993b). This type of human-resource deficit is evident in many fields, for example, in policy making and program planning as well as social services. The shortage of skilled professionals on reserve is exacerbated by the fact that many well-trained Aboriginal people leave reserves to seek further education or jobs in Aboriginal organizations or the public service. There is, of course, nothing to prevent First Nations from hiring professionals from outside their own community – indeed, this is often done. But increasingly, there is a move toward hiring and promoting Aboriginal people in general, and band members in particular, and toward recognizing life experience in lieu of other professional training. Even the most cursory review of First Nations human resources suggests a need for a concerted political commitment, at all levels, to provide training and professional development for First Nations. This is an important reason why self-government will not be exercised in the short term even if new powers are recognized or legislated (see also chapter 6).

First Nations are in direct competition with tribal councils or PTOs for key human resources. In the short term, therefore, cooperation in research, policy making, and program planning is absolutely critical. And inevitably, the shortage of human and financial resources that exists at the First Nations level makes individual bands reliant on tribal councils or larger, regional organizations, for much of their strategic planning, policy analysis, and political advocacy, thereby creating an uneasy alliance between First Nations, which are invested with statutory political authority, and tribal councils or provincial/territorial tribal organizations (PTOs), that have administrative and policy expertise, but only delegated authority.

Every First Nation possesses highly motivated, energetic, and skilled individuals who provide capable leadership. But this core group is often overworked and overburdened with the many initiatives occurring on reserve – initiatives that include crisis intervention, government negotiations, treaty research, and program design. The nature of Aboriginal community life and the lack of human resources mean that most communities are capable of handling only two or three major initiatives at any one time – for example, health care reform, land claims, or economic development. But self-government entails a huge range of jurisdictions. As a result, individual First Nations are faced with difficult choices about community priorities at any given time. This is one reason why self-government must be viewed as a process, as well as an end. Native leaders are well aware that years of community discussion, consultation, and human resource development will be necessary in order to obtain the level of community support and capacity that are necessary before self-government becomes a reality.

The small size of reserves makes it difficult and unrealistic, in my assessment, for First Nations to seize control over all services and financial resources necessary for self-government – the economies of scale simply will not allow it. For this reason, many functions – for example, higher education, training, policy development – may be invested in other, more regional, organizations such as tribal councils and PTOS.

First Nations are commonly linked together by government initiative, geography, convenience, or history into organizations commonly called tribal councils. There are currently eighty tribal councils in Canada, which range in size from two to sixteen bands, with an average tribal council comprising seven First Nations (Depew 1994c: 13). Only 106 bands, or 18% of First Nations are unaffiliated (ibid). The predominant Aboriginal political ideology, however, emphasizes First Nation status and rights. There is, therefore, a conflict between First Nations' desire for political autonomy and strategies to deliver services in a cost-effective way at a regional level. The parochial nature of First Nations politics, coupled with criticisms made against tribal councils or other neighbouring First Nations, are a major obstacle to self-government.

I believe tribal councils are the appropriate political unit to exercise a range of Aboriginal jurisdictions and to deliver a variety of services. These organizations, that represent perhaps three to five thousand people living on reserve, are the only units that, given the economies of scale, can marshall the resources – both human and material – required to address the many problems that exist on reserve.[22] But in many parts of the country, these units are often incipient in nature, and years of work, organization building, and political negotiations will be needed for Aboriginal people to develop the political capacity to sustain self-governing institutions. Depew notes the critical strategic importance of tribal councils for the long-term devolution of political and administrative power to Indian communities (1994c: 3–4). He notes that the Department of Indian Affairs and Northern Development (DIAND), and the federal government generally, have long been criticized for the complex administrative relationships with First Nations – relationships that are often 'cumbersome, and poorly focused, but cost-inefficient' (ibid). A major goal in proposals to dismantle the DIAND is to reduce the levels of administration that so constrict decision making and bind First Nations in red tape, while passing real dollar savings to First Nations through the elimination of positions within federal and regional bureaucracies.

A critical first step in this process must be the establishment of healthy Aboriginal political organizations at the regional level. As Depew notes, the DIAND has a vested interest in the organizational success of tribal councils. Successful tribal councils reduce the number of administrative linkages that the federal bureaucracy must wrestle with, and potentially offer significant improvements in cost efficiency and management. While it can be argued larger organizations are also important for the development of tribal allegiances, tribal councils seem to represent ideal groupings, that are small enough to truly represent local interests, while delivering services in a cost-efficient manner.

Although generalizing is difficult, Mamaweswen, the North Shore Tribal Council (NSTC), can be considered fairly typical; my description of this organization in the following chapters is illustrative both of the problems and unquestionable potential of tribal councils. The NSTC is one of the strongest and most progressive regional organizations in the country. But throughout its history it has experienced a variety of difficulties, including tensions between the member First Nations. The tribal council represents a total population of 6,547 people, with a total land base of about 220,599 acres. Six of the seven communities belong to the Anishnabek Nation, while a seventh community, Batchewana, belongs to another PTO, the Association of Iroquois and Allied Indians (AIAI). In self-government negotiations, for example, Batchewana held observer status, but did not actively engage in negotiations with other North Shore First Nations.

Aboriginal political organizations have evolved through colonial practice; they are government initiated and supported. McDonnell's study of the Cree (1992a) demonstrates that the form and function of Aboriginal organizations have evolved naturally as an extension of the state. First Nations' councils are a creation of the state. The Indian Act was used to wrap traditional, informal modes of leadership in the rigid cloth of Western-style democracy. McDonnell demonstrates how the organizational structure of Cree councils is oriented to the state. Lines of accountability, hierarchical arrangements, and financial relationships all function to make Indian organizations responsive to federal or provincial authorities. This makes service reorganization or political restructuring extremely difficult.

Does the existence of tribal councils threaten the power and jurisdiction of First Nations? In theory, tribal councils, which comprise chiefs and councillors from their respective First Nations, act only by delegated authority from the First Nations, in areas of corporate or regional interest. Invariably, however, the practice of tribal councils is such that any decision – whether it is to hire an individual, develop a program, or enter into various negotiations – can run contrary to the preferred position of an individual First Nation. And although tribal councils may attempt to act only after consensus is achieved, consensus may in fact exist by default; that is, it is reached only through the withdrawal of a First Nation's representation at a given time.

The authority of First Nations is also threatened by a number of other regional service organizations. For example, in the North Shore area, Nog-Da-Win-Da-Min Child and Family Services and the Anishnabek Treatment Centre are regional institutions governed by volunteer boards. These boards may or may not include chiefs as members. The organizational relationship between bands and tribal councils, which are *political*, and boards, which are service oriented, is exceptionally complex, and sometimes problematic, in part because the jurisdictional or policy base between these organizations is undeveloped or ill-defined. Mamaweswen has conducted extensive research and consultation in order to clarify the roles and relationships between various organizations (NSTC 1994b).

Tribal councils experience a number of political and administrative problems, but little evaluation of these organizations exists. There are some indications that serious problems arise because tribal councils are both *political* organizations and *service* deliverers. These dual mandates sometimes conflict. Depew suggests that the lack of serious organizational study of tribal councils prevents us from assessing if problems are systemic or not – that is, whether they stem, in part, from the nature of these organizations, or merely from a lack of experienced staff or a lack of organizational development. As Depew notes, problems may be underestimated or dismissed by the suggestion that tribal councils are young organizations, or that they must go through a period of growth before becoming more efficient (ibid: 4, 22). Consultants I have spoken to agree that, like many organizations, tribal councils must proceed through periodic crises – crises that often force major restructuring or re-alignments – in order to progress to a more efficient and innovative organizational form. There is at least scattered evidence to suggest that tribal councils are in an early stage of development and that they must be given time to increase their organizational capacity and efficiency.

Equally true, and evident to anyone who has worked at either the tribal council or First Nation level, is the lack of administrative rigour in daily practice. It is common for tribal councils, regional boards, and staff to work without written mandates or policies, and for roles and responsibilities to be ill-defined or not defined at all. And of course, informal roles are often in conflict, particularly where different agencies or councils compete for scarce resources. It is possible, therefore, for a chief or councillor to sit on several boards, all of which are concerned with, for example, developing a new program for children. There is a great need for tribal councils and First Nations to spend time and energy increasing the efficiency and competency of staff-board or staff-council relationships, to clarify mandates and jurisdictions, and to increase the professionalism of workers within various organizations. As well, First Nations and tribal councils must commit to the ongoing evaluation of services to reassess whether they are best delivered on a regional or local basis.

In most parts of the country tribal councils have less than a ten- or fifteen-year history. They have become easy targets for the diverse complaints and fears of community members. Along the North Shore, as in other parts of Ontario, for example, it is common to hear the tribal council described as a mini-Indian Affairs department, a criticism that has less to do with the increasing responsibilities that regional staff have taken on, and more to do with the lack of trust and suspicion that exists between individual First Nations and the new Aboriginal bureaucracy being created at the regional level. These criticisms may indicate that these organizations are in danger of becoming 'meaningless or dysfunctional for the communities that they are intended to serve' (Depew 1994c: 8) or, more simply, that they have become the focus of discontent and rising expectations that are a natural part of the shift to Native control. But whatever the difficulties facing tribal councils, there is reason to believe that their long-term role in Aboriginal government will only increase. Stable and effective tribal governments are, of course, one key to self-government. It is important to recognize that a financial commitment is necessary to enhance organizational development over the next decade. Failure to invest in Aboriginal leadership and political organizations will lead to expensive failures.

My analysis is concentrated at the tribal council and First Nations levels, though I will have occasion to refer to initiatives that take place in PTOs. PTOs comprise regional groupings of bands, often based on tribal and language affiliations, as well as historic treaty relationships. In Ontario, there are four such PTOs, which represent various Iroquois, Cree, and Ojibwa communities.[23] Most of my experience has been with the Anishnabek Nation, also known as the Union of Ontario Indians, which represents forty-two First Nations in south-central, north-central, and northern Ontario – from the foot of Georgian Bay through to the north shore of Lake Superior. PTOs are important culturally, because they link together communities that share a common cultural history. Yet none of these Ontario organizations represents the complete range of communities belonging to a particular tribal area. PTOs are critical to political advocacy, lobbying, and strategic planning. They help to shape provincial and federal government policy, and are essential in developing a wide number of services, for example, in the fields of health, education, and social welfare. The Anishnabek Nation, for example, was instrumental in establishing specialized Native Community Care training programs at Cambrian and Mohawk colleges. These PTOs, along with their urban counterparts such as the Federation of Indian Friendship Centres, played a critical role in the development of a provincial Aboriginal Healing and Wellness Strategy (chapter 4). In future, PTOs will assume responsibility in developing regional health authorities, Aboriginal research and training institutes, and economic development banks. PTOs are commonly directed through boards composed, once again, of chiefs who have been nominated at regional assemblies or grand councils. Staffs of these organizations often play an important part in the policy development and research necessary for long-term development of Native-controlled services. The degree to which PTOs are involved in direct service delivery varies considerably around the province.

Nationally, Aboriginal peoples are represented by various status and non-status Indian organizations. The most powerful are the Métis National Council, which represents Métis and non-status Indians as well as Native people living off reserve; Inuit Tapirisat Canada, representing Inuit peoples; and the Assembly of First Nations (AFN), which represents the aspirations of status Indians. The AFN is actually an organization of chiefs;

the leadership is not selected directly by community members but rather by an election of chiefs – for example, in Ontario, through the All Ontario Chiefs Conference. Significantly, these organizations are currently contemplating developing more traditional, or more democratic forms of representation – for example, by having elders' councils play a greater role in the selection or monitoring of leadership or by having community members vote directly for a national leader.

As the major organization representing status Indians, the AFN is an important national voice for Aboriginal people. With the support of a head office in Ottawa, the AFN conducts research and develops policy in support of a wide range of self-government initiatives. For many Canadians the rhetoric of self-government is closely associated with the statements of such leaders as Ovide Mercredi, the past national chief of AFN. These leaders, and the organizations they represent, can play a major role in setting the tone or atmosphere for ongoing confrontations or negotiations across the country, and therefore the political rhetoric they espouse is central to the relationship between Aboriginal people and the Canadian public. As an editorial in the *Toronto Star* noted: 'There is a deep well of sympathy – or perhaps it's guilt – among Canadians for the plight of our [sic] Native peoples. That translates into toleration of blockades, sit-ins and smuggling that otherwise would prompt swift public condemnation. But Ovide Mercredi, national chief of the Assembly of First Nations, risks eroding that sympathy with his mutterings this week about becoming "more aggressive, more militant" in pursuit of AFN goals' (20 July 1995, A22). This editorial suggested that 'what's bugging Mercredi' is the pragmatic approach assumed by the federal Liberal government, an approach that has ignored the AFN objective of constitutional entrenchment of the right to self-government and has instead pursued self-government agreements 'behind his back, with chiefs around the country.' Leaving aside the paternalistic tone, this editorial contains an essential truth – while organizations like the AFN can play a critical role in shaping important federal policies; the nuts and bolts of the self-government movement are to be found in tribal council and First Nations environments. This reality ensures that self-government will take on many different forms throughout the country. The integrity of First Nations authority plays right into the hands of the federal government, who, by negotiating self-government with individual First Nations or tribal councils, can seek to 'divide and conquer' and so limit the overall jurisdiction of Aboriginal government. Indeed the diversity of First Nations ensures that a certain degree of dissension will exist over almost every major national initiative (ibid: A13). The authority of First Nations to act independently – whether in concert with or against tribal council, PTO, or AFN positions – remains the fundamental precept of Aboriginal politics. Thus, the long-term division of political jurisdictions between PTOs, tribal councils, and First Nations remains a major issue, which will inevitably be determined by federal strategy and the economies of scale.

Conclusion

Without increased public education there is little hope that self-government will be palatable to non-Native Canadians. Misunderstandings about Aboriginal people are pervasive throughout society – they are common even among the well educated. I once sat on a committee that met to consider a proposal by the Department of Social Work at McMaster University. The proposal was to create a different admission process for Aboriginal people wishing to enter the social work program; not surprisingly, this created concern that academic standards might be compromised. What I found interesting was that while there was considerable understanding of the fact that Aboriginal people were disadvantaged in society, there was little knowledge of Aboriginal people's unique status, and considerable ignorance – freely admitted – about the nature of Aboriginal people in general. To my dismay, our discussions invariably fell back on inappropriate comparisons – to the special needs of disabled students, or to the suggestion that this proposal would result in special requirements for other ethnic minorities. In the end, however, the proposal passed with unanimous support. This small experience confirmed for me that, with sound information and rational debate, misunderstandings can be overcome, and an environment for social justice created.

Central to the creation of such environments is increased understanding and the willingness to debate complex ideas. In this chapter I have outlined some of the common assumptions held by mainstream Canadians about Aboriginal people, and Aboriginal affairs. At the same time I have tried to move the discussion away from simplistic characterizations of Aboriginal life, to more complex and informed questions about just how much work needs to be done before self-government can become a reality.

As a rhetorical device, self-government is a powerful concept. But it is also an elusive concept, one easily misused by both opponents and advocates of Aboriginal people. The concept is dangerous because, in lacking definition, it can promote fear of an as yet unknown state of affairs – of potential change that comes without a price tag. Ian Cowie states: 'At the 1987 Constitutional conference – the last failure in Indian Affairs at the constitutional level – you'll recall a number of the ministers, pointing at the Aboriginal leaders across the table and saying "you tell us what this actually means, draw us a picture of how this is going to work."' This is not to suggest that Aboriginal leaders have not been explicit in their description of the range of jurisdictions self-government entails (see, for example, Cassidy 1991). But at the level of individual communities, and within the government bureaucracy, there is a desire to clarify just what self-government means (see also D. Smith 1993: 60–90).

The following chapters attempt to ground the concept of self-government in the pragmatics of community life. As suggested by Bentley Cheechoo (see above, 19), for self-government to be meaningful, community-wide healing must occur. It would be a serious error to focus on obstacles to community healing (and they are many) within Aboriginal communities, without also demonstrating that family and community problems are, to a great extent, produced by the state's intervention in community life. The state must provide financial resources for healing to occur, while at the same time vacating the field so as to allow communities the freedom to develop innovative solutions to the problems they confront.

But in order for this to occur, public support for the Aboriginal agenda must increase. At some point sufficient pressure must be brought to bear on politicians so that the aims and ambitions of Aboriginal people are recognized as legitimate. This pressure will be possible only if the general discussion of Aboriginal self-government is elevated and if public opinion about Aboriginal issues is more fully informed. What is needed is the creation of a supportive political environment for long-term structural reform and decolonization. Aboriginal aspirations rest on a fundamental notion – that of Aboriginal rights – that underpins the unique status of Aboriginal cultures within the Canadian state. These rights are inherent. They require the Canadian state to begin to treat, in politics and law, Aboriginal communities as equal partners. My concern in this book is less with a rarefied, academic, or legalistic understanding of Aboriginal rights, and more with how Aboriginal people are working to heal themselves and their communities so that self-government can become a reality. The reality of self-government is unthreatening once it is grounded in an understanding of the contemporary nature of Aboriginal communities.

2

The Challenge of Community Healing

Children have dreams. We dream of a world where our parents have opportunities to earn a decent living by working at traditional or non–traditional jobs. Our survival as a distinct people should not be dependent on a welfare cheque. The welfare cheque destroys our dignity as a people. It encourages dependency ... We are not making human beings human. Educate us to be a guide, a friend, a companion, to our parents, our people and to all Canadians. Children have dreams. Children trust grown-ups. Please, don't let us down. (Iqaluit NWT. 92-05-25 88. Tara Lindsay. PG 92)

Introduction

In 1994 I participated in Healings within the Circle, a session on Aboriginal health that was part of an International Symposium on Health Management, sponsored by McMaster University Health Sciences. Chief Earl Commanda, chief of Serpent River First Nation and chair of the North Shore Tribal Council's Health Board, also participated. He is a remarkable leader, whose knowledge of Aboriginal health issues and, specifically, of the politics of community health, is unmatched in the province. Chief Commanda was gracious in his remarks concerning the help that McMaster University had provided to the pre-transfer health project (see chapter 3); he acknowledged that consultants or academics could assist Aboriginal people in a transitional period when many communities still lacked skills necessary for research or community-based planning. But he suggested that the time must eventually come when Aboriginal communities act alone in research, planning, or policy making. Comments by other presenters and members of the audience also served to question the role of outsiders in the quest for self-determination; they questioned whether non-Natives could truly help Native people without perpetuating colonial relationships.

John O'Neil, writing for the Royal Commission on Aboriginal People (RCAP), has argued that the attempt to document Aboriginal health conditions can be detrimental when the interpretation and use of 'statistics' is controlled by outsiders, especially the state (1993). There is a danger in portraying the ill-health of communities, because it may create an 'image of sick disorganized communities that can be used to justify paternalism and dependency' (ibid). O'Neil adds that, while this image is created ostensibly to support lobbying efforts to secure a larger share of national resources for community development, it can also help to form the stereotypes of Aboriginal people held by the general public, and *even become internalized* by Aboriginal communities, reinforcing dependency relationships (emphasis mine). Ultimately, O'Neil argues, this image will only be overcome as Aboriginal people assume control over the ways in which their communities are portrayed, through undertaking independent research on health issues. Some of this research is now being conducted by communities under Health Transfer (see chapter 3). In Ontario, the Za-ge-do-win Information Clearinghouse, located at Whitefish Lake, has been created to share information on Aboriginal health conditions and programs. Aboriginal control over health information is rapidly becoming a reality.

These issues serve as a backdrop to this chapter, that outlines the parameters of the 'social health' of Aboriginal communities.[1] There is a risk in generalizing about community health status. The reader should remember that many stereotypes of Aboriginal communities involve images of ill-health, dysfunction, and disorder. It is easy to paint a dark portrait of the ill-health of communities. Instead, I wish to sketch the broad outlines of the work that needs to be done in order to meet the challenge of community healing. The accuracy of images of community health or 'ill-health' goes to the heart of the dis-ease between Aboriginal and non-Aboriginal people. Aboriginal people realize that, collectively, they live in conditions that would be intolerable to most Canadians. They also acknowledge there is a danger that in presenting these facts they will be perceived as 'whining,' or that in identifying colonialism as a *cause* of their living conditions they will be perceived as placing blame for their plight on mainstream Canadians. There is a desire on the part of Aboriginal people to move beyond blame, to recognize the historical determinants to current problems, and to assume responsibility for the solutions to these problems.

Unemployment and Welfare Reliance

The relationship between health status and economic well-being is well established. Since the Whitehall study of civil servants in Great Britain, health researchers have known that health improves as income levels increase. This is true even when researchers correct for specific health behaviours (for example, the greater incidence in smoking among lower-income groups). One reason for this relationship seems to be that economic well-being provides people with a greater sense of control over their health, and health-related behaviour. Clarke has shown how the notion of 'locus of control' is central to Aboriginal perceptions of health (1992). This factor is particularly important in the Aboriginal context where individuals and communities have historically lacked control over their social health.

Elias has investigated the relationship between 'social pathologies' and worklessness in Aboriginal communities. His analysis, which draws on RCAP testimony and a review of the literature since 1980, documents how unemployment is linked to a number of social problems, including poor health and feelings of dependency and powerlessness (1996: 14). He notes how negative behaviours, once entrenched, are passed from generation to generation. Ultimately, he argues, the cause of these pathologies must be linked to 'near-global' and broad local causes, including government action that results, over time, in Aboriginal people losing access to land and resources (ibid: 16). The economic conditions faced by Aboriginal people are the direct result of long-term oppression, systemic racism, and discrimination.

There is a clear relationship between the ill-health of Aboriginal communities, poverty, and welfare reliance. Unemployment rates on Northern reserves commonly range between 60% and 90% (Boldt 1993: 231). Those who remain on reserve often have only temporary or seasonal employment. In Ontario, Indian reliance on General Welfare Assistance is about nine times higher than that of other Ontarians (Ontario 1988: 437–8). Only 44% of adults living on reserve received employment income compared to 64% of non-Indians living in similar remote or northern locations. Unemployment is especially acute among Indian adolescents. Only 24% of Indians aged 15–24 are employed (AFN 1988b). Annual income is 50% that of non-Natives and is well below the Statistics Canada poverty line: 83% of Indians who work have incomes of less than $10,000 per year (see also Ross and Shillington 1989). Native women earn about 36% of the average Canadian male income; single mothers are under enormous pressures to adequately feed, clothe, and house their children (Nicholson 1987: 14–16).[2]

Dupuis (1993) has reviewed the literature on employment equity with regard to Aboriginal communities. He states that Aboriginal people 'are under-represented throughout the Canadian work force from every point of view'; 'Aboriginal representation in the private sector increased from 0.7 per cent in 1987 to 1.0 per cent in 1991. The same period saw an increase from 1.8 per cent to 2 per cent in the public sector. It is worthy of note that one-quarter of Aboriginals working in the public sector are employees of the Department of Indian Affairs and Northern Development (19.4 per cent) and of Health and Welfare Canada (4.8 per cent), which are directly responsible for providing services to the Aboriginal peoples. If we exclude the Department of Indian Affairs, total representation of Aboriginals in the public sector declines to 1.7 per cent' (4).

Even where Aboriginal people are employed, they are more likely to have lower-paying positions in most occupational groups. Aboriginal workers also have more difficulty remaining in their jobs, and are more likely to quit than non-Native workers – a fact that is easily attributable to employment conditions and discrimination faced in the workplace. Dupuis concludes that efforts to recruit Aboriginals to the workplace cannot be described as satisfactory and that the overall representation of Aboriginals remains below their availability rate. This poor collective employment record was singled out by the Canadian Human Rights Commission and by a 1991 House of Commons Special Committee examining the Employment Equity Act (ibid).[3] Dupuis argues that systemic prejudice and a lack of understanding of culture by employers are at work in the failure to hire Aboriginal workers. Prejudice takes many forms – a lack of commitment by management, resistance by labour unions, and most insidiously, ' the refusal to see the discrimination that existed and still exists toward members of the designated groups' (ibid). Discrimination also results in Aboriginal workers' refusal to identify themselves as members of a minority for fear that this might influence their possibilities of promotion within organizations. This is a critical observation because it suggests that Aboriginal people may 'pass' as non-Natives. That is, in the face of discrimination, some Aboriginal people are forced to deny or hide their cultural identity in order to succeed in the workplace.

Dupuis concludes that while there is no consensus concerning the need for mandatory employment legislation, several pragmatic steps are required to improve Aboriginal employment. These include the elimination of necessary barriers including academic requirements for Aboriginal employees and trainees; new forms of training and development; special support mechanisms within businesses and organizations to help Aboriginal employees adjust to new jobs; and improved documentation to discover the reasons (presumed to be related to discrimination) for the high quitting rate among Aboriginal employees. These recommendations speak for the need for government commitment to retraining programs for people currently on various forms of social assistance, and to the need for employment equity legislation to promote Aboriginal people in the workforce. These 'needs' fly in the face of the current conservative political ideology aimed to eliminate the bogeyman of 'reverse discrimination.' In Ontario, for example, the Harris government rescinded equity legislation introduced by the NDP and aimed at protecting Aboriginal peoples and other visible minorities in hiring practices.

Perhaps the most significant way to increase Aboriginal employment is to invest in Aboriginal education. According to George and Kuhn (1993), roughly a third of Aboriginal adults complete high school, compared to about one-half of the general public. The Aboriginal drop-out rate is approximately 70%. A number of studies document the obstacles Aboriginal students confront. These factors include prejudice and discrimination, inappropriate curriculum and teaching styles, and the lack of high schools on reserve. Despite increased Indian control over education at the grade school level, the majority of Indians must still leave their communities to attend high school. George and Kuhn argue, for example, that there are clear benefits to be derived from an investment in post-secondary education, that greatly enhances Native people's chance of employment, and increases their earning power.

But there are promising signs of Aboriginal economic development. Considerable growth in Aboriginal economies has occurred despite the obstacles confronting communities. David Newhouse (1993) notes:

> ... Aboriginal societies are undergoing a process of modernization. This process is resulting in the development of new identities, and new social, political, cultural and economic institutions within Aboriginal societies. These institutions, in my opinion, will be primarily western in nature and will be adapted to operate in accordance with Aboriginal traditions, customs and values. One only has to look at the rapid development of organizations over the last decade to see evidence of this

process. The 1990 Arrowfax directory of Aboriginal organizations lists 3,000 for-profit businesses and 3,000 not-for-profit businesses. The 1992 edition of the same directory has shown a significant increase in the number of listings. Many of these organizations were not in existence a decade ago.

Growth in Aboriginal businesses can be facilitated through proactive government policy. For example, under a recent federal initiative the government commits $40 million a year to Aboriginal companies bidding on federal contracts. We must remember that opportunities for small business vary greatly among First Nations. But a number of solutions to economic development have been proposed by Native and non-Native experts. Submissions to the RCAP, for example, suggest the need for the creation of Aboriginal-controlled financial institutions to support local business initiatives, the radical renovation of the Indian Act to remove disabling legal obstacles that confront Aboriginal entrepreneurs, ways to ensure that taxation is returned directly to First Nations, and the development of cooperative business that could be community controlled and owned (see also Canada 1989a).

As Elias notes, long-term community-based initiatives, that are aimed at providing meaningful work, and which account for the history of powerlessness and the contemporary effects of social problems, are needed. As noted in the previous chapter, the long-term development of sustainable economies is greatly facilitated by the settlement of land claims and/or the provision of sufficient financial compensation in lieu of land. All of these proposed 'solutions' to Aboriginal economic development, therefore, must be set against the government's intransigence in recognizing the need to reform land-claims policy.

My intent here is to point out that systemic discrimination leads to structural economic inequality between Aboriginal and non-Aboriginal communities. The absence of meaningful work, poor educational experiences, and a reliance on welfare creates an overall economic burden that is critically linked to patterns of poor physical and mental health. Poverty influences the health of children in diffuse and subtle ways and limits people's ability to respond to stress, illness, or social problems (Mitchell and Aitken 1993). Lack of income, for example, can severely restrict a woman's ability to leave home when faced with emotional or physical abuse. Poor employment opportunities force Aboriginal people to migrate to cities in search of work. Those who remain on reserve often move between temporary or seasonal employment and various forms of social assistance. Lack of employment opportunities, coupled with prejudice and discrimination, create feelings of helplessness and powerlessness in both children and adults – feelings of a lack of control over life – that are at the root of many mental health problems, including alcohol use and various forms of abuse.

At the same time, a significant portion of reserve population – as much as 20% or 25% of working-age adults – are employed directly by bands in various health and social services. This Aboriginal civil service, along with a small group of politicians and small-scale entrepreneurs comprise a significant and powerful minority. Boldt suggests political and employment patterns result in a two-tiered class system on reserves; he suggests there are few people who comprise a 'middle' class between the haves and have-nots (1993: 124). This economic disparity is often intertwined with ties of kinship. Jealousy and resentment over material lifestyles, employment opportunity, and perceived political favouritism have arisen in many communities. The high level of unemployment in Aboriginal communities results in a reliance on general welfare or other forms of social assistance. As Tara Lindsay, the Inuit youth quoted at the beginning of this chapter, states: 'welfare cheques destroy our dignity as a people.' Welfare reliance is not a problem unique to Aboriginal people. Many parts of the country – for example, the Maritimes – are also heavily reliant on social assistance during parts of the year – a fact that has prompted the federal government to look at innovative ways of restructuring the social-service net. But the problem in Aboriginal communities is endemic. Here entire generations have been reliant on government assistance. Welfare dependency creates apathy and despair within communities, and by virtue of forced migration, tears at the fabric of extended families. Welfare assistance also undermines fundamental Native values concerning self-reliance and erodes important ties of mutual support within communities.

The Department of Indian Affairs and Northern Development spends $1 billion a year on social assistance to Natives, and this figure is increasing by about 10% per year (*Globe and Mail*, 3 Dec. 1994, D5). In 1991–3, 43% of on-reserve Indians received assistance. The Auditor General noted that reform is needed to this program because the social assistance does not seem to have had an effect on the general welfare of the Indian population. What can be done to reverse this situation? There is little question that Aboriginal economies, particularly those of the remote North, are severely constricted by many factors – most noticeably distance from markets and the high cost of transportation. But several studies have documented the vibrancy of traditional hunting and trapping economies. For example, George, Berkes, and Preston have shown that the economic value of hunting in Moose Factory is more than $700,000 per year (1992: 21). Indeed, wildlife harvesting is an integral component to the development of sustainable regional economies for Aboriginal communities (see Berkes et al 1994). A study by Kitigan Zibi Anishnawbeg (RCAP 1993a) indicates Northern communities already possess traditional economies that contribute significant resources so as to decrease reliance on general welfare.

These studies do much to dispel the suggestion that Aboriginal communities are totally dependent on government subsidization. Economic support is needed, as an alternative to welfare, for individuals who wish to engage more actively in these traditional lifestyles. Under the terms of the James Bay agreement, for example, Cree hunters in Quebec receive an income supplement when they are engaged in traditional pursuits (see Feit 1991a). Chief George Wapachee, the vice-chairman of the Income Security Program for Cree Hunters and Trappers, notes that the objectives of this program are to ensure that hunting, fishing, and trapping remain viable ways of life and that individuals who undertake these activities can survive in the contemporary economic environment. In 1991–2, the program assisted 1,213 families – 29% of the entire reserve population (Wapachee 1993). Wapachee is clear in stating that the program has 'helped maintain a way of life which is both cultural and economic.' He advocates increasing the efficiency of the program and expanding it so that it could increase opportunities for training, and encourage fur marketing and commercial fishing. Such programs would no doubt be beneficial for Aboriginal communities throughout the North.

Not all First Nations have sustained their traditional economies in this manner. But most communities wish to develop alternative approaches to decrease their reliance on welfare and offer individuals new opportunities to contribute to local economies. An Ontario review reaches similar conclusions, but places welfare within the system of collective rights that are so important within Native culture (Ontario 1991). This study, conducted in consultation with Aboriginal people, notes that the idea of *individual* welfare payments undermines Aboriginal notions of sharing and reciprocity, and limits bands' power to innovate in welfare reform. Aboriginal arguments in favour of welfare reform are not simply analogous to mainstream arguments concerning 'workfare.' Such a suggestion would fuel arguments in support of the idea that those on social assistance should be made to do some sort of work in return for government assistance. Such programs, which have proved unwieldy and expensive in large urban centres, may prove to be pragmatic alternatives in small Aboriginal communities, *assuming Aboriginal control over welfare decisions, and a commitment to collective economic development programs.* As one presenter to the commission noted: '"Aboriginal self-sufficiency" encompasses the ability to be self-sustaining in accordance with the community-oriented and holistic values inherent in the cultures of the First Nations ... in order to ... attain and maintain Aboriginal self-sufficiency, we must recognize the interdependency among all things, and realize the need to maintain the good of the community as opposed to the good of the individual. Self-sufficiency, in the Aboriginal experiences, is a goal of the community as opposed to a goal of the individual' (Prince George BC. 93-06-01 6. Archie Patrick. PG 216–17). The Ontario study demonstrates that Aboriginal people are seeking innovative solutions to the problem of welfare dependency that so plagues their communities. The creation of community-based and culturally meaningful work, particularly in remote communities, will come only when there is support – most likely in the form of subsidization from existing General Welfare Assistance payments – of traditional economies.

Aboriginal communities must have diversified economic and employment strategies – traditional pursuits alone are not sufficient to sustain reasonable levels of employment. But the development of healthy land-based economies is central to the creation of vibrant cultural communities; meaningful access to the land has proved to contribute to the overall health and well-being of families. In part this is because such subsistence economies sustain patterns of exchange and reciprocity that are the very fabric of community life.

Other innovative solutions to the economic problems of communities will include the development of co-management regimes, which are only now being seriously considered and studied by academics and government ministries. Co-management agreements allow First Nations to have a legitimate and meaningful part in decision-making concerning the use and development of resources in the Crown lands surrounding their reserves (see Berkes 1989). These agreements, such as that recently agreed to in principle with the Nisga'a, could also ensure greater Aboriginal access to jobs in such industries as forestry and mining, and would renumerate First Nations for the rights to timber and minerals, thereby allowing them a financial resource base to pursue other economic activities, such as tourism and small-scale manufacturing.

Infrastructure and Housing

People's needs are holistic ... For a person to be healthy, they must be adequately fed; educated; have access to medical facilities; have access to spiritual comfort; live in a comfortable home with clean water and safe sewage disposal; be secure in their cultural identity; to have an opportunity to excel in a meaningful endeavour ... (Yellowknife NWT. 92-12-09 81. Henry Zoe, Dogrib Treaty 11 Council, MLA. PG 62)

There is a correlation between poor housing and family illness. In a report of the Standing Committee on Aboriginal Affairs, Schneider (1992: 7–9) directly links poor home environments and well-being. Tom Iron, vice-chief of the Federation of Saskatchewan Indian Nations, notes that infant death among First Nations is nearly twice the national average and is at least partly contributed to by poor housing, lack of sewage disposal and potable water (Wahpeton SK. 92-05-26. PG 143). Although the relationship between poor housing and ill-health has been little studied, anyone who has worked on reserve understands that inadequate housing is a key factor in the overall health burden of Aboriginal communities.[4] Testimony before the royal commission makes it clear that inadequate housing has both physical and psychological impact on children and families. Eric Large, a councillor from Hobbema, Alberta, notes that:

The average home now houses ten people, which in itself becomes a health and safety problem. Currently 50 per cent of all housing facilities on the reserve are greatly overcrowded. This in turn has a negative effect on the average life span of the homes involved ... It is important to understand that on-reserve housing is newer than that of the Alberta Housing Programs, but of a lower value and lower quality ... The problems and the poor quality is reflected in the policies of the Department of Indian Affairs ... Over-crowded situations means the loss of privacy, over-used home facilities and the basis from which numerous social problems develop, i.e. marital strife, poor hygienic conditions, emotional and social disruptions, children with poor study habits, etc. (92-06-10 172. PG 232)

Substandard housing conditions also produce higher than average incidence of death due to fire, as Indians rely on cooking stoves and wood stoves (Young 1979). Twenty-three per cent of all houses on reserve in Canada are in need of repair; 73% of houses are inadequate; 37% have inadequate bathroom facilities; and 3% have no bathroom at all (AFN 1987). Thirty-four per cent of houses lack a piped waste disposal system or septic tank; 18% have no kitchen sink; the number of dwellings lacking central heating is more than 50%. The lack of adequate water and sewage systems increase the risk of infectious disease such as gastro-enteritis and streptococcal infection (see also Barnes 1985; T.K. Young 1979; Canada 1983; Scott, McKay, and Bain 1989: 14–15).

Crowded housing conditions are exacerbated by high birth rates and by the return of women and children to reserves under Bill C-31. In 1986 the proportion of crowding in Aboriginal dwellings was eleven times that of non-Native households in nearby non-Native communities (Schneider 1992: 11). 'The housing on most Indian Reserves across Canada is in a state of crisis. Two or three families sometimes live in a three bedroom bungalow, designed for a single family. These crowded conditions serve as a hothouse for irritability and family violence. One of the most serious crimes that can be committed on an Indian reserve is arson because the community is outraged that the precious housing has been destroyed, sometimes putting three or four families into the cold environment' (Brant 1993). The housing crisis on reserve has so many implications for Aboriginal well-being that it is difficult to do justice to this issue here. The impact of overcrowding on mental health and domestic violence is largely unknown and unstudied. But it is obvious that many health problems, for example, the spread of infectious disease, can be attributed to overcrowding and poor ventilation. Similarly, many mental health problems, such as poor educational performance, are surely associated with overcrowding and poor housing conditions.

A lack of infrastructure, including office space for service provision, directly impacts on Aboriginal lifestyles. Great improvements in Native child care have been made in many provinces during the past decade. However, many existing day-care centres in Ontario operate in old and inadequate buildings and there is a need for additional capital funding to build new centres. Poor housing, which does not meet provincial standards for licensing day-care facilities, also impedes the ability of Aboriginal people to offer day care from the home. Overcrowding directly affects on the availability of Native adoption spaces on reserve.

Significantly, when family violence arises, lack of housing means women have nowhere to turn to find a safe haven. Reserves commonly lack many of the basic amenities that are associated with the 'social safety net' so familiar to Canadians. Safe houses, day-care facilities, halfway houses for offenders, and 'second-level housing' facilities for the disabled are all in short supply (Schneider 1992; Warry and Moffat 1993). Where some of these facilities have been built, they are often shared between several communities or are located off reserve in neighbouring towns, so that people must leave reserve, and move away from their support networks. The lack of infrastructure – medical facilities, recreational facilities, offices, and so on – is readily noticeable on most reserves and greatly adds to the burden of health and social service professionals who attempt to deliver services to clients. Investment in these facilities can pay huge dividends. The building of a new day-care centre, gymnasium, or health centre can act as a major stimulus for community action, and stand as an important symbol of community pride. But, given the absence of any coordinated policy to provide funding for these initiatives, communities must spend years on government waiting lists before such facilities are constructed.

These problems are the direct product of federal policy. The government simply does not see housing or infrastructure programs as a treaty obligation, only as a matter of social policy (Schneider 1992: 23) and it refuses to provide adequate funding to increase the number of dwellings on reserve.[5] Charlotte Wolfrey expresses the frustration of many Native leaders in recounting the visit of a former federal minister to her community in Rigolet, Labrador:

> The [housing] units that were done were done under a demonstration program. The program lasted for five years. Rigolet got a total of eight homes under this project. Allan Redway, the then Minister of Housing for the federal government, visited Rigolet in 1989. The council stressed the need to Mr. Redway for more housing. They took him out on a tour of Rigolet. He saw the overcrowding. He saw the poor living conditions. He listened to our concerns, the same concerns that we bring to this table. Again, I stress the fact that funding for housing has been drastically cut. And what we really need is access to more funds. We feel that there should be more dollars put into more housing programs in northern Labrador, not less. (Makkovik NF. 92-06-15 219. PG 176]

The lack of funding for housing is not limited to northern reserves, but is a common problem right across the country, one that will only increase in future given the young age of the Aboriginal population. No single strategy could so easily lead to long-term improvements in the health and well-being of Aboriginal people as the provision of adequate housing. Given this fact, the government's announcement of a cut in federal aid for Aboriginal housing can only be met with disbelief. This action shows a basic misunderstanding of the socioeconomic determinants of well-being, and a highly compartmentalized understanding of the problems that exist on reserve.

The Nexus: Environment, Physical and Mental Health

Numerous studies have documented the poor health status of Aboriginal people (Hanvey 1993; Warry and Moffat 1993; O'Neil 1993; K. Scott 1993;

Warry 1991a; Muir 1991; T.K. Young 1983). It is fair to describe the living conditions of many Aboriginal communities, particularly in the remote North, as equivalent to those found in the Third World. The problems confronting Aboriginal communities, in fact, parallel those that Third World countries must grapple with – poor educational and employment opportunities, inadequate housing, poor water supplies and sewage disposal, concomitant high rates of infections, parasitic or respiratory diseases. The existence of a 'fourth world' (Manual and Posluns 1974) within Canada is often cited by Aboriginal advocates who ask that Canada first tend to its own backyard, before increasing the level of foreign aid.[6] In this section I document the relationship between social health, in its broadest community definition, and reserve environments.

In part because of high fertility rates and low life expectancy, the Indian population is extremely young – 35 to 40% of Aboriginal people are under 14 years of age. Fifty-eight per cent of Natives in Canada are less than 24 years of age, as compared to 39% for the Canadian population as a whole (AFN 1988b; Canada 1987a: 12). Native families are larger than non-Native families, and a considerable number (19%) are headed by a lone parent, usually a woman (the non-Native figure is 11%, Nicholson 1987: 15–16). These numbers should be borne in mind when thinking about issues such as health or unemployment, for if Native children and youth are at risk, then Indian culture as a whole is at risk (Warry 1990). Aboriginal peoples clearly see children as 'precious commodities,' integral to nation-building and central to the future of a self-sustaining Indian culture (ONWA et al 1983: 8). The proportion of Aboriginal youth will continue to grow during the next decade.

The health of children and youth is impoverished by any standard. Though significant gains have been made in decreasing infant mortality rates for Aboriginal people, the number of infant deaths remains 2.2 times that of the national rate (Muir 1991; Edouard et al 1991). These mortality rates, which are particularly high in the first 28 days of life, reflect lower socioeconomic status and less than adequate access to health care for many Aboriginal people. The leading causes of death for Indian infants from 1985 to 1988 include congenital anomalies and birth asphyxia, but also such environmental illnesses as gastro-enteritis, pneumonia, injuries, and poisonings. Such deaths are largely preventable and reflect not only poor environmental conditions, but also acute problems concerning access to medical care (Warry and Moffat 1993). The rate of sudden infant death syndrome (SIDS) among Aboriginal people in Canada is three times the national rate (Muir 1991). A high proportion of deaths occur before the health care system becomes involved, suggesting the need for improved access to health care or midwifery programs in remote communities (T.K. Young 1983; Weller and Manga 1988: 142). In short, there is a need to improve the delivery of health services, and to develop community-based alternatives, including paraprofessional programs, to hospital-based services.

Many infectious diseases are linked with nutritional deficiencies among Aboriginal infants. In the 1950s, when biomedicine in North America encouraged artificial feeding, many Aboriginal people shifted to bottle feeding – a problem similar to that experienced by Third World mothers, one 'fed' by multinational corporations promoting the use of infant formula (see Van Esterik 1985). In the 1970s when the protective effects of breastfeeding against infectious diseases were well established, Health and Welfare initiated a breastfeeding promotion project. However, in 1988 only 18% of Aboriginal women were still breastfeeding at six months (Moffat 1991). While humanized formulas are considered to be the highest quality for artificial feeding, they are either unavailable or very costly in Northern Aboriginal communities. Many people rely on evaporated milk, which is not iron fortified (ibid).[7] Other health problems for children and youth include poor dental health due primarily to a lack of fluoride in the water of many Northern communities, as well as high consumption of sugar and refined carbohydrates (Scott, McKay, and Bain 1989: 13).

For a number of demographic and socioeconomic reasons, the infectious disease burden has also remained high in Aboriginal communities. Waldrum et al (1995) utilize *The Aboriginal Peoples Survey* (1991) to demonstrate the continuing poor health status of Aboriginal populations. Sporadic outbreaks of tuberculosis in Aboriginal communities have continued throughout the 1980s and 1990s. Tuberculosis rates are *43 times higher* among Aboriginal people than among non-Natives. As one editorial noted, these startling statistics are equivalent to rates found in Africa, and are directly related to the abysmal social and economic conditions found on reserve (*Spectator*, 30 Nov. 1994, A8). Denise Avard, executive director of the Canadian Institute of Child Health, has stated that TB should not exist if a society is looking after the 'minimum human social needs' of its members (ibid). Likewise, there is continuing high prevalence of diarrhoeal disease, pneumonia, and respiratory infections – health problems also associated with the Third World. Recent studies also point to the growing incidence of AIDS among the Aboriginal population (see Waldram et al 1995; McGill AIDS Centre 1992; Myers et al 1993). Perhaps the major health problem facing Aboriginal people today (if we ignore, temporarily, mental health issues) is diabetes, which is of epidemic proportions in many First Nations, and has been linked to obesity associated with changing lifestyle patterns, dietary and nutritional practices (see Waldrum et al 1995; T.K. Young et al 1990; T.K. Young and Sevenhuysen 1989).[8]

These problems are potentially influenced by the quality of care – particularly early diagnosis – that is available. Many of these health problems are directly related to environmental conditions, including poor housing and sanitation, and nutritional deficiencies. For example, respiratory problems are exacerbated by poor housing and poor air quality, including second-hand smoke from tobacco and wood stoves. Overcrowding increases the likelihood of transmission of airborne viruses. Other health problems are linked to socioeconomic issues and the quality of life on reserve. In remote communities the high cost of fresh fruits and vegetables makes it difficult to feed children properly, particular if parents are on government assistance. Health problems such as Fetal Alcohol Syndrome are associated with lifestyle choices including, for example, parental use of tobacco and alcohol (see chapter 3). It is here where the lines between physical health and mental health begin to blur and where individual health and well-being is intimately linked to the lack of control and dependency experienced by individuals, families, and communities.

Mental Health

The academic literature on Native mental health is sketchy at best; but Aboriginal front-line workers consistently stress a number of problems that point to a general spiritual, emotional, or psychological malaise in Aboriginal communities. Personal testimonies also speak eloquently of problems people have faced and conquered – substance abuse, physical and sexual violence, incarceration, and family breakups. At least in part, these problems are also 'environmental' in origin. Crowded housing conditions contribute to irritability, interpersonal conflict, and family violence (see Schneider 1992: 7–9). More broadly, chronic unemployment and underemployment results in enormous pressure on individuals and families. Infrastructure deficits also contribute to mental health problems. For example, there are very few recreation centres on reserves; those that do exist are often poorly maintained and equipped. Front-line workers comment that young people seem idle and bored. Young people easily turn to risk-taking behaviour, including solvent inhalation and other forms of substance abuse – either from sheer boredom, or through a desire to escape a variety of peer and family problems.

Native children are five times more likely than non-Natives to die before they reach the age of sixteen (*Toronto Star*, 29 Nov. 1986, G8, cited in Warry and Moffat 1993). Major causes of death for children under fifteen are accidents and violence. Forty per cent of child mortality in the Sioux Lookout Zone is due to accidents and violence (Scott, McKay, and Bain 1989: 12; see also Muir 1991; Linwood et al 1990). One of the most horrific, and best documented, indicators of poor mental health is the prevalence of suicide. According to Health and Welfare data, in 1987 suicides accounted for 36% of status Indian deaths. The Aboriginal suicide rate is more than three times the national average (RCAP 1994; Brant 1993; Kirmayer 1993; Minore et al 1991: 3; Bagley et al 1987, cited in Charles 1991: 12).[9] There is reason to believe that the age of those who attempt suicide has declined over the past decade – in Northern Ontario children as young as ten years have attempted to take their lives. Many reasons have been suggested for the high incidence of suicide. These include interpersonal problems, lack of support from family, exclusion of youth from community decision-making, feelings of hopelessness over job or life opportunities, and significantly, problems associated with cultural identity (RCAP 1995; Kirmayer 1994: Warry 1993; Minore et al 1991). A recent study by M. Ross et al (1996) clearly documents the link between addictions and suicide and stresses that among Aboriginal women the lack of access to the basic necessities of good health – for example, clean water, educational and employment opportunities – 'engender feelings of hopelessness, depression and despair.'

Since Durkeim's classic study it has been assumed that explanations of suicide, and the precipitating causes of it, include feelings of anomie and powerlessness that can only be understood within the context of collective social life. As Brant notes, in the Aboriginal context this includes the deterioration of social supports and the 'state of disorganization' that exists on many Indian reserves as a result of the process of colonialism. 'The old methods of coping, the old philosophies and religions, which taught resilience, survival and a sense of being at one with nature, have been denigrated and destroyed by the dominant culture and discarded by many Native peoples' (1993a). While suicide is the starkest indicator of the stresses faced by Aboriginal youth (see chapter 3), alcohol and solvent abuse are also constant reminders of the collective malaise that grips many communities. Native rates of alcohol abuse vary dramatically from community to community; it is estimated that 50 to 80% of some adult populations have alcohol-related problems (Heidenrich, cited in Merskey et al 1986: 46; see also Leland 1976; Warry 1986a, 1990). Factors associated with substance abuse include physical and geographic isolation, unemployment, and lack of recreational opportunities – common features of Northern communities in general, and Native communities in particular (Warry 1990). High alcohol use also increases the risk of Fetal Alcohol Syndrome (FAS) in infants. Bray and Anderson (1989) point out that there is no established epidemiologic evidence that FAS occurs more frequently in Aboriginal populations than in non-Aboriginal populations. But while the incidence of FAS is yet to be determined, it is clear that Aboriginal people are greatly concerned with the overall effects of alcohol use on children of all ages.[10]

Reliable statistics on substance abuse among Native children and youth are also unavailable. However, solvent abuse, including gas sniffing, is generally regarded as a significant problem in many Native communities (Warry and Moffat 1993). For some Northern First Nations this problem is a major concern, involving 30% to 40% of all Native youth. Reports of two suicides in Attiwapiskat, a community of 1,500 persons, for example, suggested that there were fifty hard-core sniffers in that community (*Toronto Star*, 4 Oct. 1994, A8). Solvent and inhalant abuse is learned behaviour: patterns of substance abuse are passed to younger generations. Solvent abuse is a temporary substitute for alcohol; but early reliance on solvents also preconditions Native youth to lead lifestyles that rely heavily on the use of alcohol to obtain rapid, severe states of intoxication (Warry 1986a).

Patterns of Native substance abuse are highly influenced by social and cultural factors (see Leland 1976). A loss of cultural esteem is often at the heart of Native alcohol abuse, and culturally appropriate programs emphasizing traditional Native values are the most successful treatment strategy (Westermeyer and Neider 1984; Warry and Moffat 1993; Councillor 1992). The use and abuse of alcohol and drugs are strongly connected with the malaise of Aboriginal youth. Youth alcohol abuse is connected with family alcohol abuse and violence, and points to a need for more mental health and drug abuse treatment facilities. There is a lack of recreational activities for youth in Northern communities (Gregory et al 1992; S. Smith 1992a). In Ontario, the establishment of an Aboriginal Healing and Wellness Strategy in 1994 provided opportunities for communities to develop innovative crisis intervention and treatment focusing on the development of traditional skills, and healing lodges that serve as the focus for spiritual healing (see chapter 3).

Abuse, Violence, and Conflict with the Law

Information concerning the physical, sexual, or emotional abuse of Native children is also lacking. This issue is an extremely sensitive one, and the validity of existing studies must be seriously questioned. Several early studies suggested that Native child abuse rates were lower than national American or Canadian averages (see Yates 1986: 1136; Painter 1986; Leung and Carter 1983). But more recently, spousal assault, sexual abuse, and child neglect have been more openly discussed in Native communities, and research conducted by Aboriginal people points to higher incidences (see, for example, LaRocque 1993; Manotsaywin 1990; Indian and Inuit Nurses of Canada 1990). A study conducted by the Ontario Native Women's Association in 1987 and 1988 (cited in Muir 1991: 50) surveyed family violence among Aboriginal people in Ontario. Eighty per cent of the respondents stated that they had experienced family violence and 84% indicated that it occurred in their community. Fifteen per cent said they did not have access to a telephone and 31% did not have adequate transportation out of their communities in crisis situations. A second survey in North Central Ontario,[11] which defined abuse to include psychological and emotional harm, found incidence of violence in three of ten Aboriginal households; caregivers suggested that the incidence of family violence might be as high as 50% (Manotsaywin 1990: 28). Significantly, the vast majority of victims (80%) experienced family violence before the age of ten years (ibid: 12). Calvin Morrisseau, former executive director of the Za-ge-do-win Information Clearinghouse, notes that sexual abuse, which was rarely mentioned in these early studies, is now generally regarded by many front-line workers to be a significant concern (personal communication).

The RCAP defined family violence as a 'serious abuse of power within family, trust or dependency relationships' (1996d: 54–6). The commission notes that the pattern of 'family violence experienced by Aboriginal peoples shares many features with violence in mainstream society' but that 'it also has a distinctive face that is important to recognize as we search for understanding of causes and identify solutions.' (ibid, 56). 'First, Aboriginal family violence is distinct in that it has invaded whole communities and cannot be considered a problem of a particular couple or an individual household. Second, the failure in family functioning can be traced in many cases to interventions of the state deliberately introduced to disrupt or displace the Aboriginal family. Third, violence within Aboriginal communities is fostered and sustained by a racist social environment that promulgates demeaning stereotypes of Aboriginal women and men and seeks to diminish their value as human beings and their right to be treated with dignity' (57).

Family violence is perhaps the most vivid example of a behaviour that requires the development of interventions that link programs compartmentalized under justice, health, and social services. The neglect of children is often attributable to highly stressful family environments resulting from a combination of social, economic, and health conditions. A matrix of mental health problems – family violence, alcoholism, solvent abuse, and suicide – can also be directly linked to the intergenerational effect of colonial practices, including, most notably, what has been termed 'native child abuse by the child welfare system' (Andres 1981; P. Johnson 1983; Bagley 1984, 1985; Warry 1990). Aboriginal people also link many family problems to learned behaviour or traumatic experiences in a variety of institutional settings – be they jails or the residential schools (Canim Lake BC. 93-03-09 104. Patrick Prestage. PG 374). There is now general recognition of the cumulative effects of the 'residential school syndrome,' that debilitated a generation of parents. And while it is clear that many Indians who attended residential schools show no ill-effects from this experience, many others have carried the trauma of physical, psychological, or sexual abuse with them throughout their lives. Aboriginal people often note, for example, that many people lack parenting skills – having been taken away from their home environments for years, they were denied the opportunity to learn, firsthand, Aboriginal parenting skills.

Finally, as part of the general pattern of ill-health, Native youth experience conflict with the law at higher rates than the average Canadian child. During the 1970s, one study noted that Saskatchewan Indian boys had a 70% chance of at least one stay in prison by the age of 25, as compared to only 8% for non-Native boys (Hylton 1983). In Ontario, Native admissions to correctional facilities in the 16–25 age range account for almost half of all male admissions and 44% of female admissions (Asbury 1986: 25). A third of Native adults incarcerated were first convicted as juveniles – the first conviction occurring on average at about 16 years of age. These incarceration rates are repeated throughout the country. For male youth, reality involves a high probability that they will be arrested for minor offences, placed on probation, and, after a series of minor infractions (including breach of probation) serve some time in jail. Aboriginal conflict with the law is often alcohol related, and in Ontario a high number of jail terms are served for public drunkenness, or rather, for the inability to pay fines for public drunkenness (see Jolly 1983; Asbury 1986; Warry 1986a).

Aboriginal conflict with the law is predominantly associated with offences such as break and enter, minor theft, and assaults. The majority of crimes are committed while the wrongdoer is intoxicated, and emerge from dysfunctional family situations and impoverished community environments. One of the most common crimes, vandalism, is often committed by youths – often against band property such as schools, recreational facilities, and offices. These crimes can only be understood against the background of frustration and despair that exists on reserve. The vast majority of Aboriginal people who appear before courts plead guilty, not from any misunderstanding of the meaning of the word, but precisely because their cultural system, which emphasizes respect for authority, does not equip with them with the tools to render a fight that non-Natives expect within an adversarial system of justice (in contrast, for example, to the non-Native practice of pleading *not* guilty even when crimes have been committed).

Elders suggest that many negative behaviours found on reserve are the product of institutional experiences. Chief Tom Sampson comments on how non-Native institutions conflict with holistic approaches to health: 'I am not condemning white people, by the way. I do not want the media to take that as a condemnation of the white way – that is wrong. I am just saying it does not suit us. It does not fit into the holistic approach to life that we understand. You look at their institutions. Every one of their institutions are separate from one another. Ours are all together, not separate from one another. Their schools are separate from their homes. Even their justice system is so fragmented and separated they do not know who is responsible for anything in there, because they are separate, they are fragmented in their own way' (Esquimalt BC. 92-05-21 5. Chief Tom Sampson. PG 24–5). Many Aboriginal people would argue that the criminal justice system should be radically changed to provide for community support and treatment of people who have problems with alcohol *before* negative behaviour is reinforced by jail sentences (see chapter 5). It is absurd to jail Aboriginal people for a variety of minor offences when these resources might instead be made available for community healing. But we must remember that the criminal justice system remains a primary tool through which the government controls, disables, and disempowers Aboriginal people.

Here, as everywhere, there is hope. Many jails and correctional centres, remarkably, have given birth to Native Sons and Brotherhoods, where Aboriginal inmates come together to talk, and to rediscover traditional ways (Waldrum 1993; Warry 1986b). And while many offenders take years to break free from the cycle of repeat offences and jail terms, a small percentage now leave the jail or prison anchored in their culture, to move on to become important leaders in urban centres or on reserve. In a sense, this phenomenon is representative of the wider rebirth that is taking place across the country – of people caught in desperate conditions who somehow find the strength to move on to a centred life, a life that revolves around their renewed sense of personal and cultural identity.

The Burden of Colonialism

Indigenous groups epitomized the state of human health and environmental harmony with sophisticated systems of kinship and exacting medicinal practices. But with the encroachment of Euro-American influence, captivity and dysfunction resulted. Captivity is a complex web of geographic, economic, legal and social isolation which significantly segregates Indigenous peoples so they cannot benefit from the range and quantity of human services enjoyed by other Canadians. The dysfunction is nowhere more apparent than in the health status of Indigenous peoples (K. Scott 1993: 9).

This quotation conjures up an image of pre-contact perfection that has recently been challenged by many anthropologists and historians. Partly because of our own romantic images of Aboriginal people, we are apt to see pre-contact culture as disease free, and entailing none of the stresses of contemporary living. As Waldrum et al show, more and more evidence accumulates to suggest that this disease-free image is 'partly conjecture and partly myth' (Merbs 1992: 4, cited in Waldram et al 1995).[12] While it is unquestionably true that the health status of Aboriginal people declined dramatically with the onset of epidemics that were 'imported' by early explorers and settlers, it is not true that Aboriginal people lived in a pristine state of health, or that their indigenous systems of medicinal knowledge could adequately respond to the many illnesses that existed *in situ* before contact (see Waldram et al 1995: 23–30). Before contact Aboriginal people experienced a variety of health and mental health problems, including respiratory illnesses, infections of various types, family disruption, violence, and suicide (ibid; see also Kirmayer 1993).

Scott's statement, however, correctly asserts a causal relationship between colonialism, poverty, and ill-health, a relationship that has been documented by numerous studies for more than thirty years. The poverty of Aboriginal communities is directly attributable to their marginalization within the economic structure of Canadian society, as well as to the direct impact of racism and discrimination. Indian explanations of individual and community ill-health stress the negative effects of social and institutional processes originating in the dominant society. Problems of social health are ultimately linked to colonial oppression. For example, while it is impossible to state that residential schools 'caused' a variety of problems (everything from truancy, sexual abuse, and teenage pregnancy to conflict with the law) in children and youth, anyone who has experience working in Aboriginal communities recognizes that residential schools are attributed with having produced a generation of adults who lack parenting skills and, in some instances, who have carried with them patterns of physical and sexual abuse first learned in institutional settings (Sampson 1992: 63; Metcalf 1978: 4–12; see also Schuurman 1994). Similarly, Native elders often suggest that the incarceration of Aboriginal offenders over successive generations has contributed to an increased incidence of physical and sexual abuse on reserves – that is, that this behaviour is *learned* through the experience of institutionalization. More generally, the integrity of Native culture has been assaulted through mainstream educational systems that encourage written communication, typically ignore Native language and oral tradition, and continue to rely on outdated, often stereotypical curriculum.

From an Aboriginal perspective, individual and community problems do not stem simply from poor socioeconomic conditions, but are also directly attributable to low cultural esteem, or to a lack of cultural identity, which is critical to feelings of self-worth. As previously noted, a feeling of control over one's life is an essential element to positive self-image and physical well-being. Psychologists have used such concepts as 'learned helplessness' and 'acculturative stress,' to explain a variety of Native mental health problems (Warry 1990). Front-line workers describe these psychological conditions as resulting from 'internalized oppression,' the psychosocial process whereby individual Natives internalize the collective experience of colonization and experience feelings of powerlessness, low cultural esteem, and poor self-image (see RCAP 1994). There is, however, a recognition that solutions to this collective burden of colonialism – however non-Native in origin – are now the responsibility of First Nations. Aboriginal people wish to move beyond blame, and to assume responsibility for breaking the intergenerational cycle of violence. The re-valuation of Aboriginal culture, therefore, is viewed as critical to processes of individual recovery and community revitalization. Self-determination is not simply an abstract political concept, but one that is integral to the social, physical and mental health of individuals and Native communities as a whole.

Colonialism is also responsible for the rapid erosion of indigenous medicine, including herbalism and forms of spiritual healing. In many parts of the country the conversion to Western medicine occurred very early after contact, simultaneous with the loss or decline of Aboriginal religious leaders, shamans, who can be thought of as indigenous spiritual doctors. As Titely notes, Indian Act amendments proscribing traditional healing ceremonies 'were sponsored by missionaries and Indian agents concerned that these ceremonies were a threat to the conversion of Aboriginal populations to "hard-working" Christian farmers' (1989; cited in O'Neil 1993, n.21). Missionaries, themselves the carriers of many infectious diseases, also possessed medicines that could be used to treat the ill and dying (see Brody 1987). In communities that lost between 20 and 40% of their families to disease, there was a crisis in faith – both with traditional religious beliefs and traditional medicinal practices.

Whatever the reasons for the early conversion to Western medical care, the dominance of Western medical ideas became entrenched, as white institutions – hospitals and clinics – began to serve as the loci of illness care for Aboriginal communities. Beginning in the early part of this century, and accelerating after the 1960s with the growth of socialized medicine, Aboriginal people have slowly been assimilated into the Canadian illness-care system. Native people have internalized many notions about health and illness – ideas concerning the power of germs and medicines, of pregnancy and birth, of mental illness, and of the need for institutionalized care. In the process, interest in many traditional health practices declined. For many Natives, the power and efficacy of Western medicine is taken for granted. For example, one of the concerns Aboriginal people raise about assuming control over health-care delivery is that there may be a diminishment of access to mainstream medical care, or that somehow Native control will result in a loss of freedom – for example, the right to choose a family doctor. As I show in the next chapter, the efficacy of Western medicine is so valued that many Natives question the need to revitalize traditional health practices.

Aboriginal people experience a greater health burden and a lower level of service in their communities. These two factors are critically and causally linked. Not only do Aboriginal people have poorer health than the 'average' Canadian, they also have poorer access to health-care services – particularly services associated with tertiary (hospital) care and the expertise of medical and psychiatric specialists. Many of these access issues are the direct result of geographic isolation and costs associated with transportation. Because it is difficult to get doctors to work in the remote North, the number of doctors per 1,000 population in remote communities is very low – equivalent to that found in Third World countries. There are currently only 49 Native physicians, and another 25 Native medical students in Canada (*Spectator*, 14 Nov. 1994, B5). Though remote reserves have access to nursing stations, many reserves access physician services through urban-based institutions located in southern Ontario.

It is inappropriate to provide psychiatric care, outreach services, or medical training for remote Cree and Ojibwa communities from Toronto, Hamilton, Kingston, and London. But this is where teaching hospitals are located. Federal and provincial policy has perpetuated just such a Southern bias (Weller and Manga 1988; see also Armstrong 1978; Timpson 1983). The creation of innovative solutions to the complex health problems of Native people will only be accomplished through the creation of regional health care systems as advocated by Weller and Manga (1988) and by the establishment of community health planning, management, and evaluation at the reserve level. Aboriginal communities wish to establish culturally appropriate service delivery that is responsive to local needs. 'The issue of cultural appropriateness and the mechanisms to integrate Native culture into the delivery of services were non-existent, insufficient or under-developed. Overall, the existing service delivery agencies lack a holistic approach ... The cycle of dependency and hopelessness must be broken. To break the dependence, the inherent strengths of Native individuals, of families and communities must be recognized. It is imperative that the political and community development process include everyone's participation – single-parent families; youth; women and the elderly ...' (Thunder Bay ON. 92-10-27 112. Bernice Dubec, Chairperson, Thunder Bay Native Interagency Council. PG 173).

The ill-health of communities must be specifically linked to the failure of the federal government to recognize access to health care as an Aboriginal right. Tom Iron suggests that Aboriginal health status is an 'international disgrace'; the Aboriginal right to health has become 'another empty promise' as federal and provincial governments abandon their responsibility to provide adequate health care.

First Nations' people have a higher mortality rate than the national average. We die younger than other Canadians. Our life expectancies at birth are nearly a decade less than those of the general non-Native population. Cancer, diseases of the circulatory and respiratory systems, infectious diseases like tuberculosis which has been all but wiped out in the non-Aboriginal societies, diabetes and heart disease occur at the minimum of twice the national average among First Nations. Factors that contribute to the illness and mortality rate include poor quality housing, lack of adequate infrastructure (such as clean water supply and sewage facilities), poor access to medical services and increased exposure to disease. As well, the poor health of the mother, inadequate nutrition, and lack of pre-natal care as well as the adverse effects of drugs and alcohol also contributed. (Wahpeton SK. 92-05-26 228. PG 141–3)

Embedded in this quotation is an appreciation of the complex nature of individual and community health, and an understanding that the continuing burden of ill-health is related to inappropriate bureaucratic regimes that thwart Aboriginal attempts to develop holistic approaches to health-care delivery. Vice-chief Iron acknowledges an essential component of government practice is to provide services in such a way as to 'all but negate the traditional holistic approach to wellness'; government financing for health care, however limited, is premised on a western 'prescription' (ibid).

Hope and Holistic Solutions

To summarize, there is a pattern of risk in Aboriginal communities where children are subject to health problems during infancy and where the potential for early-childhood death through illness or accidents related to poor socioeconomic environments is much greater than for other Canadians. For older children and youth, physical health problems remain, but they seem trivial compared to a variety of mental health problems that exist. Poor educational and employment opportunities, racism and discrimination, substance abuse among peers and family, combined with poor social conditions, make for teenage years where the likelihood of violence against both self and others is all too common (Warry 1991a).

It is the solutions to this general pattern of ill-health that, to a great extent, constitute the hard work of community healing. Aboriginal people often speak of the need to return to tradition or create holistic solutions to the problems faced by their communities. 'Holism' is often poorly defined or understood. More often than not, 'holistic' is a buzzword that is easily tossed around by academics and Aboriginal people either as a criticism of compartmentalized government initiatives, or as a label to distinguish any Aboriginal approach. What, then, is precisely meant by wholistic (the common Native spelling) or holistic solutions to community problems? Typically, the term denotes approaches that integrate spiritual, physical, mental, and emotional needs. These are the core qualities associated with the four directions of the medicine wheel, the circle of healing that comprises any attempt to link and integrate these qualities. Individual action, recovery, awareness, and volition are believed to derive from the balance or harmony among these qualities (see, for example, Four Worlds 1984a; 1984b). To take the example of alcoholism, individuals are thought to overcome the need for alcohol when they are 'centred' or strike a balance among these qualities. Hence Native alcohol programs focus on making people aware of internal emotional states, as well as thought processes. They address people's spiritual awareness (via a return to cultural understanding) as well as their physical activity – for example, by improving diet and exercise to relieve stress.

Native people also identify 'macro' historical processes with 'micro' behaviours associated with individual personality. I am constantly enlightened when, in response to my asking an open-ended question about individual issues, people automatically speak of history, or colonialism, or cultural esteem as the root cause of problems:

> Our perspective of healing is a holistic one in that it deals with the complete person as a functioning member of society and does not treat only the symptoms of the problem. In order for us to heal individuals and communities, it is vital that we pursue all possible ways in which we can bind our communities back together with a clear knowledge of who we are and where we have come from. In this way, we may be better able to chart the course of where we are going from this point onwards. (Akwesasne ON. 93-05-04 274. Barbara Barnes. PG 432)

> A holistic approach that encompasses emotional, mental, physical, spiritual, social, cultural, and sexual attitudes will need to be developed. Historically and culturally we, as Aboriginal people, are one with nature and its elements. It only makes sense to approach health care with a view towards community-based health care in the development and implementation of programs and services. (The Pas MB. 92-05-19 62. Chief Flett. PG 70–1)

In these quotations, 'holism' connotes a broad understanding of the socioeconomic and historic determinants of health.[13] This meaning of 'holistic' is close to that used in anthropology, where analysts attempt to link behaviours that at first glance seem to be disconnected. Here a holistic understanding implies one where analysis crosses artificial conceptual boundaries – social, political, or economic – to encompass an explanation incorporating all these factors. Anthropologists have traditionally studied in small-scale societies where, for example, law, economy, or politics are 'embedded' in social relations, particularly in kinship, rather than articulated in specialized institutions.

Holism may be translated as an attempt to find comprehensive solutions to problems, as opposed to Band-Aid approaches that treat the symptoms of social dis-ease. The solution to alcohol abuse might be found in the provision of employment, adequate housing, or recreational opportunities, strategies that confront the root cause of people's dissatisfaction with life, rather than through the provision of alcohol counselling programs. In community action, a holistic understanding is most easily demonstrated in approaches that transcend specific program areas. It is possible, for instance, to speak of coordination of services or case management that approach family issues from different angles, or through team approaches that are based in consultation and collaboration.

Many of the RCAP quotations in this chapter speak to the concept of holism. The speakers mention, for example, the interrelationship between people, land, and the broader environment. They speak of the linkage between housing and human health, and of political institutions and social development; they speak of education in relation to spiritual well-being. The notion of holism also embodies inclusion, of contributions to community life by all segments of the community, whether young or old, male or female. Approaches to family violence, for example, are adequate only if they address the needs of victims *and* offenders, and serve to re-value the nature of families:

> Family violence – There is a vast philosophical difference between what kind of services are provided by the existing non-Aboriginal service providers. This is creating problems. The Aboriginal approach to violence is holistic healing as opposed to the non-Aboriginal approach, which is individualistic, utilizing the feminist approach where abuse is an expression of power and dominance by men over women. They usually suggest choices to the women such as leaving her husband, which usually excludes the abuser in the treatment process. This is viewed as a negative factor by Aboriginal women, as they want to involve their husbands and children in a long-term holistic approach to the problems of family violence. Aboriginal family bonds are very strong and we feel that we must help one another so that we can be stronger. Our philosophy is that strong healthy families make strong healthy communities. (Winnipeg MB. 92-04-22 63. Evelyn Webster, Vice-President, Indigenous Women's Collective. PG 256)

Note that Webster questions not so much the feminist characterization of abuse as an expression of power and domination, but the associated 'solution' that separates men and women. Holistic approaches are based in *relationships*. Significantly, the idea of holism speaks to collective well-being, the recognition that individual wants or needs must be contextualized in the needs of the family or larger community. Holistic solutions, then, are integrally tied to the idea of community healing.

Perhaps the greatest harm caused by the intrusion of mainstream institutions into Aboriginal communities is the 'fragmentation' of holistic practices that were so integral to the nature of traditional society (see, for example, Castellano 1982; Warry 1993). There is a compartmentalization of services on reserve that is a product of bureaucratic funding arrangements and of an overly specialized approach to service. The nature of service delivery can in fact negatively impact on the quality of community health. As Clare Brant noted, the competing aims and jurisdictional disputes of federal and provincial agencies generates a 'remarkable' level of tension among families and service providers who are involved with the system (1993). On a mundane level, the flow of money along ministerial lines creates inherent divisions between service providers and serves to thwart the search for integrated approaches to social problems that might naturally occur if First Nations had the financial control to designate dollars to more comprehensive, integrated institutions. As another example, the penetration of the mainstream justice system, with its emphasis on policing and punishment, is viewed as compartmentalizing the concept of 'justice,' and divorcing it from its essential purpose – that of re-establishing social harmony that is necessary for community healing. As I show in chapter 5, Aboriginal justice initiatives seek to rebuild and reestablish the linkage between law and health that has been severed in communities.

Conclusion

This chapter has laid a foundation of evidence to suggest that the conditions on many reserves, and among the Aboriginal population in general, are dismal. The research is clear: Aboriginal people live in impoverished conditions, and the challenges that they face on a daily basis – discrimination, unemployment, welfare dependency – are enormous. It is not surprising that these conditions manifest themselves in poor health, social problems, minor forms of acting out through criminal behaviour, and sadly, self-inflicted violence.

It is my experience that the stoic image of the Native person is, to a great extent, accurate. Native people do not complain about their personal experience – they certainly do not suggest to an outsider how difficult their lives are. I have had several experiences where, after people have taken the time to be interviewed, or have attended community meetings, I have found out that they were struggling with some personal trauma – the illness of a child or the death of a close relative. Some Canadians may suggest that Aboriginal people 'complain' too much, or that they are tired of hearing about the problems that Aboriginal people face – and certainly tired of calls for greater resources to address these problems. But these calls are made by committed leaders and advocates who are tired of the decades, if not centuries, of neglect that have created the socioeconomic conditions on their reserves.

What are the true human costs of the statistics outlined in this chapter? How do we translate these numbers into a meaningful awareness of the challenges facing Aboriginal fathers, mothers, and grandparents? What is the cumulative and collective strain that is indicated by this evidence? The answers to these questions are much more difficult to give. Aboriginal communities are small. They are composed of extended families where cousins are treated like siblings and where social memory, commitment, and responsibility extend to even the most distant kin. Picture, if you can, living in a small community where tragedy is the norm. Imagine living life in a dark shadow, burdened by the knowledge of violence or abuse in your own or your extended family. Imagine living with little hope for employment, and daily reminders of discrimination. Such situations are not isolated or episodic events for many Native people. They are endemic life experiences.

From the perspective of the average Native person, there is no outcry, only dignified, quiet management of lives lived in the face of difficult conditions. What is truly amazing to me is the capacity of Aboriginal people to cope in the face of these pressures. Even against a backdrop of personal tragedy, a great many Aboriginal people are prepared to help their family, their neighbours, and to continue to give of their time to make life better for children and elders. There is, remarkably, hope for the future. In any community there are individuals who have returned to their spiritual ways, people who draw on a deep wellspring of faith or political commitment that their children's lives will be better than their own.

The reality for many communities is both despairing and bright. I vividly recall walking the frozen paths of Attawapiskat, late at night, when the temperature reached minus 40°C. Huddled in the lee of the local church I saw several youths whose clouded eyes and blank expressions testified to deep intoxication from I know not what – alcohol, drugs, or solvent use. But just down the road, perhaps a hundred metres away, these stark reminders of hopelessness were overwhelmed in my mind by the laughter of children chasing a puck on a flooded rink in the cold winter night. The reality of Aboriginal life is that of multiple pathways to the realization of human potential or its destruction. The task at hand, both for Aboriginal governments and the government of Canada, is to foster an environment of healing and hope that will allow children and youth to realize their potential.

Following the failure of Meech Lake an essential shift occurred in the rhetoric of self-government – a shift that began to emphasize the need for Aboriginal communities to 'heal themselves.' There came the growing awareness that Aboriginal communities must first, and foremost, heal themselves so that they obtain the collective capacity to do the real work of rebuilding their communities. The meaning of community healing is more fully analysed in chapter 6. But an essential component is the development of holistic approaches to community problems, approaches that encourage self-reliance, reinforce a sense of community control, and re-establish links to traditional values and practices. In recent years there has been an attempt to retrieve many key values that can serve as a source of support for this process of revitalization. This collective recovery and revitalization is well under way, but is not without its own risks, including ideological conflicts and political competition. The creation of environments for individual wellness and community healing is being accomplished through hard work, sensible planning, and the dedicated involvement of community members. This is the true challenge of community healing, and the subject of the next chapters.

3

Vision and Illusion: Health-Care Planning and Community Control

Dr Ed Connors, a Kahnawake band member and psychologist, asked why we have been unable to apply a holistic model of health in our communities. 'Perhaps it is because we haven't been thinking holistically.' He said that Aboriginal people base their understanding of health and holistic health on definitions created by the outside world, and said that as long as we continue to do this 'we will miss the mark.' Professionals in Western health all have different labels and mandates for care. They often work at odds with one another, leaving clients and families confused. By the time a suicidal person has been referred over and over from one professional to another, all of whom think someone else is better mandated to help, the person might be dead, 'We must dialogue to develop our own definition,' he said, suggesting as a starting point the Ojibway term for health, which means 'good life.' (RCAP 1993b: 333)

Introduction

Shortly after joining the Anthropology Department at McMaster University in 1989 I received a call from Donald Cole, a medical doctor in the Faculty of Health Sciences. The Regional Services Program, which assists communities in health research and planning, had passed on to him a request from Keith Lewis, Health Transfer Coordinator for the Anishnabek Health Board of the North Shore Tribal Council. The board needed help in developing a community needs assessment that would lay the foundation for health planning under the federal government's Health Transfer policy. Over coffee, Donald introduced me to two other physicians, Rosana Pellizzari and Doug Sider, and shortly thereafter, in January 1990, the three of us met with Keith to discuss the needs assessment. At the time, I assumed this project would be quickly completed, perhaps within six months; but much to my surprise, the Health Transfer process seemed to take on a life of its own and developed into a complex series of community consultations and negotiations extending over a period of five years. The project's evolution illustrates several issues associated with the nature of community-based research and planning, with the bureaucratic relationship between Aboriginal communities and the federal government – in this instance, the Medical Services Branch (MSB) of Health and Welfare Canada, and with tribal council politics. As a small example of participatory-action research (PAR), the transfer project demonstrates how research can stimulate the planning of community-based services and initiatives and become something more than an academic enterprise. The actual research and planning for health services proved more difficult than I had imagined, and the idea of Health Transfer more contentious than anticipated. In the end, the success of this process demonstrated the incredible commitment and discipline of Aboriginal people in the seven North Shore communities. It is their vision and planning, placed against the background of government conservatism and intransigence, that is the focus of this chapter.

The non-specialist may find this discussion overly detailed; but I wish to convey a sense of how a great many people are engaged in difficult work to improve their communities. Although health care is by no means a high priority for many Aboriginal politicians – their time is consumed by advocacy on other issues, including land claims – it is a natural starting point for community revitalization. If Aboriginal communities cannot tackle such problems as poor nutrition or substance abuse they will be incapable of fostering the healthy environments that are a necessary base for self-government. The complexity of health-care reform demonstrates the labour-intensive task of long-term planning required by the Canadian and First Nations governments if self-government is to become a reality. The difficulties associated with the revitalization of traditional healing, in conjunction with physician services, not only challenges mainstream bureaucratic systems, but also the beliefs of many First Nation members. For this reason, health-care reform is a significant indicator of the 'environment for change' that exists at the local level, and more broadly, within federal and provincial governments.

The task facing First Nations during the next decade is nothing short of the redesign of community-based systems of health-care. The Health Transfer process is a first step toward the objectives of self-government, and a major test for Aboriginal people, one that indicates their capacity to assume control over their own affairs. The design and delivery of culturally appropriate health-care also represent a dangerous first step, because according to many observers it is in this area the federal government is seeking to limit or even abandon their responsibilities to Aboriginal people. Health Transfer demonstrates the government's acceptance of a restricted vision of Native control, and for that reason this discussion will help to ground the pragmatic difficulties of obtaining self-government across a broader range of jurisdictions.

Aboriginal 'Control' and Health-Care Reform

Kim Scott, a senior policy analyst for the RCAP, addressed the issue of health-service development (1993). Her paper, focused on the transfer of 'colonial' medicine, serves as a valuable starting-point for a discussion of Aboriginal health-care delivery. As Scott notes, the poor health status of Aboriginal people has been identified since the 1960s, but the critique of health-care delivery began in earnest only during the 1970s, when the National Indian Brotherhood (now the Assembly of First Nations, or AFN) pressured the government to reconsider the provision of non-insured services (now called non-insured health benefits, NIHBs). This advocacy resulted in the federal government's development, in 1979, of the 'Indian Health Policy.' Before this policy, the federal government had taken steps to improve Aboriginal involvement in health-care by creating the National Native Alcohol and Drug Abuse Program (NNADAP) (ibid; see also Young and Smith 1992). This program established community-based alcohol abuse prevention and treatment projects on reserve. As Scott notes, this program, despite many failings, has contributed to the emergence of some of the most significant Aboriginal health initiatives in the country, including the Four Worlds Development Project, the Nechi Institute, and the Alkali Lake prohibition strategy.

The 'Alkali Lake Story,' which has been documented in the video *The Honour of All*, epitomizes the transformative potential of Indian communities, and is now universally hailed in Aboriginal communities as an example of community healing and revitalization (Johnson and Johnson 1993). The community had experienced exceptionally high unemployment rates and alcohol abuse rates. Within the span of only a few years this community, which was referred to as 'alcohol lake' by non-Natives in nearby communities, was able to reverse its fortunes through a variety of community development strategies. Leaders prohibited the sale of alcohol, offered a variety of social assistance to recovering alcoholics, and, over time, drastically cut the unemployment rate (ibid). Central to the community's success was the fact that these initiatives were designed, implemented, and controlled by Native peoples themselves, rather than being imposed from the outside.

In recognition of such community-based successes and in response to increasing calls for increased administrative control over other services, the federal government developed, in the late 1980s, its Health Transfer initiative. This initiative aims to transfer administrative control over a variety of community-based health services to Aboriginal First Nations. As Scott notes, however: 'Administrative transfer is devolution only and not the morally independent, self- directing freedom that Indigenous groups seek in human service delivery. Therefore, any transferred health funds come with imposed legislation, rigid programmatic guidelines and accountability requirements. In cases where transferred administrative control comes with programmatic flexibility, there is room for greater sensitivity to community health priorities. The "bottom line" decisions, in any case, remain the sole responsibility of the governments which issue them. These decisions, although not entirely arbitrary, show extreme variation' (ibid: 96).

Health Transfer, then, does not result in true control over health services. The initiative aims to 'give' Aboriginal people the opportunity to plan services that are more responsive to local needs. But transfer allows de facto community control. Solutions to common problems can be developed locally. Community members can no longer complain about externally designed or 'culturally inappropriate' services. In this sense, the transfer of administrative control promotes self-reliance in health planning. At the same time, however, as Scott indicates, this control is restricted in several ways by governments, which impose guidelines on the delivery of dollars to finance services, and so set the parameters of health-care delivery. The NSTC Health Transfer experience highlights the degree of innovation that is occurring in communities, their ability to ignore government directions, and, at the same time, the government's continuing narrow vision of what constitutes appropriate health-care for Aboriginal people.

Health Transfer Policy: Government and First Nations' Expectations

The Health Transfer policy provides First Nations with funding to conduct health-care needs assessments, to develop community health plans, and in a restricted sense, to create health-care authorities responsible for the delivery of services (Canada 1989b; Gibbons and Associates 1992: 38–49; Speck 1989; Gregory et al 1992). The post-transfer period begins with successful completion of negotiations to arrive at expenditures; these theoretically include funds that MSB formerly spent on health-service personnel, training and support, facilities, vehicles, and equipment. Post-transfer requirements include agreements that the community continue to provide communicable-disease control services, environmental-health services, and treatment services, and that they maintain an emergency response plan (Canada 1989b).

Health Transfer concerns the administrative control of a limited number of primary health-care initiatives: alcohol prevention programs (NNADAP), Community Health Representatives (CHRs) nursing, and the like. The policy clearly states that there is no provision for enhancement of programs; that is, communities are supposed to assume control over existing services, but cannot expect additional dollars for new services. The policy has been the subject of some controversy. Both Natives and non-Native advocates have criticized Health Transfer as 'window-dressing' for the federal government's 'hidden agenda' to reduce spending in the area of Aboriginal health services (see Speck 1990; Assembly of First Nations 1988a)[1]. Critics of the policy share a common concern – the suggestion that, despite federal government claims that the policy will enhance the path to self-determination, the policy in effect allows the federal government to retreat from its fiduciary responsibility for Aboriginal health.

The initiative was implemented in 1989. As of 1993 there were 25 transfer agreements involving 69 First Nations, and another 74 pre-transfer projects under way involving 218 First Nations. Despite criticisms, therefore, the policy has met with considerable acceptance in Aboriginal communities. One reason for this acceptance is that it enables First Nations to engage in community-based research and planning. The policy does not attempt to develop holistic services; for example, housing, employment strategies, and mental-health counselling all fall outside the mandate of the initiative. Early criticisms – that the policy did not provide for program enhancement, that it made little accommodation for traditional health practices, and that it did not include provisions for a variety of services – including physician services and mental-health programming – were all valid. But as the following case study demonstrates, some of these problems have been overcome as communities documented their needs and made well-reasoned arguments about services to the federal government. In short, the federal government has been at least partially responsive to the development of new programs.

In the NSTC area, transfer was a regional initiative under the direction of the Anishnabek Health Board, an unincorporated body that reports to the tribal council through the chair of the board, but is an arms-length organization, discrete from the tribal council itself. The Health Board is responsible for planning and coordinating regional health services, providing training, evaluating nursing services, and monitoring health status. The board includes two representatives from each band; these individuals may be a chief, a councillor holding a health portfolio, or health employee.[2] At the time, the Health Board employed a small staff, including a health director and a coordinator-consultant who provided training to NNADAP workers and CHRs.[3]

The division of health services creates an uneasy alliance between First Nations and the tribal council. Some smaller communities, such as Thessalon First Nation, for example, share nursing services with other bands. Other communities are large enough to employ a health director, nurses, and other staff. The Health Board operates on the principle of respect for First Nations' autonomy in decision-making, while at the same time trying to ensure quality and integration of services across the member First Nations. The tug and pull between local and regional needs, therefore, is an important component in all aspects of health-care delivery. Health Board decision-making can be slow, as members take tentative decisions or positions back to their council for approval or revision. Board members must constantly strive to balance the needs of their own and other communities. The decision to engage in Health Transfer as a regional initiative, therefore, was an important step in the creation of regional health-care delivery, and as a symbol of First Nations' solidarity. But in the end, this unity proved difficult to sustain.

Federal government expectations were evident in the type of consultation process that MSB was initially prepared to fund. The original letter of agreement with the Health Board, for example, outlined a process where a needs-assessment survey would be held, to be followed by a single meeting in each community to agree on health needs, and the preparation of health plans by staff hired under the project! In other provinces such limited consultations often occurred – in some cases external consultants[4] assumed responsibility for preparing health plans, which led to administrative takeover of existing health services. Along the North Shore, key consultants suggested that people were dissatisfied with programs, in part because they had been imposed by the MSB bureaucracy. People stressed the need for community involvement in programming if Health Transfer was to be meaningful. As a result, after much discussion, including debate about the nature of participatory research among health staff and the McMaster consultants, the Health Board decided to ignore the MSB's research agenda and to develop a framework for community discussion of research findings and program planning. This decision was not without risk – there was general confidence, but not certainty, that MSB would agree to additional funding to ensure a longer period of community consultation. To their credit, once presented with an argument for community consultation, MSB agreed to provide additional funds, and to expand the project from an initial period of 15 months to more than 27 months to cover a period of community-based planning.

The Health Board viewed transfer as an opportunity to create a comprehensive vision of health-care. They ignored the limitations of the transfer policy, and concentrated on determining what type of health-care system was actually needed to deliver quality, culturally appropriate health-care. They would plan health-care services *not* included in the policy – for example, mental-health services, physician services, and a traditional medicine initiative. They refused to be restricted by the transfer policy and sought additional funds to supplement MSB's financial commitment. This decision is just one example of how First Nations are capable of *acting* to realize self-determination, even in the face of restrictive government policy. The Health Board realized that there was a risk in this strategy – for example, that the research and planning would raise false expectations about services that would not be met by MSB's financial commitment. But these decisions were based on an assessment of the federal and provincial political and policy environments. The Health Board realized that, unlike other provinces, no communities in Ontario had successfully completed transfer, and that the MSB wanted proof of the success of the policy in Ontario. The provincial political climate under the NDP was such that Aboriginal health was a high priority. The Health Board was confident that Mamaweswen had a solid reputation as a tribal council, and that the federal and provincial governments wanted to demonstrate a model at the regional level, so as to prevent the fragmentation of policy and programs that might occur if transfer occurred on a First Nations' basis.

The Research: Perception and Need

The consultants' role in this project involved regular visits to the North Shore for periods of several days to two weeks, and in the case of Dr. Pellizzari, for a period of about two months. Consultants acted in a variety of capacities: as trainers, project coordinators, interviewers, facilitators, and planners. Much of our work involved discussing and modelling group processes that were then continued by staff and volunteers who assumed responsibility for the ongoing transfer activities, including the strategic planning process. Howard Chambers, engineer for Chi Gaming Technical Services, costed the capital facilities and equipment requirements for transfer. Joanne Doyle, a medical administrator, assumed responsibility in the latter stages of the project for the human-resource costing and operating expenses. The majority of the work was conducted by North Shore staff – Marlene Nose, Lisa Meawasige, and Bill Greer – and a number of dedicated volunteers in each community. Marlene Nose, the health director who replaced Keith Lewis as coordinator, shouldered the majority of daily responsibilities for the process, and was instrumental in sustaining the community-based planning process.

The project included a community needs-assessment survey, conducted by Native interviewers, of 235 randomly selected individuals. The interviews, lasting on average two hours, included a large number of open questions. The survey was partially modelled on the Ontario Health Survey and included questions concerning perceptions of individual and community health, health status, environmental and occupational health risks, assessments of current and future program needs, attitudes to traditional medicine and contemporary health services. The data set was large, with each of the 235 interviews having 507 variables. Focus groups involving children and youth were also conducted to supplement the adult survey data. These survey techniques were balanced by key consultant interviews involving sixty Native health professionals, elders, and First Nations' councillors. Key consultants provided expert information on health-care needs and appropriate models for health-care delivery. The involvement of key consultants affirmed the expertise of local practitioners in the research and planning process. This process was also the first step to engage community members in the Health Transfer process and was designed to recognize the expertise of local practitioners and to encourage their future involvement in the planning process. That is, we used key consultants to establish a core of volunteers who became involved in planning.

I note only a few of the main findings concerning the health status in the NSTC area (mental-health status is detailed in the following chapter).[5] The survey confirmed that diabetes is a major problem in the North Shore. People living with diabetes have poorer self-rated health, and more frequently report other chronic health problems[6] (NSTC 1995a; cf. T.K. Young et al 1990; T.K. Young and Sevenhuysen 1989). People with diabetes also experience poorer mental health than other people interviewed during the needs assessment, and reported more past alcohol problems. Most people who were living with diabetes were overweight and were less active than their peers. These and other findings supported the need for the continued introduction of nutrition, health promotion, and recreational programs.

Other findings included an extremely high incidence of smoking; 48.3% of respondents reported they were daily smokers (compared to the OHS findings where 23% of respondents were daily smokers), and 15.4% were occasional smokers (NSTC 1995a). The high prevalence of smoking, especially in younger age groups, points to the potential for a high future burden of illness in NSTC First Nations. Another key finding was the perception that many community problems could be associated with alcohol abuse (NSTC 1992b: 8: 1). Alcohol was considered to be an important contributing factor to personal and family problems, as well as conflict with the law. About 60% of survey respondents said that alcohol had caused personal, family, and/or work problems. These findings served as a rationale for a variety of alcohol treatment and aftercare programs, as well as reconsideration of existing NNADAP programs.[7] Mental-health issues, particularly those associated with children and youth, were found to be of great concern to communities and the largest gap in existing services. In addition, the survey pointed to the need for a variety of mental-health programs dealing not simply with stresses felt by individuals, but with approaches to family and community mental well-being (see chapter 4).

Community attitudes to health services were positive. People were very satisfied with existing physician and nursing services, and there was little evidence that prejudice or discrimination exists in the provision of health services on the North Shore. Community members wanted to learn more about traditional medicine and to develop traditional healing, though, as I detail below, there was also considerable difference of opinion about the *nature* of traditional medicine. Community members also linked community health to larger issues of the environment; there was a general perception that the pollution of rivers and industrial development such as uranium mining (at Elliot Lake) somehow affect people's health. The range of issues arising under 'environmental health' suggested the need for a more broadly based mandate for an environmental-health program than had been previously offered by MSB.

Respondents also consistently stressed the needs of children and youth. The survey indicated that this population should be a special and ongoing focus of community health-promotion strategies. Priorities for child and youth health promotion include education about smoking, alcohol and drugs/solvents, and sexually transmitted diseases. More broadly, nutrition and diabetes programs were considered a health-promotion priority; these findings translated directly into the provision of a nutritionist and health-promotion services at the regional level. The need for traditional values in health-promotion activities was another recurring theme.

Data analysis was very time-consuming, in part because we did not sufficiently attend to the training of local staff in various aspects of computer data analysis. This resulted in a reliance on external data analysis (conducted by the consultants at McMaster), and meant that much of the raw data remained inaccessible to local staff. In fact, because of many problems too difficult to detail here, a final data set was not available to the communities until two years after the needs assessment was completed. The random sample of the various communities also produced reasonably valid regional data, but very poor data on a band-by-band basis (the numbers of interviews in some First Nations were too small to support valid statistical analysis). This attribute of the survey analysis may have reinforced people's perception that the research undermined First Nations' interests and was designed to foster regional or tribal council health strategies.

Because of these and other constraints we decided to develop community profiles for each of the seven First Nations. These consisted largely of descriptive statistics and a summary of key consultant interviews that allowed volunteers to prioritize the perceptions of health needs and develop programs aimed at various forms of intervention. The profiles gave a snapshot of First Nations specific data concerning perceived health conditions, needs, and priorities. At the same time we began to develop a picture of regional programs and services.

Significantly, the research indicated great consistency between communities. Health status, perceptions about community care, problem areas, administrative suggestions, and health-promotion strategies were similar in all the communities. What differences existed between First Nations were based on the distance and/or proximity to urban centres, community size and corresponding level of service or facilities, and concern for specific environmental problems. There was agreement that communities needed to assume control and ownership of their health programs. A key research finding was the need for the development and activation of First Nations' Health Committees.

The Planning: Community Participation in Health Care

What emerged as the most successful part of the project was the development of a community-based planning process that utilized the community profiles drawn from the survey. People volunteered to participate in Health Planning Circles (HPCs), which were modelled on focus groups (Morgan 1988:11). The HPCs, one in each community, met to review the community profile and to prioritize issues for each community. In some communities the circles of five to ten volunteers met as often as once every two weeks for about two hours. In two communities, either because of poor staff facilitation or a lack of community interest, participation was poorer and more sporadic. As a result, one community 'fell behind' in the planning process, and latter claimed that they felt pressured into making decisions to proceed to negotiations.

At each meeting people selected one or two program areas and discussed plans according to a simple 'who, what, where, when, and why' format. The HPCs suggested solutions to specific health needs, determined who should be responsible for the intervention, identified other community members who could assist staff deliver the program, and established basic (often qualitative) evaluation criteria for each intervention. Special representatives also participated from time to time; for example, the input of people living with diabetes was sought for particular health-promotion discussions. Consultants and staff sometimes facilitated meetings and also reviewed the literature on Native health programs and community-based health-care so as to provide information to planning circles.

The HPCs prioritized community needs based on the research. They then generally *ignored* the survey findings and relied on their own knowledge of the community in the planning process. In other words, the initial review of the research results acted as a stimulus to discussions about priorities, and provided each circle with a common body of knowledge on which they could base their planning. But the actual process of program planning rested on people's pragmatic wisdom about what approaches might work best in their community. The results of these discussions were then taken by staff and developed into comprehensive regional and First Nation health plans, which were then taken back over the course of several months for revisions by health committees and councils. Because each community developed its own approach to a given health area – for example health promotion, or environmental health – a number of strategies emerged that were unique and could be shared with other communities.

This process was extremely successful and resulted in the production, over the course of a year, of comprehensive health plans for each of the communities. The Health Board also developed a regional service-delivery plan. Each community plan, totalling more than a hundred pages, included a number of objectives, program areas, program rationales, and strategies to improve the health of community members. Volunteers decided who in the community should be responsible for the delivery of programs and what additional human resources were needed. This exercise challenged volunteers to identify where new staff were needed, or where linkages to regional services were required. Each program area outlined a variety of strategies to address a wide range of issues – from the creation of well-baby clinics, to the need to develop suicide intervention programs. In fact, communities mapped out strategies for tackling a much more comprehensive range of interventions than we had initially anticipated – everything from safety and nutrition services to recreational programs and occupational health programs. These plans became the central rationale for negotiations aimed at enhancing local services. But they also became important resources that have been used to set yearly plans for health staff, or to assist First Nations in the reorganization of programs. Quite aside from their role in Health Transfer, they have also been used in a variety of proposals to support requests for new financial resources from federal and provincial governments.

As a final step in the planning process, health staff, consultants, and Health Board members held a retreat to plan the organizational structure necessary to deliver these programs. These plans were also taken to the HPCs for feedback and revision. The regional organizational structure was developed after a discussion of the traditional values that the Health Board regarded as important. The Health Board used the medicine wheel concept to develop a non-hierarchical organizational structure, which linked various programs into management teams. Finally, HPCs determined the type of staff they needed to address priority issues. Joanne Doyle then costed the human-resource requirements considering population and need. That is, the plans were used to assess the difference between existing and needed staff, and to project the type of staff positions that would be required to deliver all of the new programs. New initiatives were identified in a variety of areas. These included the need for First Nations' health directors, additional nurses and nurse practitioners, a health-promotion specialist, and a nutritionist to support community initiatives.

First Nations also identified the need for mental-health workers; these positions were to be supported through a regional program that would contract the psychiatric services and provide crisis intervention.

For the region, the Health Board also identified the need for a community-development specialist, a traditional-medicine adviser, a mental-health coordinator, and a researcher/evaluator. All these new positions were to be provided with support staff. Many of these programs were developed *even though they were beyond the mandate of the Health Transfer initiative.* Similarly, under the regional plan, a new initiative in primary health-care was developed, which would have the tribal council directly hiring a primary health-care director who would supervise doctors, as well as a nurse practitioner, a chiropodist, a registered nursing assistant responsible for foot care, and a midwife. This latter initiative became the basis for a proposal for a provincially funded Aboriginal Health Access Centre (see below).

The human-resource assessment provided the basis for First Nations' and tribal council budgets, which included capital costs for new offices and equipment. In what proved to be a painstaking process, these budgets were then again discussed by community members and councils and taken to negotiations. Not surprisingly, the inclusion of a number of new initiatives increased the 'price tag' for what was, essentially, an ideal health-care delivery system. And even though it was always clear that many of these new programs could only be delivered by obtaining provincial resources, this approach had the effect of raising expectations in several communities concerning the negotiations. One important aspect of negotiations focused on the relative benefits to First Nations versus tribal council control over programs.

The Politics of Health Care: The Negotiations

By the end of the planning process, the Health Board had seven First Nations' health plans, and a regional health plan in place. Community consultations continued even as the Health Board prepared for negotiations. Marlene Nose and I facilitated community and council meetings where the final plans were discussed. In several communities the plans were easily accepted, ratified by First Nation Councils, and became the basis for program delivery. In several other communities, much to my surprise, both the plans and the entire transfer planning process were criticized. Criticism of the process ranged from the complaint that communities had insufficient time to complete their plans, to the contention that, once on paper, the plans were 'written in stone.' In one community, we also heard the suggestion that the planning had not been inclusive enough – that membership in planning circles had not included sufficient community representation. Many of these complaints were difficult for me to understand. Consultants and staff, for example, had taken great pains to stress that the plans were 'organic' documents that health committees would change over time to reflect community priorities. It seemed that we had been trying to build a process for community involvement in health-care, but that communities were only seeing a particular 'product' of this process. And while participation in the planning process was uneven across the communities, this was the result of *local* health committee process – in my assessment the Health Board staff had consistently tried to facilitate participation, despite being pressed for time and having limited resources. Staff used numerous techniques – presentations to schools, information sessions with councils, and newsletters – to inform communities about Health Transfer. But despite these strategies, misunderstandings remained among people who did not participate directly in the planning circles. Some people, for example, were concerned that the transfer project would contribute to a deterioration of services. This view cannot be dissociated from people's larger concerns about self-government, or from their perception that communities are not prepared to assume control over their own programs.

As it turned out, some of these criticisms were intertwined with the personal circumstances of regional and local health-care staff. There was the legitimate concern, for example, that staff positions might be eliminated, or that new positions would potentially alter the current structure of authority and responsibility among health-care staff. There was also considerable trepidation that the new program initiatives (essentially a restructuring of health priorities) would require workers to change roles, to seek additional training, or to abandon certain responsibilities. In short, there was some reticence about the unforeseen 'side effects' that Health Transfer would have on people's professional well-being.

The individual political priorities and diverse nature of North Shore communities make it difficult to describe in any detail the nature of political concerns that emerged over several years. During the transfer project, each of the First Nations held three elections, resulting in turnover of key chiefs and councillors. Two communities temporarily withdrew their membership in tribal council, and questioned their participation in transfer and other tribal council initiatives. It became evident that those communities that were experiencing internal factionalism, or that were in need of organizational development, were unable to fully contribute and participate in Health Transfer and other regional initiatives. Conversely, political conflicts within tribal council, including those related to self-government negotiations and issues arising around tribal council finances, infiltrated the Health Transfer process (see also chapter 6). In short, the Health Transfer project became embroiled in more deeply seated and complex political issues.

From my outsider's perspective, there were also concerns within the Health Board. Representatives needed training in board organization and development – certain members often seemed unsure of whether or not they had the delegated authority to make decisions on behalf of their community. The board also lacked many basic policies and seemed to depend on a few key members who assumed the majority of decision-making. But these were problems familiar to many non-profit organizations. More positively, the core board membership remained relatively constant during this time, which allowed for coherent decision-making over the course of the Health Transfer process.

Some of the criticism of Health Transfer reflected wider concerns about the nature of regional versus First Nations' interests, and concern about the preparedness of communities to move forward into the implementation phase. What eventually became clear was the concern of several First Nations that Health Transfer would solidify the role of tribal council in the delivery of health-care, to the detriment of First Nations' control of services. In several communities, for example, people commented that the comprehensive health plans would establish a 'mini-MSB' at the regional level. This complaint parallels criticisms of tribal councils as new Indian Affairs departments, which are perceived as self-sustaining 'small bureaucracies' that dictate plans to First Nations.

This issue was exacerbated as negotiations with MSB began. Understandably, the 'bottom line' for Health Board representatives was that, if a reasonable level of financial resourcing could not be secured to deliver *both* regional *and* First Nations programs, then a priority should be given to maximizing resources in *individual* First Nations. This, of course, is consistent with the principle of the integrity of First Nations to design, control, and implement services. This emphasis was also reasonable because Health Board members were aware that MSB would be unlikely to fund new regional services (for example, mental health and traditional medicine) and that other provincial funds might be forthcoming that could support the regional organizational structure – most notably, funds requested under the Aboriginal Health Access Centre (primary care) initiative and the provincial government's Aboriginal Healing and Wellness Strategy (AHWS) and Long-Term Care initiatives (see below, 125).

It is a testimony to the strength of the Health staff, particularly Marlene Nose, and to the quiet leadership of Chief Commanda, the Health Board chair, that the communities were able to sustain their cooperation throughout the negotiations, which consumed more than two years. The Health Board maintained its commitment to compromise and consensus decision-making. I was not part of the negotiating team, and my understanding of negotiations is based on conversations with Marlene Nose and Earl Commanda, as well my occasional attendance at Health Board meetings. The arguments presented by MSB and Health staff at these meetings were very complex, and I was greatly impressed by the astuteness and political acumen of Health Board members, who at times were under enormous pressure to make difficult decisions while faced with what seemed a bewildering array of financial estimates, funding formulas, and cost-sharing arrangements. To greatly simplify, initial estimates by MSB suggested that as much as $3.7 million might be available for the entire NSTC transfer – an amount that was more than double the level of pre-transfer funding. This estimate gave hope that a number of new regional and local programs could be initiated and that, with the addition of provincial funds (of approximately one million dollars) for AHAC funding, the Health Board's comprehensive vision could be realized. This budget is similar, if not meagre by comparison, to that of any Northern community health centre servicing similar populations.

But the MSB was unable to deliver on this early estimate. The final MSB offer, which included start-up costs, but not capital funding for new facilities, was $2,609,460 for the seven First Nations. Individual First Nations budgets ranged from about $100,000 to $600,000 (NSTC 1995c). And although this amount is greater than pre-transfer project resourcing, it does not represent any significant enhancement of services, but rather, can be attributed to normal increases of staffing and salaries that occurred during the life of the project. This amount includes a share of the former MSB administration budget on the basis of a formula driven by community population. In addition, the Health Board was to assume control over the environmental-health program, formerly run by MSB. The major enhancement was the provision of dollars to hire part-time or full-time health directors for First Nations, and minor enhancements to CHR, NNADAP, and nursing positions that might have occurred naturally over time. The federal government refused to fund mental-health programs, a traditional medicine initiative, and the regional administrative infrastructure.

It will strike the reader as extremely ironic to learn that MSB representatives, after encouraging the development of regional approaches, reversed their position during the final stages of negotiation, and suggested that the MSB was prepared to sign agreements with individual First Nations, rather than a single agreement with the Health Board. After years of Health Board discussion and dialogue about the need for communities to work together, to share resources, and to create a regional vision of health-care, individual First Nations could now apparently 'go it alone.' Several Health Board members interpreted MSB's position as a divide-and-conquer strategy.

From MSB's perspective, this new position was assumed for two reasons. First, the MSB representatives, recognizing the continuing shifts in allegiance to tribal council and the Health Board, wanted to ensure that Health Transfer proceeded in at least those communities that were prepared to move forward. But this new MSB position further undermined the position of those Health Board members who would have preferred to advocate for strong regional services. Second, MSB's new offer responded to First Nations' desire to directly administer health services.

As a result of this new arrangement, First Nations needed to determine which services they wished to continue at the regional level. The First Nations decided that they would enter into individual agreements with MSB and then would 'buy back' regional programs by contributing to shared services they believed they could support after allocating their individual health budgets. Such an arrangement acknowledges the integrity of First Nations, while still allowing for the delivery of regional support services. These shared contributions, to support Health Board meetings, the environmental-health program, and regional coordination through Health Board staff, was estimated to cost approximately $288,000. This amount was divided on the basis of on-reserve population, which meant that larger reserves would pay more to support a 'basic' regional organization.

Was the North Shore's initial proposal cost efficient? While I do not believe a 'price tag' can be attached to various self-government initiatives (see chapter 7), it is important to stress that much planning went into the efficiency of service delivery. The North Shore's proposal was very reasonable, particularly when measured against the cost of operating local clinics, mental-health programs, and hospital-based services. Any service cost is dependent on pre-existing services, the size of the community in which it is delivered, and the distances that need to be travelled. Canadian taxpayers accept the principle that certain 'less advantaged' parts of the country must have services subsidized by more wealthy regions; southern urban centres will naturally have better and a wider range of services available to them; and, in rural and remote regions, the costs of service delivery will be higher, and the range of services smaller. These factors are critical to arguments about 'economies of scale' – the relative and reasonable costs that can be associated with the delivery of services in different localities, across different population sizes. Clearly, there are also inefficiencies in the system. Services can be delivered in more cost-efficient ways, and less expensive alternatives to current practices can be found.

When the North Shore tribal council submitted its best vision of a holistic, integrated health-care system, it came with a 5-million-dollar price tag – a price that excluded capital costs but included new staffing for community development, support for traditional medicine, and the development of community-based mental-health workers who would focus on crisis intervention and family violence. This amount – four times the prior allocation by Medical Services Branch – was regarded as exorbitant by federal negotiators and, through negotiations, was eroded to $2.6 million. I have little doubt that the balance of these funds (roughly $2.4 million) will eventually be realized. The difference will be made up, gradually and over successive years, through provincial funding; for example, through Aboriginal Health Access Centre funding, through Long-Term Care funding, and through new federal and provincial initiatives announced to tackle, in however a piecemeal fashion, the special physical- and mental-health problems of Aboriginal communities (NSTC 1994c).

The NSTC's vision of regional health services was developed in full awareness of the economies of scale and with a firm appreciation for the need to deliver efficient services. Human-resource requirements, including staffing and training budgets, were based on a pragmatic, program-by-program review of the costs of services commonly delivered in other settings. In fact, salaries and program costs were low in comparison to non-Native services. What was disappointing to community members and to the Health Board leadership was that their global vision, which was based on solid research and community discussion, could not be grasped by federal bureaucrats or, more pragmatically, was simply beyond the federal mandate for Aboriginal health. Perhaps most frustrating was the lack of recognition that Aboriginal communities were prepared to act in specific areas – such as mental health, traditional medicine, and environmental health – where the federal government *had not yet developed* program or policy initiatives.

This review of a four-year-long research and planning process cannot do justice to the complexity of the work that occurred in each community.

The difficulties of conducting participatory-action research (PAR) and community planning in seven separate communities are many and varied (see also Ryan 1995). Inevitably, for example, some communities progressed at a faster rate than others. Election results mean that staff and volunteers must constantly retrace their steps in order to apprise new chiefs or councillors of initiatives. Staff and Health Board members also needed to convince new chiefs or councillors that their predecessors were correct in supporting the transfer process. There were a great many political issues that, had it not been for the acumen and subtle diplomacy of tribal council staff, Health Board members, and chiefs – most notably Chief Commanda, a strong advocate of regional integration – would have jeopardized the project at several stages.

The integrity of this community-based process was sustained despite these and other problems – temporary shortages of human and financial resources, staff turnover, miscommunication, and the personality clashes that are a natural part of any organizational reform. The NSTC Health Board continues to rethink its long-term vision of a comprehensive health-care-delivery system. Mamaweswen, through provincial funding, will over the course of the next decade deliver the services that many communities have envisioned.

Culturally Appropriate Care: Traditional Medicine

Before turning to the role of provincial government in health-care, I examine what for many Aboriginal people is the keystone to the holistic delivery of culturally appropriate health-care – traditional medicine. Many of the actions taken by the NSTC Health Board under Health Transfer aimed at the provision of 'culturally appropriate' health-care. The incorporation of values associated with the medicine wheel into the structure and organization of health-care delivery is an example of how Aboriginal people are attempting to adjust a Western health-care system to Aboriginal needs. The emphasis on environmental health within the NSTC health program is an another example of holistic approaches, as is the attempt in the community health plan to develop interventions that deal with individual, family, and community well-being.

Many people, however, equate culturally appropriate care with the revitalization or enhancement of traditional Indian medicine. Writing for the RCAP, O'Neil notes, '... the term "colonial medicine," as an alternative reference for Western, scientific medicine, serves to remind us "Western" and "scientific" are terms laden with cultural meaning which imply that the medicine they describe is somehow superior to other forms of medicine. To assume that science is uniquely a Western phenomena, or that scientific approaches to medicine are only found in the West is the epitome of cultural arrogance' (1993: 39). O'Neil notes that the history of contact between colonial medicine and Aboriginal communities was in many instances positive. Drawing on the work of Vanast (1991) he notes that the efforts of doctors and nurses, often in the face of negative state policies and practice, did much to alleviate the health burden of many Native communities. But colonial medical practice in Aboriginal communities has, according to O'Neil, transmitted new ideologies that convince their recipients that their own values and beliefs are no longer valid (ibid, see also Nandy 1983).

The RCAP final reports speak of 'two great traditions' of health and healing, yet the commission is cautious in recognizing the importance or efficacy of biomedical approaches for Aboriginal communities. Instead, it points to areas of convergence between the biomedical and Aboriginal health-care systems; specifically, it argues for an enhancement of primary health and the placement of human (individual health) into wider community and environmental systems (1996d: 221). The RCAP speaks of the potential for 'transforming human health' through the sharing of insights and building of partnerships between Aboriginal and science-based knowledge (ibid: 223).

The ideological power of the biomedical system is enormous, and Aboriginal people have internalized many Western medical values. Biomedicine is accepted, valued, and respected, perhaps more so than other aspects of Western culture. Consequently, talk of health-care reform is sometimes greeted with suspicion by some community members. Two common concerns raised during Health Transfer discussions were that existing physician services might be lost, or that increased Aboriginal control would actually restrict people's ability to choose a family physician.

The statistics cited in the previous chapter make it clear that, for complex reasons, the current 'illness care' system has failed to adequately address the needs of Aboriginal people. For many people, increasing the use of traditional medicine is an important aspect of improving health-care delivery. Traditional medicine encompasses approaches to physical, spiritual, emotional, and mental well-being. It is also focused on health promotion, illness prevention, and treatment. As a holistic system, traditional healing transcends the compartmentalized boundaries of biomedicine that separate medical and spiritual practice. It is important to remember, therefore, that even where Native people believe in the power of traditional medicine to prevent illness or cure diseases, there is also a deep appreciation for biomedicine. People often seek out physicians when their own health practices fail – and vice versa. In short, it is appropriate to speak of traditional medicine as a complementary and parallel system of health practice;[8] but it is wrong to assume that faith or belief in Aboriginal health practices is uniform or universal in communities. And it would be a mistake to see an increased use of traditional medicine as a substitute for continuing improvement of western health-care delivery to First Nations.

The penetration of Western biomedicine into Aboriginal communities makes attempts to revitalize Indian medicine extremely problematic. One of the critiques of Health Transfer is that insufficient recognition and financial support is available to support traditional medicine approaches. This is certainly true. Over the course of the Health Transfer project we found considerable interest among government officials for the idea of a traditional medicine initiative, but this interest did not translate into financial commitment. In the survey we asked a short series of questions concerning traditional medicine. In addition, we discussed traditional healing with all key consultants. Finally, the Health Board hired Tom Biron, a Native researcher with interests in medical anthropology, and together we held focus groups in each of the seven communities.

Interest in traditional medicine was strongest among key consultants, for example, councillors and service providers, whom we interviewed. This is not surprising, for these are individuals who are best versed in the ideology of community revitalization. There was support for the building of healing lodges, and for integration of Western and Aboriginal approaches – for example, for notifying patients that herbal medicines, as well as Western drugs, are available as treatment options. This attitude was also true among elders who were interviewed – most felt that there were ways that traditional healers and physicians could work together in an 'integrated' system. But it was clear from focus group discussion that while most people felt traditional approaches were complementary to mainstream approaches, they also felt ways should be found (for example, in training and education) to emphasize the distinctiveness of Aboriginal approaches so that they could be regarded as a true alternative to Western treatment options.

Herbal remedies were used by over half the people surveyed and were found in all communities. But when people were asked whether they had ever used traditional healers or practices to deal with problems of the body, mind, or spirit; *only 8.5% of people stated they had done so* (NSTC

1995a). Many key consultants also seemed to be uncertain about the use of 'spiritual' healing, for example, the use of purification lodges, and there was disagreement about individuals who should be considered medicine men. Traditional healers were clearly identified in three of the seven communities. Other communities, however, relied on medicine people from outside the region, and there was concern about the 'authenticity' of healers who were not well-known. Focus group participants suggested that some self-proclaimed healers were charlatans, 'plastic medicine men' who use the idea of healing for their own benefit.

One of the most significant aspects of Aboriginal community life is the conflict between 'traditional' and Christian beliefs.[9] The influence of Christianity, coupled with the penetration of Western biomedicine, has left many people with distrust, if not fear, of traditional medicine. For example, we interviewed a number of individuals who vehemently denied that traditional approaches had any value, or who associated the revival of such practices as purification lodges or other forms of spiritual healing with paganism, 'the devil's work,' and 'bearwalking,' or what is commonly known as 'bad medicine.' These attitudes are interesting because belief in traditional medicine contains a spiritual or religious dimension that seems potentially threatening to some Christians. Likewise, traditional medicine threatens the world-view of many Western health practitioners who rigidly adhere to psychological or psychiatric models. Dr Ed Conners, whose views on holistic health are quoted at the start of this chapter, has elsewhere noted how spiritual healing and Western psychology function by drawing on key cultural metaphors and beliefs in order to assist patients in reformulating and re-integrating their sense of self (UOI 1993a).

A holistic view of healing stresses that a person's life can be radically altered through a variety of medical and/or spiritual experiences. Despite widespread change in Native communities, and the influence of Christian beliefs on reserves, one fundamental constant remains – that a person's belief system is integral to healing processes. It is for this reason that modern psychiatry and traditional medicine practices have much in common. And it is for this reason also that many religions – including the older Catholic and Anglican faiths as well as more recent Pentecostal churches – have spiritual healing in their belief systems. Indeed, many Native professionals believe that the aspects of many traditional healing practices exist within contemporary religious beliefs.

Attitudes toward traditional medicine are connected to the particular pattern of colonialism experienced by people in North Shore First Nations. In Ojibwa society, the primary institution that safeguards traditional knowledge about healing is the Medewiwin, or Grand Medicine Society. The Medewiwin does not appear to have been sustained or to be active in the North Shore area – at least I am not aware of any organized collective of healers. I interviewed several key consultants interested in revitalizing traditional medicine, or active in ceremonies, but I could find no evidence of any in-depth knowledge of this tradition.

Significantly, however, during a different project two years later, I found several individuals who were knowledgeable about a variety of traditional practices, and had greater understanding of this tradition. One community had even conducted a research project to document traditional medicine practices (Sagamok Naadmaada Research Project 1994b). I mention this only to suggest that the inability to discover knowledge of the Medewiwin during the transfer project may have been due to a failure in methodology, or simply of a reluctance of consultants to discuss this issue. Much of the knowledge possessed by medicine people is sacred and private and is passed down through apprenticeship to individuals who have demonstrated a lifelong commitment to traditional healing arts.

Today there is a general belief that many people who call themselves traditional healers practice their medicinal arts with good intention. There is concern, however, that many people who are self-professed medicine men (or women) do not have either the power or expertise of their traditional counterparts, and that much of the traditional knowledge has been lost. There is also disagreement about the practice of traditional ways in general and about the nature of bad medicine in particular. Nishnawbe medicine people are known as *wabano*, *djiskid*, and *mide* (or *midewidjik*).[10] Those who possess supernatural power and use it with good intention are called *wabano*. The *wabano* is distinguished from ritual specialists, *djiskid*, and from the *mide*, who practice good or bad medicine (ibid). Today, however, many people do not have knowledge of these different roles. Traditional medicine people received gifts in return for doctoring. Today, people who accept gifts for medicines are sometimes accused of 'selling' medicine and this can be taken as an indication that a person's practices are unauthentic or that he or she is practicing bad medicine.

Traditional healing stresses the individual's ability to gain knowledge of his or her world and use that knowledge to lead a healthy lifestyle and, when ill, to heal themselves. There are a number of individuals – both within the NSTC area and beyond – who are spiritual healers, herbalists, and medicine people. Such persons are believed to have exceptional knowledge and healing gifts. Traditional healing gatherings at Birch Island attract several hundred people each year from around the NSTC area. Some Native agencies draw on traditional healers as needed, to assist people who are experiencing a variety of personal problems. But collaboration between traditional healers and clinicians is still rare. Quite separately from the Health Transfer initiatives, one traditional healer, Dan Pine, of Garden River, was instrumental in developing the vision for a traditional healing lodge. With great persistence, he was able to secure funding from the provincial government's Native Affairs Secretariat to build it. Today, the lodge is almost complete, though sufficient funding for operations has yet to be secured.

The question of how to best recognize or promote traditional medicine is very difficult. As noted above, people have conflicting ideas about whether or not traditional medicine should be integrated with or remain separate from the Western medical system. By and large, the healers we identified remained isolated from the Health Transfer process. In part this was because there was insufficient staff and time to assume a more one-on-one approach with healers, which might have brought them into the process. But these individuals also did not express interest in the transfer initiative, which they saw as irrelevant to their own work or interests. Mr. Biron suggested that traditional medicine should not be included in the transfer process because it might become compromised. He argued that great care needed to be taken so as not to institutionalize traditional medicine through its association with a Western health-care delivery system. Waldram et al (1995: 224–6) note the potential threats (as well as benefits) to traditional medicine implied in increased collaboration or formalization with the mainstream biomedical system. The NSTC focus groups revealed that people consider it inappropriate to formalize or institutionalize traditional healing *at present.* People believe that the idea of a 'program' in traditional medicine was inappropriate – healers cannot be regarded in the same manner as doctors, CHRs, or other health professionals. In some communities, for example, people noted that the teaching of traditional medicine cannot be done through schools; rather, it can only take place through apprenticeships with healers. Again, there were also concerns that Health Transfer was a tribal council initiative, and there was the desire of at least some First Nations to pursue traditional medicine on their own terms. Others saw Health Transfer as tied to the federal government, and eschewed any linkage between traditional practices and government services. The message was clear: traditional healing as *an informal system* of holistic practice transcends the boundaries of biomedicine, integrates medical and spiritual practice, and cannot be 'captured' by institutions.

However, as Marlene Nose notes (personal communication), this is not to suggest that traditional medicine cannot be practised within the confines of an institution, only that the locus of control for Aboriginal medicine must remain within the community. She notes that, where Western practitioners and administrators accept and respect traditional medicine, it is possible for traditional medicine to be practised in hospital and other institutional settings. On Manitoulin Island, for example, a native council has been created to advise the hospital board on traditional practices, and healers are given consent to practice within Western facilities.

Discussions about revitalizing traditional medicine concern the nature and authenticity of culture. Many people who believe in the efficacy of traditional healing are also concerned that these practices should be authentic, that is, derived directly from local Ojibwa traditions. Renewed interest in traditional healing is tinged with caution and skepticism. Because of the deeply sacred nature of this information people believe they must proceed cautiously, in a manner that is in keeping with customary law, which stresses, for example, the relationship between healing practices, the role of guardian spirits, and relations to Mother Earth. These views are intermixed with concerns that traditional ceremonies have been compromised by whites, most notable by 'New Agers' infatuated with the trappings of Aboriginal culture. There is concern, for instance, that traditional spiritual practices are being appropriated for misuse by the colonizers – the last in a long line of appropriations of Native culture. Those who share this concern point out that the practice of Indian medicine is rooted in a person's serious, long-term commitment to spiritual growth. And they fear that many ceremonies now being investigated by Aboriginal people will be tainted or compromised by those who try to cater to non-Native 'believers' (*Spectator*, 13 July 1995, A13).

To summarize, the focus-group discussions revealed a cautious attitude toward the revitalization of traditional practices. People suggest that the experience of those who practise traditional medicine should be verified lest they take advantage of individuals or cause spiritual harm. They want traditional medicine to be 'home-grown' and built on local knowledge and expertise, and at the same time, recognize that there is a shortage of knowledgeable practitioners. People also stress the need to rediscover authentic traditional knowledge. It was suggested that First Nations document and protect specific sites where medicinal plants grow. With the elders' agreement, videotapes or other interviews might be made to document traditional practices. Additional research into the efficacy of traditional healing practices might also be conducted. Many people mentioned the need for a 'safe' or non-threatening environment where people could come together to learn about traditional medicine. And they suggested that this learning must take place in appropriate ways – through storytelling, coming together around a fire, or at social gatherings rather than through workshops or formalized training.

In the end, therefore, the Health Board decided to approve a traditional-medicine initiative to promote the revitalization of Anishnabe health practices. The tribal council proposed to support First Nations' efforts to conduct research in this area, to invite traditional healers to communities, and to make them available to individuals who expressed a desire to consult these healers rather than physicians or psychiatrists. This initiative was also designed to foster a slow and conservative approach to public education so as to enhance people's awareness of issues associated with Indian medicine. It called for the hiring of a traditional medicine adviser who would consult with healers, document traditional medicine sites, and provide guidance to staff and board on how healers might be linked to other health-care initiatives – or how they might act as an alternative option for people seeking medical care. The initiative did not include salaried or other monetary arrangements with healers. But it proposed a number of indirect supports for traditional activities – for example, funds to provide food for traditional gatherings, to assist elders with transportation, to pay students to assist healers in gathering medicinal plants.

The Health Board approved an initiative that would attempt to increase the use and awareness of traditional medicine over a three-to-five year period – a suggestion that met with 'mainstream' community attitudes and was a pragmatic beginning that would eventually lead to greater discussion and community education about the idea of traditional healing. Despite the fact that the initiative did not receive federal funding there remains considerable optimism that these or similar activities will be supported in future, perhaps through core provincial funding for the Garden River Healing Lodge.

Until very recently, Canadian governments had failed to recognize the validity of Aboriginal health science (see O'Neil 1993; K. Scott 1993). This lack of recognition stemmed from a simple ignorance of Aboriginal culture, and from ideological blinkers that sustained the belief that western biomedicine was inherently superior to other indigenous health systems. Fortunately, the past decade has seen a remarkable shift in the perceptions of mainstream medical practitioners and health-policy analysts – a shift that is mirrored in the increasing acceptance of 'complementary' medicine among the general public (for example, herbalism, acupuncture, and other forms of holistic medicine). In the mid-1980s, a small number of programs were implemented that emphasized the inclusion of spiritual and cultural awareness in alcohol and drug programs, or the development of cultural interpreter programs in Northern hospitals (see O'Neil 1988). Today, the use of traditional medicine is an essential component of the Ontario Aboriginal Healing and Wellness Strategy (AHWS), and traditional healing lodges are being funded throughout the province.

From a Native *political* perspective, the revitalization of traditional medicine is viewed as a critical motif within the mosaic of self-government. The RCAP has called for a new Aboriginal health and healing strategy to ensure that Aboriginal people experience 'equal outcomes,' that is, the same level of health and well-being as the general population (1996d: 202). Many components of this strategy are already established at the community level and evident in initiatives such as Ontario's Aboriginal Healing and Wellness Strategy – a commitment to holistic approaches, culture-based programs, and a renewed focus on traditional healing (see below). Recognition that indigenous health science is a central component of Aboriginal *control* over health systems is constantly restated by Aboriginal peoples. As O'Neil notes:

> Traditional Aboriginal medicine clearly is undergoing a renaissance in the country and is making an enormous, but undocumented contribution to community well-being. While documentation should be done only by Aboriginal scholars according to Elders' regulations, I believe it is in the context of traditional medicine where issues of self-government, socioeconomic development and environmental protection are best integrated with community health development for most Aboriginal communities. Even in situations where traditional medicine has been severely colonized, the underlying principles of balance, harmony, and respect, common across the Aboriginal world, provide the foundation for development (1993: 45).

The NSTC area is an example of communities that, in O'Neil's terms, might be described as 'severely colonized.' But even here there is cautious optimism that traditional medicine can be revitalized and returned to its rightful place as a system of healing that would complement Western biomedicine.

Health-Care Delivery: The Bureaucratic Realities

The federal government's Health Transfer policy is so limited that First

Nations are forced to rely on a combination of federal and provincial monies in order to ensure an adequate level of health services for their members. As Chief Earl Commanda has remarked, the federal government provided dollars for First Nations to design a Cadillac health-care system, but was only prepared to deliver a Volkswagen. For example, despite the obvious need for mental-health services, there are no provisions for such initiatives. Nor does Health Transfer provide for physician services – these must be developed through provincial initiatives. In the North Shore's case, Health Transfer decisions were being made as a number of provincial initiatives were emerging – most noticeably the development of a comprehensive Aboriginal health policy, a major family-violence consultation, recognition of Aboriginal Health Access Centres, and a Long-Term Care initiative. The Health Board pursued all these provincial funding opportunities. They tried to assess how the complete vision of a new health-care delivery system could be realized by melding together, under one funding umbrella, various provincial and federal initiatives. In short, the Health Board sought to accommodate a Native vision of 'holistic' health to a bureaucratic reality that was shaped by both the federal and provincial governments.

Jurisdiction for Indian health care is poorly drawn, a fact that affords both the federal and provincial governments the rationale for failing to provide adequate services to various Indian communities. Section 91(24) of the Indian Act states federal responsibility for Indians and lands reserved for Indians, but Section 92 devolves responsibility for establishing and delivering human services to provinces. Aboriginal people argue that health care is a treaty right. But this position has never been accepted by the federal government, which maintains that health-care provision is simply a matter of policy (see K. Scott 1993). The government's position was dramatically revealed when Health Minister Diane Marleau refused, at the last moment, to sign an agreement with the Assembly of Manitoba Chiefs when the chiefs would not include a line stating that the federal government would not recognize health care as a treaty right (*Spectator*, 17 Feb. 1995, A9).

Provincial governments recognize the federal government's responsibility for health-care delivery to status Indians. The provinces recognize off-reserve Indians as 'ordinary citizens' and provide services accordingly. The provinces finance Aboriginal health care through physicians on a fee-for-service basis (for example, through OHIP billings) and hospital services.[11] In special circumstances 'where numbers warrant' the federal government has contributed funding to Aboriginal Health Centres or

Treatment Centres that serve groups off reserve. In special cases arising from historic agreements, Medical Services Branch provides hospital services, for example, in Moose Factory and Sioux Lookout, Ontario. MSB provides funding for hospital operations, but all insured services, for example, physician services, are reimbursed to Canada from provincial operating grants. The cost of Aboriginal health programs is also shared through human-services agreements under the Canada Assistance Plan (CAP) and Established Programs Financing (EPF) for health care,[12] that is, through transfer payments from the federal to provincial governments.

Although difficult to estimate, current costs for Aboriginal health care are shared relatively equally between the provinces and the federal government. Waldram et al (1995) note that the Health and Welfare expenditures were $36 billion in 1991/1992. MSB's budget of $700 million represents less than 2 per cent of expenditures (recall that the RCAP places the Aboriginal population at 2.7 per cent). Waldram et al note that a major portion of these funds were for non-insured health benefits (NIHB), which include health-insurance premiums, prescription drugs, dental care, eye glasses, prosthetic devices, as well as the costs of patient transportation that are not covered by provincial health-insurance plans. The total amount of NIHB escalated from $36 million in 1979/80 to $442 million in 1992/93, a per capita annual increase of 7 per cent (Waldram et al 1995: 186–7). As Waldram et al note:

> From the Aboriginal perspective, there is solid reason on constitutional and political grounds that NIHB should be an integral part of the federal government's responsibilities towards Aboriginal peoples. Yet, for NIHB – which have at best only a marginal impact on the health status of Aboriginal Peoples – to constitute such a substantial portion of total health expenditures on Indian and Northern Health Services, in a climate of fiscal restraints, can only skew and distort overall health priorities. The vast amounts paid to diverse dentists, optometrists, pharmacists and taxi companies can surely be better spent on the development of preventative dental programs, vision screening, a formulary of essential and efficacious drugs, and a triage/referral/evacuation policy. (ibid)

That is, as with other bureaucratic systems – for example, justice or social services – the appearance of federal expenditures for Indian health services is deceptive. Communities continue to lack control over how monies are allocated, and a major portion of health-care dollars is spent on services located off reserve, rather than in direct, community-based services.

In Ontario in 1994, MSB began discussions concerning the devolution of control over administration of NIHBs to First Nations. Along the North Shore, some First Nations have begun negotiations to assume direct control over this program. Other communities have yet to engage in this process, in part because they are concerned that, at the moment, they lack the human resources necessary for the proper administration of these dollars. Here again, the administration of these services is best managed on a regional (PTO) or tribal council basis. There remains a dearth of Aboriginal people trained in health management and administration. Perhaps more significantly, MSB has shown little inclination to support regional staff and programs that would provide an umbrella organizational framework for the administration of NIHBs. This leads some Aboriginal leaders to suggest MSB policy is designed to fail – there is the suggestion that the federal government is encouraging a transfer of NIHBs without the financial resources to properly administer the system.

Some First Nations have resisted provincial involvement in the delivery of on-reserve services. Communities can be reluctant to engage in tripartite negotiations because they want to protect the federal government's fiduciary responsibilities for health-care. But as Carrie Hayward, project manager of Ontario's Aboriginal Healing and Wellness Strategy (AHWS) notes, this is also the interest of the provinces. Ontario, for example, openly acknowledges that the federal government should assume its responsibilities for Aboriginal health care and that this would maintain or limit provincial costs. At the same time the province wishes to ensure that health standards for Aboriginal people are the same as for other residents and so the province is forced, in the absence of federal monies, to try to ensure an adequate level of service. In reality, the federal government fails to assume responsibility for urban or off-reserve natives. The province generally assumes costs for these populations through physician care, hospital services, and so forth. Currently, though it is difficult to track, the monies spent on status Indian (on reserve) health care in Ontario are divided, at best 60–40, at worst 50–50, between the federal and provincial governments respectively (Carrie Hayward, personal communication).

Ontario recently became the first province to develop a comprehensive Aboriginal Health Policy (AHP). This policy may be followed by other provincial initiatives that will entrench the role of provinces in Aboriginal health care. There will be criticism that these policies will undermine the federal government's fiduciary responsibilities and provide Health Canada with the opportunity to further limit its role in the delivery of services. As Ms Hayward notes, however, Ontario has taken the position that the provincial role is in addition to, not instead of, federal responsibility.

Thus, in the absence of any comprehensive self-government agreements or constitutional recognition for health jurisdiction, the federal government is able to restrict, at every turn, its fiduciary responsibility. From an Aboriginal perspective, the reality is that with the introduction of the AHP, communities select from alternative federal and provincial funding opportunities and, at the community level, attempt to integrate and enhance existing services.

Ontario's Aboriginal Healing and Wellness Strategy (AHWS) resulted from the merger of the Aboriginal Health Policy with a major family-healing initiative (AFHJSC 1993; Ontario 1994, 1996).[13] The AHWS was the result of sixteen months of consultation with PTOs, and included off-reserve organizations. At times this was a contentious process, and at many points it appeared endangered as Native political organizations threatened to withdraw their support for the initiative. Without detailing specific arguments, it is fair to suggest that differences arose during the process between urban and reserve Indian organizations, and between coordinating groups such as the Indian Social Services Council – which comprise social services directors – and the health directors about the processes to develop the initiatives and the direction and overall wording of the final policy. But in the end, the strategy, which is governed by a joint government-Aboriginal steering committee, serves as an example of how Native political organizations can work cooperatively through collective forums with government in the development of policy and implementation of programs.[14]

Though the development of the AHWS was the result of a collaborative effort of many individuals and organizations, Carrie Hayward is to be commended for 'stick handling' the policy through the provincial bureaucracy. Ms Hayward, a former health director of the Union of Ontario Indians for eight years, recognizes that her success owed much to her previous experience and her knowledge of Aboriginal decision-making processes. She notes: 'It is about process, and I think that is part of the conservative nature [of bureaucracy], of not realizing the very different way of working, whether it is Nation to Nation, or even in moving along the spectrum to Nation to Nation. Government can't just go away and do its own thing and then say "here it is take it or leave it." And there are a lot of people who have difficulty with a different approach.'

Provincial bureaucrats, Ms Hayward argues, must bring a fundamental respect to their dealings with Aboriginal people – a respect born of the realization that representatives of First Nations should be treated as equal partners in decision-making, and as representatives of distinct Nations. To date, however, the reality is that government officials assume responsibility to decide for First Nations, and to act 'as if' Indians were wards of the state. A respect for 'healthy process' also means that bureaucrats must be willing to spend considerable time and effort consulting with individual First Nations. As in the case of Health Transfer, policy or program consultations initially designed to take six months, may take three or four times that period. Part of the development of the MOH process, following a lengthy series of community consultations, was to hold two major retreats to bring together Aboriginal representatives and leaders in order to arrive at the language and intent of the health policy. This collaborative approach, though suited to the Aboriginal stakeholders, conflicted with traditional Ministry approaches aimed at controlling and claiming 'ownership' over the policy-making process.

In making the transition from an Aboriginal organization to the government bureaucracy, Ms Hayward also notes she moved from a highly decentralized, informal, and consensual decision-making environment to a centralized hierarchy, which is consumed by formalism, detail, and documentation. Within government ministries a single letter may take months to approve, as it must pass through several 'approval levels' before being presented to the Minister for signature. A record of meetings, correspondence, and decisions must be maintained; this administrative load influences the amount of time that can be spent in direct negotiation or consultation with communities. Ms Hayward also notes that the lack of knowledge of Aboriginal communities and culture among government decision-makers also makes innovative policy initiatives difficult to develop. In addition, there is an inherent bureaucratic conservatism that sustains the status quo. When this is reinforced by conservative political platforms the chances of innovative policy reform are remote.

The success of the Aboriginal Health Policy and the implementation of the AHWS under the NDP and Conservative governments demonstrate that these and other obstacles to change can be overcome if people are willing to develop policy-making processes that place Aboriginal governments on equal footing with mainstream governments. Several ministries and departments – the Ministry of Health, Community and Social Services, the Native Affairs Secretariat, and the Women's Directorate – deserve credit for recognizing the need for funding arrangements that transcend the artificial boundaries of government ministries. But it is important to note that other key ministries, most notably the Attorney General and Solicitor General, did not view Aboriginal health as within their mandates, and so refused to contribute to this initiative, even though one focus of the AHWS is family violence and the need for alternative justice programs. This attitude, as I suggest in chapters 5 and 6, indicates a continued narrow understanding of the problems existing in Native communities, despite government rhetoric that suggests the need for the development of integrated services.

The money committed to this strategy – $33 million on operations in the fifth year of implementation – is a fraction of what must inevitably be committed to resolve the problems noted in the previous chapter, and much less than the $137 million that Aboriginal communities originally sought for the family healing initiative alone. This is a paltry sum when measured against global health-care expenditures. To place this financial commitment in perspective, at about the same time the AHWS was announced, the NDP government also announced plans to build or expand three urban cancer treatment centres at a cost of $100 million.

None the less, the AHWS monies will be used to develop many key strategies for Aboriginal health care including the funding of Health Access Centres, additional family crisis shelters, traditional healing lodges, alternative justice programs, and a variety of new community-based health-care positions. The provincial initiative will create approximately 600 new health-care jobs in Aboriginal communities (*Toronto Star*, 2 Nov. 1994, A10). Significantly, there is also provision for the development of an Aboriginal Health-care Information network, Za-ge-do-win, to be developed by Manotsaywin Nanottojig, based in Whitefish Lake, which will allow communities to share knowledge about successful strategies for addressing health problems. And finally, the initiative provides key developmental dollars for the establishment of Aboriginal Health Authorities (AHAs), which will afford First Nations a greater degree of control over policy development and administration of health services.

The scope of the strategy, and the financial resources allocated to its implementation, therefore, can easily be criticized. For example, despite arising from a concern over family violence, the strategy contains no comprehensive approach to the creation or delivery of community-based mental-health services; such an initiative awaits further provincial review. But the Strategy sets an important precedent. AHWS is built around three complementary concepts: holistic health, life cycle, and continuum of care. The Aboriginal health policy's strategic direction attempts to enhance the environment for the development of integrated services through improving access to existing services, developing new approaches to improve health status, and respecting traditional Aboriginal health knowledge and practices. When combined with federal transfers over health care, and other federal initiatives in the area of mental health, the AHWS presents First Nations with great opportunities to realize their distinctive visions of health-service delivery over the next five to ten years.

This initiative has already resulted in new challenges for status- and non-status organizations. The NSTC's proposal for an Aboriginal Health Access Centre (AHAC), which evolved from the transfer planning process, was aimed at providing a new model of primary care that included physician services. The NSTC will now provide services in conjunction with off-reserve populations, specifically, those people served by the Sault Ste Marie Indian Friendship Centre. As a result, the tribal council set up a separate Health Access Centre Board, which is composed of Health Board, as well as Indian Friendship Centre, representatives. The AHAC, therefore, will include a satellite office to provide services not only to NSTC members living off reserve, but to all Aboriginal people seeking health services who reside in the area. This type of collaboration to develop 'seamless' services between off- and on-reserve communities requires new Aboriginal organizations that extend beyond traditional First Nations or tribal council boundaries.

The development of Aboriginal Health Authorities (AHAs) at the PTO level will result in different models of health-care delivery. These health authorities may eventually assume responsibility for allocating funds and evaluating service needs within their regions. These authorities should prove to be more responsive to First Nations and tribal council needs than the Ministry. They may develop policy and service-delivery mechanisms to respond to different geographic and cultural needs. A major prerequisite to the long-term development of these agencies, as Ms Hayward notes, will be the need to think through the philosophy of community ownership and control over health services. It is here where building the capacity of community-based health-care delivery systems becomes paramount. For Ontario, the challenge of the next decade is to formalize the government-to-government relationships so that Aboriginal control over health care can become a reality.

Conclusion

The North Shore Health Transfer experience, though not without problems, demonstrates the incredible dedication and tenacity of community members and First Nations leadership to come together and create programs that reflect a holistic vision of environmental and community health. Health Transfer was the start of a longer, ongoing process that will lead to community implementation and evaluation of new health programs over the coming years.

The vision of what constitutes culturally appropriate health care remains partially obscured by conflicting views about the efficacy of Western versus traditional health practices. But the resurrection of traditional medicine will be an essential component of community revitalization. This fact has been increasingly recognized by federal and provincial governments during the past decade, and today, traditional healing lodges are springing up across the country in cities and on reserve. The movement 'back to' traditional holistic health-care practices is also a trend in keeping with changes that are beginning to occur within the mainstream health sector. Western health practitioners have much to learn from health workers in Aboriginal communities. But long-term improvements to Aboriginal health status can only be accomplished through improved access to the Western biomedical system – for Aboriginal people will continue to rely on the provision of many health services that are located off reserve.

The NSTC's implementation of their vision for health care will be accomplished over the next decade. The development of traditional medicine lodges, Health Access Centres, and Aboriginal Health Authorities all comprise important pieces of this ongoing effort. It will be evident from this discussion that many challenges remain. But as the Health Transfer case study demonstrates, Aboriginal people are prepared to meet these challenges. Communities are planning community-based services based on research and widespread community consultation. Aboriginal institutions are being developed in the face of acute shortages of financial and human resources, and with an awareness of the need for ongoing evaluation and efficient delivery of services.

One method of achieving holistic health is to integrate and coordinate various aspects of service delivery. The North Shore experience speaks to the need to develop integrated health and human services. The following chapters continue to analyse this theme by examining mental health and alternative justice programs.

The next decade is full of opportunities and incredible challenges. At a macro level these include the definition of an Aboriginal jurisdictional base that includes health, and that integrates Aboriginal health policy with environment and justice policies. At a micro level, there are challenges associated with supporting families and promoting healthy behaviour, which will require front-line workers to work together and to plan together. In fact, policy sectors such as education, housing, health, and human services remain largely independent, so that the realization of holistic or environmental health is extremely difficult. But First Nations are experimenting with ways of providing holistic services. The uniqueness of Aboriginal First Nations makes them ideal places for innovative, community-based initiatives that can integrate health and human services. And there is growing awareness, at both the federal and provincial levels, of the potential for learning from these experiments that are occurring at the margins of mainstream society.

4

Mental Health: The Failure of Government Practice

... we also have a vision, we also have dreams in which we want to build a better future for our people, so the quality of life is there, so that we know when our children walk out the doors, that no harm will come to them, so that we know that when they go to school, that they will be embraced over there and that love will be given to them, so that we know that our women won't have to suffer from physical abuse, that we as a people won't suffer from spiritual abuse, so that we can rid our communities and begin to understand how much alcohol and drug abuse has prevented our people from developing as well, and it is we as a people that can only do that, that no other government, no other agency, no other outside influence can solve our own problems. We do, however, ask that they join with us because they do have access to resources that we don't have so that we can do this. (Sault Ste Marie ON. 92-06-11 189. Chief Darrell Boissoneau, Garden River First Nation. PG 169–70)

Introduction

As I indicated in chapter 2, there are a number of mental-health issues that are of critical concern to Aboriginal communities. Personal psychological or spiritual problems manifest themselves in substance abuse, family violence, and suicide. Concern about family violence was a major reason for the development of the Ontario Aboriginal Healing and Wellness Strategy (AHWS), which includes a variety of initiatives including crisis-intervention workers, shelters, and family violence programs both on and off reserve. Mental-health problems are clearly connected to conflict with the law – the vast majority of Aboriginal crimes, for example, are petty offences associated with alcohol abuse, or involve various forms of minor assault that are connected to interpersonal problems.

Given the difficulty of maintaining confidentiality in a small community, people are often reluctant to seek help for personal problems – for example, to visit counsellors or psychologists or to attend self-help groups. A certain stigma surrounds even the use of the term 'mental health.' Front-line workers, such as nurses, NNADAP workers, and CHRs, have tried to reframe the issue of mental health in proactive terms – for example, to speak of creation of healthy environments for individuals to obtain spiritual and psychological well-being. And increasingly, the idea of personal recovery – of overcoming alcohol abuse, surviving childhood abuse, or escaping family violence – has become accepted as a keystone to community healing.

Discussing mental health as a 'special' topic, of course, undermines an attempt to present a holistic picture of health. In future chapters, I attempt to overcome this analytic separation by addressing the relationship between individual and community healing. Here I focus on two specific problems, alcohol abuse and suicide, which are commonly associated with Aboriginal people through stereotypes and media reports. A common thread in both these examples is the fact that emotional, psychological, and spiritual health are intimately connected, and for many people, are linked to cultural awareness and identity. I conclude the chapter by examining the ways in which, despite poor resources, Aboriginal caregivers are attempting cope with these problems.

The Gap in Services

A number of programs exist to address mental health; most notably the NNADAP program and associated alcohol- and solvent-abuse treatment centres located both on and off reserve. In Ontario, the Aboriginal Healing and Wellness Strategy offers the potential of developing a range of services to assist individuals and families. Despite these initiatives, Aboriginal mental-health services remain seriously undeveloped. The federal and provincial governments have failed to develop any comprehensive policy or funding envelopes to address the mental health of Native individuals and families. The RCAP recommendations called for a new Aboriginal health and healing strategy that clearly addresses the many facets of mental health (1996d: 201–53).

Until 1992, Medical Services Branch of Health and Welfare Canada had no national mental-health initiative. Following a three-year consultation with First Nations and Inuit organizations, including the Assembly of First

Nations Health Commission, MSB developed a framework for Aboriginal mental health. This consultation, detailed in *Agenda for First Nations and Inuit Mental Health* (Canada 1991b), provided some direction for the development and provision of community-based mental-health strategies that would encourage the use of traditional healing and be linked to other health and human services. But federal funding of Aboriginal mental-health programs – for example, through the Better Futures initiatives – have been piecemeal at best. Community Mental Health/Child Development Programs and more recently the Healthy Communities initiative followed, but again fell well short of Aboriginal expectations with regard to financial resources and Aboriginal control. They provide only meagre resources that more often than not were used for small-scale, temporary prevention programs, rather than the development and support of sustainable programs.

The federal government, then, has recognized that it has some responsibility to act in the area of Aboriginal mental health. It spends approximately $104 million for its community mental-health initiative (RCAP 1994: 72, n.116). Under Health Transfer, federal funding has also supported planning of mental-health services. The NSTC survey revealed mental-health programming to be the largest single gap in services. Key consultants identified a number of specific problems – for example, family violence, suicide, depression, and bereavement – as areas that needed to be addressed. As a result, a regional mental-health program was developed. The price of this program, about a half million dollars for seven communities, though cost effective when measured against the ongoing utilization of counselling and hospital services off reserve, proved too great for MSB negotiators, who deferred the funding of this program for an undetermined period.

While the recent introduction of the Healthy Communities initiative is to be lauded, there are no guarantees of Native control, nor any assurance, given current budget constraints, that new monies will be made available to fund long-term strategies (ibid). This initiative remains embedded in the colonial context of the Medical Services Branch bureaucracy. What is required, then, is a dramatically increased financial commitment to fund the implementation of new community-based and community-controlled mental health strategies.

Aboriginal leaders and front-line workers have highlighted the issue of mental health, and specifically, suicide, for well over a decade. Communities are dealing with many complex issues associated with emotional and spiritual well-being. They are undertaking mental-health initiatives despite meagre financial support. As Darrell Boissoneau notes above, First

Nations are reaching out to non-Native communities and agencies that have resources that are desperately lacking on reserve. Aboriginal self-sufficiency is clearly demonstrated in the area of individual and community mental-health. It is perhaps because of this huge gap in mental-health services that Aboriginal people have turned to many forms of self-help to provide support to people who are confronting personal problems. The Aboriginal self-help movement is infused with the ideas of self-identity and recovery, as well as approaches (such as AA) that initially developed outside of 'mainstream' mental-health organizations. Front-line workers note that as self-help and other health-promotion activities begin to take hold, people begin to end the denial associated with substance abuse, family violence, and sexual abuse. There is then an even greater need for direct services, including crisis intervention, counselling, and treatment. Front-line workers are confronted with 'clients' (often family members or friends) who require counselling for complex personal problems. But they often feel poorly trained in counselling skills. This is one of the commonest complaints of First Nations' staff, along with the criticism that there is no continuum of care for people who must temporarily leave the reserve for treatment.

Aboriginal Mental Health

The use of the term 'mental health' in mainstream biomedical practice is associated with considerable stigma. The term is often regarded negatively as a label that some individuals use instead of mental illness – it often seems to connote the 'problem' side of mental-health issues, not the promotion of psychological 'wellness.' Ideally, First Nations people use the term 'mental health' in the broad sense of describing behaviours that make for a harmonious and cohesive community and for the relative absence of multiple problem behaviours such as family violence, substance abuse, juvenile delinquency, and self-destructive behaviour (Canada 1991b).

The notion of *Aboriginal* mental health raises complex issues associated with cross-cultural psychology and the search for culturally relevant solutions to psychological dis-ease. Many of the projects I have been involved in over the past decade have allowed me to discuss the issue of Aboriginal mental health with physicians, Native and non-Native psychiatrists and psychologists, and a variety of Aboriginal counsellors. Native people experience culturally specific symptoms and problems; the solutions to these problems also differ from those offered through mainstream treatments.

Culturally relevant approaches to Native mental health stress that assistance to clients must be situated in the context of Aboriginal community life. The likelihood of misdiagnosis or inappropriate therapies increases whenever counsellors or therapists fail to account for the nature of family or community life, or when they ignore cultural beliefs and values. It is imperative, therefore, that Southern professionals who provide services to remote communities invest the time and energy in understanding Aboriginal culture (see, for example, Armstrong 1978, 1993). The causes of many Native mental-health problems may require an understanding of the spiritual life of Aboriginal people, or an appreciation of Native values and norms of behaviour (Brant 1990). Timpson et al, in a careful examination of a case from Northwestern Ontario, for example, noted how Western conceptions of 'depression' are better understood in terms of grief or spiritual illness (1988).

Aboriginal explanations of mental illness differ from those offered by Western psychology, which tend to focus on pathology, dysfunction, or coping behaviours that are rooted in the individual.[1] Aboriginal mental health is relational; strength and security are derived from family and community. Mental illness is, to a considerable extent, the result of damaged or disrupted relationships. As previously noted, Aboriginal people's explanations of individual and family dysfunction also emphasize the influence of colonial history and the impact of state domination on individual and community cultural identity. This explanatory model emphasizes the intergenerational effects of the Western assault on Aboriginal culture through state policies, including, for example, the impact of residential schools and the seizure of children by the child welfare system. This perspective is demonstrated in the following statement concerning family violence by the Aboriginal Family Healing Joint Steering Committee (AFHJSC: 1993, 10): 'The Aboriginal People in Ontario define family violence as consequent to colonization, forced assimilation, and cultural genocide, the learned negative cumulative, multi-generational actions, values, beliefs, attitudes and behavioural patterns practised by one or more people that weaken or destroy the harmony and well-being of an Aboriginal individual, family, extended family, community or nationhood.' Such explanations also emphasize a holistic understanding of mental-health issues and place individual problems firmly within the matrix of socioeconomic problems, including welfare reliance, that exist on reserve. And significantly, Aboriginal solutions to individual problems stress the importance of cultural revitalization and draw a critical link between personal well-being and the achievement of self-determination at a community level. The improvement in people's mental health is an important first step that needs to be taken to improve community capacity for collective action.

In keeping with this holistic view, Aboriginal consultants also stress the underlying psychological and emotional causes of illnesses. The following quotation by one informant during pre-transfer interviews indicates this view: 'Programs that are designed to help bring about sound "mental health" should be the primary focus of the health department. They are not. Drug and alcohol abuse, smoking, obesity, family violence, elder abuse and disproportionate high incidence of most mainline diseases here are only symptoms of far deeper problems. Where the mind goes, the body follows ... [there is an] abysmal lack of self respect, low self esteem, apathy, despair ... which in turn has been brought on by centuries of negative conditioning' (NSTC 1992a, 8, p. 4). For many reasons, there is not a great deal of information on the mental-health status of Aboriginal peoples. In particular, it is difficult to suggest whether specific incidences of problems such as schizophrenia, depression, or other Western 'diagnoses' occur at the same, or higher, rates than among the general population. In part this is because Aboriginal people who suffer from such problems must travel off reserve to clinics or hospitals for diagnosis and treatment – and such records, which are difficult to access, do not necessarily record the Aboriginal status of patients. Even where Aboriginal status is known, for example, through client intake at alcohol treatment centres, records are often confidential. It is clear, however, that individual and community perceptions stress the significance of mental (or spiritual) illness as a major issue confronting Aboriginal people. As noted in chapter 2, there is also a danger in over-generalizing about the *degree* of problems, for example, of people experiencing some form of substance abuse, for risk of stereotyping Aboriginal people in general.

As part of the NSTC's health needs assessment conducted in 1991, we asked a random sample of 236 individuals a series of questions concerning their perception of mental-health issues (NSTC 1995a, 1992a). The questions covered a self-assessment of individual mental well-being, and issues associated with family and community mental health. These indicators are very subjective. For example, we asked people whether they were 'happy some of the time,' 'most of the time,' or whether they were 'not very happy.' At the suggestion of our consultants, we also asked people whether they experienced 'bad times,' and whom they turned to for support during such times. Responses depended on people's willingness to communicate their feelings, as well as on the quality of their family relationships, personal networks, and personal circumstances. That is, the structure of the Health Transfer survey, with its emphasis on short answers, was insufficient to truly capture people's opinions or their illness experiences.

None the less, survey results revealed a number of important findings. The majority of people (79%) responded that they were happy 'most of the time.' People were more likely to report lower levels of happiness (that is, 'happy some of the time,' 'not very happy') if they were male, or if they reported poor physical health or experienced chronic illness. Unemployment and marital status were *not* associated with lower reported happiness. Almost two-thirds of the people had experienced bad times during the past year. Women experienced bad times more frequently than men (71% vs 51%). The most common experience associated with 'bad times' was the death of a family member or a friend, which 15.5% of people surveyed had experienced in the previous year. Other personal problems reported included lack of money or a job (12.5%); trouble with alcohol, drugs, or the law (7.5%); and medical problems (5.5%). Sexual abuse or family conflict were reported by only 2% of respondents – a result that is probably attributable to the survey method (see below).

Young people, particularly those aged 18–24, appeared more likely to report lower levels of happiness. Females were more likely than males to report experiencing stress on a daily basis. Again, those in the 18–24 year category, or who were students, reported the highest levels of daily stress. The lowest levels of daily stress were reported by those 65 years of age or older; people who were separated, widowed, or divorced also reported lower stress than those married or living together (NSTC 1995b). We also asked questions about whether people experienced symptoms of poor mental health such as emotional problems, anxiety, sleep difficulties, or depression. These symptoms were most often reported in those who were older, with poorer self-rated health. This relationship between poor physical health and mental health is an important finding, particularly given the higher-than-average incidence of respiratory diseases, diabetes, and other illnesses noted in chapter 2, and points to the need for programs that, again, take into account a holistic approach to well-being.

This needs assessment did not include an alcohol-use assessment scale, but instead asked whether or not alcohol use had caused 'upset' within the home and work environments. In this context, alcohol-related problems were extremely common, and the general perception that alcohol use was a community problem was recognized in each First Nation. Drinking problems were more common in people with chronic illnesses and were associated with those people reporting poorer physical- and mental-health symptoms, but significantly, they were still frequent in those individuals who reported good health. Almost three-quarters of the people interviewed thought that reducing drinking was important for improving their health.

From the perspective of program development, perhaps the most significant finding from this survey was that people generally relied on family or friends for support during crises or other bad experiences. A small number of men (20%), and even fewer women (5.5%), stated that they kept things to themselves and did not seek assistance from others. Very few people turned to other professional sources of help within or available to their communities, that is, to CHRs, NNADAP workers, religious leaders, or elders. People are reluctant to turn to professional care-givers for fear of being negatively labelled, and this suggests that programs aimed at assisting people in times of crises should focus on supporting families and social networks that might assist clients. The survey confirmed that very few people use health programs and services to help cope with stress. People were more likely to turn to traditional healers than to counsellors, though the number of people using any assistance beyond family and personal networks was very low (about 8%) (NSTC 1995b). The survey data also indicated that 'stress management programs should focus on enhancing individual and family/community skills and resources, and offer a variety of activities within communities, especially related to exercise and recreation' (ibid).

Individual perceptions of community mental-health issues revealed concern about three issues: problems with alcohol and drugs (70%), unemployment (15%), and violence and vandalism (6%). Alcohol use is often seen as a 'causal' factor - that is, many Aboriginal people see alcohol use as a problem in and of itself rather than as a symptom of other issues. However, when asked about the sources of community stress, respondents recognized unemployment(31%) or violence (11%) as sources of stress for their communities. Again, these perceptions link individual problems to the larger socioeconomic environment.

Although it is difficult to generalize, the overall picture that emerged from this survey was a relatively positive one, where the majority of individuals reported positive feelings of mental well-being. This characterization is useful if it helps to combat stereotypes that conjure up images of Aboriginal communities as dysfunctional. In fact, given the degree of racism, prejudice, and discrimination faced by Aboriginal people, the survey results seem to indicate that people, though experiencing occasional periods of emotional distress or feelings of psychological malaise, were able to cope with personal problems and stresses by drawing on a circle of friends and kin rather than through appeals to external professionals or agencies.

Personal Journeys: The Challenge of Individual Healing

During a subsequent consultation conducted in 1995, a number of people spoke of difficult and long-term problems they had experienced. It became clear that loss of individual mental well-being was intimately connected with negative life experiences that occur over long periods of time, and that surface in times of major crisis in communities. In every community, there are a number of people who are in deep pain. The vitality of Aboriginal communities seems to be constantly threatened by the *potential* for crises, as deeply buried problems surface to temporarily disable individuals or networks of kin.

This information was revealed because the consultation, concerning individual and community healing, was focused on people's life experiences, and was framed in the context of a number of recent events and crises that had occurred in specific communities. It may also be that during the short passage of time since the 1991 survey, there had been a growing awareness of the need for individuals and communities to deal more openly with many difficult issues. This awareness was also encouraged through related initiatives – health-promotion campaigns focused on the issue of family violence and sexual abuse, and increased media attention to the problem of suicide and abuse experienced in residential schools.[2]

Many individuals were remarkably open and honest about sharing their feelings with us during individual and group interviews. It became clear that many people carry with them complex experiences – problems associated with bad relationships, concerns about children or relatives, alcohol and drug abuse, a history of child neglect or abuse, or problems associated with the loss of friends or relatives through suicides, accidents, and violent deaths. It is not my intention to repeat or outline the many difficult experiences that people shared. People linked these personal problems to their own loss of identity, and to the loss of culture through colonialism. They emphasized, for example, that many of the negative behaviours or instances of dysfunction they witnessed in their own lives and the lives of fellow community members, were connected to behaviours learned through contact with mainstream institutions such as residential schools or correctional facilities, or to even more 'mundane' experiences with racism and prejudice learned in school. Over and over, people suggested that they carried around 'pain' or 'stress' that had its origin in either the abuses experienced during childhood or the abuses experienced by past generations. As the following quotations indicate, it is up to the individual to identify the source of his or her pain for a healing journey to begin:

> A healing journey is about dealing with those issues that you are carrying, that pain. We can always shove that pain back but after a while there is so much inside ... that is why we have so many people drinking because it temporarily numbs the pain.[3]

> It starts at the person. He has to heal inside first then deal with the people round them. People have to see this and they will start looking at themselves.

> Individuals dealing with their own issues is about things like abuse in childhood and how that colours your perceptions when you are an adult.

The first step in the healing journey is 'ending denial'; that is, a person must recognize that he or she has a specific problem. This belief reflects Aboriginal notions about self-reliance. For example, it is often stated that counsellors cannot assist a client unless the client is ready to be helped. Individual healing stories also include reference to repeated failures in treatment or other programs, which are followed by more personal revelations of why a problem exists. Denial also refers to community-wide processes. Aboriginal communities are now recognizing the deeply embedded negative behaviours and processes that sustain community factionalism, and ending community denial is perceived to be a critical first step in the long road to recovery. For example, in every First Nation, people acknowledged that they had to develop better methods of openly and honestly talking about community problems (Warry and Justice 1996).

There is much in the rhetoric of healing that echoes the literature and discourse of the self-help movement. There is little doubt, too, that the long-term impact of the NNADAP program in general, and the widespread use of Aboriginal AA groups, has influenced people's thoughts about personal recovery, which is the essence of the healing journey. Similarly, increasing recognition of the intergenerational and familial causes of many problems has no doubt been shaped by people's involvement with self-help groups such as Al-Anon or Adult Children of Alcoholics.

But the language Aboriginal people use to talk about healing is unique in emphasizing that the moment of realization that leads to 'ending denial' is often associated with an epiphany of cultural awareness. For a great many people recovery and cultural esteem go hand in hand. Healing journeys are spoken of as lifelong searches for personal identity, cultural awareness, and spiritual understanding. These journeys often begin with some sort of critical realization. Individuals speak of dreams and visions, or other symbols of spiritual awareness, which were instrumental in igniting their own understanding. A healing journey might begin with a purification ceremony, or simply by words of encouragement from an elder. For some, the journey began in correctional facilities, with meetings with Native brotherhoods who talked about their culture. There are elements of spiritual revelation and transformative thinking in people's accounts of their personal healing journeys, all of which are closely tied to a person's search for his or her cultural identity (see also chapter 6).

Drinking Is Not Indian

For many people the relationship between culture and healing is most clearly evident in the rejection of alcohol. Anyone who has lived or worked in Aboriginal communities knows that alcohol abuse is a problem. My own involvement with Aboriginal people began with an attempt to design a culturally appropriate treatment program for Aboriginal offenders housed in provincial jails and correctional facilities – the vast majority of inmates have alcohol-related problems, and commit offences while intoxicated (Warry 1986a, 1986b). The issue of Aboriginal alcohol use and abuse is exceedingly complex. Ideas about recovery from alcoholism are closely connected to the need for cultural awareness and cultural esteem: a relationship succinctly summarized in the common phrase 'drinking is not Indian,' which stresses the need for Aboriginal people to pursue a traditional lifestyle of total abstinence.[4]

When, during the course of several consultations, people have spoken about their vision of a healthy community, they invariably stress a view of community life where there is much less alcohol use than at present. Alcohol abuse is regarded by many as *the* critical mental-health issue for communities. It is sometimes regarded as the cause of other problems (such as family violence), and, most certainly, as a manifestation of a variety of personal problems. As one front-line worker stated: 'All of the issues I deal with here have to do with alcohol. Abuse, fighting, abandoning the kids. It is very unhealthy. Today there are some people remaining sober. They have to see the problem and want themselves to heal.' Abusive drinking is a way of dealing with pain; it is a short-term method of coping with problems and a (misguided) alternative to the more difficult and long-term path toward individual healing (Justice and Warry 1996). While under the influence of alcohol, many people act out their anger and pain – for example, drunkenness allows people the 'courage' to say things that they couldn't otherwise say. As one informant expressed it, 'Native people don't like to talk about their problems unless they are drinking.' Alcohol abuse greatly increases the chance for social conflict. Not surprisingly, in most communities conflict with the law is intimately connected to alcohol use. One peacekeeper estimated that at least half the domestic violence on his reserve was alcohol-related and that all other assaults were alcohol-related. Alcohol-related quarrels sometimes involve the show of firearms or other threatening behaviour. And alcohol use is seen as a pressing problem for youth, who may themselves be the children of alcoholics. For some communities teen solvent abuse is a major concern and one linked closely to issues associated with suicide (see below).

Over the past decade, NNADAP and other alcohol-related prevention and treatment programs have had a positive influence on reserve. Some, though not all, communities have shown a measurable decline in alcohol abuse. This success has stemmed not simply from the increased availability of culturally related treatment programs (often located off reserve) but also to the sustained efforts of recovered alcoholics who sponsor AA and other self-help groups. As one councillor stated: 'Here there is a lot of us who have been sober for quite a while. But there is still drinking going on and there are incidents of fighting etc. Still, drinking is getting more controlled. Some people drink on weekends. But you don't see people anymore on those one or two week binges, though they do still walk around drinking beer ... we still have a way to go yet. It [total abstinence] needs to be strived for even if it never will be achieved.'

Alcohol use can divide communities. The decision to serve alcohol at social events, for example, can take on political connotations as, inevitably, this action excludes or includes certain individuals or families. When alcohol is available, social events may lose their positive impact: 'When you mix the alcohol, events are not [positive]. When there are fights, it is because people have come with a personal issue and then they drink and the issues builds and then a little push will set them off.' Alcohol use is prohibited, for example, before and during a variety of ceremonies. Bands may try to create policies concerning 'dry' events (for example, powwows), but these policies must be gently enforced, lest they create friction among certain community members. As one person explained: 'There are signs saying no drinking. The people have to respect the other people and the visitors that are coming and not drink. One family that we asked to leave were really mad but they came back the next year and they were not drinking.'

Many people have begun their healing journeys by giving up alcohol or other drugs. And Aboriginal treatment programs commonly stress a return to traditional spirituality as a key element in the recovery from alcoholism. For this reason abandoning alcohol and understanding traditional spirituality are closely linked. Abstinence is also a quality that is often associated with appropriate role modelling, and, as a result, social drinkers who find themselves in leadership roles often feel pressure to stop drinking, or to do their drinking in private. Of course, social drinkers, for whom alcohol seems to have no ill effects, question the sharp association between abstinence and being a 'traditional' person. And those who, because of their status, are naturally considered role models to children and youth risk being criticized 'just because' they drink. As one chief said: 'I hear that (leaders should not drink) from the membership and from the service providers. I hear what they are saying, but I disagree. I enjoy things to a moderate degree. I don't find it too hard to deal with. I know the limits. You have to govern yourself. Each person has to be how they are.'

Because alcohol use is so intimately connected to a history of individual and community problems, it is a subject that many people hold strong opinions about. Success in tackling alcohol abuse is highly symbolic of both individual and community healing, and an essential component to the rediscovery of traditional ways – witness the almost mythical status of Alkali Lake among service providers across the country (see York 1992; Four Worlds 1986). But there is every indication to suggest that though most communities have not experienced the 'rapid' (that is, ten-year) success of Alkali Lake, a gradual and significant decline in serious alcohol-related problems seems to have occurred in many communities. Many people seem resigned to a certain level of alcohol abuse in individuals or families – an unfortunate, if pragmatic assessment – but seek to limit the influence of alcohol in community events. The use of alcohol, the relationship between abstinence and cultural identity, and the degree of tolerance for different lifestyles, then, are complex social and political issues that are constantly being debated among people intent on revitalizing their communities.

Suicide: A National Tragedy

So I ask myself a question. I said, 'What is this new Royal Commission of Aboriginal Affairs?' And I said to myself I hope that if I do make a presentation and all my people come here and make presentations, it seems that every time the government is in a bind, it sends out Royal Commissions. It sends out people that study our people, more studies, more studies. While in reality we live, our people die, they commit suicide, they hang themselves, they die from overdose, we see them splattered all over the highway sometimes. It's a slow death, this, what Canada has done to us. Our children are being ridiculed in a society because of the lack of knowledge of Aboriginal people. (Charles Joseph Bernard, Jr, Eskanoni, cited in Warry 1993; RCAP 1995)

This quotation demonstrates the frustration Aboriginal people feel with government inaction in the face of self-inflicted violence occurring in their communities – violence that they directly link to long-term colonial practice. The issue of suicide is a touchstone for change, because, as George Erasmus has stated, 'The despair and hopelessness of Aboriginal people, especially youth, requires urgent solution ... We cannot have healing, self-government, new relationships or self-sufficiency while the hope of the future – our young people – are killing themselves in depression and despair' (cited in Warry 1993).

Canada has the third highest rate of youth suicide in the world, yet the incidence of Aboriginal suicide is dramatically higher – three to four times that of the general population (RCAP 1995: 11). This figure would be even higher if mysterious and accidental death – which may disguise suicides in certain cases – were included. Suicide and other forms of violent death are symptomatic of the historic domination and chronic malaise of Aboriginal communities. The ability of Aboriginal communities to respond to the challenge of suicide will act as a stimulus to community revitalization. No single issue better demonstrates the need for personal and community control and empowerment.

In June 1993, I was approached by Marlene Castellano, Co-Deputy Director of Research at the RCAP, to write a background paper based on a series of special consultations that had been held. My task was simple: to review the transcripts and place the issue within the context of existing literature and policy concerning Aboriginal mental health and to make recommendations that could be reviewed by the commissioners. The commission had come under increasing pressure to address this issue – suicides in several areas, including those in Big Cove, Davis Inlet, and

Nishnawbe Aski communities, had been the subject of major news coverage. The commission was to make this issue a priority and to offer a report in advance of its final recommendations.

I had previously written about suicide and crisis intervention (UOI 1993a; Warry 1990). I knew that no Native person was left untouched by suicide – virtually every Aboriginal person I had worked with, spoken to, or interviewed could relate some personal account of a friend, family member, or loved one who had taken his or her own life. I wrote the paper over the summer; before the paper was completed, two more suicides occurred in NSTC communities.

My paper was only a small part of what grew into a major RCAP initiative, ending in the report, *Choosing Life* (1995), which reviews this issue and offers recommendations for government action. The reference to 'Unfinished Dreams' in the title of this book, is taken from that research paper, which took a highly rhetorical tone in attempting to 'push buttons' and even to play on the guilt that I believe many Canadians feel when they learn of the poverty and hopelessness on many reserves (see also Boldt 1993). The paper began:

> There is a crisis of tragic proportion in Canada. Aboriginal youth are taking their own lives in unprecedented numbers. The voices of Aboriginal peoples appearing before the Royal Commission are filled with desperation and expectation that something can be done to call attention to this epidemic which tears at the fabric of community life, and stymies the potential for self-determination ... But given that this tragedy has been identified for over a decade only two questions need be posed. Why has the collective understanding of Aboriginal peoples, social scientists, and government researchers not led to change; and what hope is there that the reiteration of these facts in light of the current crisis will lead to a committed political and moral strategy that seeks to end this human tragedy? (Warry 1993)

Looking back, I see my analysis was partially driven by my frustration at trying to understand a crisis of almost unfathomable complexity. I remain upset that the existence of extraordinarily high rates of Aboriginal suicide have been documented for more than a decade and that, despite considerable awareness of what strategies might be effective in attacking this problem, there is little political will to provide the financial resources to implement these strategies.[5]

In the end, the release of *Choosing Life* was given short shrift by the media. Release of the study – with its statistics citing this appalling tragedy – appeared in a brief page 4 column in *The Globe and Mail* (10 Feb. 1995,

A4). The front-page news of the day included a piece on how Calgary vehicles were crashing through the winter ice on a nearby lake and a full account of former vice-president Dan Quayle's decision not to run for the GOP presidential nomination – a story, no doubt, of immense importance to Canadians. The two leading television newscasts covered the release of the report superficially, in both instances merging it with an account of the breakup, by the RCMP, of the Aboriginal tax-protest camp on Parliament Hill. A week later in editorial coverage, the *Spectator* (14 Feb. 1995, A10) while noting the tragedy of Aboriginal suicide, put its own conservative spin on this problem by noting the 'waste' of money in land-claims negotiations and other social-assistance programs, and suggested that no new money should be allotted to suicide prevention.

The reader might suspect my reaction to this press coverage is biased. I cannot help but think that my country's sense of priorities is horribly confused when what must surely be regarded as a great Canadian tragedy is so uncritically and unsympathetically covered by the media. For most Canadians, Aboriginal affairs – and the lives of Aboriginal children – appear to be insignificant, and the continuing tragedy of Aboriginal suicide is, in itself, an insufficient stimulus to jar the Canadian consciousness from its staggering apathy.

The *Choosing Life* findings were not without their detractors, which included Paul Chartrand, a Manitoba Métis lawyer and a RCAP commissioner, who issued a three-page dissenting opinion. He voiced concern that the report's recommendations failed to account for differences between communities, and rested on the 'creation of a symbolic characterization of the relationship between Aboriginal people and Canadians generally' in asserting that suicide was one of a 'group of symptoms' that included family violence and alcohol abuse and that were expressions of the burden of loss, grief and anger experienced by Aboriginal people. Chartrand is correct in asserting that this 'generalized' explanation of Aboriginal suicide often dominates the specific determinants of suicidal ideation in the RCAP report. But there is no doubt that the Aboriginal *perceptions* of the causes of suicide consistently and coherently link suicide and other problems to the historic domination of communities. Chartrand also suggested that the community-based focus of some recommendations could actually be dangerous, and cautioned against the risk involved in having untrained 'resource' teams responsible for crisis intervention (RCAP 1995: 95–7; *Globe and Mail*, 20 Feb. 1995, A3). This perspective risks perpetuating the colonial belief that only mainstream biomedical practitioners such as physicians or psychiatrists are capable of intervening in crisis situations. As I have written elsewhere (UOI 1993), there is good evidence that, once trained, community members themselves can assume responsibility for crisis intervention – indeed, this is an essential and established tenet of crisis-intervention planning (see below).

Rather than reiterate the conclusions of *Choosing Life*, I outline some difficulties associated with the development of holistic strategies to tackle this issue, and emphasize the relationship between suicide and self-determination. The effects of suicides, and suicide attempts, are much more devastating in Indian communities because of their small size, and the close-knit nature of kinship relationships (Warry 1990; 1993). Aboriginal suicide patterns involve a ripple effect; they are often characterized by serial suicides or suicide clusters by friends and peers. These localized epidemics have long been reported throughout Canada. The nature of Aboriginal suicide is such that communities can remain relatively untouched by suicide for many years, only to then experience a rapid succession of suicide attempts and deaths. These events reverberate through many communities via kin and friendship networks. In Davis Inlet, for example, *46 people out of a population of 500* had attempted suicide during a single year.

There are few published accounts of Aboriginal suicidal ideation that would suggest a simple pattern of suicidal behaviour that is unique to Aboriginal youth. Front-line workers, particularly those serving remote Northern communities, have suggested that in some instances depressed individuals report sensations that include spirits of the dead invading a person's body, disturbed patterns of sleep and dreams, and hallucinations. Aboriginal youth may receive visions from peers who have committed suicide; they sometimes say that deceased friends try to encourage them to commit suicide. This is not to suggest that Aboriginal youth are 'driven' to suicide by the voices of their peers, nor to suggest that visions are not part of suicidal thoughts in non-Aboriginal populations. But these visions are undoubtedly an expression of Inuit or Indian spirituality. Aboriginal key consultants stress that guardian spirits have only a positive influence on people's behaviour. Yet Aboriginal spirit beliefs are complex, and there are accounts of spirit possession, spiritual visits during dreams, and malevolent spirits – such as in *windigo* possession – which influence youths' behaviour (see Timpson et al). Front line workers suggest that many youth lack an awareness of the role of visions in traditional spirituality and so may actually misinterpret the meaning of these messages.

Lester (1989; 1992) has carefully outlined the many precipitating causes of suicide. These include poor relationships with family and peers, broken love relationships, confusion about sexual identity – problems common to youth everywhere (see also Kirmayer 1993). Aboriginal youth, like their non-Aboriginal counterparts, are sometimes consumed with interest in rock music, which has as a central motif a preoccupation with death and violence. Peer participation in Satanic cults also occurs in some communities. Youth interest in the occult, or Satanic cults, is not surprising given that Aboriginal religious belief often includes an active role for spirits and for Satan – a fact that is fuel for fundamentalist Christian crusades. A 1994 *Fifth Estate* report highlighted the deep spiritual cleavage between traditionalists and Christian fundamentalists in the community of Pikangikum. This rift was exacerbated by the death of a youth, himself a member of a hard rock band, who, it was argued, was influenced by Satanic beliefs. But in Aboriginal communities, such personal problems are often set in a background that includes the loss of a parent or care-taker, or the deaths of peers or relatives through suicide or violent death. That is, suicidal ideation among Aboriginal youth must be understood against the collective psychological burden of families, peer groups, and communities.

There is some indication that suicides tend to occur among Native youth who are better educated than their peers. Kirmayer suggests that such suicides may be precipitated by feelings of frustration or hopelessness created by failed expectations or the inability to compete for jobs or recognition in mainstream society (1993: 48). Thus, in a very tangible way, hope is a dangerous thing for many Aboriginal youth. And we must remember that as community expectations about healing, self-government, and Aboriginal rights grow, there is the potential for increased frustration born from people's inability to realize rising expectations.

Significantly, as Lester (1989) has noted, a person's belief that they lack control over their life (external locus of control) has been correlated to suicidal thinking. Many Aboriginal youth feel that they have little control over their futures, and the reality of continuing oppression and discrimination only enhances a general malaise that Aboriginal youth experience concerning their life outcomes. We must recognize the legacy of colonialism, and the overall environment of despair that exists on many reserves – an environment that includes the welfare dependency, unemployment and poor educational experiences outlined in previous chapters. As Clare Brant, an Aboriginal psychiatrist, noted, an environment 'of poverty, powerlessness and anomie produces the triad of alcohol and other substance abuse, suicidal ideation, suicide attempts and depression' (Canadian Psychiatric Assn 1985: 1). Thus, while many of the causes of Aboriginal suicide are similar to those found in non-Native populations, there are added cultural factors that influence individual decision-making and suicidal ideation. These cultural factors include 'cultural stress' (RCAP 1995: 25, n.32; cf. Berry 1993), that is, the internalized effect of colonialism and post-colonialism, and racism, which leads individuals to question their personal self-worth and the value of their culture (Warry 1993).

It is difficult to imagine the frustration and feelings of alienation that must accompany Aboriginal youth on a daily basis as they face an uncertain future, a future where they have only a modicum of control over their ability to achieve and contribute to society. Feelings of a lack of personal control are critical to the generation of suicide epidemics. And it is here where notions of self-determination and self-government bear directly on the potential solutions to the crisis of Aboriginal suicide. As previously noted, Aboriginal ideas of health emphasize the need to promote lifestyles that attend to the physical, spiritual, and emotional needs of children and youth in processes of human development. This holistic vision places human volition, decision-making, autonomy, and feelings of control at the heart of personal identity (Four Worlds 1984a; 1984b). The link between perceptions of health and feelings of personal control is also substantiated in recent health-promotion literature. It is important to acknowledge this explanatory tenet as a key element of Aboriginal health science and perceptions of health (J. Clarke 1992). Perceived control is a major component of healthy childhood development and can be considered a major buffer against risk. Youth who are exposed to positive educational experiences, who have access to recreational outlets, and who benefit from an awareness of cultural traditions often thrive despite the presence of other risk factors. Unfortunately, these protective factors are all too often lacking in Aboriginal communities.

Aboriginal people sometimes speak about how suicide is 'violence turned inward.' The violence, they have remarked in frustration, might better be turned outward, against their oppressors. This, however, is not how it seems to work; there is no evidence to suggest that Aboriginal protests, occupations and the like are a harnessing of the negative feelings that seem to preoccupy so many young people. Rather, we are better to suggest, as many Aboriginal care-givers do, the need for individual and community healing. As more individuals come to deal with how they have internalized the colonial experience, as they overcome their personal demons and recover a sense of themselves as cultural and spiritual beings, the more the community heals. The question then becomes how communities can support individuals and families who are at risk, and how they can foster a sense of hope and accomplishment in children and youth. Ways must also be found to continue support to those individuals who have ended their denial and begun their healing journeys so that their energies and experience can be harnessed to assist others.

The findings in *Choosing Life* suggest that community development, cultural revitalization, improved economic opportunities, and Aboriginal political control may all have direct and positive impact on youth mental health: 'Commissioners are firmly of the view that, in the long term, only the development of self-determining Aboriginal governments and institutions and reconstruction of the fundamental building blocks of Aboriginal cultures will reverse the personal, social and economic conditions that lead some Aboriginal people to take their own lives' (1995: 76–7). If we assume a direct relationship between individual mental health and the wider social environment that is necessary to promote feelings of self-worth and self-control, then the link between Aboriginal community control, in the form of self-government, and individual mental health is undeniable. The current reality for Aboriginal youth is one of an environment of unrealized expectations, disturbed nightmares, and unfinished dreams. In this sense, the crisis of Aboriginal suicide can be viewed in essentially metaphoric and symbolic terms. The solution to this crisis will be a major touchstone of change. But for this change to occur, Aboriginal people must be given the time, resources, and power to control their own lives and improve their communities, and this will require political will, and vision from mainstream Canadians and their leaders. Suicide is a visceral and tangible reminder of the despair and desperation of Aboriginal people. At its most basic level, suicide is a major marker of the ill-health of Aboriginal people. And the reduction in Aboriginal suicide rates may well prove to be a major indicator of renewed and revitalized Aboriginal communities.

Toward Solutions

Research suggests many remedies to Aboriginal mental-health problems – for example, *Choosing Life* lists forty recommendations for First Nation and government action (1995: 90–4). These range from obvious political actions – for example, the need for a shared government–First Nation commitment to prevent suicide – to highly specific and pragmatic suggestions, such as the call for funding of a small secretariat to coordinate the actions of a National Forum that would publicize, coordinate action, share information, and evaluate strategies taken in response to this crisis.

The implementation of any comprehensive federal or provincial strategy is dependent on the provision of new monies. If youth are to play a critical role in the revitalization of their communities, they must have access to financial resources proportionate to their population and potential (Warry and Moffat 1993). First Nations councils must refuse to pay lip service to the needs of youth, and instead promote ways of enhancing youth participation in political processes, including those directly related to self-government – for example, through the creation of youth councils. The RCAP called for an investment in cultural institutions that would allow youth to be engaged in building the capacity of their communities, specifically for resources for youth centres (on reserve and in urban communities), and for cultural and recreational programs with a youth focus (1996e: 154–5, 159).

At the risk of oversimplifying, the 'solutions' outlined in *Choosing Life* and the final RCAP recommendations, as well as in previous health consultations (1996d: 51; AFHJSC 1993; Canada 1991b), can be grouped into three broad strategies: the development of community-based crisis intervention; the sustained commitment to culturally appropriate, holistic health promotion; and long-term community healing strategies to improve the overall mental-health environment for Aboriginal children, youth, and families. In chapter 6 I analyse the idea of community healing in some detail. I conclude this chapter with a discussion of problems associated with crisis intervention and holistic services, and, in so doing, attempt to reveal the degree of preparedness, commitment, and control that already exist in many communities.

Crisis Intervention

A crisis is a situation that has the potential to end in serious injury or death. Unexpected deaths, family violence, suicide, or other crises can have devastating impacts on a community. As one front-line worker explained, 'It isn't just the immediate family that is affected by a crisis – it ripples out through the community like a tidal wave' (Justice and Warry 1996). Crises also disrupt long-term initiatives such as prevention and health-promotion work and, as a result, staff feel frustrated that, despite their best efforts, they are having little positive influence on the community.

Ironically, in the aftermath of tragic deaths, communities pull together. People come together to support families and to provide emotional and economic support. Crises, then, can provide impetus for change. As one staff person said: 'Whenever there is a crisis ... I think this is the beginning of things. [After a recent community crisis] this is the first time in my memory that there is consensus to do something and *that the response should be internal'* (ibid, emphasis mine).

When viewed as a positive opportunity, then, a crisis can become a natural starting-point for a healing journey. It is often during times of crisis when a person's problems first become revealed, or when, because of the seriousness of a situation, family and friends feel compelled to act to assist those in need, or to intervene to change behaviour. In a suicide attempt, crisis intervention allows counsellors to address patterns of suicidal ideation, and to instil in a person a sense of personal control over his or her situation.

It is easy to say that communities must effectively and immediately respond to crises. Unfortunately, crisis intervention is incredibly difficult in practice. Workers lack adequate training that would provide them with the confidence to intervene in difficult situations. Police or peacekeepers are often the first on the scene in times of crisis and central figures in crisis intervention. Yet the relationship between police and the wider community may be ambivalent at best, and problems of communication between police and other service providers are common. Long-term follow-up care, therapy, and counselling for those involved in crises are often unavailable – indeed, facilities such as family-violence crisis shelters are extremely rare. In Ontario, shelters and other family-violence initiatives have been greatly enhanced under the new Aboriginal Healing and Wellness Strategy (see chapter 3).

Crisis training must also foster culturally appropriate interventions. Some Aboriginal people have questioned whether or not Native values are fully compatible with the notion of *direct* intervention. Clare Brant, an Aboriginal psychiatrist, described a number of Aboriginal ethics and rules of behaviour (1990). These include the ethic of non-interference, beliefs about sharing, non-competitiveness, and emotional restraint. Aboriginal intervention is soft or indirect. The emphasis in Aboriginal culture is on providing support and fostering self-esteem. Workers walk a fine line between concerned intervention in the affairs of others and unwanted interference in people's lives (ibid; UOI 1993a). The ethic of non-interference is often cited as a stumbling block to developing crisis-intervention techniques. Front-line workers express doubts about appropriateness of intervening in crises when family members or friends are involved. In part, this doubt stems from a concern that individuals may lack sufficient training in crisis intervention. But the concern also arises because people suggest that they might be criticized by others for a 'holier than thou' attitude – particularly when it is common knowledge that those intervening may themselves have personal problems.

But intervention was a part of traditional Aboriginal cultures, and is a necessary part of community care. And health- and social-service professionals believe that training can allow people to intervene in risk situations in a culturally appropriate manner. The fact remains that many Aboriginal people are willing to help, but they lack knowledge of the specific skills that would enable them to proceed with confidence in times of crisis or community trauma. This skills deficit is perpetuated by reliance on outside 'experts,' whether Native or non-Native, who are often called into remote communities in times of crisis. Northern reserves continue to be serviced by urban-based mental-health programs. The inappropriateness – and increased cost – of providing psychiatric care, outreach services, or medical training from urban centres for remote Inuit and Indian communities would seem to be obvious, but such urban-based intervention programs continue to dominate the scene. As Darrell Boissoneau notes, governments have chosen to fund urban institutions, rather than Aboriginal community-based care [92-06-11 189. PG 169–70].

Those who attempt suicide are not *necessarily* in need of psychiatric therapy or long-term medical care (Hawton and Catalan 1987: 4). A formal psychiatric assessment may be required to determine the need for specialized help, but in keeping with the tenets of community psychiatry, it is generally the case that community care can greatly help individuals who attempt to take their own life. Non-specialists can also intervene in other crises. Given appropriate training, non-medical practitioners can be as successful in managing cases of attempted suicide as therapists (ibid). Currently, the removal of youth from the community for treatment often occurs only because of a lack of appropriate community resources. This option should be reserved for individuals who have been clinically diagnosed as in need of psychiatric assistance. And this decision should be made in consultation, where available, with traditional healers to ensure that other treatment options have been considered. These and other choices concerning 'culturally appropriate' treatment can only be made at the community level.

Clearly, community-based training is critical for successful crisis intervention. Workers require basic assessment skills so as to identify individuals who need to be referred to traditional healers or non-Native specialists. Crisis intervention requires specialized approaches that can build on pre-existing skills and afford people the confidence to intervene in times of crisis. Such information would include, for example, conflict-resolution techniques, the warning signs of suicidal behaviour, skills to engage the community in grieving and communication, and facilitation skills for youth involved in peer counselling (UOI 1993a).

Sagamok Anishnabek, a North Shore community, developed one such crisis-intervention strategy, which, with the aid of provincial funding, is now operational. The program was developed in response to recent suicides in the community. In the aftermath of these deaths, which deeply affected many staff and community members, Sagamok health- and social-services contacted Wikwemikong First Nation, one of the few reserves with long-term experience in crisis intervention and mental-illness prevention. This experience was itself gained in the aftermath of a severe suicide epidemic in the 1970s (RCAP 1995: 44–8). Over the course of twenty years, Wikwemikong set in place a number of programs, including a recovery centre. Most recently, in conjunction with the Network North Community Mental Health Group, they established the Nandmadwin Mental Health Clinic, whose catchment area includes Manitoulin Island and the surrounding mainland communities, including parts of the North Shore. As a result of this shared relationship, Sagamok was able to access the services of an Aboriginal mental-health counsellor for one day a week.

The core of the initiative, however, is the development and training of a volunteer crisis-intervention team (CIT) (Justice and Warry 1996). At first, Sagamok health- and social-services staff did 'double time,' acting as volunteers on the CIT, because it was difficult to attract and keep Native volunteers. In part this was because people felt reluctant to intervene in situations where they were closely related to victims or offenders (for example, in instances of family violence) or felt insecure about their own skills. But, as staff noted, the key to this initiative is giving people the confidence to get involved, and acknowledging that *any* person can offer empathy and support in times of crisis. CIT members suggest that empathy and support can do much to alleviate the pain and stress inherent in crisis situations. The CIT team coordinates its activities with Native peacekeepers – both to ensure their own safety, and to ensure quick access to people who are in crisis. The Sagamok volunteers are not counsellors; they are there to provide support to anyone in crisis, whether to victims, offenders, friends, or kin. The volunteers have some training in crisis and suicide intervention, which is really designed to give them the confidence to intervene in difficult family situations. They also receive first-aid and CPR training, as well as information about safety and protecting themselves in potentially violent situations. Because they lack funds, the CIT is currently relying on peer-training; people who receive specific training or attend workshops off reserve return and share this information with other volunteers. A team of two volunteers is on call to respond to any crisis, but to date, because of a lack of human and financial resources, the program only operates throughout the weekend (when drinking and incidents of violence are most common), though there are plans to expand the service.

Sagamok Council has fully supported this initiative; it has provided the CIT with its own radio system, and recognized the involvement of volunteers through special events. No monies are available for even the most basic reimbursements – for example, gas money. Because the band, through Health Transfer, is now controlling its own health budget, staff are also examining options to restructure services so as strengthen this initiative with existing human and financial resources.

This program presents difficult challenges. Staff and volunteers are concerned about issues of confidentiality and personal safety. Volunteers feel scrutinized by the community at large, and are fearful that they may say or do something that will only exacerbate existing problems. Quite naturally, there has been considerable attrition in volunteer involvement – from an initial roster of about 90 people to now about 50. But this number of volunteers is a remarkable achievement in a community of 1,200 people.

This initiative is taken in full awareness of the risks – both personal and professional – that come with involving oneself in the affairs of other families. Without access to external financial resources, or even local resources, the effort draws on the ordinary courage of volunteers, and the dedication of staff. There is no crisis shelter at Sagamok, little access to consulting psychologists, or, with the exception of one day per week, even a mental-health counsellor. Treatment centres have long waiting lists, and even when individuals in crisis recognize the need for assistance, it can be months before such help can be found. But this collective effort demonstrates that, in the absence of institutional support, the natural skills and involvement of community members can substitute for formal professional training.

This community response came at a time when both federal and provincial governments were beginning to support new initiatives in mental health. The program continues to rely on urban institutions for support. Many First Nations are poised to act in the area of mental health, and, significantly, have chosen to act even with minimal resources. Along the North Shore, several communities have prepared mental-health plans –

complete with job descriptions, program objectives, and budgets – as a result of the pre-transfer health initiative. With adequate funding, a variety of crisis-intervention and mental-health programs could be implemented immediately.

This is but one example of how Aboriginal communities along the North Shore are assuming responsibility in the absence of government-supported mental-health programs. It is difficult to overestimate the amount of time, effort, and commitment First Nations leadership, staff, and volunteers must make in order to bring such initiatives to fruition. The concerted efforts of many individuals is necessary for a period of years, and even where this effort exists, people often face frustration and disappointment when trying to convince governments to expend resources to meet pressing and significant gaps in services. Sagamok First Nation has turned tragic and traumatic crises into new community initiatives. Although the funding is inadequate, they have re-allocated staff time and resources, and made crisis intervention a priority. Like many other communities this First Nation has melded separate provincial and federal initiatives in order to construct full-time mental-health programs. By demonstrating this type of self-reliance communities also position themselves well for any new initiative in the field of mental health that governments might develop.

Crisis-intervention strategies do not necessarily require large institutional supports. Thus, as Waldram et al note (1995: 8–22), it may be necessary for MSB to provide ongoing support for psychiatric consultations. But I would argue that it is a mistake for Aboriginal people to rely on external resource people in developing Aboriginal mental-health programs. What is needed is community-based intervention and community mental-health support. Contrary to the opinion of Chartrand noted above (144), the risks of utilizing local volunteers to deal with crises are risks that must be taken to promote community well-being. Indeed, it can be argued that people are already coping with these crises in the *absence* of specialized training – relying only on their practical knowledge and a deep commitment to community members who are in crises. What is now required is the honing of such informal support networks and their enhancement through medical or other training. The experience of First Nations demonstrates that community members and existing staff can be trained to assume responsibility for crisis intervention and that training or specialized resources (that is, psychiatric referral) can be coordinated by tribal councils or regional mental-health services.

Finally, crises are complex events, embedded in the psycho-social life of communities. Specific crises may spark memories of other previous crises, and give rise to additional stressors, most notably feelings of unresolved grief and loss. For this reason alone, crisis intervention cannot be seen as an end in itself, but rather as a critical point around which comprehensive mental health support and intervention programs must be built.

Holistic Prevention and Treatment

Crisis-intervention strategies must be accompanied by a focus on holistic health promotion directed toward the physical, cultural, and spiritual needs of youth. Youth appearing before the RCAP offered many specific suggestions for prevention of mental-health problems, including, for example, mentor programs to encourage school completion, and the creation of better links between elders and youth to enhance cultural awareness. The need for recreational facilities was a constant theme for youth appearing before the commission. The failure of government action in this area is particularly disturbing, because the provision of adequate recreational opportunities is a simple and effective physical- and mental health-promotion strategy.

Youth also advocate the development of youth organizations at the community, regional, and national levels. These organizations would develop leadership skills and would allow youth a voice in educational planning and input into school curricula. Feelings of self-control and self-worth are best promoted through youth's participation in community life. If they feel isolated, part of that feeling is undoubtedly their dislocation from community decision-making and problem-solving. It is critical that Aboriginal children and youth are engaged as agents of change. Suicide-prevention strategies, for example, might focus on peer behaviour. Specifically, children and youth might be encouraged to approach elders or health- and social-service providers when they believe their peers are at risk. Youth may sense that their friends are depressed or despondent. But whether through misunderstanding, cultural prescription, or lack of confidence, they feel unable to bring these problems to the attention of those caregivers who might be able to help. Preventive approaches, then, must tackle the stigma associated with mental-health problems, and must openly confront assumptions that lead people to hide such problems as physical and sexual abuse rather than seeking the assistance of caring professionals.

People also suggest that youth committees and youth councils should be activated to oversee recreational programs, or to organize cultural events. In some communities such committees exist, but youth often experience the same frustration and anger that their elders have, when faced with a shortage of financial resources to purchase even the most rudimentary recreational equipment. And, unfortunately, where youth act, video games, recreational halls, youth centres, or other symbols of success can quickly become the target of vandalism, as youth who feel disenfranchised from those involved in the decision-making take aim at the symbols of their peers' success. These problems are indicators of continued despair and alienation. Yet Aboriginal people persist in their attempts to involve youth in activities that teach and model the principles of holistic health. North Shore communities, for example, have initiated bush-recreation programs where youth receive instruction from elders and spiritual leaders (NSTC 1992a). Elders take youth on nature walks to teach them about medicinal herbs and plants. The provision of meaningful recreational alternatives, including those that emphasize land skills and traditional environmental knowledge, are perhaps the simplest and most effective suicide-prevention strategies. Traditional drum and dance groups are increasingly common throughout the country. Elsewhere, programs such as the Fly-In Sports Camp, in which Aboriginal youths are employed as leaders-in-training, have been very successful in northern communities in Manitoba (S. Smith 1992). Healing circles provide people with a non-threatening and supportive environment where they can voice their personal experiences. These self-help groups are widespread. In so far as they promote open communication and confront the stigma attached to seeking help for social and mental-health problems, they can be very beneficial. But here again, training is needed for staff and volunteers who may act as facilitators to these groups.

Another key to long-term holistic prevention and treatment of mental-health problems is the reestablishment of traditional healing practices. As noted in the previous chapter, this exercise is fraught with difficulties, not least of which is the current shortage of established and recognized healers. But traditional healers are much more capable of understanding the nature of Aboriginal family and community life than non-Native physicians or psychologists. And where spiritual questions or confusion are a part of a patient's illness experience, a traditional healer may be the *only* person capable of assisting the patient in sorting through complex psychological states (ibid). Diagnosis may include discussing a person's dreams or visions, determining whether or not a person has experienced bad medicine, or delving into thoughts about childhood experiences, or family relationships. Treatment may include having individuals attend purification lodges, fasting, or holding other spiritual ceremonies, or more simply, may involve explanation of various components of Aboriginal spirituality, including instruction in the meaning and use of sacred plants. But referrals to Aboriginal healers are far from routine.

The potential value of such referrals is increasingly recognized by mainstream health practitioners. Innovative programs such as those offered through Network North and Lake of the Woods Hospital now offer patients the opportunity to consult with traditional healers. The choice of whether to consult an Aboriginal healer, or a mainstream mental-health worker is left to the individual. In Ontario, also, the Healing and Wellness Strategy is funding cultural translator projects and healing lodges in all regions. What is now required is increased access to healers through the establishment of regional referral networks and the provision of resources to assist patients and healers with travel and other ancillary costs. The actual costs of such services are much less than the sums commonly expended by governments on psychiatric consultations, and the corresponding benefits of appropriate diagnosis and care are greatly increased.

A number of other innovative projects exist across the country. In the Fort Frances area, for example, Big Grassy/Big Island First Nations are developing innovative healing approaches to family and youth violence that are closely associated with concepts of restorative justice (see chapter 5). But to date there has been insufficient evaluation and information sharing about specific programs. In Ontario, the development of Za-ge-do-win Information Clearinghouse should facilitate the sharing of information between First Nations about the successes and failures of alternative approaches. Government policy-makers also need to encourage an experimental approach to the funding of new programs, and will be required to assume a hands-off approach to new initiatives, and to accept the self-evaluation of experiments by Aboriginal people.

The Stress of Change: Healing the Healers

Aboriginal leaders cite the dangers of the collective frustration that exists on many reserves because of stymied expectations concerning self-government. Incidents like those at Ipperwash and Oka suggest that a climate of frustration exists among certain segments of many communities. These feelings may have negative consequences for community well-being. This frustration stems in part from the slow pace of land claims or other forms of government action. High expectations for self-government are also fuelled by the rhetoric of local or national political leaders. The stress manifests itself, for example, in youth's criticism of Aboriginal leaders. Youth may also feel that political action, in any form, is useless, and so experience feelings of hopelessness and apathy about the political process. These feelings are insidious, and cause Aboriginal youth to question the utility of participating in community affairs.

First Nations may experience a number of new stressors as they move toward self-government. Communities that are in the midst of land-claims negotiations, for example, experience enormous stress from increased prejudice and discrimination in surrounding communities (see chapter 1). There is evidence in the testimony before the RCAP that many communities, and their leaders, fear the potentially harmful effects of the transition to self-government. The stress on leadership and staff is already noticeable in communities that have assumed control over health and other human services. In short, front-line workers and political leaders often feel pressured as they go about the work of moving their communities toward self-government. This stress is increased where staff lack sufficient experience or training to assume responsibility over Aboriginal-controlled institutions. Some people fear that constitutional reform will result in self-government 'overnight,' and that First Nations, without adequate preparation, training, and skills, will have to rapidly assume control over a number of jurisdictions.

As communities end the denial surrounding various problems, health- and social-service staff face new challenges. Aboriginal leaders and front-line workers are sometimes reluctant to address serious problems such as violence or abuse when they suspect that a relative or prominent community member is involved. Culturally appropriate counselling based on Aboriginal ethics and cultural norms can help staff and community leaders to overcome these feelings of discomfort and to deal with the stigma associated with many negative behaviours. Particularly where perpetrators of abuse are well-respected elders or community leaders, it may be important for victims to be able to speak to professionals outside their community in order to break the cycle of abuse. These fears, and the community dynamics that promote them, point to the need for long-term community development and community healing.

These concerns speak to the need for 'healing the healers,' an idea that has gained increased attention over the past decade. Service providers are key role models in communities, and they themselves must be healed in order to assist the community in the healing process. 'Healing the healers' has become the catch phrase for the need to attend to the complex stressors that influence how service providers operate within their own community.

For example, the need for occupational mental-health programs has been increasingly recognized. Aboriginal service providers experience stress and anxiety because they work in closely knit communities. Jennifer Dawson has examined this issue in detail, as part of a study concerning southern and local service providers in Moosonee and Moose Factory (1995). She notes that many diverse expectations and perceptions are at work when Aboriginal people offer support within their own community. These include their own personal struggles with identity, exceedingly high demands on workers' time and energy (the feeling that workers are always 'on call'), sensitivity to community criticism, and concerns about their own skills and professional training. Workers are also subject to the stressors felt by other community members, including the grief that accompanies suicide or other traumatic crises

Aboriginal workers often assume positions of responsibility at a young age. The majority of care-givers are also women, many of whom are single mothers and who often assume the burden of health- and social-service provision while raising children in the absence of appropriate child-care facilities. The RCAP recognized that women often assume primary responsibility for family and community healing, and that women place a priority on the need for improved health and social services (1996e: 56). Consequently, RCAP recommendation 4.2.2 calls for Aboriginal governments to ensure 'full and fair' participation of women in the governing bodies of all Aboriginal health and healing institutions (RCAP 1996e: 60).

There is growing concern that political leaders and service providers feel the stress that comes from unreasonably high community expectations about their performance. Elders and traditional healers may also experience stress as they are increasingly called upon to travel to community after community in order to revitalize ceremonies, promote spiritual understanding, or deal with personal illnesses.

Given that the strain on existing human resources is already being felt, it is reasonable to expect that the transition to self-government will generate in staff considerable turbulence and stress. Aboriginal leaders anticipate that the progression to self-governing institutions will be slow, deliberate, and well planned. But increased control over institutions will bring new stressors to communities. For this reason it is appropriate to suggest that occupational health programs and other efforts aimed at supporting leadership, healers, and other role models should be a priority. Governments should invest in the development of human resources through culturally appropriate training, retraining, and educational opportunities for volunteers and workers. These initiatives would ensure development of adequate supports to reinforce the relationship between healthy family and work environments. To date this type of social scaffolding has not been developed in anticipation of the construction of self-governing communities.

Conclusion

Unfortunately, until recently the government has only been willing to provide funds for crisis intervention or mental-health services post facto in response to serious crises. Aboriginal leaders are placed in the unfortunate position of appearing to exploit, as pressure points, the deaths of Aboriginal youth in order to obtain dollars for mental-health initiatives. In fact, Aboriginal leaders have consistently argued that mental-health programming is a major gap in human services. Aboriginal people should not have to see children die in order to demonstrate to the government that there is a need for suicide-prevention programs.

While the current fiscal reality confronting federal government must be acknowledged, it cannot account for the dire shortage of programs that could help address the crisis of Aboriginal suicide. For more than a decade the government has been aware that youth suicide rates are of epidemic proportions. But despite this fact, and despite tragedies of solvent abuse and violence that are regularly reported in the media, the government has failed to produce any comprehensive policy framework for Aboriginal mental-health programs. There is growing recognition that any long-term solution to these problems must lie in the provision of community-based and culturally appropriate prevention and intervention services.

What Aboriginal leadership has continuously requested are comprehensive federal and provincial policies that would enable communities to develop proactive, holistic approaches to mental health and individual healing. The creation of innovative strategies to deal with the complex mental-health problems of Aboriginal peoples will only be accomplished through the creation of regional health-care systems that allow Aboriginal communities to link their services to institutions located off reserve. The Ontario Aboriginal Healing and Wellness Strategy is an important initiative in this regard because it provides First Nations and urban Aboriginal organizations the opportunity to collaborate in a variety of physical health, mental health, and justice services.

Government policy-makers must also recognize the wealth of indigenous expertise that exists at the community level. Community care will only be successful if governments provide First Nations with adequate resources to train and retrain existing staff. Aboriginal communities are clearly capable of making decisions, and forming linkages to mainstream and Native mental-health agencies in order to provide training and expertise to their communities. Indeed, First Nations have demonstrated such initiative in spite of a dry and desolate funding environment. Communities are prepared to develop new strategies to address the current crisis of suicide. The North Shore experience demonstrates that communities are searching for ways to redistribute existing resources, to better coordinate services, and to experiment with new programs to address the factors that lead to suicides. The development of holistic approaches to community mental health requires a rethinking of health-care delivery systems, a redesigning of existing services, and a retraining of existing staff to better address a wide range of social issues. Many communities, including those on the North Shore, have already accomplished this planning, but remain frustrated by the government's failure to make mental-health funding a priority.

Aboriginal health perceptions lead to a commitment to illness prevention and health-promotion approaches that include spiritual and cultural components, rather than to the reactive 'disease' model of health, which emphasizes only the physical determinants. Accepting the Aboriginal world-view of health and mental health as valid is a critical first step to the legitimation of Aboriginal cultures in Canada. From the Aboriginal perspective, a person's feeling of having control over his or her life cannot be separated from the larger issue of community political controls. Self-government and self-determination are linked to solutions to suicide or other social health problems.

The solutions – or, at the very least, the long-term strategies – to enhance individual and community well-being are well known. What is required is leadership to make issues of mental health a priority. Chiefs and councils must help provide a better environment for healing by ending the denial about family violence and sexual abuse. This denial corrupts the fabric of community life. Leadership is required to restructure services and to develop case-management and crisis-intervention skills. Many Aboriginal communities have demonstrated that they are prepared to act even in the face of inadequate resources and continued intransigence by the government. Aboriginal service providers, no less than other professionals, are increasingly committed to open fiscal policies, and with ways of delivering health and social services that are accountable to their community.

Ultimately, leadership must also be taken by the federal and provincial governments, not to recklessly fund a new layer of Aboriginal mental-health institutions and organizations, but to provide communities with monies for training in crisis intervention and dollars to build on and develop existing counselling and aftercare services. In short, resources are needed to enhance, rather than stifle, the resourcefulness and initiative that is already being shown across the country as Aboriginal communities struggle to create an environment for healing. The emphasis on community care, self-help, and preventive approaches offers, over the long term, extremely cost-effective alternatives to the current reliance on mainstream mental-health and social services.

There is a subtle difference between creating a supportive atmosphere for healing – that is, an environment that promotes self-reliance – and promoting approaches that 'institutionalize' the healing process, and, in so doing, continue the colonization of community life. Innovative approaches to the problems of Aboriginal communities require policy-makers to escape the hegemony of medical and psychiatric institutions that dominate the field of mental health. Thus, while linkages to urban-based mental-health programs are important, the focus of mental-health activity in the community should be on enhancing the skills of existing staff, improving supports for families, and, wherever and whenever possible, enhancing traditional medicine initiatives.

First Nations are only as strong as their membership, and their capacity for self-government is intimately connected to the mental health and well-being of the children and youth who will lead in future generations. Clearly, the overall environment in which children and youth are raised must be improved. The need for community and economic development to overcome the dire circumstances and life opportunities facing many Aboriginal youths has been identified, firsthand, by Canadians faced with grim reality of Aboriginal suicide – for example, by the jury in the inquest into the suicides of Donnie Sanipass, Anthony Sacobie, David Augustine, and Keith Augustine at Big Cove Reserve, New Brunswick. One aspect of this tragedy is that the names of these Aboriginal youths, and countless others, fade away so easily and never seem to make an impression on the collective consciousness of our society. In the memory of these youths we might ask ourselves what political action needs to be taken to transform the unfinished dreams of Aboriginal youth into the reality of community healing and the achievement of Aboriginal self-government.

5

Restoring Justice: Conflict with the Law

What is the use of studying values that were discarded, ignored as irrelevant, and otherwise completely swamped by the imposition of a totally foreign justice system if that system will continue to operate and exist under the complete and total control of the dominant society? Why go through the agony of enumerating these values if the dominant authorities will be the only ones picking and choosing which ones are compatible and which ones are not? To spare us the futility of such an exercise, we first have to be provided with an answer to this fundamental question: To what degree will Inuit have control over the justice system in their ancestral homeland? How much self-government will be accorded to facilitate this dream? Once this question is adequately answered, it would take a thorough series of in-depth ethnological and anthropological studies to do justice to the fundamental values, norms and concepts which the present system presumes to want to know about. But until then, we have to be wary and genuinely sceptical about getting drawn into an exercise which will come to naught if the administration and implementation of the system remains firmly in the hands of foreigners who will never have an adequate appreciation and respect for these values. (Ottawa ON. 92-11-25 13. Zebedee Nungak. PG 60–1).

Introduction

I have been interested in traditional tribal law since my Ph.D. fieldwork in Papua New Guinea. There, in a nation that includes more than seven hundred distinct cultures, a system of traditional law (or tribal courts) exists within the umbrella of a national system of justice modelled on that of the British (see Warry 1987a; 1990). In 1985, as an employee of the

Ontario Native Council on Justice (ONCJ), I met people who were advancing the idea of a parallel justice system for their communities. Having lived in a country where a plural system of justice existed, I found the idea of a parallel system to be natural and logical. However, the lawyers and public servants whom I talked to at this time thought that the idea of a separate system was impractical at best, mere fantasy at worst. Since then I have had a number of opportunities to visit courts throughout Ontario and in the Arctic. I have spoken with criminal justice system personnel and Aboriginal people about the existing justice system, and their hopes for Aboriginally controlled justice programs (SPR 1989). Marcia Hoyle, a Ph.D. candidate at McMaster, has conducted research on traditional law in Sagamok, and we have worked together to assist Sagamok in obtaining funds to begin planning an alternative justice program (Hoyle 1994; 1995). During the past decade I have seen a modest amount of change in the existing system, and grudging acceptance on the part of government officials that the idea of a parallel Aboriginal justice system might become a reality.

At first glance 'justice' would seem unrelated to many of the issues associated with health or mental health. But in its most basic sense, 'law' is about establishing agreement on appropriate conduct within a community. Aboriginal ideas about justice are, at least in ideal terms, very much about individual healing and reintegrating offenders into the community. The issue of Aboriginal justice is also seminal to the conception of self-government: it is difficult to conceive of a nation that does not have the right to determine its own laws, and to determine a course of action for people who break those laws.

The notion of separate justice systems seem to be a lightning rod for opinions about Aboriginal issues. A 1988 Environics poll showed the public favoured a parallel system by a margin of 53% to 34%. But in 1990 (following the Oka confrontation) 51% of the population opposed an Aboriginal justice system, with only 40% in favour (Simpson 1994: 221). This decline in support probably reflects a general concern that Aboriginal justice threatens to undermine the system of 'one law' that is presumed to exist in Canada. These views were evident in the crises at Ipperwash and Gustafson Lake, when media panels and letters to the editor invariably emphasized the need to 'enforce the law' (see, for example, *Spectator*, 14 Sept. 1995, A9).

The idea that there is 'one law' in Canada is a major psychological block to the implementation of alternative justice programs. The spectre of a 'thousand laws' is intolerable for many people, who see criminal law in particular as a major philosophical plaster to the Canadian mosaic. For example, an editorial about parallel systems in the *Sault Star* cited the Charter of Rights, called the idea of separate systems 'a ridiculous idea,' and called for its rejection by the federal government. The editorial position rested on two common assumptions: the existence of separate courts would create a different set of laws and penalties for Natives, and it would entail a 'huge added expense' for the government and taxpayers (*Sault Star*, 31 Jan. 1995, A4).

The current administration of justice, however, serves as a focal point for Aboriginal discontent. Protests in Davis Inlet, where the community refused permission for RCMP and court officers to land in their community, demonstrate that Aboriginal people wish to directly control police and justice services (*Toronto Star*, 11 Sept. 1994, A1, A5). At the time of this conflict, Newfoundland Justice Minister Ed Roberts articulated the beliefs of many Canadians when he stated: 'They're quite willing to take the benefits of being Canadians. They must also take the responsibility of being Canadians – and that means we're subject to the rule of law' (ibid). Federal Justice Minister Alan Rock endorsed the idea of a separate justice system for Aboriginal people, but remained noncommittal as to what such a system might entail (*Spectator*, 15 July 1994, A13). A RCAP report strongly recommends that federal, provincial, and territorial governments recognize the right of Aboriginal nations to establish and administer their own justice systems (1996f: 312; see also 1996g). The report outlines the ways in which sufficient 'conceptual and constitutional space' might be created to allow for the development of Aboriginal courts (1996f: 177–249). Yet within days of the release of this report, the federal government had distanced itself from many of the recommendations. Instead, the government chose a more conservative course: to maintain its support for the Justice Department's Aboriginal Justice Directorate, an $18 million commitment that allows the federal government to fund and monitor justice pilot projects in Aboriginal communities.

In this chapter I examine the nature of Aboriginal law in order to provide a rationale for the development of policies that would promote a Aboriginal system of justice. An 'alternative justice system' – which may or may not include courts – is a logical and an efficient alternative to the current system. In examining Aboriginal law, I focus on the minor advances in Aboriginal justice during the past decade, as well the more radical vision of a parallel system. As a policy field, Aboriginal justice is a decade or more behind other areas such as education and health care. The lack of progress in this area is partially explained by the fact that the criminal justice system is inherently conservative, and a primary instrument of colonial practice (Arno 1985; Havemann et al 1985; M. Jackson 1988). To date, the majority of those involved in the criminal justice system, unlike their medical counterparts, have failed to seriously consider the possibility that complementary systems of justice might coexist with mainstream approaches.

When Aboriginal people speak of community healing, justice issues are naturally raised. Aboriginal ideas about 'justice as healing' should be of great interest to mainstream society. The notion of 'restorative' justice, for example, provides us with a universal language for thinking about the purpose of law. In this sense, my argument is not simply about the separation of justice systems, but also about the search for areas of accommodation and agreement.[1]

The Need: Conflict with the Law

Previous chapters have documented many problems of conflict with the law. Family violence, drunk driving, assaults, vandalism, break and enters – breaches of criminal law occur in Aboriginal communities on a regular basis. Currently, whether these events are considered minor, and result in charges, and how they are treated in court – as summary, hybrid, or indictable offences – is determined by various state criminal justice authorities. The essence of a parallel justice system, therefore, lies in the community's ability to identify offenders of the public order, and to punish – or treat – these individuals.

Alcohol is involved in many current offences. The relationship between alcohol abuse and conflict with the law is undeniable. Don Auger is an Ojibwa lawyer with Nishnawbe-Aski Legal Services, a legal-aid clinic serving 30,000 to 35,000 people in Northern Ontario. He has noted that a survey of more than 30,000 police reports and court dockets from 1988 to 1991 revealed several trends typical of the Aboriginal pattern of conflict with the law (RCAP 1993a: 92-10-27 50. PG 65). Police respond to a variety of general calls, most of which involve minor offences such as break and enter, but also a fair number of minor assaults. About 46% of all disturbances that police investigated involved alcohol or other drugs. When charges are formally laid, however, alcohol is involved in virtually all incidents. The involvement of alcohol in so many offences clearly indicates that 'crime' can in many instances be interpreted as a signal for help.

Native people are greatly over-represented in all phases of the criminal justice system, from arrest through to incarceration (Asbury 1985). Aboriginal people are twice as likely as non-Natives to become involved with the criminal justice system, and constitute one-quarter of the combined federal and provincial inmate population (see, for example, LaPrairie 1992a). Although they constitute roughly 3% of the Canadian population, they comprise 10% of the federal inmate population. Provincial incarceration rates (sentences of two years or less) are even higher, particularly in western Canada. Incarceration rates vary regionally, reflecting not only demographic differences, but differences in arrest rates, as well as sentencing patterns. Certain areas, for example, Kenora, have generated a great number of Aboriginal jail terms – in part because of the high rate of public drunkenness charges. But the incarceration of Aboriginal people is greatest in the area west of the Ontario/Manitoba border, where it commonly involves status Indians living in urban centres (see Depew 1994a, n. 41; LaPrairie 1992a). Depew notes that urban Natives commit more crime and disorder offences than similar groups of non-Natives, and more than status Indians living on reserve, though they also commit fewer *violent* offences than those on reserve. On reserve, there is a much higher proportion of violent-offence reports, about one quarter of offences as opposed to 10% in other rural and urban areas (Depew 1994a: 43–6, n. 45). It appears likely that on reserves many crimes and offences are reported, but go unprocessed. In urban centres, perhaps by nature of their visibility, offences are subject to more criminal justice processing (ibid: 38).

In some instances, however, it appears that conflict rates on reserve are comparable to 'high-crime' areas in urban centres. This is not to suggest that Aboriginal people somehow naturally commit more crimes than non-Aboriginal people. Indeed, the pattern of offences that occur, their location and their method of reporting are all subject to great variation. As Depew (1994a) and LaPrairie (1992a) note, there is a great deal yet to be learned about Aboriginal offence patterns. Carol LaPrairie has been conducting research on various aspects of Aboriginal law, criminal behaviour, courts and policing for more than a decade. She participated in a collaborative study among nine Cree communities in the James Bay area, analysed police daily reports, and drew on community-based interviews (LaPrairie et al 1991). The research, which needs to be confirmed through comparative studies, documents what has been suspected by many for a long period – that rates of interpersonal violence, crimes against the person, and other offences such as mischief are extremely high on reserve. Elsewhere LaPrairie (1987) has suggested that emerging information indicates an association between family violence, physical abuse, and rates of Native conflict with the law. Her study suggests that rates of interpersonal violence on reserve may be six to eight times higher than those reported in the general population (the probability that many incidents of violence in the general population also go unreported must be acknowledged here). She found, for example, that more violent offences occur on Indian reserves than are reported, and that many offences that occur do not become subject to court scrutiny. She notes that many Aboriginal communities, particularly those that are geographically isolated, have considerable time and scope to deal with problems of law and order because of the infrequency of circuit courts (personal communication); that is, much of dispute processing is informal in nature, beyond the influence of the state.

Marcia Hoyle conducted justice research in Sagamok Anishnabek First Nation, in the NSTC area (Hoyle 1995: 5–6). Sagamok is a reserve with a population of just over one thousand. Hoyle found that both residents and justice personnel thought that Sagamok was a 'quiet' community and that crime was not a serious problem. Yet her research shows that, when criminal code violations were considered in relation to total population, the Sagamok 'crime rate' was higher than the Canadian average (176 reported incidents per thousand, as opposed to 100 per thousand in Canada). Hoyle also notes that many other incidents went unreported, and that community tolerance or acceptance of crime may not in fact reflect many other concerns about the nature of community order. Hoyle also found that when assaults were calculated as a percentage of the total incidents, the incidence was nearly double the rate of that for the general population. Significantly, domestic violence is the most frequent type of violent conflict, yet local band constables are seldom called on to intervene in such incidents (Hoyle 1994; cf. LaPrairie et al 1991 regarding Cree parallels). LaPrairie (1992b: 130) has detailed the complex factors, including the desire to sustain the family in the face of violence, which contribute to the low reporting of sexual assaults and family violence. Incidents of family violence, in conjunction with the role played by alcohol in conflict on reserve, point to the need for crisis intervention such as that discussed in chapter 4 and for justice systems that are integrated with other health and human services on reserve.

For many Aboriginal youth, particularly male youth, conflict with the law involves a high risk of incarceration. In Saskatchewan, an Indian boy turning sixteen had a 70% chance of at least one stay in prison by the age of twenty-five (Hylton 1983). Comparable figures are unavailable for Ontario, but Native admissions in the 16–25 age range account for almost half of male admissions and 44% of female admissions to Ontario correctional facilities (Asbury 1986: 25; see also M. Jackson 1988). A third of Native adults incarcerated were first convicted as juveniles – the first conviction on average occurring at 16.5 years. Children between the ages of 7 and 11 represent a high-risk category with conflict rates eight times greater than non-Indian youth (Jolly 1983; 1985).

The experience of incarceration, then, is all too common for many Aboriginal men. It is interesting to note that, although the roots of the community healing movement are difficult to trace, inmate self-help programs have clearly played a role in the healing journey of many individuals. Since the early 1980s, groups such as Native Sons or the Native Brotherhood, based in correctional facilities, have stressed traditional spiritual approaches to recovery from alcohol abuse or other abusive behaviour. These groups have raised awareness about the many inadequacies and injustices of the criminal 'justice' system. Networks of inmates and ex-inmates have been influential well beyond the prison walls in promoting traditional values as a means to recovery and healing. There is a particularly deep and poignant relationship between incarceration and healing. Many Aboriginal inmates first become aware of pipe ceremonies or sweat lodges through contact with elders who visit correctional facilities (Warry 1986a, 1986b; Waldrum 1993). In many senses this type of recovery encapsulates the larger Aboriginal experience: incarceration within a total institution epitomizes state control and oppression; personal (re)discovery of self- and cultural esteem through self-help and cultural awakening occurs despite institutional controls.

Many Native inmates are very much attuned to ideas concerning colonialism, state oppression, spiritual healing, and reconciliation with mainstream society. Darrel Breton, of the First Nations Freedom Network (FNFN), a brotherhood and sisterhood attempting to address the issues of over-representation and recidivism in the correctional system, synthesizes many of these concepts in the following statement to the RCAP (1993a): 'In our endeavour to overcome the great Canadian lockup ... my people are taking me through a healing process. They need to continue the healing process. The FNFN helps our people in the transitional phases from incarceration to reintegration into their Native culture and also into the overall society. The [RCAP] commissioners speak of reconciliation. This is part of the healing process. This is a step toward maturity. Canada is a young country ... As Canada matures, I become more and more confident in my future and the future of my people' (Edmonton AB. 92-06-11. PG 205)[2].

Aboriginal people have developed alternative correctional programs.

But where these exist, they bear little resemblance to mainstream institutions or facilities. Ontario has recognized the need to fund innovative corrections experiments on a small scale. Okunongegayin, a bush camp and traditional healing program for chronic solvent abusers near Kenora is one such example (Councillor 1992; Ontario 1992c). The federal government has also recently built a healing lodge for female Aboriginal offenders. Other Aboriginal approaches have involved bush camps and wilderness programs for offenders that are aimed at teaching traditional skills and spiritual practices. It is reasonable to assume, therefore, that Aboriginal control over justice would result in a variety of innovative programs that might better be considered as treatment facilities rather than as jails or correctional institutions.

The need for Aboriginal justice systems, then, is clear. Aboriginal peoples' over-representation in all phases of criminal justice processing – from arrest to incarceration – is at the heart of the call for parallel systems. (Morrow 1992: 3–4; Rudin and Russell 1991; M. Jackson 1988; see also Havemann et al 1985). Aboriginal people often suggest that systemic racism (in sentencing or the judicial process) as well as discriminatory police practices account for the high incarceration rates cited above. Underlying these explanations, as Depew notes, are models of culture conflict suggesting differential treatment (1994a: 85–9). Depew notes that these models underlie 'corrective' change by policy makers – for example, the belief that if only the system can be made more culturally sensitive, or more culturally relevant, then incarceration rates will decline. The missing link in justice research, as Depew notes (ibid), is the *quality* of contact between police and Aboriginal peoples. Although the disproportionate involvement of Aboriginal peoples in the justice system is clear, it is still unknown whether Aboriginal people receive different treatment than non-Aboriginal peoples, whether greater police attention to Aboriginal reserves results in higher crime rates, or whether Aboriginal communities are over-policed in comparison to non-Native communities (ibid).

Finally, we must acknowledge that systemic racism in the justice system has been documented, for example, by the Manitoba Aboriginal Justice Inquiry, a provincial royal commission (Hamilton and Sinclair 1991). However difficult racism is to prove, discrimination can be inferred in the absence of other explanations that would account for the over-representation in jails. It is certainly well documented that the court process is culturally insensitive and that many Aboriginal offenders proceed through court without ever pleading not guilty or questioning the authority of criminal justice personnel (see SPR 1989; Ross 1992). In remote fly-in courts, dockets may include forty or more offences. An offender may have only a few seconds with duty counsel before pleading guilty. Because of the cost of travel between reserves and towns, Natives also have a great deal of difficulty obtaining legal aid, and as a result Aboriginal offenders generally rely on duty counsel.[3] Conversely, lawyers seldom have sufficient information about the circumstances and context of a case, nor do they have the time and resources to identify witnesses to mount a serious defence. Once before the court – and recall that most charges are minor in nature – the vast majority of Aboriginal people charged with an offence, some 90%, plead guilty. In serious cases, an Aboriginal offender is less likely than a white person to receive bail, and therefore spends time in jail awaiting trial (M. Jackson 1988; Warry 1986a).

Incarceration rates are also directly linked to poverty. A great many jail terms are the result of fine default – the inability of Aboriginal offenders to pay fines. Jail terms also result because offenders have a long record of minor offences – they receive jail terms as a result of their breach of probation, or as a result of their reappearance before the court on similar charges. In sum, Aboriginal crime is the product of poverty, social problems, and interpersonal conflict. The 'quality of law' available to Aboriginal offenders is very poor and is saturated with cross-cultural misunderstanding and institutionalized discrimination. The desire to end Native people's disproportionate involvement with the law is a central motivation behind the search for workable alternatives to the adversarial model of law currently employed in Canada (Alberta 1991; LaJeunesse 1991; Warry 1991a). It is suggested, for example, that the pattern of over-incarceration would be reduced by the development of alternative courts.

But alternative justice is also a political issue. Many Aboriginal people view the current system as a foreign system, resting on non-Native assumptions and values. From the Aboriginal perspective, alternative justice is about being able to decide whether certain events should be labelled crimes and about how the community should deal with people in crises. Aboriginal justice is about appropriate community responses to disputes, arguments, and fights. This perspective challenges the state's right to intervene on reserve and to define what constitutes inappropriate or 'deviant' behaviour. It is possible that, even over the long term, alternative systems of justice may have only a *minimal* influence on conflict rates. There is no evidence to suggest that the number of charges laid would decrease under an Aboriginal system. And currently, there is Aboriginal support for a continuing role in serious offences for the criminal justice system. But given the pattern of repeat offences by a small number of

Aboriginal offenders, it may be that alternative measures would serve better to 'correct' the behaviour of offenders charged with minor offences and so would decrease incarceration rates over the long term.

From a cost-benefit perspective, even a slight decrease in legal-aid costs, court costs, or incarceration rates would be sufficient to fund alternative approaches. *The potential of Aboriginal justice systems lies in the long-term restorative quality of law for Aboriginal communities.* Alternative approaches have the potential to re-integrate communities, and offer offenders, particularly young ones who experience first offences, better prospects for rehabilitation or the correction of inappropriate behaviour. Aboriginal justice is very much about healing and ideas of social competence. Hoyle suggests that solutions arising out of a Native holistic philosophy are aimed at treating causes rather than punishing behaviour. As one councillor stated: 'The basis for our beliefs is not punishment ... we need to encourage the offender to understand they did wrong and make them understand why they should not do wrong again. We need to revive our spiritualism and our traditions. It should be such a system that offenders are tried by their peers' (cited in Hoyle 1994: 29). These sentiments, particularly the desire for rehabilitation, are no doubt shared by many non-Natives who wish to improve the criminal justice system. But there is also the emphasis here on the involvement of peers, that is, on community standards and sanctions. The type of solution envisioned here, with its emphasis on reconciliation and rehabilitation, requires a flexibility not offered by existing courts (Hoyle 1994). For example, in cases of vandalism, people often express the opinion that young offenders would be far less inclined to repeat their offence if they had to face the community directly to explain their crime, rather than be dealt with in an impersonal court system. Again, the emphasis is on restitution (Hoyle, personal communication). To date, however, there is little evidence to suggest whether such approaches would be effective given the complex kinship relations that exist on reserve (see chapter 6).

Hoyle's research in Sagamok initiated a community dialogue concerning the meaning of 'traditional' law (see also Ryan 1995). Plans for an alternative justice program are only now beginning, but they call for community and workers to be involved in a process that will lead to justice programs that are fully integrated, from intervention to sentencing and referral, with existing health and other social services. As Morrow notes, the creation of alternative justice programs raises the fundamental question of what laws are to be recognized and enforced (1992: 31). For many

Native people, the answer to this question lies in the restoration of traditional law and its recognition by the Canadian state (see Crawford et al 1988; G.S. Clarke 1990). The nature of Aboriginal law is such that it is embedded in other forms of behaviour – there is no discrete body of rules to which people can point and say 'this is law' (see Roberts 1979; Coyle 1986). As a result, restoring the customary bases of law would require not only anthropological and community-based research to establish a body of legal processes or values, but considerable community consultation and program development aimed at asserting community participation in informal justice (see also Ryan 1995; Hoyle 1995).

Customary Rules, Traditional Law

The literature is full of comparisons, by both Aboriginal and Euro-Canadian writers, between the *contemporary* Western and *traditional* Native legal ideas. These analyses occasionally set up false dichotomies, where the adversarial nature of modern-day courts become a straw man. The formal rule-bound nature of Western law is compared to the informal 'situational' nature of traditional Indian law based in consensual decision-making (RCAP 1993c). These comparisons are invidious in that they rest on a false assumption about the nature of culture change – for example, we might instead require analysts to compare traditional Aboriginal law with its seventeenth- or eighteenth-century English equivalent. The resulting comparison, though equally facile, would reveal a 'Western' court that was much less formal, less rule-bound, and less bureaucratic than present-day courts (see Van Velson 1969). Such comparisons also ignore the many experiments within the mainstream system that would aim to increase the use of less formal and non-adversarial processes to encourage mediation of disputes (see Merry and Milner 1995).

But what, then, does the notion of traditional law entail? To date, the most detailed elaboration of traditional law is to be found in Ryan's description of the Lac La Martre justice project (1995). Here Dene notions of law, of 'doing things the right way' include not only ideas Euro-Canadians would associate with 'criminal' justice, but also with family law (including divorce and family violence), political life, and resource 'rules' that extend to the ways animals and other wildlife are treated. Common to 'correction' for those whose behaviour was considered inappropriate was instruction in correct behaviour through various means, indirect and direct, including story-telling, ridicule, shaming, and, in more serious instances, putting individuals 'in the circle,' where elders would use harsh words, and demand a change in behaviour before meting out the ultimate sanction of banishment (ibid: 60–3).

How viable are traditional Aboriginal values for contemporary legal process? For example, what is the significance of Dene customary marriage and family rules for contemporary life? Formerly, marriage partners were chosen for people by their family or by elders. The status of women was also derived from a gender ideology that supported the isolation of women at first menses (ibid: 36–46).[4] These specific practices may have been abandoned, yet many of the values (respect for elders' experience or for women's procreative power) remain. It is clear from Ryan's account that the people of Lac La Martre are working with a fluid understanding of traditional law. When they considered what aspects of law should be brought forward, people focused not on specific 'rules' but rather on the core values – of sharing, caring, respect, and self-discipline – which are critical to 'doing things the right way' in a contemporary world (ibid: 66–72).

These issues, of course, are another version of the 'culture and tradition' argument I have previously addressed. Here, the distinction – and the confusion – between past custom (a particular cultural practice) and tradition (the appeal to values and actions that sustain customs or provide continuity to a social group over time) is important. Ryan, for example, attempts to dispense with the anthropological distinction between custom and tradition by suggesting that they can be seen as an 'integrated process that encapsulates the continuity between generations, conceptual continuity and persistence of cultural practices' (1995: 112). At the risk of splitting hairs, I would argue that the distinction between custom and tradition (whatever the terminology) is useful and should be maintained. It is important, for example, when attempting to conduct discussions about the nature of traditional revival in modern communities. Ryan's interpretation, in my view, runs the risk of overemphasizing continuity and persistence of traditional culture and of dispensing with the conflict that is so critical to the generation of changes within a community. In reality, however, communities are not homogeneous, there is considerable ideological disjuncture and conflict between generations, and shattered discourse (and much hair-splitting) about the relevance of various customs or cultural practices for contemporary life. And these ongoing debates are important to how or whether beliefs or practices persist and contribute to the resistance of outside influences.

This distinction is thrown into relief by the example of customary sanctions, which some people would like to revive or sustain. For others, customary punishments – including banishment from the reserve to remote bush areas – are considered inappropriate given contemporary standards. I believe that the use of practices such as banishment are perfectly feasible, particularly when agreed upon by offenders through mediation (and where traditional punishment is adapted, for example, to allow the 'banished' offender to obtain supplies or be visited by friends and family). Based on the few examples to date, however, it seems that as an experiment in 'traditional law' banishment is sometimes unenforceable (offenders refuse to adhere to the sentence and return to society) or politically insupportable (neighbouring communities will not accept offenders from Aboriginal communities).[5] Just as important, such sentences, even when attempted, are often directly opposed by the state as an affront to legal practice. In northern Alberta an offender in a sexual assault case agreed to be banished to a remote island for a year, with only monthly visits for supplies. But the Crown appealed the sentence (by a non-Native judge in a sentencing circle), claiming that banishment constituted a 'non-sentence' in criminal law. The offender was subsequently given a ninety-day sentence, with his traditional punishment being considered part of his probation. In other words, the Crown could not contemplate *any* sentence, however consensual or culturally appropriate, if it violated the letter of Western law.

The question, then, is whether customs should be abandoned, modified, or adapted given contemporary circumstances. A rigid appeal to custom sometimes alienates individuals who otherwise might be attracted to traditional beliefs. Indeed, this simple distinction is often the marker between 'fundamentalist' and more liberal ideological interpretations. For example, a person's position on banishment can distinguish an Aboriginal legal reformer as a 'hardliner' or 'moderate.' The distinction between what is 'really' traditional, and what is authentic and culturally appropriate, therefore, is subject to debate (see also chapter 6).

It is also possible to assert that customary law is not relevant to the establishment of a parallel system in some communities. Aboriginal justice systems could simply be established by recognizing Aboriginal jurisdiction over the administration of laws borrowed or adapted from the mainstream system. But for many people, an approach that sustains core values via tradition is the preferred road. This is the centrist view in most of the communities with which I am familiar. It is this view that Rupert Ross, a crown attorney with years of experience in Aboriginal communities, notes (1994: 2; 1992) when he states that the 'restoration' of traditional law need not imply the reconstruction or re-creation of traditional ways; rather, it represents the desire to 'incorporate traditional *values* into processes tailored to meet today's challenges' (1994: 2). Aboriginal people wish to preserve the essence of legal practice and process – whether that entails an appeal to compensation, for example, or to consensual decision-making.

In other words, it is useful to distinguish 'customary' processes, rules, or penalties, which may or may not be relevant to contemporary life, from 'traditional law,' which is a system of values embedded in social relationships, rather than a domain separate and discrete unto itself. The essential quality of what is referred to as traditional law is, as Depew notes, 'morally-defined role relationships and practices, and their underlying principles of order and control which have their origin and context in the cultural organization of social, economic and political relations and the nature of on-going social interaction' (1994a: 20–1).

A critical feature of Aboriginal law is the view of disputes as arising naturally from a long history of individual experiences and community life – including past quarrels and disagreements (Warry 1991a). Aboriginal justice emphasizes the *context* of legal events. In this sense, whether a specific law was broken or not is often a rather meaningless question. The major concern for the community is why there has been a disruption in the community peace, and how best to restore community harmony. For this reason 'traditional' legal process attends to relationships, and must be flexible enough to discover the complex antecedents to contemporary events. This holistic conception of law gives rise to a much wider conception of evidence, greater latitude in the hearing of testimony from offenders, witnesses, and victims, and a more complex notion of responsibility than is possible in a guilty/not guilty system of justice. From this perspective, it is important for those involved in mediating disputes to sort through complex and often competing interpretations of events – and this may include assessing the individual personalities conveying those facts. This type of 'deep' legal knowledge requires that mediators or arbitrators have an intimate knowledge of all parties to the dispute and of the community as a whole. These qualities distinguish Aboriginal law from its Western counterpart in fundamental ways.

As previously suggested, 'traditional values' may reflect an idealized conception of social rules or some previous normative order. Depew cautions those interested in the (re)establishment of Aboriginal law to recall that 'customary law' was flexible, dynamic, and subject to contestation (1994a: 21). It is normal not only for conflict to arise as a part of even the best-functioning and stable communities, but also for legal practice to be constantly challenged. We should expect the formation of Aboriginal courts, police forces, or correctional services to threaten certain segments of the community, and to be challenged by others, just as we should expect the 'outcome' of court cases or disputes to be the subject of debate and disagreement. As MacDonald (1992a, cited in Depew 1994a: 22) acknowledges, 'social life is intrinsically problematic' and a degree of tension and conflict is normal, even within tightly knit, kin-based communities. Culturally appropriate dispute-resolution strategies can serve to reintegrate and revitalize communities by affording community members the opportunities to debate community standards. We must accept the daily perturbations in community life, and appreciate law for its ability to play a harmonizing function in society. And for precisely that reason it is imperative that law evolve naturally from communities rather than being imposed from outside.

The possibility of a parallel system gives rise to the need for what Morrow has called the development of 'interface mechanisms' to integrate Aboriginal and mainstream systems at critical junctures (1992: 26–7).[6] But many Canadians see alternative systems that entail different legal roles or different sentencing patterns as inherently problematic.

One Law, Many Laws: Legal Pluralism

For many federal and provincial policy makers, the concept of alternative systems remains a radical notion. As recently as 1991, Kim Campbell, then the federal justice minister, reiterated the federal position: there is no intention to create separate justice systems for Native people. The justice department stated 'that solutions must be found within the Constitution of Canada, present and future, as interpreted by the Supreme Court of Canada. In this sense, it does not envisage an entirely separate system of justice for Aboriginal peoples, although community justice systems, for example as connected to Aboriginal self-government, are both possible and desirable' (Canada: 1991c). This is classic political rhetoric, a message of the forked-tongue variety, which reinterates the federal government's commitment to Aboriginal solutions, while retaining control over justice for the state. While it is true that many of the implications of alternative systems are only now seriously being contemplated by government planners, limited control over law and order is part of ongoing self-government negotiations. Tribal court systems are constitutionally feasible and well within the legal parameters set down in the Indian Act

(Morse 1980). Several government inquiries and independent commissions have called for the establishment of some form of parallel system (RCAP 1993c and 1996g). These reviews have been sufficient to demonstrate that despite potentially thorny objections concerning local jurisdictions, or the issue of incommensurable jural norms, there are few, if any, major jurisdictional or constitutional impediments to major reform or the development of separate systems (RCAP 1993c: 7; Webber, in RCAP 1993c: 133–60). Aboriginal notions about legal process are compatible with mainstream experiments aiming to de-emphasize the adversarial nature of criminal courts, to enhance mediation processes, and to ensure the rights of victims through increased involvement in sentencing and through compensation (see Coyle 1986; Warry 1990). Even a cursory review of community-based justice projects in the United States reveals a number of alternatives to the mainstream system that are more radical than any Aboriginal experiments currently being conducted and that are perfectly compatible with Aboriginal calls for legal control (Merry and Milner 1995).

To date, the major thrust of government action has been to reform the current system by improving Native people's access to court services on and off reserve. The state asserts that the vast majority of serious criminal code offences should continue to be the responsibility of the criminal justice system. This view is consonant with the federal government's stand on self-government: that First Nations be restricted to powers commonly associated with municipal governments. As MacPherson notes, discussions sponsored by the RCAP were unable to provide consensus on the part of academics, policy-makers, or Aboriginal people themselves as to the need or pragmatics of fully independent Aboriginal justice systems (RCAP 1993c: 10).

Morrow has reviewed the range of models that Aboriginal communities might consider in the delivery of alternative justice (1992). These include enhancing existing Native justice of the peace programs, developing courts under section 107 of the Indian Act, or creating new institutions based on Aboriginal customary law. It is important to realize that even the development of parallel or tribal courts (for example, those modelled on the Navaho experience) would simply continue the hegemony of Western legal institutions. The creation of any parallel system of 'carbon copy' courts that would replicate non-Native processes or substitute Native for non-Native personnel will only serve to sustain the legitimacy of mainstream laws.

Aboriginal people have always maintained that a plurality of justice approaches is a necessary and a natural outgrowth of both traditional and contemporary Aboriginal cultural diversity (ibid; Giokas 1993: 184–231). But the federal government has resisted the development of alternative justice programs on the basis that they would be difficult to integrate with the mainstream legal system or that they would threaten universal notions of individual rights under the law. That is, the government seems willing to accept a degree of variation in legal process, so long as it can sustain the idea of a common body of law that protects, and is applied to, all citizens.

Rupert Ross assumes that Aboriginal cultural, historical, and political diversity is such that approaches that are successful in one community may be a failure in the next (1994). He suggests that any formulae for promoting justice reform must be flexible enough to permit a wide range of unique community responses. In Canada the notion of legal pluralism entails two pluralities: differences between Aboriginal legal traditions, and differences between these systems of law and those promoted by the state. LaPrairie (1994a, 1994b: 28, n. 24) emphasizes the internal diversity within communities as the primary stumbling block to the development of effective justice systems. She notes how portraits of Aboriginal communities that stress a collective or egalitarian ethos often mask complex divisions based on gender, power, or access to economic resources (1994a 16–17; see also chapter 6). This is an important point. It may be that, during the initial period of implementing and evaluating alternative programs, internal conflict poses a major threat to a program's success or acceptance. LaPrairie argues that all too often the call for reform is based more on an idealized vision of communities as sharing common values. This view neglects, for example, internal divisions while asserting a need for approaches that encourage community revitalization. I share these concerns, but would add that external conflict with the state, which refuses to accept the *idea* of legal alternatives, is the major obstacle to change.

Not surprisingly, efforts to expand Aboriginal jurisdiction in the area of criminal law have collapsed under the weight of the rigidity and formalism of legal specialists, including judges and lawyers. Ross, for example, notes that discussions about the transfer of criminal-law jurisdiction to First Nations often begin with a categorization of offences that Aboriginal people will, or will not be 'allowed' to handle in the community.[7] The contemporary reality is that few police, lawyers, or judges – and Aboriginal people – would contemplate, *at present,* allowing Aboriginal adjudicators to process indictable offences such as murder and sexual or aggravated assault. But the limits of Aboriginal legal authority, however restricted at present, will naturally expand as communities demonstrate their expertise in processing minor offences – indeed, this has been the case in tribal courts in other countries (Warry 1987a; 1991b). At present, however, criminal justice personnel see state intervention as necessary to ensure equal punishment of offenders in indictable offences, and to permit the accused equal access to an adequate defence – that is, a defence based on Western legal principles, including the right to a jury trial. The ability to decide 'serious' cases is linked to the presumed superiority of Western legal practice and ideology. The continued hegemony of the mainstream justice system, which rests on this assumption of superiority as well as the structural dominance of legal professions, continues to infiltrate and undermine attempts to innovate in the area of Aboriginal legal reform. As Turpel notes, the failure to develop grass-roots justice systems is in part related to the inability of mainstream reformers to understand the intrinsic difference of Aboriginal culture – difference that includes unique assumptions about the nature of punishment, legal process, correction of social behaviour, and other cultural norms (1993: 161–83).

Ross notes that much violence is already hidden or 'withheld' from justice authorities. Aboriginal people are already exercising their jurisdiction in some instances by withholding knowledge of conflict from the state. Many Native *victims* refuse to appear in court to testify against the accused, and some offences, particularly those associated with family violence, go unreported, or where reported, do not result in charges (see R. Ross 1994: 3). Ross notes that any system that identifies offenders with any regularity, will be an improvement on the current system. But this perspective misses the point if it is meant to suggest that increased Aboriginal participation in the justice system will increase the identification of offenders in *Western* courts. The critical point is that Aboriginal people have the right to identify what constitutes an offence in their community. Failure to notify the external system must be interpreted as instances of individual or collective resistence to state justice. The question that remains is how to directly sanction – or assist – offenders and victims within the community. And an Aboriginally controlled system is most likely to lead to this solution.

Many concerns exist about the implementation of Aboriginal legal systems. Ross suggests that 'an overnight withdrawal of the western justice system would not be followed by the immediate substitution of effective Aboriginal approaches but by significant violence,' given the social illness that exists in many communities (1994: 2). Ross's concern, then, relates to the speed of transition, not whether Aboriginal justice systems should be attempted. In my opinion, this cautionary note is unnecessarily alarmist given the practical and conservative approach to change that predominates in communities. Ross's view develops from a concern with the protection of individual rights, and is another version of a conservative and transitional view of change – one that rejects radical implementation of self-government until the ramifications of Native legal authority are understood. This is also the view of the majority of Aboriginal people, who also seek reassurance that the mainstream legal system could continue as a system of appeal or final resort. In arguing for 'compromise' by both Aboriginal communities and state authorities, Ross suggests that what is required is that governments must relinquish power without having a precise blueprint for the changes that will occur and, further, that governments must also expect problems and failures to occur (ibid).

More serious opposition to Aboriginal systems derives from deeply held beliefs about the superiority of Western law – for example, the notion of judicial independence, or the fundamental importance of courts or juries. Ross, for example, suggests that offence categories could be abandoned in favour of a 'process-based' analysis of cases, which, over time, would allow Aboriginal people increased input into bail hearings, plea discussion, or 'pre-trial' processes (which involve defence and crown attorneys who determine whether a charge is appropriate and what range of sentences should be suggested to the judge) and sentencing options (such as the previously discussed sentencing circles). He makes the pragmatic observation that the vast majority of cases – some 90% – involve guilty pleas and do not result in trials. His suggestion offers the potential for the greater involvement of Aboriginal people in the justice system, and for the development over time of Aboriginal alternatives to these court-based procedures. However, any transitional reforms should question the need for Aboriginal participation in court-based processes; that is, the idea of restorative justice raises the possibility of alternative legal processes that bear little resemblance to those associated with trials, courts, or hearings.

Still other concerns about a pluralistic legal system emerge from basic moral premises. The notion that religious or cultural beliefs might serve as grounds for defence in criminal cases was recently floated in a Justice Department discussion paper. This suggestion was roundly denounced as offensive and unworkable in editorials across the country. Such an idea, it is argued, would undermine the principle of equality under the law, and would compromise the protection of the public. But such defences are already part of the legal discourse, at least in Aboriginal communities, where judges routinely try to take into account the different reality of Aboriginal culture and community in meting out sentences. The potential for conflict emerges in cross-cultural settings whenever people choose between lines of action embedded in contradictory normative orders. Theoretically, it can be argued that, from an Aboriginal perspective, any decision rendered in a Canadian court against a Native offender carries no legitimacy, given the fact that there is no Aboriginal word for 'law' or 'guilt,' or that the defendant does not recognize the validity of an 'offence' such as hunting out of season on crown land. In practice, however, only certain offences carry this type of political content and many cases are settled appropriately and in keeping with Aboriginal values.

It is the pragmatics of dispute settlement – the demonstration of fair and just settlements – that makes the realization of a plural system of justice possible. And there is little doubt in my mind that Aboriginal control over justice systems would enhance the quality of law. For example, because conceptions of Native health are holistic and relational, illness is often viewed as the result of damaged or disrupted relationships. Thus, although Native and non-Native alike may be able to agree that violence between spouses should be condemned, they are also likely to disagree on what is an appropriate course of action when incidents of abuse are revealed in a community. Legal action taken against a spouse may further damage the relationship, and hence affect the health of both partners. It is this type of situation that requires a legal process where Native family values and gender relations can be fully taken into account. This example also raises the danger, voiced by Aboriginal women's organizations, that a male-controlled or -dominated Native justice system might endanger women's rights under the Charter. The royal commission (RCAP 1996) also signalled the importance of ensuring that women participate in all aspects of justice reform, including the evaluation of any alternative programs.

The possible creation of family or criminal courts where Native mediators would determine neglect, order intervention, establish criminal negligence or medical liability, points to the need for open dialogues concerning the cultural values that determine ethical action. Community support for alternative systems can only come through experimentation and debate. And while it will be necessary in the interim to ensure appropriate interface mechanisms exist – for example, appeal systems or options to allow Native offenders to appear before non-Native courts – there is little doubt that the development of community-based justice systems will be more responsive to a wide range of complex dispute and crisis situations than the existing system.

The State's State of the Art

Throughout the 1970s and early 1980s, state innovation in criminal justice reform was limited to programs to indigenise criminal justice personnel, to provide more culturally sensitive programs to inmates and offenders, and to provide 'cross-cultural awareness training' to criminal justice personnel. Aboriginal organizations fought hard to place many of these initiatives on the government's agenda. For example, during the 1980s, the Ontario Native Council on Justice (ONCJ) consistently urged the Ministry of Correctional Services to ensure that Native elders were treated similarly to other religious leaders. The ONCJ received numerous reports that elders' sacred bundles were being searched, or complaints about the use of sweet grass, which guards mistook for marijuana. The level of cultural understanding among guards in some institutions was, to say the least, distressing. Cross-cultural awareness sessions are now routinely conducted for police officers, corrections workers, judges, and more recently, members of the armed forces (see *Globe and Mail* 16 Feb. 1995, A8; SPR 1989). Even where participants in these studies favourably evaluate their experience, the long-term effect of this education is impossible to measure. None the less, my own experience suggests that such programs can be extremely important in laying the foundation for longer, more systemic change within the bureaucracy.

Since the late 1980s the federal government, through the Department of Justice's Aboriginal Justice Directorate, has funded a number of research and demonstration projects across the country (see R. Ross 1996). The concentration of these projects has been greatest in the Northwest Territories, where the Justice Department has direct responsibility for the administration of justice. Provincial governments, too, have funded a number of projects both on and off reserve. I cannot extensively review here the many projects that have been implemented, but can draw attention to several emergent lessons. The three central government strategies for Aboriginal justice are indigenisation, delegation of minor powers, and a surface acknowledgment of Aboriginal culture.[8] To date, 'radical' government reform has consisted of initiatives aimed at using panels of elders to address sentencing, or the introduction of Native justices of the peace, who receive training by mainstream justice officials and are responsible for hearing only minor offences (see, for example, RCAP 1993c). Initiatives that have been based on traditional law have simply been ignored by provincial and federal authorities or have met with active opposition and resistance by the legal profession (see Keenan 1993: 397–8). Academic and professional discussions about Aboriginal justice, including those sponsored by the royal commission, have been dominated by models (such as the American Navaho justice system) that encourage the development of 'carbon copy' courts, or advocate the principle of low-level diversion of minor offences from mainstream courts (see RCAP 1993c, specifically the contributions of Yassie 1993: 407–16; and Zion 1993: 309–25). The RCAP justice report, while maintaining this orientation, also documented the importance of 'justice as healing' initiatives such as family conferencing and healing circles (1996: 120–1, 159–67, 172; see also 187 below).

Indigenisation is the process of substituting Native for non-Native personnel, while preserving the fundamental structure of mainstream systems. Indigenisation has long been associated with colonial practice. In Canada this strategy has been pursued most vigorously in Aboriginal policing (Canada 1992b, 1992c). While policing agreements have been signed with various levels of Aboriginal organizations, the training and certification of Native constables (or special constables) has remained the responsibility of the RCMP or provincial agencies such as the OPP. This training, and the chain of command that ties Native police officers to external authorities, perpetuates mainstream policing patterns. The mere fact of having a Native person in the role of constable may improve the quality of policing on reserve. But many Aboriginal people think police should act as peacekeepers, that is, as individuals who would assume a role combining qualities of social workers, prevention workers, and mediators, rather than simply as law-enforcement officials. To date, however, the role of Aboriginal police remains largely undocumented and evaluated. For example, there are no community-based studies that would clearly document whether Aboriginal police behave differently from non-Native police while patrolling reserves. In other words, it is difficult to assess the extent to which the peacekeeper role is actually practised. In my own experience in Ontario, Native constables have expressed the concern that they do not have sufficient training to assume this type of role, and that, at any rate, their image as police officers prevents them from assuming a wider role. Only those constables who are also from the community they police seem to naturally assume this role – and then it is often an informal one, without band council or community recognition. This is significant, because the role of peacekeepers must devolve from, and be legitimated by, community members.

Diversion projects afford communities the opportunity to divert offenders involved in minor offences from the mainstream system. In these programs, the crown attorney agrees to release the offender to a diversion program where the case is considered by a panel of community members and appropriate action is suggested – commonly community service, restitution, or compensation of victims. Even though diversion programs deal with only a small percentage of potential cases – those designated summary offences by the Crown – these programs are successful because they allow Aboriginal people to express their concerns directly to offenders, and also allow greater recognition of victims' rights. In sentencing panels, a roster or panel of elders sit, along with a judge, hear the details of a wider range of cases, and advise the judge on the appropriateness of various fine options or other sentences. In Ontario, the Ministry of the Attorney General has funded two such programs, in Sandy Lake and Attawapiskat. The initial evaluations of these experiments raise a variety of concerns, most noticeably with the training of elders, the discretion exerted by crown attorneys in deciding which cases should be diverted, and the lack of understanding of the court process by the community (Obonsawin-Irwin 1992b).[9] Such sentencing panels were the precursor to circle courts (sometimes called circle sentencing), which have been embraced by several judges and crown attorneys as an important innovation in the administration of Aboriginal justice (see, for example, *Globe and Mail*, 25 June 1994, A1, A4).

The conservatism of the criminal justice system is evident in the acclaim given to 'circle sentencing,' (a term coined in Yukon courts) widely practised throughout remote Aboriginal communities. Circle courts seem to have arisen in different parts of the country in response to community pressures to make courts more understandable and less foreign to participants and observers (see R. Ross 1992: 110; 1996; Lilles and Stuart 1992). Native elders, clan leaders, or wider networks of community members – in some instances up to seventy-five participants – are involved in the sentencing of people involved in minor offences (see Davies 1992; Lilles and Stuart 1992). The name 'circle court' is taken from the attempt to make the court more hospitable to community members by moving chairs and tables into a less formal arrangement, for example, a circle. The goal is to increase participation by community members, particularly in the sentencing phase. Circle courts are essentially community forums that occur around trials, and allow for the input of family members, peers, or others into the sentence that is handed down by a judge – often in consultation with a small panel of elders or other advisers. Compensation to offenders or public acknowledgment of poor behaviour may be entertained at such circles. Victims are allowed to speak, if not confront, the offenders and, in the process, participants can reach a shared understanding of the social or personal damage that an offender's action has caused.

The strengths of circle courts, and they are many, include an attempt to break down the formality of court settings; a recognition that differential sentencing (measured against standard, national, or 'typical' sentences) is to be expected and promoted; a slight modification of the traditional role (but not the authority) of judges and lawyers; and, significantly, community input into sentencing, which can lead to better utilization of existing rehabilitative and counselling services or to an increased awareness of victim needs and restitution orders (Lilles and Stuart 1992: 4). Perhaps the greatest potential of such procedures lies in the creation of support groups and referral networks among justice and social-service personnel, which offer the promise of local rehabilitation rather than externally imposed punishment or incarceration for offenders.

Advocates of sentencing circles (see, for example, Arnot 1994), stress that this process not only produces better sentencing, but allows a wide range of people to express their feelings and concerns about individual disputes. It is through community participation that sentencing circles can become a vehicle for community healing and reintegration (LaPrairie 1994b: 6). Stevens (1993) stresses that community participation in dispute processing, for example, in instances of family violence, allows offenders to better see abuse for what it is, and to acknowledge a *history* of behaviour. The potential of sentencing circles lies in its use as a forum for community development. As Judge Stuart notes, this process 'improves the capacity of communities to heal individuals and families and ultimately to prevent crime' (cited in LaPrairie 1994b: 9).

Circle courts have been greeted with considerable enthusiasm by Aboriginal people as well as by progressive members of the judiciary; yet as LaPrairie cautions, there has been little or no evaluation of this approach. Several cautionary notes have been raised – for example, the possibility that circles might impose sentences inconsistently across Native communities, or that community values might actually lead to the imposition of harsher sentences. LaPrairie also notes that, unlike family conferencing (see below), which is based on a theoretical (experiential and experimental) model, circle sentencing has emerged without any 'precise theoretical formulation' and in response to political pressures and the environment created by the push toward self-government (1994c: 27). This, however, may be a strength of the approach – circle courts seem to be evolving according to the pragmatic wisdom and evaluation of community participants. LaPrairie argues, however, that there are no clear guidelines on how these circles should best be developed or operated, and no criteria for success. Indeed, there has been a general lack of attention to program evaluation, which, as LaPrairie notes, is partially explained by the fact that programs are often developed in recognition of an obvious gap in services, and then quickly become institutionalized as they 'symbolize fairness, access and equity' (1994c: 38). LaPrairie acknowledges that the need to develop uniform evaluation criteria, and to implement evaluations fairly and dispassionately, is a major challenge for government and Aboriginal planners as communities move toward developing innovative justice services (ibid). Systematic evaluation is necessary to assure mainstream planners and program funders that Aboriginal approaches are efficient, and that tax dollars are being wisely spent. Moreover, evaluation allows successes and failures to be shared across diverse communities.[10]

But what is most obvious about the implementation of circle courts in particular, and state-sponsored programmatic change in general, is *the appearance of radical change when in fact the state has abandoned absolutely none of its control over dispute processing.* As Judge Lilles notes, circle courts do not constitute a 'truly new direction' in sentencing. They can be considered only a small first step toward community justice systems (Lilles and Stuart 1992). Indeed, the circle court perpetuates the adversarial nature of dispute resolution during the trial, retains the final authority of judges, and limits community input to only the most minor of criminal offences. As LaPrairie describes, both family conferences and circle sentencing remain integrated in a very formal legal process – one dominated by police reports, external judges, and authorities (1994b). In fact, there is nothing at all 'radical' about these courts – all authority remains with the crown attorney and judge. There is a danger that the attention and acclaim accorded to circle courts, however warranted, will undermine more broadly based and holistic justice initiatives. Indeed, by suggesting 'flexibility' on the part of the existing system, and by catering to the ideal of community inclusion in the justice system, circle courts serve to sustain the institutional bases of Western law, and continue to entrench the criminal justice system in Aboriginal communities.

It can be argued that such small-scale adjustments to existing practice offer communities the opportunity to debate the nature of change. But attempts to extend provincial courts on reserves, through the use of

Aboriginal elders or justices of the peace, may also impede a community's ability to develop home-grown responses to breaches of family or community peace. Western courts continue to undermine indigenous philosophical systems of law that might serve as the foundation for systems of mediation and reconciliation. The time and effort spent by community members on state-sponsored diversion programs might be better directed toward developing holistic approaches to promote social competence through the development of crisis-intervention programs or to the search for new educational, spiritual, recreational, and employment alternatives for youth.

From the perspective of the wider public, these small-scale changes provide provincial or federal governments with the appearance of having acted in the area of self-government. For example, a media report under the title 'Self-government for natives takes vital steps' drew on a DIAND news release to suggest the establishment of an Aboriginal justice system in Garden River First Nation (*Spectator*, 20 Sept. 1994, A7). But this DIAND initiative – funded to the tune of $25,000 – was in fact the remnant of failed negotiations between the department and the North Shore Tribal Council. In the aftermath of these negotiations, Garden River agreed to proceed with a small initiative to create a diversion program that would result in alternative sentences for Native offenders. In other words, what appeared in news media as a rapid advance in the area of self-government, was a mere chimera when judged against the political stalemate over truly alternative justice systems.

Work by the RCAP suggested the need for more radical reforms (RCAP 1993c; 1996g). As Nungak argues in the quotation opening this chapter, what is required is government recognition (by way of comprehensive policy or constitutional amendment) of the cultural and philosophical foundations of Aboriginal law. Given the conservative nature of the law, such recognition may be necessary before bureaucrats and criminal justice personnel will seriously entertain alternatives to the current system. However, there is reason to believe that ideas of restorative justice are already taking hold, and that arguments about cost efficiencies of alternative approaches may, in fact, drive legislative or constitutional changes.

Restorative Justice

There is no reason why justice in Aboriginal communities has to come from the same premises, perspectives and processes that prevail in the western justice system. Moving from one system to another, however, is no easy task, especially when communities are mired in extensive social turmoil. (R. Ross 1994: 29)

In speaking to Aboriginal people about justice, I am impressed by how quickly the conversation moves toward concepts that mainstream Canadians would normally categorize under the rubric of health or personal development. Aboriginal notions of law are intrinsically linked to ideas of social well-being and to the restoration of positive relationships. Ross recounts how Sandy Lake elders, when involved in sentencing decisions, 'seem to do their best to convince people that they are one step away from heaven instead of one step away from hell' (1992: 166–9; 170–1). This characterization points to essential differences in legal philosophy and process – the difference between treating offenders with respect rather than disdain, between approaches that build on good behaviour rather than punishing bad behaviour, between justice as healing and justice as punishment.

Ross's perspective, as evident in the quotation that begins this section, is important because it raises the possibility of an Aboriginal justice system based on truly alternative ways of knowing – a different legal foundation. Ross's pragmatic suggestions for change embody compromise rather than radical reform. For example, he suggests that the government create regional teams that would be trained in Western and Aboriginal ways and would facilitate the development of community-based justice teams throughout the North. This approach seems reasonable as a transitional measure. But like many experienced lawyers, Ross seems attached to the idea of independent legal authorities (external judges) and questions whether diffuse community control over law is possible (1994: 22). In fact, Ross's analysis seems to be 'all around' ideas of *kin-* and *community-based decision-making.* We must recognize that legal authority can be exercised in small communities without bias – at least bias as it is understood by Westerners.

Most people recognize that intimate knowledge of an offender's family or community history may actually improve the quality of judgment in legal cases. In many cultures, the possibility of 'bias' is overridden by the understanding that friends and kinsmen have an intimate knowledge of the offender and that they, better than strangers, can weigh the complex factors involved in disputes. But it is difficult to move from this understanding to an appreciation that Aboriginal justice programs might dispense with the idea of independent (that is, unrelated or detached) legal authorities altogether, so as to promote mediation systems that are founded in the moral and ethical suasion contained in trust relationships. This, admittedly, is a highly speculative suggestion, and certainly one that will only be realized after much long-term experimentation. But it is possible that traditional Aboriginal legal systems could be based on mediation within extended family and community contexts. This would require Aboriginal people to reexamine the western assumption that legal professionals – 'strangers' – are necessary to settle even the most minor dispute in a community.

Quarrels, disputes, arguments are complex psychosocial events that can be viewed as an opportunity for community intervention. Often the criminal justice system may not be the most appropriate way of dealing with a crisis. For example, the physical neglect of children is often attributable to highly stressful family environments. But as Ross notes, the neglect of children is not easily dealt with under federal law – it is difficult to lay charges against parents who leave children alone, for example, when they are binge drinking (1992: 109).[11] There is little opportunity, given current jurisdictions, for social intervention to be linked to community sanctions. Attempts by front-line workers to develop holistic approaches to assist offenders and victims are ruptured by the nature of Western law. Family violence is perhaps the most vivid example of a behaviour that requires the development of interventions that link programs that have been compartmentalized under justice, health, and social services (Warry and Moffat 1993). The law's emphasis on punishing offenders often interferes with holistic family healing approaches.

A holistic view of justice, then, would shift legal responsibility from external experts to the community. Ideally, community-based justice systems would link individual and community health and would stress the re-establishment of harmony following any rift in the public order. Such a system has been summarized by the Aboriginal Family Healing Joint Steering Committee: 'The focus of the current justice system on the offender alone, rather than the family and community and the offender's accountability to the family and community, restricts the ability of the system to promote a healing approach. The Steering Committee has concluded that a criminal type of process will likely always be required to deal with some individuals and some offences. However, through the development of community-based systems, and community-based and controlled alternatives based on a healing approach, the levels of violence and dysfunction should decrease and the need to resort to the criminal justice system would be reduced' (Ontario 1993: 7–8). This quotation is in keeping with the concept of 'restorative' justice, which rests on a longer tradition of 'popular' or communitarian justice. LaPrairie notes that three important principles of this tradition are the use of informal community processes rather than criminal justice personnel; the inclusion of victims in legal processes; and the treatment of crime as a (social) injury, rather than as simply 'law-breaking' (1994b: 5). She further notes that, given that victims' rights are central to ideas of restorative justice and that victims of offences are predominantly female, it will be essential to assess the degree of satisfaction of women who are most likely to be affected by the implementation of community-based justice systems (LaPrairie 1994c: 27–8).

Ross recounts the example of an Aboriginal youth who, while intoxicated, was given the keys to the family car. The youth subsequently rolled the vehicle, causing the death of a passenger (1994: 16). While there was some question as to whether the youth was in fact driving the car at the time of the accident, it became apparent during the ensuing investigation that the community felt the family was responsible for allowing him to drive, and that the son's conviction, in bringing shame to the family, was an appropriate punishment. That is, Aboriginal values may appeal to wider notions of responsibility or to collective rights, if not 'guilt' in the Western sense.

Shame was an important control mechanism in traditional Aboriginal communities. Many Aboriginal people would approve of techniques that would publicly identify offenders. For example, they would approve of bringing offenders before community meetings to acknowledge their crimes, or to posting the names of offenders on community billboards. Significantly, people suggest that when crimes such as vandalism or fighting occur, the entire family must be the focus of community intervention. Braithwaite (1989) has carefully explored the nature of shame in a South Pacific context, and suggests that systems of justice that set offences within a broader social context of the extended family have enormous potential. LaPrairie has explored the potential of 'family group conferences,' which have been widely embraced in New Zealand and Australia. She notes that these approaches, and those associated with sentencing circles, share a common concern for understanding crime in its broader social context: 'The driving force for new approaches is that the criminal justice system as it presently operates ignores the social context in which crime and disorder occur and, in so doing, decontextualizes the offence and marginalizes various players. By contrast, restorative justice ... is designed to provide the context for ensuring that social rather than legal goals are met ... Restorative justice promises a new paradigm, a new and better way of doing justice, when justice becomes everybody's business.' (LaPrairie 1994b: 2, citing Shearing 1992).

Family group conferences are still an extension of existing courts; operational procedures make it clear that they are meant to be convened only where a crime has been committed and the offender has admitted guilt (see McDonald et al 1994). They are primarily designed to address problems of young offenders, and to ensure group participation in decisions around reparation, compensation, and reconciliation. A key aspect of this approach is the use of peers, role models, or others whom the offender holds in high regard, so that he or she can be made to feel shame (see LaPrairie 1994b: 7; Braithwaite 1989). The rationale for this approach, as articulated by Braithwaite, is that people are law-abiding because they are moral agents – conscience and fear of public disgrace are integrated in the concept of shame, which can be thought of as preventing poor or socially unacceptable behaviour. The use of 'reintegrative shaming' and the expression of remorse can be useful tools for deterrence in the aftermath of crimes. The principle of reintegrative shaming underlies processes that are being labelled 'ceremonies of reintegration,' in which offenders are made to recognize the unacceptable nature of their behaviour, while at the same time being made to realize their value within a community. Ideally, then, the motivation to change or 'correct' behaviour comes from personal realization rather than from the imposition of external deterrents (such as fines or jail terms) (see also LaPrairie 1994b: 6–8; D.B. Moore et al 1994).

If these approaches are to be adapted to reserve life, they must take into account Aboriginal notions concerning conflict itself – ideas that stress avoidance, non-interference, and indirect action. These Native ethics, or rules of behaviour (Brant 1990), make open discussion of personal, family, and community problems or tension difficult, if not impossible. This makes the development of informal systems of justice, based on indirect forms of communication, even more essential. It may be, for example, that Native mediators or peacekeepers could pursue solutions in semi-public or private settings to provide for one-on-one negotiations to obtain a personal commitment from offenders.

Though still embedded in the existing criminal justice system, family conferences would seem to offer greater potential for the transition to Aboriginal justice than sentencing circles, for several reasons. First, they are based originally in Maori concepts of conflict resolution and on recent theoretical work about the role of shame in social control and reintegration (LaPrairie 1994b, Braithwaite 1989). These basic premises, derived from tribal law, seem well suited to Aboriginal communities.[12] Second, family conferences integrate justice, health, and human services and thus provide a holistic approach to conflict, one focused at the level of the family rather than the individual. Third, and most important, family conferences offer the potential for the natural development of Aboriginal systems – an entry point to a truly home-grown form of conflict resolution. To date, family conferences, like sentencing circles, remain linked to external authorities, that is, to summonses or court orders. But they might just as easily be used prior to any formal court intervention or be developed as a natural extention of peacekeeper roles.

The phrase 'justice as healing' might be considered the Aboriginal label for restorative justice – it describes a range of perspectives that are broadly aimed at rethinking the meaning of conflict resolution in Aboriginal communities and developing techniques that restore community order (see, for example, Depew 1994b, Hoyle 1994, LaPrairie 1994b; R. Ross 1994). 'Justice as healing' has at its core an adherence to Aboriginal values about appropriate behaviour and a respect for traditional spiritual practices – including traditional medicine. Sentencing circles are generally thought to be based on Aboriginal healing or talking circles, though they have in fact been heavily influenced by non-Aboriginal self-help approaches. But, as previously argued, these approaches are neither traditional nor about community healing, given the location of legal authority in the external system.

I do not know what a truly separate system of justice based on the principles of restorative justice might look like. But a 'justice as healing' approach can only be developed as part of more broadly based community strategies (see chapter 6). In its simplest iteration, the idea of restorative justice in an Aboriginal context might include procedures to encourage offenders to be given treatment by Native healers, rather than standard punishments associated with incarceration or fines (*Toronto Star*, 11 Sept. 1994, A5). A wide range of other options is conceivable. For example, Aboriginal peacekeepers, working in tandem with elders, social workers, healers, and other volunteers might decide to attempt to mediate family disputes, or set new guidelines for the behaviour of parents and children *before* sending a case of family violence or youth vandalism to a circle court. There are many options for located authority within such a system – certain communities might chose to have peacekeepers mediate a dispute, while others might prefer to involve social workers or elders. An important component of systems of restorative justice are the creation of initiatives to promote positive behaviour. In the Aboriginal context, these would include storytelling forums, cultural programs, and adult-education programs (however informal or indirect) aimed at addressing issues around parenting or family violence.

In short, many Aboriginal people can envision an informal system of restorative justice that is not dependent on a court. Indeed, I suspect that any alternative system that, at first appearance, looks like a court system cannot be based on Aboriginal traditional law or on the principles of restorative justice. This position is similar to that put forward in chapter 3 concerning the relationship between traditional healing and the mainstream medical system. Any Aboriginal court would run the risk of limiting in spatial, conceptual, or behaviourial terms the 'boundaries' of traditional law. But as with traditional medicine, I would argue that there is a place for actual court settings, however informal, as a *complementary* system or as a forum of last resort before referral to the mainstream justice system. Courts might also exist simply as public legal forums where offenders were subject to 'strong talk' from community leaders, or where the community could talk about problems of community life in general (Ryan 1995).

The fact of the matter is that many Aboriginal people have little moral connection, and no social investment, in the mainstream system. We often take for granted, for example, that the role of the crown attorney is to represent 'community standards' in sentencing or in determining the severity of a crime. But which community does the crown attorney represent? In sentencing, the deterrent value of a fine or jail term is one that comes from a foreign system, and is imposed on an Aboriginal person. *For many Aboriginal offenders, the Western legal system is without moral or social relevance.* In contrast, within their own community, Aboriginal offenders are situated among family, friends, and kinsmen, and are scrutinized by the moral gaze of the community. When this community is invested with judicial authority, the Aboriginal offender is much more likely to take the consequences of his or her actions seriously, and to respect community decisions.

Both Aboriginal and mainstream society are searching for innovative ways of dealing with conflict with the law that place less emphasis on punishment and retribution and more emphasis on the provision of social support so that offenders can be reintingrated in communities. Given the social determinants of conflict, alternative justice programs must be flexible enough to assist in the re-weaving of the social fabric of communities. Aboriginal justice, therefore, cannot simply duplicate institutions or programs within the criminal justice system and should not be developed as an adjunct to existing criminal justice programs – for example, as a method of siphoning off 'less serious offences' or decreasing pressure on already overburdened courts. These may, of course, be results of Aboriginal justice programs, but they should not be the rationale for the development of such programs. Rather, Aboriginal justice initiatives should be developed with an eye to community healing – as methods through which community members can comfortably and confidently gather to sort through local problems and assist offenders and victims. Aboriginal justice and community healing are linked by the need to foster a sense of social competence in individuals and families so as to ensure their effective participation in community life. Crimes that result from the many interpersonal problems Aboriginal peoples experience can be punished, or they can be taken as the first sign of the need for community intervention in the process leading to recovery.

Obstacles to Success: Government and Community Attitudes

The government seems content to minimize criticism of the current system and to demonstrate that the existing system can appear responsive to the needs of Aboriginal people. Any government desire for 'reform' is constructed on the conservative notion that Aboriginal people are poised to assume control over a Western system of justice. What appears absent in government initiatives to date is the recognition that legal change could potentially serve as a focus for community development through reintegrating conflict resolution into the life of the community. Federal and provincial government initiatives, while producing an array of pilot projects and programs, have failed to yield a coordinated, comprehensive policy on Aboriginal justice, though such comprehensive policies have been pursued, with considerable effectiveness, in such areas as health care and education.

The criminal justice system compartmentalizes law as a special domain of knowledge and activity, and focuses on individual behaviour, deviance, and wrongdoing, rather than addressing the socio-economic determinants of community conflict. As Depew (1994a: i) notes, this perspective helps to 'obscure' promising focuses for change – the development of programs that might be derived from community standards of law and order.[13] Depew's observations, in the context of Aboriginal policing, reflect his training as an anthropologist. He believes that greater attention must be given to the analysis of the behaviour of policing patterns with the 'unique forms of interaction' that exist in Aboriginal communities –

patterns of behaviour that are shaped by a complex of environmental factors of a cultural, social, demographic, economic, and political nature (ibid). Put simply, much of what alternative or restorative justice is about is 'beyond the mandate' of the criminal justice system. For innovative policy reform to occur, a paradigm shift has to occur that will allow policy-makers to understand the holistic nature of traditional law, so as to escape the artificial confines of existing justice programs. Such an understanding is needed to ensure the development of innovative funding envelopes that would, for example, see the Attorney General or Department of Justice fund programs that many might consider to be the mandate of the Ministry of Health or of Community and Social Services. The research conducted by Hoyle, Depew, LaPrairie, Ross, and Ryan, cited above, has produced examples of the long-term and innovative work that can enhance the project of Aboriginal justice. But it is also clear that much of this advanced thinking has yet to find wider acceptance within the justice system itself, nor have these ideas been translated into action.

The notion of restorative justice is given impetus by more general changes that are occurring to restructure the system. Part of this impetus derives from increasing public concern with the rights of victims and with renovation of the Young Offenders Act (*Toronto Star* 4 Dec. 1994, D4). For example, for reasons of fiscal restraint the federal government is particularly concerned that a real shift to rehabilitation occur for young offenders, especially in non-violent offences. Community programs are cost-effective when compared to institutional care. Currently the federal government spends about $200 million a year on youth justice – $150 million of this amount supports institutional care (ibid). But these proposed changes take place against a backdrop of public opinion, fed by media reports of violent crime, which calls for harsher sentences and a 'punishment' mentality with regard to young offenders. The challenge of social science is to make the inherent logic and cost-efficiency of community alternatives evident to the general public, so as to foster an appropriate environment where community-based experiments will be embraced.

What is clear, however, is the lack of federal and provincial support for innovative programs that might demonstrate such savings – savings in dollars and human lives – over time. The reader should recall, for example, that to date there has been little government support for the creation of funding envelopes that would transcend the artificial boundaries between health and justice. For example, in Ontario, even though Aboriginal organizations identified justice issues as central to the Aboriginal Healing and Wellness Strategy, three key justice ministries – the Attorney

General, Solicitor General, and Corrections – refused to participate in the ongoing funding of the initiative.

Testifying before the royal commission, Don Auger notes that the cost of remote courts, coupled with the expense of keeping convicted offenders in jail for the fifteen days, is between $25,000 and $30,000. This expense, he states, is without any rehabilitative effect (92-10-27 50. PG 71). Jonathan Rudin (Ottawa ON. 92-11-25 111. PG 259) notes that a sentencing pilot project in Attawapiskat received $100,000 from the Ontario Attorney General. This financial commitment supports the hiring of a coordinator, costs of the elder panel, and office expenses (Ottawa ON. 92-11-25 99. Reg Louttit. PG 244). Rudin states that offenders involved in the program might have otherwise ended up in jail at a cost of $60,000 or $70,000 a year. Even if the program results in community sentences for five or six people per year, such programs potentially save the correctional-services system hundreds of thousands of dollars. But Rudin acknowledges 'that is not how the accounting system works because that is $100,000 of the Attorney General's money and the $350,000 that Corrections gets to save doesn't get factored in' to assessments of the cost of new or experimental programs. In fact, any economic assessment is complex because the Ministry of the Attorney General, which funds the project, operates with a separate budget and bureaucracy from Correctional Services or, to put it more bluntly, because the government is incapable of innovative thinking that would transcend these artificial boundaries. Rudin suggests an overall saving of $350,000, based on an range of five to seven person years of jail time at a cost of $60,000 to $70,000 per person. This is a conservative estimate, because it does not include the costs of travel, salary, and legal-aid fees for lawyers, judges, or native court workers that might be saved by developing a fully controlled community-based system.

The current, if unstated, policy of the Ontario Ministry of the Attorney General is that alternative programs should be developed 'at low cost or no cost.' There is concern, for example, that even if the ministry were to fund a single program in each of the 130 Aboriginal communities in Ontario, at an average cost of $100,000, then the total cost to the ministry would be in the vicinity of $13 million. Would the overall savings to the Ontario taxpayer exceed this amount? Most certainly, the answer is yes. But this is only part of the picture. As we have seen, Aboriginal people are also seeking local control over correctional programs – the development of bush camps and other small-scale facilities that would supplant or replace jails.

What would happen if Aboriginal people had control over their own justice system? Over the long term, there would have to be a downsizing and reorganization of correctional facilities – perhaps even the closure of some institutions, such as the Kenora jail, where the majority of the inmate population is Native (see RCAP 1996g: 292). There is, of course, much at stake here. The development of Aboriginal systems clearly threatens many interests in what is a massive, $10 billion criminal justice industry.[14] And while there is hope that fiscal arguments will make community-based systems more attractive, it is easy to understand how criminal justice personnel have a vested interest in maintaining the status quo. As many Aboriginal leaders have noted, Indians are big business, and the long-term development of self-government will result in the loss of non-Native jobs in many service industries, including health and justice. But as the royal commission's analysis of 'cost' of justice makes clear, even after several major Aboriginal justice enquiries, the government has been unable, or unwilling to provide a baseline figure for justice services against which analysts could measure the cost of reforms (1996g: 294).

To date, community-based research into traditional law and community dynamics has been swamped by the work of lawyers, criminologists, and political scientists who have focused on the nature of Aboriginal conflict with the law. As Havemann et al note, despite the constitutional feasibility of Native courts, the bureaucratic and political realities of creating such courts have not been addressed by social scientists (1985: 88; see also Lajeunesse 1991; Rudin and Russell 1993; Warry 1991a). Much more community-based research is required to establish how Aboriginal justice systems might operate in practice, and to determine how justice programs can be integrated with other human services, and what interface mechanisms can be created to complement the mainstream system.

Within Ontario, communities vary dramatically in their experience with, and reliance on, provincial courts and policing. Differences between communities are particularly evident between Southern and remote 'fly-in' communities in the North. There are communities that have signed Native policing agreements or have already developed justice committees, elders' panels and Section 107 courts, and communities that continue to rely on the provincial courts held off reserve. In the far North, there are communities that continue to sustain traditional systems of justice, that have refused to allow police onto reserves, and where appeals to external criminal justice authorities occur in only the most serious cases. Stenning (1992: 2–3; cited in Depew 1994a) notes that one remote community had only three to four investigative visits over the past ten years; the community leadership simply took the view that police activities were not appropriate or desirable for their community. In contrast, there are other communities, such as those in the North Shore area, where OPP patrols have been a regular part of reserve life for years, and where the state legal system is well entrenched.

The state's control over conflict resolution is an example of 'structural communication' that reinforces inequality between Native and non-Native authorities and allows state authorities to influence local ideas about social competence and deviant behaviour (see Arno 1985; Warry 1991a). The extension of justice and policing systems into Native communities is a primary means through which the state exerts its control over Native communities. Not surprisingly, many communities are highly resistant to the notion of legal change. Because the potential for violence is a part of their life, they expect a strong police and judiciary to control offenders who would threaten the fabric of community life. The reality is that, after decades of involvement with Western police and courts, many Aboriginal people have assimilated Western notions of law and order – just as they have ideas about medicine. LaPrairie notes how many community studies, including her own research among the Cree, show that Aboriginal people are often concerned about the leniency of the mainstream system (personal communication). My experience in the North Shore area confirms this view. We must recognize, then, that many Aboriginal people see much that is good in the Western legal system. We cannot easily dismiss the fact that many Aboriginal people would call for harsher sentences, a more demanding parole system, or greater police presence on reserve. Some Aboriginal communities are deeply divided on questions of law and order. Within a single community there may be individuals who want a greater role for state police or an enhanced role for Native peacekeepers. And while many people are able to speak idealistically about the nature of restorative justice, other community members may express reluctance about accepting offenders back into their communities – particularly those convicted of serious offences. Communities may also be divided as to what kinds of offences they would like to handle themselves, and which crimes should be left to be handled by the existing criminal justice system (see Depew 1994a: 96–7; Auger et al 1992; Clairmont 1992). Many of these conflicts and contradictions arise from the disjuncture between peoples' ideals and their more pragmatic assessment of current realities. It is up to the Aboriginal leadership to ensure that their communities engage in the painstaking and politically intensive work that needs to be done to develop alternative programs.

Applied social-science research can contribute to the development of alternative justice systems. The work of Hoyle (1995) and Ryan (1995), for example, is meant to provide communities with a solid platform of information on which to base decisions about the direction of legal change. These changes must be compatible with local community standards. There is a wide array of potential options for Aboriginal justice programs. Each of these options – for example, who should be selected to sit on an elders' panel – is absolute critical and potentially explosive given the dynamics of community politics. There is a need, for example, for greater understanding of the basis of Aboriginal legal authority. To date, Native justices of the peace and elders' panels have been recruited by criminal justice personnel, rather than being elected or selected by communities. Lawyers and judges have sometimes accepted the legitimacy of elders on the assumption that seniors are automatically appropriate custodians of legal wisdom. This naïveté limits the involvement of younger people who may be respected in the community or youth who may be important peer counsellors. Not surprisingly, in certain instances, elders involved in circle courts have also demonstrated an inherent conservatism, so that sentences meted out may actually be harsher than those under mainstream courts.

These tensions point to the need for a solid understanding of the social and political environment in which alternative justice programs will be set. The legitimacy of Aboriginal systems of justice depends on community discussions and agreement about who will be given the authority to act as mediators or peacekeepers, and the roles these individuals will play in relation to chief and council. Some Aboriginal leaders have suggested that First Nations' councils should select mediators or magistrates. Such practices, however, threaten Western legal ideals concerning the 'independence' of the judiciary.

There is also a need for research and consultation into regional, as opposed to First Nations', justice programs. The RCAP suggested that non-Natives committing offences on reserve might choose between systems (Native or non-Native) to have their cases heard (1996g: 312). The RCAP suggested that tribal council, regional, or national appellate courts could be developed – with the Supreme Court as the ultimate court of appeal. Several North Shore leaders have suggested that regional mediation panels or appeal mechanisms would enhance the legitimacy of local justice programs, at least until the legitimacy of local mediators is established. In the case of informal systems, 'appeals' might take on the appearance of referrals to formal courts. But ultimately, there is a need to appeal to an Aboriginal 'higher court' to sustain the integrity of local systems. To my knowledge such a system has not yet been devised or attempted. A regional court, for example, administered by a tribal council or PTO, would potentially enhance local autonomy over conflict resolution and reduce legal and communicative dissonance between Native and non-Native courts, by providing an internal appeal mechanism for litigants who believe kinship relations, political rivalries, or other local conflicts have biased particular cases.

Finally, communities will have to enter into formal protocol arrangements to map out 'interface' systems of referral and appeal. Interface protocols are also required to grapple with incidents where non-residents commit offences on reserve, or are sued in civil actions by Aboriginal people. Although there may be communities, particularly in the remote North, which can maintain a totally separate system of justice, even these communities may prefer to ensure that the state criminal justice system can be relied upon in violent cases that are too serious or dangerous to be handled locally. Many Aboriginal people see the need for a continuing police and court role to process offences such as serious incidents of sexual assault, aggravated assault, and murder. The Canadian public, too, will demand some level of integration between state and local law, so that the notion of a totally independent Aboriginal justice system, while conceivable, does not appear to be politically palatable at present.

These obstacles, however complex in appearance, can be resolved as part of ongoing community consultation, program planning, and evaluation. They are, in fact, common problems that have been resolved in a variety of ways in countries operating with plural systems of law.

To reiterate, there is a great deal of work to be done. Given the conservative nature of the current system, the development of alternative justice programs will take decades. But much preliminary work has already been accomplished, and the broad outlines of such Aboriginal systems are clearly visible to many Aboriginal people. Many of the pragmatic issues noted here are secondary when judged against a more important obstacle – the need to shift both government perceptions and, to a certain extent, the expectations of some community members in order to establish a long-term vision of Aboriginal justice. This vision is embedded in notions of restorative justice – of holistic processes that will contribute to both individual healing and the development of healthier communities.

Conclusion

The law is a primary instrument of state power and colonial control. State control over conflict resolution and dispute processing disempowers Native communities by usurping the ability of Native people to define and debate the norms of their communities. 'Fly-in' courts, such as those existing in the remote North, epitomize this legal dependency. The Canadian state currently denies that Native people possess the capacity to competently resolve internal problems of law and order. And so communities must passively await the arrival and 'judgement' of outside experts. The process is less obvious, but no less insidious, in the South, where Native people must travel great distances by road to urban centres, to stand before courts that are constructed on Western cultural assumptions, and that appeal to 'community standards' that bear no witness to the integrity of the kin-based social order of the reserve.

In the quotation that begins this chapter, Zebedee Nungak questions the value of studying traditional law, given the continuing domination of the criminal justice system. He suggests that anthropological (or other community-based) studies will be valuable only after communities have obtained the power to determine what laws should be implemented or what values emphasized [Ottawa ON. 92-11-25 13. PG 60–1]. I understand the frustration and pragmatism contained in these remarks. I am often dismissive of research that does not lead immediately to new approaches or ideas. And in my experience, it is difficult for many Natives and non-Natives to understand a vision of an Aboriginal justice system that significantly diverges from the existing system. But over the past decade there has been a slow recognition of the value of holistic approaches to law (see, for example, R. Ross, 1996). The work of Hoyle (1995) and Ryan (1995) demonstrates how community-based research can generate dialogue and debate that is necessary in order to lay the foundation for alternative justice programs. More generally, research on alternative justice has demonstrated the cost efficiency of mediation and other community-based systems (Merry and Milner 1995).

In this chapter I have tried to convey a rather complex understanding about the nature of law in a plural society. But my essential message is simple. Aboriginal people should have the right to control their own justice services, and to determine what behaviours are 'right' or 'wrong' within their communities. But, at the same time, I do not believe that most Aboriginal communities are even remotely close to being able to reach consensus on what type of justice system they would like to see designed and implemented in their communities.

The linkage between 'criminal' behaviour, social environment, and mental-health problems makes the development of culturally appropriate justice services a key component of the quest for self-government. The relationship between law and community healing is most evident in instances of family conflict – situations that cry out for compassion and healing rather than punishment. The conservative nature of legal institutions makes it extremely difficult to 'decriminalize' individual behaviour: the state insists on punishing behaviour in Aboriginal communities, and in so doing, fails to recognize the socioeconomic determinants of community conflict.

'Justice as healing' has as its starting-point the incredibly obvious, yet often subtle, relationship between community health and the criminalization of behaviour. The criminal-justice system's traditional emphasis on 'law breaking,' policing, and corrections is at odds with the development of more holistic approaches that would encourage the integration of health and justice services, or that would take as their starting-point the development of social competence, rather than the punishment of deviance. Holistic justice systems need not be based on formal institutions like courts. Rather than replacing courts, they should be seen as complementary programs that displace, through the promotion of community competence, the need for more formal interventions.

The idea that alternative justice programs can serve as a locus for community healing and development is greatly underestimated by non-Native policy-makers who continue to compartmentalize law. Aboriginal legal values point the way to new ways of settling disputes. Aboriginal notions about law lay bare all that is wrong about our own legal system, and point to more human ways of maintaining the peace and restoring harmony to relationships when conflict has arisen. It is ironic that in Ontario in 1996 Attorney General Charles Harnick suggested that there is a need to shift to greater use of mediation. This shift is driven by arguments about cost-effectiveness. But others interested in legal reform point to the many benefits of mediation as a more flexible and less adversarial system of justice. Those interested in reform of the current system envision community justice systems where the presence of external police and judges is severely curtailed, if not eliminated.

But even where the conceptual shadows of such a justice system are beginning to emerge, communities face two fundamental obstacles to the creation of parallel systems. One of these is externally located in the criminal justice system's continuing conservatism and reluctance to relinquish control over justice. This continuing desire to perpetuate state control is masked by a rationale of concern for the protection of individual rights and the need for 'one law.' Another critical obstacle is located internally within Aboriginal communities – with the lack of capacity that would enable people to mobilize, and to agree on, a common set of values that can act as the foundation to alternative systems. There remains much to be accomplished in creating environments where political factionalism can be overcome, where public participation is increased, and where community healing can begin. It is to these issues that I now turn.

6

Visions of Community Healing

My dream for my daughter is that she will speak her language, that she will feel proud of who she is as an Anicinabe person. The only way I can make that dream come true is by healing myself. We have to start healing, and the first step in healing is talking about what happened ... We cannot heal without a spiritual foundation. Whatever spiritual foundation you choose is your business, but we have to heal from a spiritual base. Without spirituality, we will never heal. (Fort Alexander MB. 92-10-29 62. Karen Courchene. PG 88)

Introduction

The origin of the term 'community healing' is obscure. The phrase has been used by political leaders in many contexts – for example, in seeking compensation for residential-school experiences and in negotiations between Aboriginal people and Christian churches (see Furniss 1995: 118–20, appendix). Ovide Mercredi has promoted the idea that community healing is part of the self-determination movement, and the Royal Commission on Aboriginal Peoples has spoken of healing and reconciliation between Aboriginal people and the Canadian state. More recently, at a sacred assembly in Hull, Quebec, Aboriginal leaders affirmed the need to promote reconciliation with dominant institutions through education and spiritual awareness. But ideas about community healing have been emerging since the 1980s with the expansion of treatment programs and self-help groups, some of which, as noted in the previous chapter, were based in prisons and correctional centres. These self-help groups focused on how Native culture and spirituality could assist inmates in recovery from alcoholism, residential-school experiences, sexual abuse, and family violence. At the same time, communities were sharing community-development experiences, as, for example, in the case of Alkali Lake. Community healing, then, is tied to many processes – community development, cultural revitalization, spiritual rebirth, and national reconciliation.

Along with a colleague, Christopher Justice, I recently had the opportunity to consult with North Shore communities about the nature of community healing (Justice and Warry 1996). This project, conducted on behalf of the Anishnabe Health Board, was sponsored by the Solicitor General of Ontario. The project mandate was to develop a 'blueprint' for community healing in northern First Nations. The terms of reference called for the preparation of a manual that would assist front-line workers in developing community-healing projects. The project goals emphasized integrated service delivery, the use of Ojibwa values, and a holistic understanding of individual, family, and community life. We were to create a blueprint that was transferrable to other Aboriginal communities.

From an academic perspective, this project was extremely gratifying because it lent itself to broad discussions of community life. We talked with people about many questions that interest social scientists: the nature and meaning of communities, the link between individual and corporate action and complex issues of health and well-being. It became clear through these conversations that an understanding of the process of community healing has been emerging over the past decade, and continues to accelerate as communities find new ways of nourishing the spiritual and cultural well-being of their members.

In the end, we produced a discussion paper for Aboriginal and government policy-makers, staff, and leaders, in which North Shore people shared their ideas about the prospects for, and obstacles to, community healing. This discussion paper relied on people's own words to carry their vision of healthy communities to other Aboriginal people in Ontario.[1] From an applied perspective the success of this project will be determined by whether the discussion paper assists people to think and to talk about community healing, or to create specific strategies for their communities. But for those people involved in our interviews and conversations, the research process clearly had therapeutic and intellectual value – for many people it was the first time that they had the opportunity to discuss in any detail the nature of individual and community healing.

Very early in the project, we found that the word 'blueprint' lacked meaning for people. It seem to conjure up an overly formalized image of planning. People suggested that community healing was so complex a process that no single model would apply to all communities. We struggled with the idea of a blueprint *for* healing. It seemed to imply *control* over life.[2] People told us that you cannot control change in this way. We began to realize that they saw healing as occurring *naturally* in their communities. They spoke of the natural link between individual growth and the slow transformation of their communities. Community healing would be a very long process, perhaps taking generations. On the other hand, people told us that communities could be proactive. Staff and council could facilitate the healing process by providing an appropriate 'climate' or 'environment' for healing. Key consultants suggested approaches (not solutions) to community healing that are inherently personal and spiritual. Personal healing journeys involve self-discovery. They are seen as the core experiential foundation to larger community and regional processes.

Chiefs, councillors, and human-service staff also stressed that structural and social organizational change was integral to the process of individual and community healing. Political institutions can be changed or reorganized to enhance healing initiatives. Structural changes, such as those associated with the reorganization of First Nations councils and administration, are also personal processes – institutional change implies collective growth of the people who comprise the organization. Conversely, organizational problems are often the result of negative patterns of interaction that, for example, reinforce unhealthy behaviours in the workplace. It is virtually impossible to separate individual and community healing. At almost every turn we were cautioned that for structural change to occur, people need to change many basic behaviours and values. First and foremost, people need to 'end the denial' about the problems that exist in their communities and that, to a great extent, are the product of colonial history. People also need to establish constructive communication processes that will foster strong and positive interpersonal relationships. By fostering a positive environment for self-expression, communities can promote greater participation in community affairs.

We asked people directly about the relationship between community healing and self-government. The central message I took from these discussions is that self-government is less about constitutional reform or external recognition of Aboriginal rights, and more about internal creation of self-sufficiency and *exercise* of pre-existing, inalienable rights. The goal of self-government requires that people create a positive environment for change, where individuals are empowered to contribute to community well-being, and, once empowered, feel emotionally safe and spiritually centred to exercise their inherent rights.

This chapter examines a few key elements in the process of community healing. I use key consultants' thoughts on community life to revisit previous discussions of mental health, personal healing, culture, and tradition. This discussion is overlain with analysis about the nature of community life and the need for capacity building in First Nations.[3] I conclude with a discussion of how political change is related to the process of community healing.

Individual and Community Healing: Cultural Revitalization

A healing journey is about dealing with those issues that you are carrying, that pain. We can always shove that pain back but after a while there is so much inside ... that is why we have so many people drinking because it temporarily numbs the pain.

Individual healing is about overcoming personal problems that are debilitating to community life. These include such behaviour as alcohol abuse, but also negative emotions and behaviour such as jealousy or anger. In chapter 3 I briefly discussed the nature of personal healing journeys. Personal healing journeys are lifelong struggles to grapple with the intergenerational effects of various forms of abuse, neglect, or loss of identity. These journeys are the core of what we can think of as 'individual' healing. Here I am interested in the relationship between these experiences and community-level processes.

Community healing starts with the individual and then radiates out into the community and when other people see that, it spreads ... I've got three words. Ownership of self. You have to arrive at that. You can't do that through comments from others. Some people may come out and say how they see you. But the person has to pick it up themself.

We are getting stronger and people are going on their healing journeys. The more this happens the more we will heal. People must realize that we need this healing and it has to begin on the individual level. Our families are like mobiles. When one makes a different move it affects the whole family. So if I start healing it will spread.

The willingness of people to talk to an outsider about physical and sexual abuse they have experienced (or perpetrated) or to recount how alcoholism led to personal problems or conflict with the law, speaks to me of an enormous well of spiritual strength. Common to all healing journeys is the starting-point of self-acknowledgment, which leads to ending denial. This experience is sometimes spoken of, *post facto*, as honesty of self. Honesty is a core Anishnabe value and is represented as one of Seven Grandfathers or traditional teachings. The concept is central to self-actualization.

Over the past decade, there has been an increasingly open dialogue about social problems that promises more direct forms of acknowledgment and intervention in future. Front-line workers now speak of how some communities are in denial and how the open and honest evaluation of family violence, sexual abuse, or alcoholism is critical to the development of healthy patterns of interaction. During the past decade, for example, the issue of sexual abuse has become more openly discussed, and Native researchers have openly addressed this issue in order to lay the foundation for a variety of child and family initiatives (see, for example, Manotsaywin 1990; LaRocque 1993). What now concerns workers is that as awareness programs succeed, and denial of social problems ends, the need for intervention and direct service increases. This is because people who have ended their denial require counselling and other types of support, which in turn require workers to obtain new professional skills.

Once a person has acknowledged their need for healing, the next step is to share their experience with others – at first to seek support and, later, to offer knowledge that might be of value to others. This sharing takes place through a number of approaches – for example, through AA meetings, treatment programs, and, increasingly, in healing or talking circles. Individuals may also share their experiences indirectly with community members who they suspect might be in denial. But as noted in chapter 4, for many Native people directly intervening in another's life is problematic. Some people feel, for example, that it is arrogant to offer even the suggestion that what has worked for yourself may also be appropriate to a friend or family member's healing journey. A more appropriate strategy is to live a good life, that is, to act as a role model to others in the community.

We heard people use the phrase 'relationship communities' to emphasize the interconnectedness of all individuals on reserve (and beyond). They spoke, for example, of how the hurt of one person was felt by all.[4] This emphasis on relationships, rather than on individuals, became an important focus in our discussions. People stressed that individual behaviour must be viewed within the context of family and community life. As mentioned in the previous chapter, there was a pervasive sense of collective responsibility, which overshadows any notions of individual wrongdoing. People stressed that it was the responsibility of communities (and not simply of families) to teach children language, culture, and spirituality in order to inculcate in them cultural values that are essential to the promotion of good behaviour and positive self-esteem.

Some people mentioned how this collective ideal is at odds with the values of the dominant society, which promote individual status and rights. They suggested that many people did not feel a sense of communal responsibility and that, in fact, communities were fragmented (see below). For example, several individuals bemoaned the fact that they seldom sensed a community spirit that is evidenced in 'random acts of kindness' (what anthropologists would refer to as generalized reciprocity) such as shovelling the snow off a neighbour's driveway. Indeed, people suggested that it was only in times of crisis that a community spirit was evident. At the most basic level, then, people's statements about healing journeys comment on the relationship between individual and group behaviour, or between individual and cultural identity.

Anthony Wallace analysed the relationship between personal transformation and participation in larger revitalization movements. Wallace offered the concept of 'mazeway' in order to describe the manner in which individuals discover personal meaning and connect themselves to ideologies of change, which arise when societies are undergoing rapid sociopolitical and religious transformation (1956a, 1956b; see also 1969).[5] In the mazeway a person struggles with their personal identity but emerges with a new sense of self, which has been influenced by ideas taken from a larger social movement. For example, a person's understanding of a new religion can resonate with their sense of identity and help them to find new understanding of the world. People emerge from the mazeway reborn, if you will, to be adherents to a new vision of society and active participants in a social or religious movement. Wallace was suggesting ways in which people experience conversion to new ideologies – often through revelatory moments – which seem to offer hope for sorting out complex and contradictory messages in a rapidly changing world.

The concept of the mazeway has a certain analytic appeal in trying to assess current Native conceptions of personal and community transformation. The mazeway metaphor speaks to temporary setbacks, reversals, and the confusion that can accompany any search for personal or cultural identity. The metaphor of a healing journey reminds us that these personal spiritual searches can entail a lifelong struggle and gradual growth. Both images link individual and community revitalization. There are certainly elements of conversion, spiritual revelation, and transformative thinking in people's accounts of their personal healing journeys. Individuals speak of dreams and visions containing eagles or other symbols of spiritual awareness, which were instrumental to their own healing journeys. A healing journey may begin through a random meeting with an elder on a bus, on the street, or not so randomly, at a Friendship Centre or a powwow. The gift of tobacco, an eagle feather, or simply words of encouragement can ignite a lifelong process where individuals struggle to understand their culture. For others, these journeys results from the shared experiences of recovery that are nurtured through AA or other self-help groups. Personal healing journeys – what might be glossed as illness-to-health experiences – are rife with images of movement, discovery, and exploration. Conversations about healing often include references to extensive travel throughout Canada, from reserves to cities, or to the four directions. Ultimately, these journeys speak of returning Home – whether it be to an actual reserve, to a reunion with family, or, more metaphorically, to the centre of a culture. And at every turn people are sparked to make major changes in their personal lifestyles because they come to an awareness of their cultural identity.

Wallace's analysis, I think, is too suggestive of irrational or unconscious psychological processes to fully apply to the contemporary Aboriginal reality. Wallace analysed syncretic movements such as the Ghost Dance and the Handsome Lake movement, which arose during a time when Aboriginal populations were experiencing rapid decline from disease, forced assimilation, and resettlement onto reserves. His analysis was based on a view of Aboriginal culture as passive and under assault from Western ways – the creation of new forms of belief and behaviour was ultimately tied to the need to assimilate Western ideas. With hindsight and a contemporary understanding of Aboriginal resistance to the dominant culture, it is clear that Aboriginal people are active participants in a process of decolonization. People pragmatically borrow elements of Western culture while protecting Indian ways that can serve as the basis for their cultural identity.

Today, individuals speak of personal, spiritual awakening and how this awareness allows individuals to contribute to community revitalization in general. The everyday actions of healthy individuals contribute to the sociopolitical objective of self-determination and self-government. Wallace spoke of conversion to new syncretic ideologies that incorporated elements of Western or Christian belief and afforded indigenous peoples the opportunity to create new norms to replace those lost through the attack on traditional systems of meaning. The contemporary flux of ideological and spiritual change in Aboriginal communities reverses this process: many people seek to abandon Western ways to rediscover traditional Indian values and return to authentic Aboriginal culture. And it is here that much confusion arises – for there remains great debate in Aboriginal communities about the best or most appropriate way to revitalize traditional practices for contemporary community life. As I suggested in chapter 3, some people are concerned that many traditional ways have been permanently lost, or are at risk of being lost with the death of a generation of elders who are viewed as keepers of traditional knowledge. There is suspicion that even basic ceremonies and practices are not authentic, because they represent not Ojibwa, Iroquois, or Cree ritual ways but some amalgamation of pan-Indian practices. There is concern that some people who represent themselves as traditional teachers or medicine men are poorly motivated or are 'making things up' as they go along. And there is the fundamentalist Christian's concern that a return to traditional beliefs is a return to superstition, paganism, or devil worship.

When asked to suggest the one thing that is central to community healing, people often reply that they must 'know their culture' or utilize traditional values, such as honesty, respect, caring, and sharing, in their everyday lives. And when pressed about the authenticity of ceremonies, people often suggest that there is no right or wrong way of conducting a specific ceremony so long as the ritual is done with good intentions or a 'good heart.' People realize that there are many paths to personal healing. And this recognition brings with it a tolerance for other people's personal beliefs, and the expectation that 'fundamentalist' attitudes – be they the self-righteous indignation of Christian Pentecostals or the rigid adherence of traditionalists who criticize ceremonies that do not follow some 'correct' and local traditional formulas – are to be avoided.

Media images of drumming, dancing, and Native arts may suggest to non-Natives that communities are awash in opportunities for individuals to participate in traditional ways. But knowledge of tradition or traditional practices is by no means uniform within communities, or across them. I have been taken aback, as happened recently when a woman told me she had never even heard of a purification (sweat) lodge until the previous year. She then spoke with astonishment of her first experience in the lodge and of how she was ignorant of Native spirituality. She talked with some disappointment about how she had not experienced some personal revelation while in the lodge. And she spoke with wonder at how naturally her young daughter, who was not yet five years old, had said she had seen spirits 'as if watching them on TV' while in the lodge. Similarly, some individuals are only now beginning to learn the fundamental tools for talking and thinking about their culture – the name of their *dodem*, the sacred plants, or the way to smudge. For some people the return to traditional ways involves some initial unease as they acknowledge their lack of understanding of Indian culture and take the risk of being criticized as they begin to participate in ceremonies. In other words, Aboriginal cultural revitalization, though gaining momentum, is a process that needs to be fostered and nourished. One of the most fundamental challenges facing communities is to create environments where people can participate in ceremonies or learn traditional ways.

Colonial History, Community Dynamics

North Shore reserves developed gradually over the century following the signing of the Robinson Huron treaty. In the latter half of the nineteenth century, extended families were dispersed geographically and communities developed near trading posts, near the borders of small towns, or close to major rivers and lakes. Some of these extended families operated small farms; others engaged in a variety of seasonal employment, including fishing, trapping, and forestry. Movement between communities was common. There was considerable movement between Manitoulin Island and the North Shore area, as well as across the border into the United States. There was always some intermarriage with non-Native families, including traders and farmers residing in local communities. Children were sent off reserve to a variety of residential and industrial schools, where they lived for eight to ten months of the year. People moved off and on reserve with considerable ease – in order to pursue work, to be closer to towns, and for a variety of other personal reasons. Families remained separated in geographic space, unconnected by roads, and economically self-sufficient. Until the 1960s, interaction between families was much less than it is today. Even visiting another family could entail a difficult walk, particularly in winter. Often families came together only for funerals or to celebrate marriages.

During the historic period, as Jamieson notes (1986: 118), band administrative records were poorly kept, and were subject to the whims of Indian agents who had various views on the morality of mixed marriages. Often names were confused – some members used their Indian names, or translations of Indian names in English; others took the names of their white fathers, many of whom lived on Indian land with their Native wives. Not surprisingly, over several generations considerable concern, if not rivalry, developed between various families concerning the nature of Indian status. These rivalries were rekindled in the late 1980s with Bill C31 and the return of Native women who, along with their children, and occasionally accompanied by their white spouses, began to reclaim their status and return to the reserve.

By the 1940s and 1950s reserves had also become divided by Catholic and Anglican missions, who vied for converts and took responsibility for education. The battle for Native souls was at times fierce and unforgiving. Elders speak of how they attempted to send their sons and daughters to mission schools located near their homes, only to have their children turned away because they belonged to the wrong denomination. Parents were subsequently forced to ask their children to walk many kilometres to an appropriate school or to send their children to residential schools, or were forced to abandon their hopes for their children's education. Not surprisingly, these and other small acts of religious conflict became the seeds of harsh memories and fuelled the development of religious antagonisms that still overlie family divisions today. Further confusing the development of religious differences was the continuing allegiance, to varying degrees, to traditional ways. Some Christian families came to abandon traditional spiritual ways, and even to denigrate them as pagan. Other families managed to sustain a belief in traditions or to blend their conception of a Christian God with the Native Creator. And a small number of traditional people continued to practice Indian medicine, to act as guardians of spiritual knowledge, and to protect artefacts such as sacred pipes and medicine bundles. Most recently, Pentecostalism, with its emphasis on sobriety and self-reliance, has found an audience on many reserves.

Contemporary communities are in many ways a post-1960s phenomenon, stimulated by government social-welfare policy, that encouraged geographically isolated families to coalesce around a central location to provide housing and other modern conveniences, including water and electricity (cf. Asch 1988). Today reserve life is characterized by complex family relationships. There are those that trace their lineage through five generations to chiefs or other original signatories to treaties. In some communities these members make claims to 'original membership,' which suggests to some that they have claims to a higher status or preferential treatment. Conversely, members of these founding families may feel that others in the community do not appreciate the historical status of their family. They feel that they have significant insight into the history of the community that could be shared, or should be valued, but is instead disclaimed or denigrated by others in the community. For example, descendants of early chiefs can be blamed for converting to Christianity, abandoning their culture, or for 'selling out' through the treaty process or through relationships with Indian agents. In such cases, family history becomes the fodder for contemporary political battles. Today, colonial history is intertwined with continuing colonial policy – for example, with the access to limited resources, including band jobs and scarce housing. As one elder stated: 'They say none of us belong here. There is resentment. There is always jealousy here and so it is hard to get things done. At the band meetings there is friction. Also there is religion. Some people go to church. When you go you can feel people looking at you with resentment. Also our resources are depleting. There isn't enough houses. Sometimes you are promised a house and someone else gets it. That causes resentment. I don't go around visiting people anymore ... I don't know why. There is jealousy. People say that you're no good and stuff like that. It's hard to get along. It wasn't like that before.' I offer this brief snapshot of colonial history only to suggest that today, community life is overlain with claims of history, cultural status, language, and religious belief. In sum, First Nations are internally divided and complex.

As previously suggested, many of the causes of individual psychosocial disease can be linked to colonialism. The physical, emotional, and sexual abuse of children in residential schools is perhaps the most obvious example of direct harm experienced by many Native men and women. Less direct, but perhaps more insidious, is the anger, pain, or depression experienced by individuals who have been encouraged to abandon their language or culture. And as I have argued, many of the problems faced by youth, such as poor educational experiences, are also the direct result of prejudice and systemic discrimination by mainstream institutions.

Native people are now examining how colonialism has contributed to the ill health of communities. Community divisions present a significant obstacle to community revitalization. In our consultation, 'overcoming family divisions' was regarded as a critical aspect of the community healing process. People are now trying to come to grips with the dis-ease that exists as the result of tensions between extended family groups. People are now placing these divisions in the context of their emergence, that is, as a natural product of the colonial process. There is increased awareness of how colonial policy has produced family divisions, economic disparity, and religious and political factionalism.

Key consultants stressed the need for people to better appreciate the post-colonial history of reserve life. People are beginning to talk about how the construction of their communities – their geographic settlements, family divisions and sociopolitical structure, have been shaped by the state. For communities to heal, people must understand community history, and the ways in which European governments and institutions have influenced, and continue to influence, life on reserve. Some communities are reforming school curriculum so that students can learn local Native history and the political sociology of their First Nation. Others are sponsoring community research projects and events that allow youth to hear elders' accounts of community history. Increased historical understanding, people say, would allow families to move beyond personal animosities, and to understand that the cause of factionalism lies in the colonial process itself.

> Most of these problems arise out of our history of relations with the dominant society. This history is responsible for individual and community dysfunction.

> You have to see these family divisions in the context of why they happened. The colonial style of leadership, and money, have led to this power struggle and jealousy.

> Before we can move on we need to understand where we came from. We have to understand that we were well people at one time and that this is what has happened and this is where the unhealthiness has come from. We need to understand the multigenerational trauma that was caused by the two cultures coming together and clashing.

As these words demonstrate, there is a growing understanding of the nature of the colonial process and resistance to that process in First Nations. This understanding, while less well articulated than in the critiques of Aboriginal academics, is none the less well understood and sharply focused for many community members. And this awareness of the colonial process will prove to be critical to the process of community healing.

Restoring Culture: Values, Language, and Spirituality

Of the many responses people gave us to questions about community healing, the most automatic and unwavering dealt with the need for people to return to their language, culture, and traditions. Wrapped in this theme were diverse understandings of traditional values, and the meaning of Aboriginal spirituality. But people were in agreement that traditional values promote tolerance of other spiritual ways. They spoke of the Seven Grandfathers: respect, honesty, wisdom, love, bravery, humility, and truth. In recent years, these traditional Anishnabe values have become better known. They are are often depicted symbolically, for example, in artwork or posters. They appear in schools and are used as a framework for presentations and workshops.

Not surprisingly, there is considerable confusion about just what values comprise the Seven Grandfathers and how they should be used. Some feel the term is sometimes misused or that people pay lip service to these values, but do not live by them. But people seemed to agree that basic values – most often caring, sharing, and respect – were needed to guide people's everyday actions (see also Ryan 1995). Some consultants stressed that what was at stake was not a return to traditional values, but the adherence to *basic* values that distinguish Anishnabe life in the contemporary world.

> [Traditional values] is about awareness of your culture and your language and your spirituality and using basic values in everyday life. Basic values is what traditional teachings are about.

> We are talking about going back. Those things we want to go back to are principles. There is the reality of the present. We have to be willing to learn and to change. We have to move ahead but with our old values and principles. We have to grow and adapt.

For example, the value 'respect' can be translated into tolerance for other ways. Bravery (or courage) is a quality that allows people to openly communicate their feelings. And honesty, as noted above, is a value closely associated with ending denial or what, from a community perspective, the RCAP calls 'naming the problem'; that is, the public acknowledgment of hidden personal or family problems (RCAP 1996d: 54).

Culture is constantly adapted to contemporary challenges. When Justice or I used the phrase 'returning to culture' in an early presentation, consultants immediately questioned us about the implications of this phrase. People instead prefer to speak of *restoring* culture. For many this is a simple but important distinction. As people suggested, it is unrealistic to think that Aboriginal people can simply go back to ways of living that existed decades or centuries ago. If we think of culture as a piece of fine furniture, we can imagine the essential structure surviving centuries of neglect or abuse and then being revitalized at the hands of a skilled artisan. The word 'restore' suggests that an underlying cultural order, as maintained by language, values, and beliefs, can be sustained, and that traditions and practices can be rediscovered and improved so that they can meet the challenges of a constantly changing world.

This distinction is important in communities, like those along the North Shore, where there is a perception that in comparison to remote Northern communities, traditional ways and language use have been 'lost.' First Nations differ enormously in the extent to which they have retained their language and traditional practices. In the NSTC area, for example, there are small communities with virtually no Native language speakers and very little knowledge of traditional ways. And there are other First Nations that are large enough to have maintained a critical mass of Native language speakers and have retained traditional knowledge of medicine, law, or environmental relations. In several communities we were told that until a few years ago there was virtually no knowledge of traditional spiritual practices. Even in those communities where traditional medicine is practiced, or where powwows, drum groups, or purification ceremonies are held, many people feel they are just beginning to restore their cultural values in everyday life.

Not surprisingly then, the topic of traditional values can be highly charged, particularly when 'values' and 'spirituality' overlap. The search for Aboriginal spirituality is contested. Some people feel insulted or angry at the suggestion that they cannot be truly Indian unless they reject Christian values. Others are trying to learn about their culture, which for many years was labelled pagan by the churches. As one person said, 'tradition alienates some people.' For others restoring culture raises issues associated with the authenticity of Ojibwa traditions. People may contest spiritual or medicine practices as being non-genuine, in the sense of being pan-Indian, rather than local in origin.

> The sweat lodge that they do today is quite different from the past. The revival of tradition is not genuine. It's like they have read it in some book. My granddaughter comes home and tells me I should be doing things I have never heard of! The powwows should be bringing us together. Right now [tradition] is dividing us.

For many people the preservation of culture is linked to the use of Aboriginal languages. Throughout the country there is a shortage of Aboriginal language instructors and curriculum, and a general lack of support for the protection of Aboriginal languages by education ministries. In Ontario, for example, provincial policy fails to recognize elders as teachers or resource staff, so that it is difficult to employ them as language instructors. But despite these obstacles, First Nations are committed to revitalizing the use of their languages. Two NSTC communities have committed resources to the teaching of language and cultural practices in the community day-care centre, as well as schools.

There are important demographic and generational differences in language use in many communities. Children who are fortunate to have Ojibwa taught to them in school may have parents who are unable to speak the language in a home environment. Today within the extended family it is not unusual for seniors to speak Anishnabe with English as a second language, for their children to speak only English, and for their children's children – the current school generation – to be learning Anishnabe as their second language.[6] But it is often the middle generation that is most active in protecting and restoring traditional culture and spiritual practices.

Members of this middle generation sometimes suggest the need to distinguish between elders as persons who are sources of traditional knowledge and wisdom, and elders as seniors, who are often unconcerned with traditional ways or conservative in outlook. The following statements reveal some of these attitudes:

> The elders [seniors] are afraid of self-government. There is going to be major opposition. They say, 'how can we do that when we can't even look after ourselves?'

> I am a Catholic and I pray every day that the whole community would be united as it was. No anger, cross words. Caring, socializing, sharing. We all went to the same church. Nowadays there are powwows ... I wasn't raised like that. Powwows are new. This is the second year [they have been held]. The elders [seniors] say to stay away from things like that. There is an elder man who says you don't know if it is bad or good medicine so you should stay away. They all say the same. You won't find any elders using the sweat lodge. They might go to the powwow and watch the dancing but that's it. I don't know any more. The elders get upset if you ask them.

Ideas about restoring culture imply a spiritual or moral quality for some, and a political agenda for others. Some suggest, for example, that there is political capital to be made from capturing the rhetoric of cultural revitalization. While non-Natives may assume that demonstration of traditional practices is an indicator of community vitality, for community members the restoration of cultural ways is potentially divisive.

Is this move to traditionalism dividing the community or will it heal the community? I don't know. If it happens the right way it could be healing but right now ... There was a healer who came here and started some stuff, but he was giving bad teachings. I don't know what he was up to. When people heard about that they were concerned. A lot of people are afraid of such bad teachings.

Overall, however, there has been a growth in the numbers of people seeking to rediscover their culture, not just on the North Shore, but right across the country. Despite opposition, community healing is taking place through the restoration of cultural practices. Many people are trying to demonstrate that beliefs, traditions, rituals, and language are fluid and can change to meet new challenges. The revitalization of tradition is a painstaking process. In speaking of Native spirituality, people proceed cautiously. As the following quotes indicate, the restoration of traditional practices is slow:

Not everyone wants to go to the sweat lodge or to see the medicine person or put down tobacco. People practice other ways of spirituality, which is good because if we are a spiritual people, as we claim to be, then I don't think it matters what [spiritual] life we follow, whatever it may be. It is important to overcome these barriers and respect each other, rather than sit there and be judgmental. I think we know too well the effects of those institutions [churches] and how they created division and took things away from us. I think we have to move beyond that and respect other people's beliefs. At the same time we can't lose sight of who we are and what our beliefs are as well. We have survived for thousands of years. And we still have people who speak the language and understand the culture and tradition. That's a foundation. I think if we survived that long with these things then why wouldn't they help us today? They are going to have to be adapted to today's changed society. We are constantly changing, that's important.

As leaders in two different communities suggested:

Many people here don't really turn to tradition unless as a last resort, when all other resources have been depleted. Only about half of the community really uses the traditional way. You can see the difference between people. Maybe some people have been clouded by things like television. The tradition isn't lost here, though. People are still looking for it. Tobacco and cedar are still a big healing thing for a lot of us. But twenty years ago, people were trying to modernize themselves, and they sort of forgot about these things, and took them for granted. Now they're back.

We have come a long way. Ten years ago there was only one traditional person. He was mocked and called crazy. But he kept on, finding his own way. Then I started into it and others. Now there are about forty of us. We get so far and then it goes back again. The younger parents have gone on the vision quests. Now we are trying to get the young people to come to the drum and do vision quests.

What is the relationship between culture and healing? There is an intense link between cultural identity, self-esteem, and feelings of personal control. Discovery and understanding of one's culture can have an absolutely revolutionary and transformative effect on personality and, in particular, on motivation. Personal healing journeys often begin with just such moments of revelation. Spiritual practices such as purification ceremonies have always been part of Ojibwa health practices, but talking or healing circles, which assist many people in recovery from personal problems, are examples of contemporary practices that emphasize traditional culture – hence the interest in these practices by those concerned with models of restorative justice. Identity, spirituality, and healing are all connected in people's minds. Here are three different, but compatible thoughts on community healing.

The spiritual part of that is done in the sweats, smudging, and at sunrise ceremonies. I have made that connection of understanding and these things are healing.

I would hold a lot of circles. They would have to start slowly because of the mistrust and pain. Slowly trust and sharing would come. When the feather was going round and medicine was being burned, strength would come to share. The pain will go around and people become one in the circle.

Traditional healers are people but traditional healing is a process. There are many ways a person can do their own traditional healing: cedar baths, sweats, smudging, drinking cedar water, collecting medicines that are out there. Individuals can also do fasting and vision quests.

Justice and I were told that there are many paths to healing. But all paths are spiritual in nature. Once discovered, this spirituality gives rise to cultural identity and to a political commitment to assist others in the community, to help to improve the quality of community life. People stress that while direct participation in healing ceremonies can be important for individuals, the process of community healing is much broader: it is about the protection and preservation of language, political rights, and nationhood. Community healing is about undoing the damage caused by years of colonial oppression, which attacked Aboriginal beliefs and practices as bad, inferior, primitive, or pagan. Community healing, in this sense, is about recovering from years of oppression and exploitation by the Canadian state through revaluing and restoring Native cultural ways.

Certain types of community events can have a positive effect in promoting traditional culture. Powwows, for instance, are important vehicles for expressing culture. Even though many of the beliefs and behaviour associated with powwows are modern in origin, these are events that generate pride in tradition and culture.

At night you could hear the drums and get the feeling that this is what it must have been like years ago.

One of the visible things is the powwow we have in the summer. You feel pride there and you see sharing going on, families together. That has been a start for us, a start at sharing. You may be a Catholic but you can listen to the various things and share ... One of the things we have done is brought back the drum. That's what the kids all like now. They are learning to dance, and drumming, at school. Every year we have a ceremony where we initiate new dancers. People make regalia and people come in and teach them the significance of the regalia. There are a lot of dancers, and a lot of teaching goes on at that spring gathering.

Powwows provide people with the opportunity to cooperate in the organization of large community gatherings that promote cultural pride. These events require considerable effort, leadership, and financial resources to organize and consume an enormous amount of people's time. Significantly, they also require First Nations to communicate and plan with other communities in order to prevent scheduling conflicts, and to identify dancers, drum groups, and other resource people, many of whom travel the Powwow Trail across the country during the summer months. Individual families must also plan months in advance to arrange for accommodation and food, and to prepare costumes. Women speak with enormous enthusiasm about the effort required to make jingle dresses, or the way children practice drumming and dancing in preparation for these celebrations. Powwows are often spoken of in powerful spiritual terms. People recount how eagles – important ancestral symbols of pride and strength – appear over the powwow grounds.

Not surprisingly, not everyone favours these events. There are complaints about the commercialization of these events, differences of opinion about whether prize money should be offered to dancers, and even concern about their appropriateness or authenticity. Some Aboriginal people suggest that powwows are merely superficial celebrations that deflect attention from more serious attempts to return to cultural and spiritual practices in everyday life. But while such concerns exist, outright opposition to these events is minimal, and the majority of people view powwows as important cultural occasions, which promote pride and harmony in the community.

Powwows are also an example of a holistic event, gatherings that operate in complex ways to attend to people's physical, emotional, psychological, and spiritual well-being. The notion of holistic approaches is central to the restoration of culture. One elder told us of how she had organized nature walks that taught both Natives and non-Natives about medicinal herbs – a brilliantly simple activity, combining physical activity with cultural education, and aiding in the reconciliation between Aboriginal people and mainstream Canadians. We heard many other ideas for recreational or other activities that contained cultural and spiritual components. People spoke about ideas associated with restorative justice – for example, of educational camping retreats where police, along with elders, taught youth bush skills.

The list of cultural initiatives occurring across this small sample of communities is very diverse. Crisis-intervention teams, family-violence shelters, and treatment programs have grown out of recent federal and provincial strategies. Other approaches, such as healing circles for victims of sexual abuse or family violence, or AA groups that incorporate traditional spiritual knowledge, are sustained without government assistance. There are Anishnabe language courses, drum groups, and 'dry' socials for youth. In grade schools located on reserve, or in day-care facilities, children are taught language from an early age, and with this, considerable instruction in traditional teachings and values. There is great hope that the next generation will escape the problems of the past.

Aboriginally controlled schools are unfortunately few and far between. Where they exist, however, they are incredible resources. At Sagamok, for example, children are taught Native curriculum, free from the often negative interaction and hostility that accompanies learning in non-Native classrooms. Aboriginal students are learning their history and traditions. Classrooms and halls are filled with images of Native culture, and the Anishnabe language is everywhere – on posters, in texts, and on signs. Native schools also become important focal points for the promotion of social and physical well-being. Teachers act as facilitators in the aftermath of deaths or other traumatic events – allowing children to communicate about their feelings and to learn how to deal with grief at an early age. Peacekeepers organize recreational activities for youth, and promote socially competent behaviour in classroom presentations. At Sagamok, leaders have noticed a decline in vandalism and solvent and alcohol abuse among children and youth since the opening of the school.

Traditional knowledge, then, is as much about the future as it is the past (Justice and Warry 1996: 49–50). For many First Nations, the restoration of culture is not something that can be taken for granted, but is rather a process that needs to be nourished. It is a project that actively engages many staff and councillors. In this sense restoring culture is a personal journey for many, and a professional strategy for others who believe that culture must be part of the provision of any service. Everywhere along the North Shore, small pockets of individuals are teaching children the way to smudge, to braid sweet grass, to drum, and to dance. Traditional activities are spurred by key staff people, who teach traditional values and practices to children and youth, or bring resource persons into the community. Elders are invited into day-care centres to tell stories in the Ojibwa language to children. Teachers instruct children on the meaning of sage, cedar, and other sacred plants. And for these leaders there are great returns associated with this investment in culture. The establishment and maintenance of a drum group or a purification lodge is an important accomplishment. It is with considerable reverence that a person will mention that he or she has only recently been given an Indian name, learned his or her *dodem*, or entered a purification lodge.

Given the obvious link between healing and cultural identity, the government should invest in a range of cultural programs that would enable communities to further explore and experience their traditions. While much can be accomplished by communities through the efforts of staff and volunteers, money is needed to pay for the travel of traditional healers and other resource people, to plan and coordinate major cultural events such as powwows, and to build regional cultural centres that can serve as focal points for the cultural revitalization process. There is need for cultural coordinators, for example, to facilitate powwows, retreats, visits by elders, and many other initiatives. Currently, First Nations often have difficulty finding resources to support cultural initiatives. To date, even where governments have begun to see cultural programming as a central component of community healing, they have failed to invest adequately in these programs. I suspect this is because in the Aboriginal context, 'culture' is now viewed as natural and self-sustaining. But the reality is that, if we see a relationship between cultural integrity and community revitalization, then an investment in cultural institutions is an investment in social health.

Structural Change

Powwows and other cultural or recreational events promote community cooperation. Ironically, we were also told that tragedies – suicides, accidental deaths, or natural deaths – temporarily pulled families together. People stated that funerals were occasions that could be interpreted as positive from the perspective of community well-being – they were times when people came together, naturally assumed responsibility for sharing food, visited relatives of the deceased, and offered financial and emotional support. But when we asked how these feelings, which transcend internal divisions and family rivalries, could be sustained, our questions met with long silences, or simple statements that such a wish was unrealistic or impossible.

But when we re-examined our interviews, we found that people made a number of suggestions about how harmony in community life could be better fostered. Many of these suggestions centred around what we came to think of as 'structural' approaches to community healing. They include the learning and fostering of communicative skills, ways of enhancing public participation in decision-making, the creation of informal situations where community members could come together in unthreatening, cooperative environments. Significantly, long-term reform to political structures was viewed as central to community healing. Political leadership, staff development, and role modelling – broadly speaking, human-resource development – were seen as essential to these reforms.

Mark Nichter (1995) has noted that social scientists are often attracted to negative or problem-oriented behaviours. He suggests that social scientists could serve communities better if they focused on examples of 'positive deviance,' that is, on how positive behaviour can help to reshape communities where dysfunctional behaviour has become normalized. Dawson's research provides insight into the complicated feelings of Aboriginal workers as they try to act as positive role models in their communities (1995). The idea of 'healing the healers' is predicated on the belief that staff, councillors, or other leaders can be key agents of change, and role models for children and youth (ibid). People who have begun their healing journeys often link their personal growth to their capacity to contribute at the community, regional, or tribal levels. For example, front-line workers often state that it is impossible for communities to heal unless key individuals – human-services staff, or chief and council – are healthy, or have healed themselves.

As previously noted, part of this process would be categorized in mainstream terms as occupational health. More generally, however, people spoke to us about the need for professional development that would allow staff and leadership to obtain the skills necessary to facilitate the community healing process (see, for example, UOI 1993a,1993b). Culturally appropriate training for staff in a range of counselling and intervention techniques is desperately needed. To address individual healing within the context of family, peer, and community interaction requires effective case-management systems among health- and social-service staff. In recent years many First Nations have made concerted efforts to improve networking, information sharing, and team approaches. But there remain many obstacles to the establishment of effective case management (ibid; NSTC 1994a) .

First Nations councils, staff, and board members often work in a vacuum, without sufficient coordination of their work, with little evaluation of their progress, and without any clear set of expectations. Policy is often unwritten and ad hoc; it emerges according to particular situations. While this is understandable – indeed, it is in keeping with the informal nature of reserve organizations and the situational nature of consensus decision-making – many staff people would prefer to be operating with a clear set of expectations from their communities. Other problems arise from the internalization of Western notions about professionalism – for example, the need to maintain client confidentiality, which, while simple in large urban environments, is almost impossible on reserves where a person's actions are constantly on view for the community (see Warry 1992). As Dawson (1995) notes, there is an intrinsic catch-22 in the role of Aboriginal staff, who are at once professionals as well as family or friends to their clients (ibid). This role confusion manifests itself in many ways. For example, it is difficult for staff to share information about their clients – particularly where they know a fellow staff member is closely related as kin, or, conversely, where they suspect some type of personal animosity. Case-management approaches, therefore, are difficult to develop and sustain, and integrated service delivery, which is an important part of holistic services, can be difficult to establish and maintain.

During the past several years, First Nations and tribal councils have done a great deal of work on board development, organizational change, and policy development (see NSTC 1994a, 1994b). Many communities are experimenting with case-management approaches, and new ways of promoting teamwork that can overcome family divisions. An organizational ethic is emerging, based on the traditional values noted above, which, even if unwritten, is being conveyed to the larger community of care-givers. Among North Shore communities, for example, there is increased attention to open and 'transparent' hiring processes, to publicizing all council meetings, and to holding meetings in forums that are accessible to the entire community. There is increased attention to limiting the roles of council in program design and operation, that is, to a 'hands off' role for councils in staff affairs. There is a greater commitment to ongoing program and performance evaluations. This Aboriginal professional ethic seems to encourage an informal organizational environment and to respect the personal needs of workers.

Great efforts are being made to provide integrated service delivery both within and beyond the First Nation. The North Shore Tribal Council has examined many of its services and developed a model for integrated health- and human-services at the regional level. This model has yet to be implemented, however, in part because management dollars have not been found. The lack of funding for management positions, which would enable integrated service approaches at the First Nations level, is yet another external obstacle to community development and self-government.

Human-resources support and training are critical to the development of Aboriginal communities. But money for training is scarce. Training workshops enable people to come together and talk about such things as communication, teamwork, and conflict resolution. This is an important part of the puzzle that is community healing, and one that seldom receives much attention. As one care-giver stated: 'Training and healing go together. When you spend time with people in training then you develop relationships. It would be good for the care-givers of a community to spend time doing training together. When they can accept each others' problems they will be able to help the community.'

Improving work environments, of course, is important precisely because staff are key agents of change. Any effort that strengthens staff relations and 'heals the healers' enhances the process of community healing. Sagamok Council, for example, has held retreats with staff to create a vision for their community initiatives and to re-organize the roles of staff. As a result it was decided to begin with training to promote personal growth and development, focusing on the chief and council, as well as staff. This approach has re-energized people, and encourages leadership to model positive behaviour in the community. Such initiatives demonstrate that First Nations fully understand the relationship between personal development and community healing, and are prepared to invest in human-resource training.

Unhealthy attitudes among workers are the source of many organizational problems. Personal or family conflicts are carried into the workplace, making teamwork, open communication, and integration of services difficult. In short, many First Nations feel there is a need to improve communication and interpersonal relations in the workplace. The reality of Aboriginal organizational life (and perhaps all organizational life) is that staff often feel they lack the skills to collaborate in team approaches, or that they are working in unsupportive environments. Communication and conflict-resolution skills, in particular, are essential to the community healing process. Some people went so far as to say that communication was the only real problem and defined a healthy community as one where people can openly communicate their feelings without fear of criticism or reprisal.

More generally, people acknowledged poor communication skills within families or the larger community. Anger is often internalized, only to emerge when people drink. People routinely personalize criticism, unable to distinguish between a critique of ideas or political ideology and an attack on personality. Band members feel uncomfortable voicing their opinions at council meetings. Few people feel they can go to a public meeting and express themselves openly without the fear of criticism, or the risk of bad medicine. In this context the belief in bad medicine can be thought of as disabling to communicative life on reserve. Rumour and gossip are used as ways of influencing behaviour: 'Now if you go to a meeting and say what you really feel, later you will definitely hear gossip about what you said. People are afraid to speak their minds. It could be very different. It is changing; there is hope. But more people need to be talking about it.' Again, these problems are also found in non-Native communities. But they are exacerbated by overlapping friendship, kinship, and professional relationships in Aboriginal communities.

The term 'conflict resolution' is not commonly used in Aboriginal communities, though in chapter 5 it was obvious that people recognized the close link between justice and healing. Conflict resolution skills enable people to defuse situations when anger, disagreements, or criticism are involved. When we used this phrase in our presentations, people talked about, or around, this Western concept in many different ways. It was acknowledged that few staff, including peacekeepers, actually have the language skills or interpersonal skills to deal with family violence or other conflicts in community life in a neutral manner, or perhaps more important, to deal with them in a manner that others will perceive as neutral. People spoke of the need to improve communication skills, to ignore criticism arising from personal animosity, and to transcend the divisions between individuals and families when trying to pursue common objectives:

> What is important is to hear all sides of a story. We need conflict resolution skills and appeal systems for decisions made. We must be able to criticize without fear and take criticism without being destroyed. I have seen people destroyed by criticisms of programs. People cannot distinguish between criticism and personal attack.

> Chief and council must learn to hear criticism without being personally hurt. It's a role every politician agrees to. Councils tend to become defensive when challenged. They don't like to be questioned.

In sum, a great deal of work needs to be done to ensure a safe and secure organizational environment on reserve that would allow staff and council to create innovative and collaborative approaches to change. North Shore communities are experimenting with new organizational structures. The process of coming together to discuss a shared vision of the future seems to be therapeutic. When staff and councillors can reach agreement that integrated services, teamwork, and coordination are important principles of organizational life, they begin to apply a shared vision of their role in community healing. Communication and sharing of information are the key to coordination of services. And in the end, communication is dependent on the quality of the relationships in an organization; the promotion of healthy relationships is critical to organizational success.

Community Healing and Self-Government

In discussions about health, Aboriginal people quickly move from individual health to the larger consideration of the community environment. They speak of relationships that normally would be considered political in nature. Community healing is about the promotion of a new sense of harmony in communities through cooperation, shared decision-making, and community participation in political processes. For this reason it is linked to the notion of self-government through the promotion of new forms of political representation that reflect community, rather than state, objectives. For some people these political aspirations are focused at the level of First Nations. For others, there is a desire to develop political organizations that represent regional, or even tribal groupings. Like the idea of restorative justice, the notion of creating new political institutions that are not reliant on the state, or that are not derived from Western notions of democracy, is for many Aboriginal people a new and radical idea.

Forms of political representation – band councils and elections – were imposed on Aboriginal people under the terms of the Indian Act. The fact is that First Nations are *incipient* political communities. To date, their identity has been defined by the state, rather than by the communities themselves. At the same time, community identity has been articulated partly by way of political philosophy *in opposition to* the state, and specifically, through emerging notions of what rights First Nations should exercise. By this I do not mean to suggest that the inherent right to self-government has not been sustained through history. Rather, I am suggesting that the sense of political status evident in the concept of First Nations is tied to state recognition of band councils, and that this political status is distinct from any sense of community identity.

Today's band councils can be dominated by one or more family factions that are never considered to be truly representative of the community at large. Menno Boldt (1993) has suggested that there is a polarization of Aboriginal communities into haves and have-nots (see also chapter 2). Small political élites exist in almost every Aboriginal community – and this élite status translates into band employment for perhaps thirty per cent of the reserve population. This group stands in contrast to the majority of residents, who rely on unemployment insurance or other forms of social assistance. This dual class and power structure, as Boldt notes, is rooted in colonial structures. Over time, those in political power have gained access to land entitlements, housing, and salaries associated with band employment (Boldt, 118–24). A significant portion of band members, then, feel shut out from political processes and reliant on this élite for any improvement in their social and economic well-being. This political division is at least partly responsible for the criticism that the behaviour of Aboriginal leaders replicates the sins of government bureaucrats (117). As we have seen, tribal council employees are particularly susceptible to this criticism.

Boldt's analysis offers a general characterization of First Nation political structure as rooted in colonial history, and accurately portrays the divisions that exist on many – perhaps the majority of – reserves. He is certainly accurate in suggesting that many of the traditional qualities of Indian leadership – an egalitarian ethos, a belief in consensus and non-hierarchical forms of organization – have been lost or supplanted through the transition to Western political processes that are entrenched in the Indian Act. But, although he acknowledges that class lines are frequently coterminous with kin-group alignments (125), his analysis glosses over the deeply personal nature of kinship divisions, and in the search for structure he dismisses the vagaries of band politics, which can lead to rapid and temporary shifts in power, as haves temporarily become have-nots.

Family divisions greatly influence political life. It is possible for councils, which are elected for a two-year term, to become dominated by a single family, or members of aligned families. Not surprisingly, accusations of political patronage are also common, as band employees related to councillors are hired. Criticism of council and staff decisions – over access to housing, welfare benefits, or even band membership – is sometimes tinged with claims of personal wrongdoing, or revenge motives. Elections are often contests between family blocs, and knowledge of key issues or administrative skills can become irrelevant in the selection of leaders. Councillors (one for every two hundred persons on reserve) are elected in a first-past-the-post process where band members cast ballots for each position. In some instances councillors need only twenty-five to thirty votes to be elected. Dramatic shifts can occur from one council election to another. The vagaries of family composition make for an unpredictable and unstable political environment. To an outsider, band politics often appear chaotic and personal.

If there is a common complaint about politics it is that the Indian Act, in requiring elections every two years, creates political instability; such an election system is unknown in other jurisdictions. Native people desire more stable leadership, which could aid in long-term strategic planning. The current situation is one of almost constant uncertainty and lack of direction. Reversals in leadership and policy direction are common to many First Nations. Councils have a hard time building any sustainable processes before they must face re-election. For this reason many communities have begun to discuss new forms of political representation that would emerge from community values, and be more authentically based in Anishnabe tradition. But there have been few concrete suggestions of what such a Anishnabe political system might look like; how, aside from elections, leaders might be selected; and how the rights of individual band members could be protected under any traditional system of government.

Perhaps the most blatant example of the penetration of state norms in community life is the adherence to democratic processes, or that version of democracy, required by Indian Act legislation, that stresses one-person-one-vote. The assimilation of Western political ideals has undermined attempts to reconstruct traditional political processes, such as organization of councils along clan lines. Many people cannot conceive of a political system that is not based in some form of election.

Political leaders continue to explore these issues. Intrinsic to the process of self-government is the right to define and determine political institutions based on traditional values and political processes. Self-government will entail rejection or reformation of institutions like band councils that have been imposed through the Indian Act. As with previous iterations of the culture argument, the conceptualization of traditional politics is full of difficult twists and turns, many of them related to the simplistic desire to return to an 'imagined golden age associated with traditional life' (Justice and Warry 1996). It is unrealistic to expect that modern political processes can be modelled on band sociopolitical organization, which emerged from a hunting and trapping lifestyle. But contemporary political processes can sustain traditional political values such as equality and consensus, or could be built on clan affiliations.

For the most part, leaders discuss the idea of returning to traditional political values with remarkable sophistication and élan. Therefore, the criticism that Aboriginal political institutions might undermine democratic processes or individual rights under the Charter appears to be simply another version of post-colonial ideology that suggests that Aboriginal people are incapable of finding sophisticated solutions to contemporary problems.

Take the suggestion by a number of North Shore leaders that family influences on political life might be eliminated. Some people immediately raised questions about the dangers of returning to customary ways: 'Election reforms are either going to eliminate family influence or it will become even bigger if custom elections go backward ... I don't know what will happen. It could go back to patriarchy and being hereditary. I don't know.' This comment suggests the potential difficulties of adhering to past customs in a contemporary world. Specifically, it warns against any method of representation that would restrict women's rights or input to the political process (see Nahanee 1993). But the fact that this danger exists is immediately recognized. Most people we spoke to questioned whether or not the word 'eliminated' was appropriate. It was natural, they suggested, that personal quarrels or animosities should enter into political life. But communities could strive to minimize divisions between families in an number of ways. The most obvious way an extended family or lineage influences political life is through electing one of its members to council. Competition for political office was said to stem from family divisions.

> It is a popularity thing, as opposed to being issue driven. It is also a family thing. Whoever has the largest family. I feel that [we must elect] people whom you can trust and who can do the work.

> It pulls the wrong strings: you don't end up electing the people with common sense and experience. It is just about personal background ... It [an election] should be on the basis of merit or ability.

For many leaders the key to self-government and community healing is in the construction of new political processes that can be seen as just, equitable, and inclusive by the entire community. Angus Toulous, chief of Sagamok First Nation, notes:

> [Self-government] is about getting the membership to understand our history and the problems we have faced, the restrictions (for example, red tape and Indian Act legislation) under which we operate. There has to be some understanding of why we are where we are today and why it is hard to take that next step. There are a lot of people still in denial. We did a retreat which was a start. We talked about these issues and we talked openly and honestly. That is certainly needed ... We are going to develop our own election procedures. The process will require extensive community consultations. We can start with certain groups to try to get the discussion going. How do they want to see candidates nominated? Do you need ten votes? Do you need to know the issues?

Toulous links the search for new forms of representation to a method for overcoming family divisions and building a more inclusive political system. Sagamok has started community consultations to solicit suggestions about what an alternative political system might look like. They are considering, for example, setting criteria for the nomination of candidates. Family, geographic, or religious divisions could be explicitly recognized, for example, so that special interest groups could participate in council.

These and other reforms can only be accomplished by changing the first-past-the-post election system and imposed council system in favour of a system based on community districts or electorates. Elections might also be supplemented by appointments to ensure representation of minority religious (and other) groups. Several communities have discussed the idea of forming youth councils and elders' councils, which would act as resources to leaders, or like a senate, would provide a forum of second thought. First Nations are also considering genealogical research to enhance people's understanding of clan systems, which traditionally held specific political responsibilities. One chief suggested that these clans be resurrected by way of political symbols or positions that would recognize different clans in the First Nations. For example, members of a particular clan would be charged with responsibility for peacekeeping and an elder from that clan would act as a resource person to council and staff.

Specific forms of customary elections or leadership will vary throughout the country. Some Iroquois communities have a traditional form of longhouse politics that has sustained an ideological base that can be used to create new political institutions. Other communities, such as those on the North Shore, where knowledge of clan membership is poor and where community politics seem dominated by institutions created under colonial rule, will require years of experimentation, consultation, and perhaps research, before consensus can be reached about the appropriate form of political representation.

Beyond questions of the selection of leaders, there are concerns about the overlapping roles of people on councils and community boards. In many communities staff members also sit on boards or on councils. This arrangement differs from mainstream organizations where staff-volunteer relationships are impersonal and where volunteers provide a vision of community needs and desires and staff implement this vision. From a Western perspective, council-staff or board-staff relationships are constantly threatened, undermined, and compromised by potential 'conflict of interest,' which fuels community criticism of leadership in many situations. It is almost impossible to convey the implications – or implied implications – of family relations on decision-making. In Aboriginal communities it is not uncommon for key staff to be councillors, and for staff or councillors to be connected as in-laws, spouses, or family members. It is inevitable that in virtually every decision people are somehow connected by kinship – the only real variable at work is the degree of separation that exists in interpersonal relations. Those readers who have experience in mainstream volunteer organizations are aware of conflict-of-interest guidelines. They are familiar with the care people take to separate staff and board roles in decision-making. But once again, analogies to mainstream organizations are inappropriate because the concepts of confidentiality, bias, or conflict of interest are *Western* constructs – ones devised to remove the last vestiges of personal or family relations from professional life.

For Aboriginal people, removing kinship from professional affairs – indeed, from 'affairs of the state' – is impossible. It is precisely because Western notions of appropriate professional conduct have been internalized through years of contact with mainstream bureaucracy that people have leave to appeal to criticisms of impropriety. This can cause people to feel insecure about their professional conduct. In my experience, criticisms of misconduct, conflict of interest, or patronage more often than not have no basis in fact. Rather, such criticisms come from those who feel locked out of decision-making, or wronged in a variety of ways. Yet complaints about unprofessional behaviour continue, even where bands go to extraordinary lengths to develop transparent hiring processes or guidelines for decision-making.

Carol Trudeau is the health and social services director for Sagamok Anishnabek First Nation. She is also a band councillor, and related by blood or marriage to several other councillors, as well as to the staff she works with on a daily basis. She contends that only a personalized sense of ethics can help Native people navigate the daily minefield of First Nations' organizational politics. Councils can do much to assist individuals by setting clear guidelines for behaviour, but ultimately a reputation for fairness must be generated from the consistent behaviour of staff. She asserts that while there may be clear instances where staff or council must remove themselves from discussions or political processes, there are also, inevitably, times when decisions are so important that the kinship relations should not dissuade individuals from contributing to what they see is a fair and equitable solution to a problem.[7]

First Nations' councils, then, are charged with the arduous task of creating positive organizational environments that provide safe spaces where people can openly and honestly communicate. Councils can be instrumental in this process by meeting openly, ending the confusion and secrecy that surrounds the work of staff, publicizing hiring processes, and setting clear guidelines to promote staff professionalism and an agreed-upon code of ethics. First Nations are being proactive by developing leadership codes and hiring policies in order to establish the legitimacy of their political processes and institutions.

In short, as part of the self-government movement, First Nations are working hard to develop new forms of political representation and new political and professional processes, which not only foster community participation but encourage community healing. Community healing is a process linked to self-government. It is a process that requires long-term vision. Staff at Sagamok First Nation spoke of their own experience at a retreat involving chief and council:

> The vision is coming from all of us. We are sitting as a group, backed by chief and council. Out of forty people we have a committee to come up with a vision. We are in the process of doing that. We are now working on a vision statement. It can start with us and filter into the community. We are looking at children who are being raised with the presence of a grandparent. We are looking at starting with the youth at a very early age in learning the skills of facilitating. We are looking at issues which are barriers to our own growth and development. We need to have a goal and be all speaking the same language. Here is the vision, how are we going to get there? It is difficult. We have to just talk things out ... everybody who works for the band and whoever else wants to sit in.

Self-government and community healing are *naturally* occurring and linked processes. As one chief summarized:

> It would have to happen in parallel. But I would think community healing has to take priority. It is a quandary to say the least. The healing will be the mechanism for political reform hopefully. Community healing incorporates the structure of selecting our leaders and deciding how to govern ourselves. Divisions along family lines find their way into politics. You have to see these family divisions in the context of why they happened. The colonial style of leadership, and money, have led to this power struggle and jealousy. In the fifties when I was growing up ... even at that time you were classified by where you lived. There are a number of contributing factors: there are geographical divisions and denominations. The spiritual revival is another one ... There is no mechanism for equalizing the distribution of representation. What I have suggested is basing representation on geographical area ... There are [many] options ... We may have two or more chiefs. When the Robinson Huron treaty was signed there were four chiefs from our community; what we want to see is an accurate documentation of the history.

These locally developed visions and initiatives are quite separate from the self-government negotiations in which many First Nations are engaged. As mentioned in chapter 1, the North Shore Tribal Council was involved in self-government negotiations for several years. But despite their hiring self-government coordinators in each community, the negotiation process remained a mystery to most people. Some people feel that the tribal council moved too fast toward self-government. As one councillor suggested: 'I ask people outright what they know [about self-government]. It is amazing. There is very little awareness ... The boat has gone adrift for a while. It [the tribal council's self-government initiative] could be revived. We have to build awareness in the communities first so people can make informed decisions.' This lack of awareness stemmed from the tribal council's failure to adequately explain, by way of community consultations, the complex legal issues associated with attempting to take control over different jurisdictions such as law, economic development, or health – a problem that was also experienced during Health Transfer.

More broadly, people do not necessarily see *state-sponsored* self-government initiatives as relevant to the process of political reform that must occur within First Nations. Self-government as a label for political reform is not a high priority for North Shore communities. People are also concerned about the unforeseen consequences of self-government. They are concerned that their leaders will be forced to assume too much responsibility too soon. Perhaps this is because many people are still locked in government dependency – unlike the more assertive leaders in major Aboriginal organizations, community members are uncertain that they have the skills required to enact self-government now.

> [Self-government] can work, but within certain parameters. Most people think about this in terms of existing systems. I am not sure that in the long run self-government may be our undoing. Our people are so used to external solutions, and we as leaders [are] too. Self-government may transfer one form of dependence to another. I worry about it. It comes down to our vision of the future and a lot of us haven't thought this through very well.

At the same time, people speak of self-government in diverse ways, which conjure up images of self-sufficiency. This is the irony embedded in the contradiction between self-government as process, and self-government as some distant institutional form. Ideas about community healing promote local self-sufficiency and autonomy, which are different from and, for many, should precede state-sponsored self-government plans.

Many people believe their leader's understanding of self-government far outstrips their own, and they are content to trust these leaders as they press forward in complex negotiations with the state. Others are more cautious, often critical of particular leaders' actions. They may be concerned that chiefs spend too much time away from home on self-government or other consultations, and as a result, are unable to help in the healing process. People distrust government-driven ideas of self-government, particularly those associated with the tribal council's negotiations, because they do not trust the government's agenda and have yet to be convinced how First Nations' interests can be protected within more regional forms of government. Many people – perhaps the majority – wish to see self-government developed from the bottom up – they wish to first find agreement about the future political shape of their own First Nation. In short, they seek self-government that is defined on their own terms, based in local reality, and emergent from the participation of people in a healthy community. The last thing people desire is self-government that is arbitrarily imposed from the outside.

As suggested at several points in this book, divisions evident at the First Nations level are carried outward to regional alignments of bands. A councillor commented on the tribal council: 'It is also about personalities of who is representing the First Nations; the structure of the tribal council was developed to help one another, but it has become a problem of control ... the disease [family divisions and jealousy] has infiltrated the tribal council.' At the time this statement was made the tribal council was involved in some turmoil, having had its chair resign and its chief administrator released. These changes occurred in response to criticism over a deficit, which, in my assessment, was small but which was taken by some chiefs as a sign of poor administration. In fact, First Nations often find themselves in deficit positions. This is to be expected where First Nations or tribal councils attempt to deal with difficult social crises, with very limited funding.

As an aside, I note that at about the same time media reports suggested that collectively First Nations were $537 million in debt. The federal government debt was $550 *billion.* The tenor of these reports, which suggested administrative incompetence on the part of Aboriginal leaders and bureaucrats, is dangerous because it suggests First Nations are incapable of good management and, therefore, of self-government. These reports create a double standard. By failing to place deficits in the context of other provincial and federal government deficits, which have been considered a natural part of doing business for decades, they create a false illusion that Aboriginal leaders cannot properly administer their affairs (see *Spectator,* 25 Jan. 1995). Unfortunately, this critique is accepted and repeated by some Aboriginal people.

As several Aboriginal consultants noted, despite ongoing criticism of the tribal council, despite political infighting and occasional uncertainty, many people were still dedicated to the development of regional institutions. As one councillor noted: '[The tribal council] has developed principles that allow the communities to develop at their own pace and toward their own goal. The [self-government] work they did does not tell us what our laws will be, etc. It is about recognizing uniqueness and having jurisdiction within their own area and within the treaty area. The problem is that the community members are not aware of this thinking. Local government at the end of the day will form the regional government based on things they decide would be better handled regionally.' This leader stresses that tribal councils must be viewed as extensions of local needs and aspirations, and cannot fall into the trap of handing down directives or forcing First Nations to react to regional initiatives – such an approach fails to respect the integrity of First Nations' autonomy.

In the end, people stressed that there was a current backing-away from specific self-government negotiations, simply because communities felt pressured, by both the Canadian government and tribal council negotiators. But none of the criticism of the tribal council, or uncertainty about the timing of self-government, could hide the fact that people believed that regional co-operation was necessary. And while there are certainly chiefs or councillors who believe that tribal councils are unnecessary, the majority recognize that tribal councils offer the only pragmatic solution to the problems of smaller communities.

> [Our community] may feel they are big enough [to go it alone] but we aren't. We have to work together because of economies of scale. Otherwise we have to purchase services from outside agencies. So there is merit in the regional government concept, whatever that may be.

Community healing implies improvement in political relationships within and between First Nations. People realize that until the tribal council is strong and stable, any version of specific jurisdictions associated with a model for self-government will be contested by individual First Nations. Opinions about the relative roles of tribal council and First Nations councils, or, for that matter, other forms of political organization, vary dramatically. The same issues associated with improving communication, establishing trust, and resolving conflict, which individuals need to address within their communities, also need to be attended to at the level of tribal councils and beyond.

In summary, people see community healing as a long developmental process, beginning with individual change, radiating out from First Nations to other communities and ending in the realization of self-government. Encouraging self-reliance and breaking the cycle of dependency is a critical first step in this process: '... we are doing self-government now ...

it is good for the community. As people participate, it heals. People need to take more control.'

We have come full circle: Participation in the politics of community life enhances self-reliance, and contributes to personal healing. Individuals are self-determining. Their health emerges from a sense of self and well-being that is connected to their cultural identity. Personal well-being, community self-determination, and the enactment of self-government are intimately linked. Aboriginal people are engaged in a process of adult education, structural reform, and ongoing community consultation in preparation for the changes that will occur over the next decade.

Conclusion

Culture, identity, tradition, values, spirituality, healing, transformation, revitalization, self-determination, self-government: a spiral of ideas and actions constitute community healing. At the most basic level, when Aboriginal people speak of community healing they suggest that there are many individuals within their community who must heal themselves before they will be capable of contributing to the many tasks that lie ahead. They talk of finding ways to help support individuals who must heal deep wounds. This can only be accomplished if people are provided with opportunities for spiritual growth and cultural awareness. More generally, people must acquire new skills so that the capacity of their communities to engage in discussion, planning, and control over their institutions is increased. There is a need to build supportive and healthy environments so that debate and dialogue can be conducted on the many complex issues that comprise self-government. Aboriginal people are engaged in a slow process of rediscovering meaning and identity through participation in processes aimed at preserving, protecting, and constantly restoring their culture in the face of colonial history and post-colonial forces. For Aboriginal people, commitment to the cause of self-government is deeply connected to their personal healing experiences.

Important ideological divisions exist in any community; conflict is a natural part of life. The many different positions on culture, community, and self-government described here should be seen as fuel for dialogue and change. The diversity of ideas, skills, and understanding that exist in communities can become a source of creative tension and change if people are healthy and if they possess the interpersonal and communication skills to harness the enormous intellectual capacity of their communities.

Community healing and self-government, as linked processes, need to rest on a solid understanding of colonial history, and a cautious pragmatism about the nature and pace of change that must occur in future. Community healing is occurring. Aboriginal people can mark the changes that have occurred in their community over the past two decades: individual healing, acknowledgment of the problems that remain, a better understanding of the nature of culture and tradition, increased control over services, leaders who are more confident, more strategic, and knowledgeable in their dealings with the state – and on and on. Community healing is part of the process of self-government; it is the cultural and spiritual foundation on which the politics of self-government must be built.

It is clear to me that self-government is inevitable. It is an ongoing process that the state cannot deny, and that, with additional resources, can only accelerate. Aboriginal people refer to prophecies that speak to some as yet indistinguishable moment when their culture will be acknowledged and appreciated, and when they will fully participate as social, economic, and political equals in Canadian life. I am more inclined to stress the hard work and pragmatism of the people who are working toward that distant dream.

I am constantly impressed by the quiet dignity and spiritual strength with which people go about the business of transforming their communities. The question for mainstream Canadians is whether to support or suppress community healing. It could be suggested that the gains over the past decade have occurred in spite of government assistance. A more honest interpretation would suggest that Aboriginal people have made the most of whatever opportunities have been provided through the reform of government policy. Self-reliance has an important place in people's conceptualization of both individual and community healing. But the process of community healing needs to be nourished, and this can be accomplished in many different ways – for example, through government recognition of cultural programs, through support for human-resources training, and through the funding of broadly based community-healing initiatives. Programs need to be developed to support individuals and families throughout the healing journey. And more generally, much more consultation is needed to stimulate political and organizational reform.

Aboriginal people have carved out sufficient political and cultural space so that most Canadians would now reject a simplistic assimilationist ideology. But there is a great deal to be done in creating and managing a new relationship between First Nations and the Canadian state. This relationship will entail many complex associations and agreements to allow for different degrees of separation and integration between Aboriginal and non-Aboriginal communities. Along the road to Aboriginal self-government, Canadians will do well to remember that the process of community healing is one that begins with the individual, and radiates out to the First Nation, and to other nations, including Canada.

7

The Nature of Change: Cleaning the Caribou

I spent some time in residential school and I'm a cynic. I'm concerned about the lack of political will in this land. The lack of visioning among those who have power ... after I came out of residential school I was fortunate to find Elders who still vision and still dream and who value others and their visions and their dreams. And I've been trying to learn about respect and sharing. I hope the Royal Commission will perceive ... that part of the process is education. And certainly the education isn't just for the Commission, but it's for the Nation. You will be participants in a process of healing, if every time you meet you sit in this circle of learning and respect. Not as objective observers, but as participants in a process that Canada must know about, because we're living with old myths and old dreams, empty visions. Words like 'two founding nations.' (Winnipeg MB. 92-04-21 32. Stan McKay. PG 126–9)

Introduction

The process of individual and community healing will continue to grow and accelerate over the next decade. Aboriginal people know that as their communities are strengthened and as their traditions are revitalized, the reality of self-government will become self-evident to the mainstream public and they will assume their rightful place in Canadian society.

Like Mr. McKay I feel frustrated by the lack of government vision. Like many Canadians I was disappointed, though not surprised, at the government's recent reaction to the final reports of the Royal Commission on Aboriginal Peoples. I sometimes find it difficult to understand why many Canadians see a threat in the idea of Native self-government. Clearly, continued public education is necessary to provide the self-government movement with sufficient momentum to overcome government inaction. The RCAP stresses that public education is a foundational element of the project of self-government (1996f: 90–100). Public awareness of Aboriginal peoples and perspectives is essential to creating an atmosphere of respect that will produce constructive dialogues on the nature of Aboriginal rights. The RCAP notes that many sectors of Canadian society – educational institutions, municipalities, religious organizations, labour unions, and others – have important roles to play in the creation of these dialogues (ibid).

I hope that this book will be regarded as a small contribution in the long-term process of healing and reconciliation that must occur between Natives and non-Natives. In this conclusion, I consider the role of social science in relation to the project of self-government. I then briefly review reactions to the release of the RCAP final reports and discuss arguments about the cost of self-government, which I take to be the final rhetorical manifestation of colonialism in Canada. I then conclude with comments about the relationship between community healing and self-government.

The Role of Social Science

My own direct involvement in the project of Native self-government has been minor. It has occurred largely through my participation in a number of projects over the past ten years in which I have acted as a technician, providing specialized knowledge about research or planning strategies, writing reports, or analysing topics of interest to First Nations or Aboriginal organizations. The preceding analysis is built on a wide body of literature and grey literature that represents the cumulative effort of social scientists, as well as the expressed opinions of many Aboriginal people whom I have spoken to over the years. This type of analysis, however, pales in comparison to the work of Aboriginal people, who are engaged in the project of self-government on a daily basis.

I am left with the feeling, which Moore acknowledges (see 2), that my description of Aboriginal affairs is soulless. Much social science falls short of truly motivating people to act positively in the world they inhabit. In part this is because the medium of writing – whether the form itself or the academic expectations that accompany the form – is restrictive. For the most part, as MacNeil has noted, the written word seems curiously unable to move us; 'speak to me and you will move me; write to me and I'll have to think about it' (1989: 186). MacNeil continues: 'We are adrift today in a sea of weightless words ... There must be some living connection between the weight of words and truth – not literal, factual truth, perhaps, but an effort at truth, like the effort of a poet, someone who struggles for truth. Today it seems words mean nothing to the person using them, have no connection to what he believes, yet are presented as though they had,' (ibid: 224–5).

MacNeil questions how words are used, their relationship to our personal beliefs, and the ability to convey truthful meaning. These are questions of great importance in the social sciences today. Explanations reflect our personal beliefs and our commitment to truth. We must be capable of moving people to act, but we must do so on the basis of the best information and analysis available. I hope I have conveyed information in such a manner that it will assist the reader in better understanding a contemporary Aboriginal reality. My interpretations, no doubt, will be regarded as bland by some, offensive by others. But I hope that the analysis 'rings true' to the reader.

John O'Neil notes that although scientists may claim that their work is value-free, this claim is usually made from a position firmly situated in the context of a white, male, middle-class, Eurocentric background. 'Aboriginal, other minority, and feminist, scholars have convincingly argued that so-called value-free science in fact supports the central values of the dominant ideology in society and that claims to independent objectivity are central to maintaining control over definitions of the normal and abnormal, and appropriate and inappropriate social behaviour' (1993). For this reason, social scientists have backed away from a vision of the world where a single interpretation is right or true. Anthropologists have seen their interpretation of other cultures contested and rejected by the members of those cultures. Many social scientists now speak of truth as 'partial' or 'situated' both historically and politically. But as MacNeil suggests, however partial our understandings, we cannot abandon the *effort* for truth. Social science attempts to discover complexity in cultural life, with all its situated meanings. Like Van Willigen (1986: 29), I prefer to speak of value-explicit research, which remains empirical. Some interpretations are more logical than others; some are more firmly based in reliable methods and empirical practice. Our search for the best or most appropriate course of action must be subject to rigorous analysis of the information at hand, to continuing debate, and in line with our sharpest sense of what is appropriate political and ethical behaviour (Warry 1992).

Native people are fond of saying that they have been 'researched to death' (Warry 1990). These feelings are very common – most researchers have had the experience of being questioned about the relevance of their work, or have been taken to task by Aboriginal people for building their career on ideas taken from Aboriginal people. To say that communities feel 'researched to death' is to state, powerfully and metaphorically, that words and ideas, like bullets and bad medicine, can kill, disempower, or destroy. As anthropologists are all too aware, research is easily associated with the colonial project. But as I have argued elsewhere, this research lament is more about the way research has been conducted (the lack of native direction and control over the research process) and about the lack of applied research, than it is about research per se. It has been my experience that Aboriginal people are more than willing to give of their time and energy to a research project – providing they see some potential benefit or return from the research. At the First Nation's level, research can improve a community's ability to understand issues and plan for the future. Research can lead to the development and evaluation of programs and to new interventions (see, for example, Depew 1994a: 84–9; LaPrairie 1994c). Currently, as LaPrairie notes, new programs are often developed in response to political pressure, or in an attempt to provide equity in services, and in the absence of empirical research (ibid). And little evaluation research has been conducted on the broad socioeconomic and political environment into which new programs are placed.

There is also the perception in Aboriginal communities that research results accumulate dust on library shelves and never lead to change – change that 'any fool' can see is necessary. Many researchers – both government and academic – continue to develop programs of basic research that have little implication for policy or program development. It may also be that bureaucrats raise the need for additional study as a delaying strategy for reform. Inevitably, the time comes when peoples' desire for change may outrun their need to have new research or another understanding of an issue. Research is then regarded as another obstacle to change. In such cases it is important to recognize the limits to social science research. Ultimately, where common sense dictates the need for reform, the only rational, human response is to act on the basis of the best available information, and to trust people's local knowledge and their ability to create new and innovative programs. Once implemented, these programs must be evaluated to determine their effects.

Federal and provincial governments have funded Aboriginal research as part of ongoing program evaluation, or in direct response to historic grievances, as, for example, in land claims. But most Aboriginal communities lack the financial and human resources to conduct long-term research that would benefit their communities. While it is possible to suggest greater liaison and cooperation between specific communities, colleges, and universities (RCAP 1996f: 98), local research capacity must be enhanced before Aboriginal communities will be fully capable of developing programs to revitalize traditional medicine, law, and politics through participatory-research techniques that engage their community. Clearly, Aboriginal involvement in all aspects of research must be increased. The government, therefore, should commit itself to the development of cultural resource centres, policy centres, and research centres on a regional basis so as to enhance Aboriginal people's capacity for self-government.

Applied research must be community-based and -controlled, must respond to local needs, and must be put to use to improve people's lives. The research model that comes closest to attaining these goals is participatory-action research (PAR) (see B. Hall 1979; Warry 1990; Ryan and Robinson 1990; Castellano 1993; Ryan 1995). PAR can be an expensive and time-consuming methodology (Ryan 1995: xi, 7–22) and one full of challenges for researchers. The Health Transfer project outlined in chapter 3, for example, which occurred over a three-year period, was very successful in engaging a reasonable segment of North Shore communities in the data analysis, public education, and dissemination of research findings. These findings were immediately used to plan programs in what proved to be a very organic and iterative project. But the 'success' of the project, both in terms of public participation (and criticism) and in the utilization of findings, varied considerably between communities. Joan Ryan's description of justice research in Lac La Martre (1995) is an excellent example of PAR in the Aboriginal context. The project was community-based and -controlled. Aboriginal researchers and a Community Advisory Committee were engaged in all phases of the research. But even here, as Ryan notes, there were inevitable conflicts between academic and local agendas or expectations, and clashes over objectives and methodology.

PAR is as much a philosophy of research as a specific method. As a philosophy there are many ideals – turning research into action, enhancing community development, skills transfer, and many more – that social scientists should value. But as an applied research method, certain aspects of PAR must occasionally be sacrificed, adapted, or amended according to the aims and objectives of specific projects (see Reimer 1993). The demands of applied research – tight time frames, goal-specific research, and the need for intervention – often serve to distort the PAR method. For example, practical or political demands can sometimes make it difficult to ensure that community members fully participate in data analysis. And other PAR goals, such as skills transfer or adult education, are sometimes sacrificed due to lack of time or resources.

Such shortcomings are natural given the nature of PAR and the demands of specific types of applied research. My own inclination, for example, when confronted with tight time lines or small budgets has been to sacrifice widespread community participation for control over the research by a small and committed group of community representatives. Such individuals can determine research goals and ensure that the research has direct practical utility to the community. The project outlined chapter 6 is a good example of how short-term research, conducted by outsiders, can assist communities in creating a vision of community wellness by providing information needed for strategic planning. The success of the project rested on the contribution of a small number of people, perhaps seventy in all across six communities, who met with researchers to discuss, brainstorm, and rethink issues associated with community healing and wellness.

There is concern among some Aboriginal people that PAR is simply a rhetoric that is being used to gain entrance into communities, but is being ignored as researchers continue to engage in their own research agendas (Flaherty 1995). I am uncertain if this is a common problem or, as noted above, if this perception is partially explained by different understandings of PAR or other research methods. But to the extent that this problem occurs at all as conscious practice it is the worst form of intellectual colonialism. Social scientists must continue to explain their methods, and the problems associated with those methods, so that no confusion or misrepresentation occurs. And Aboriginal organizations must continue to advocate finding new ways – and new monies – to train people in research methods so as to decrease their reliance on outsiders, and to enhance collaboration between Native and non-Native researchers.

Like Hedican (1995), I would like to see anthropologists practice their craft unapologetically, while sustaining the discipline's traditional strengths and outlook in the pursuit of contemporary issues. These strengths have always included practical application and advocacy in Native issues (see, for example, Feit 1991b). The time has long passed when anthropologists could speak 'on behalf of' Aboriginal communities and clients. Aboriginal people are perfectly capable of putting forward their own positions, arguments, and research agendas. But we must continue to offer our methods, theories, and perspectives to Aboriginal communities in the hopes that, as outsiders, we can be of some assistance. And we must make a better effort at conveying our analyses to the wider Canadian public, so as to combat the 'pervasive lack of knowledge' of Aboriginal peoples among the Canadian public (RCAP 1996f: 92). Our awareness of colonial processes and the misrepresentation of the 'other' has also been painfully garnered and, as a result, we are sensitive to many of the ethical issues associated with cross-cultural research. But we cannot conduct our work while walking on eggshells. It is important to pursue truth even in the face of the critique of our work by Aboriginal people. If the relationship between social scientists and Aboriginal people cannot be sustained then we are all lost – simply because if a spirit of cooperation cannot be generated in this relationship, then the chance for reconciliation between Aboriginal people and the wider public would seem hopelessly doomed to failure.

Applied social science provides communities with new information and new arguments that can be used when negotiating with governments, or attempting to resource new initiatives. Research can help people to see their communities in new ways. The most dynamic points in any interview or discussion revolve around these small revelations – moments of clarity when people suddenly recognize the validity of an observation, or when they stop and say: 'Well, I hadn't thought of it like that before, but ...' It is for this reason that much applied research can be viewed in the context of an emergent re-visioning process – as a method of providing information that assists people in strategic planning, program development, or policy reform. In this way, social research provides communities with information and ideas to help people tackle a variety of contemporary concerns, and, in so doing, contributes to the ongoing project of self-government.

Reactions to the RCAP: Investing in Community Healing

We are confident that, given adequate financial resources, we have the human resources and strength to heal our community. That is our dream. (Canim Lake BC. 93-03-09 108. Roy Christopher, Canim Lake Band. PG 392)

Aboriginal people are confident that 'given adequate resources' First Nations can realize their dream of community healing. As chapter 6 demonstrated, Aboriginal leaders want to increase the self-reliance of their communities. They are restructuring their services to free up existing resources for new initiatives. In a world of offloading, downsizing, restructuring, and cutbacks the task facing First Nations is how to develop holistic approaches to community healing in the absence of sufficient resources. Clearly, new resources are needed; but given the current fiscal reality the public is unlikely to support any call for additional resources earmarked for Aboriginal people. What argument, if any, can be made to convince the public and political leaders that Aboriginal issues should be a priority?

In view of the many problems and challenges facing Aboriginal communities, it is supremely ironic that the RCAP – at $58 million the most expensive commission in Canadian history – has been criticized as a waste of taxpayers' money. There is certainly evidence that parts of the RCAP process have been highly politicized and ineffectual.[1] But over all, the public-education value of this commission cannot be questioned. The RCAP succeeded in promoting, over a period of more than five years, a great deal of public discussion about Aboriginal affairs. The royal commission has provided a template for long-term policy reform. It will be difficult for any researcher, policy analyst, or advocate to comment seriously on Aboriginal issues without reference to the RCAP findings. For these reasons the RCAP should surely be considered an important contribution to the future of Canada.

As could be expected, the federal government reaction to the RCAP reports was cautious and negative. Not coincidentally, the prime minister was out of the country when the report was released. The government moved rapidly to call the commission's suggestion for increased financial expenditures unrealistic. At the now infamous December 1996 CBC 'Town Hall' meeting, the prime minister was asked by Alex Dedam, an Aboriginal person from Burnt Church, New Brunswick, whether the RCAP recommendations would be implemented. The prime minister, while acknowledging the comprehensiveness of the reports, would state only 'some elements of the report' were 'extremely expensive,' that the government would try to place the recommendations 'into the fiscal framework of the nation,' but would not act on the report before the next federal election. In subsequent weeks, Ron Irwin tabled amendments to the Indian Act that were *totally out of step* with the RCAP recommendations. These amendments were overwhelmingly denounced by the AFN and by other Aboriginal leaders as a continuation of the paternalistic relationship between DIAND and First Nations (*Globe and Mail*, 13 Dec. 1996, A11). Both the prime minister and minister of Indian Affairs subsequently declined invitations to attend a national conference to discuss the recommendations, which was attended by more than three hundred chiefs from across the country (*Toronto Star*, 24 Feb. 1997, A12). The federal Liberal government's stated election stance was designed not to offend: the government was 'already implementing' many of the commission's recommendations, but the government's strategy for deficit reduction would not allow for 'expensive' spending on Aboriginal initiatives at this time.

The government's reaction to the RCAP reports merely reflected their calculated assessment of public opinion with regard to Aboriginal issues. Media reaction to the RCAP final reports and recommendations was predictably superficial and dismissive.[2] Rather than acknowledging the commission's precision and comprehensiveness, many reports superficially criticized the RCAP for its length (3,500 pages and five volumes). The cost and five-year tenure of the commission were routinely cited – as if to suggest there was a bargain-basement cost to the development of social policy. In fact, when measured against the size of the Canadian public, the commission's cost of about a 'twonie' per person seems reasonable. Political commentators were sceptical. *Globe and Mail* columnist Gordon Gibson seemed uninformed, cynical, and insulting in dismissing the idea of self-government as 'racially based' and in suggesting that such ideas as treaty renovation represented a 'fixation on the past instead of the future'.[3] Jeffrey Simpson suggested that the RCAP perspective rested on an 'airbrushed,' 'embellished,' and 'misleading' view of the past and criticized the RCAP reports as 'blue skies everything,' for setting 'maximalist positions, or wish-lists if you like, that have little, if any chance of being adopted' (*Globe and Mail*, 25 Feb. 1997, A14; 26 Feb. 1997, A16). Others who were more familiar with Native affairs, like Rudy Platiel, were prepared to suggest that the reports offered a 'road map' for long-term reform whose directions the government seemed unwilling, or unprepared, to take (*Globe and Mail*, 22 Nov. 1996, A1; 26 Dec. 1996, A4).

In hindsight, and given the neglect of or outward hostility to Aboriginal issues that characterizes Canadian public opinion (see chapters 1 and 4), many of the RCAP recommendations seem idealistic and unrealistic. For example, the RCAP calls for a new royal proclamation and companion legislation as a prelude to constitutional reform (1996b: 65–6). The proclamation would acknowledge, in general terms, 'the injustices of the past' associated with paternalism and express 'regret' for the harm caused to Aboriginal peoples by colonial and post-colonial policies (1996f: 5). Such a recommendation, however well intended, ignores the government's desire for non-legislative and non-constitutional solutions to questions of Aboriginal rights, as well as the tendency of public opinion to suggest that open acknowledgment of responsibility for past injustices is a political non-starter. The government's and the media's reaction to the reports, then, seems in keeping with a desire for a cautious, incremental, policy-based strategy rather than a radical, legislative, or constitutional approach to reform. Moreover, the reaction reflected the low priority given to Aboriginal issues in the national agenda of political issues.

The RCAP recommendations do not provide a single model or blueprint for self-government; rather they suggest a range of self-governing institutions and nations. But the final reports are, by any careful reading, comprehensive, pragmatic, and hopeful. The recommendations provide a template for social policy and social action across a broad range of jurisdictions. The reports set out an agenda for capacity building – an investment in the human potential of Aboriginal communities. There are recommendations for both short-term and long-term change, including structural reform. As important, the final volume sets out in a careful analysis the financial resources necessary for renewal of the relationship between Aboriginal peoples and the Canadian state. The RCAP analysis attempts to highlight the costs of the status quo – costs associated with the economic marginalization of Aboriginal peoples, which prevents them from contributing to the economy ($5.8 billion, the costs of 'forgone production') and costs associated with government expenditures on a variety of health, social service, and welfare programs that must be incurred in the absence of healthy and productive communities ($1.7 billion in 'remedial costs') (RCAP 1996f: 24–35). Combined, the RCAP estimates these costs to be $7.5 billion in 1996. Given that the Aboriginal adult population is growing at almost twice the rate of the general Canadian population, the commissioners note that these costs will only escalate in future unless major policy changes are implemented. The RCAP details its strategy, which is framed as a twenty-year commitment involving increased expenditures of between $1.5 and $2 billion per year above current levels. The RCAP projections suggest that this investment in Aboriginal communities would have to be sustained for ten to fifteen years before the costs associated with the status quo begin to decline (RCAP 1996f: 56–9).

In response to this analysis the federal government chose to stress only the unreasonable 'costs' of the commission's strategy given current fiscal constraints. The government reaction to the RCAP in general, and to its call for a major influx of 'investment dollars' in Aboriginal communities in particular, can only be seen as short-sighted. I have tried to suggest how innovative policy and program changes in Aboriginal communities might yield long-term savings to government – and the taxpayer. But I have avoided dealing with the 'price tag' of self-government because I do not believe that this is a fair way of thinking about Aboriginal aspirations. The

RCAP testimonies clearly indicate the fear-mongering that can accompany debates concerning the 'cost' of self-government.[4] To be fair, many Canadians understand that 'a century of neglect cannot be overcome overnight' and that long-term development potentially means a reduction of many current costs, including those associated with welfare (Ottawa ON. 93-11-01 254. Helen Buckley. PG 218).

Current and future funding commitments to First Nations are, in the end, a question of national character and philosophy. I believe the rhetoric about the cost of self-government is simply the last in a long line of rationales aimed at masking the colonial project. For the foreseeable future, the financing of Indian self-government will take place in what is an increasingly difficult fiscal environment, one in which the obsession with federal and provincial deficit reductions increasingly consumes government policy, political rhetoric, and expressions of public concern (see *Spectator*, 1 Dec. 1994, D10). As McQuaig (1995) has shown, arguments about the 'importance' of the deficit are inherently political, as well as economic. An obsession with the deficit leads to an overly simplistic attack on social spending, rather than to policies aimed at increasing revenues – for example, strategies to increase employment or to tax corporate interests (ibid). In times of budgetary restraint, arguments about the 'bottom line' serve those who would wish to stymie social reform. The RCAP advocated a long-term vision for the funding of Aboriginal self-government that would see the current costs of services *decline* as Indian economic development increases, and as social problems decrease. This, for me, is an essential perspective. As I have suggested throughout, those who suggest the 'costs' of self-government may be too great, often ignore *existing* costs for Indian services, and the long-term transition to Aboriginal control that could potentially lead to a decreased reliance on welfare or other forms of social assistance. The RCAP reports also stress the long-term contribution that healthy Aboriginal communities would make to local economies. Aboriginal leaders also emphasize that there are many hidden dollars currently attached to Aboriginal administration. It can be argued that First Nations are currently supporting a huge number of non-Native employees, through administration and support of civil servants in the 'Indian business.' By some estimates the costs associated with the DIAND bureaucracy account for 70% of all monies spent by the federal government on Indian affairs [see Vernon Roote, deputy grand chief, Union of Ontario Indians, North Bay ON. 93-05-10 171. PG 126]. Aboriginal leaders seek an honest accounting of the Indian business, which includes such hidden bureaucratic costs. They would also like to see studies comparing the cost of human services to the Canadian population generally with those delivered to their communities (see K. Scott 1993). Far from demanding the moon, Aboriginal people want an honest accounting of the cost of services delivered to their communities. They wish to decolonize the number crunching. By seeking control over resources – whether direct or hidden – that are currently a part of the federal government's contribution to Indian Affairs, they are asking for a redistribution of existing monies – from old services to new programs, from mainstream institutions to Aboriginally controlled institutions.

There are many alternative ways of thinking about the investment in self-government. It has been my experience that Aboriginal people are keenly aware of the current fiscal environment. What they ask for is sufficient resources to ensure the same level of services as those received by mainstream Canadians. And they demand that in calculating the costs of new initiatives, governments be honest in assessing the costs and benefits of Aboriginal administration. The process of self-government is shackled by a lack of resources. Aboriginal people are being nickelled and dimed to death. What is required is an influx of funds – investment capital – in alternative programs that can be used to shift our current human-service paradigm to one more community based, holistic in design, and Aboriginally controlled. To not invest in these developmental costs is sheer madness, which can only serve to sustain a status quo characterized by dysfunction, pain, and incalculable costs to human lives.

Many of the issues addressed in this book comprise what the RCAP considers 'capacity building,' that is, the capacity of Aboriginal nations to 'rebuild and reclaim nationhood' and the strategies necessary for the transition to self-government (1996b: 326–9). Two essential components of this transition, as argued in the previous chapter, are community healing and political processes for consensus building (ibid: 328–9). In other words, First Nations must find internal strength, as well as their place in larger cultural entities, so as to overcome political divisions and parochialism, which stymie the emergence of political units capable of forging the institutions necessary for self-government.

Under the rubric of healing initiatives, the RCAP suggests an investment of new monies over five years, totalling $525 million, in education, health care, social services, and justice.[5] Much of this investment is earmarked for initiatives aimed at children and youth, and to enhance institutions engaged in language and cultural activities. The RCAP strategy is predicated on the notion of capacity building, the revitalization of cultural systems (including traditional healing), and the promotion of holistic health for a future generation of Aboriginal adults (RCAP 1996f: 62, 68–9). Money spent on capacity building, cultural institutions, and traditional healing centres will greatly contribute to community revitalization. The RCAP also suggests that these funds be used to develop a youth strategy, which would incorporate recreational activities, counselling, and other interventions, and which would potentially have impact on the epidemic of Aboriginal suicide outlined in chapter 4 (ibid: 68).

Federal and provincial expenditures on capacity building need to be substantially increased even in the face of cuts to health and human services in other areas. This will require governments to exert considerable resolve. Aboriginal communities will also need to ensure that money is well spent and in keeping with the search for long-term innovation in institution building. In previous chapters I have tried to point to examples of such innovations.

In sum, Canadians can continue to adopt a philosophy that views Aboriginal initiatives as an additional cost and burden on an already strained system. Or they can begin to see the resolution of Aboriginal issues as a major investment in Canada's future. Speaking to the RCAP (1993a), Dean James MacPherson [Ottawa ON. 92-11-27 98. PG 735] argued the costs of Aboriginal initiatives should be measured against the equally grievous costs of building new prisons, or the government's lavish expenditures on weapons of war or ministerial travel. Such views may sound idealistic, given that Aboriginal affairs are a low priority for most Canadians. But they point to the need to weigh the costs and benefits of various priorities in comparison to the project of self-government. In the end, therefore, an investment in self-government turns on a vision where Aboriginal people are central rather than peripheral to the renovation of a new Canadian society.

Community Healing and the Reality of Self-Government

The statistics speak for themselves. There is no denying the many problems faced by Aboriginal communities. Rather than focus on desperation and despair, I have tried to emphasize how Aboriginal people are working, often in difficult conditions and without adequate resources, to improve their communities. I am constantly impressed by the efforts of community members and First Nations leadership who come together to create programs to better serve their community while reflecting traditional ideas of holistic health. I am struck by people's patience, perseverance, and tenacity in the face of layers upon layers of bureaucratic red tape, and government negotiations that often seem designed to frustrate even the most reasonable request for new resources.

Ultimately, the processes of self-government and community healing are related. Individual healing fuses self-actualization and political commitment through a deeply spiritual understanding of one's cultural identity. This process of individual healing produces people who are firmly committed to the idea of cultural revitalization and self-determination. Those who have experienced personal recovery understand how the history of colonial relationships has negatively affected their lives and their communities. Many of these individuals are leaders in their community; their actions over time are providing important models for the next generation of children and youth. More generally, community healing is about collective approaches to change that enhance Aboriginal cultural identity. It is about family and community crisis intervention, integrated human services, political cooperation, and public participation in processes of planned change and institution building. The potential of holistic approaches for community healing is perhaps best demonstrated in the idea of 'justice as healing,' justice that restores harmony in a community and heals individuals by attending to the needs of victims and offenders. However ideal, such a legal philosophy is inherently constructive and constitutive in its orientation because it emphasizes personal development and mental health, rather than deviance or criminality. The idea that justice programs can serve as a locus for community healing is, I believe, a simple and radical notion.

Recognition of self-government would enhance community healing by enabling communities to carve out the jurisdictional space where, free from state intervention, such innovation could occur. Nothing in my argument should be taken to suggest that I am opposed to constitutional reform. There is little doubt in my mind that state recognition of the inherent right to self-government would have great symbolic and practical value for First Nations. The term self-government conjures up ideas about cultural integrity, sovereignty, and equality between nations. Constitutional entrenchment of self-government would signal to non-Native Canadians that Aboriginal culture has been sustained in the face of overwhelming assimilative policies that have attempted to put an end, literally and figuratively, to the 'Indian problem.' Pragmatically, constitutional entrenchment would provide the philosophical platform for innovative policy-making at all levels of government. The constitutional solution, therefore, has immediate implications for community healing – because no single act could so easily affirm the value of Aboriginal culture.

But barring a major revisiting of constitutional issues in the light of another Quebec referendum, constitutional entrenchment does not seem to be in the cards for the near future. The deck is stacked against Aboriginal interests. The Liberal government's reaction to the RCAP recommendations has signalled their commitment to the constitutional status quo. Indeed, as the Assembly of First Nations has recognized, a federal proposal for regional vetoes on constitutional reform virtually bars the door to any immediate revisiting of the constitutional entrenchment of Aboriginal self-government (*Spectator*, 6 Dec. 1995, A6). But even in the absence of constitutional reform, a number of other incremental strategies and policy reforms are available to federal and provincial governments. Holistic approaches require governments to be more innovative in designing policies and require funding approaches that coordinate federal and provincial initiatives. Ontario's Aboriginal Healing and Wellness Strategy is an example of a policy that begins to bring together various ministries and recognizes the need for provincial action in the community healing process.

There are many opportunities – in health, justice, and social policy – for provincial governments to support Aboriginal initiatives, both on and off reserve. But political and bureaucratic action must be built on an attitude of respect for First Nations as equal partners in tripartite decision-making. As an interim measure governments might begin to develop new funding envelopes and block grants to First Nations or tribal councils that would provide a resource base for community-based initiatives. It may be that some First Nations or PTOs may wish to forgo provincial relationships in order to stress the federal government's fiduciary responsibility to status Indians. But the majority of First Nations now recognize that the boundaries between federal and provincial jurisdictions are as arbitrary as the designations between status and non-status Indians. Similarly, in an era of institutional rationalization, Aboriginal organizations must work to overcome their internal divisions, and, where appropriate, must develop shared institutions that link urban and reserve populations.

We can expect that as community healing takes hold, a spirit of reconciliation will infiltrate government decision-making. Many public servants comment on 'how different' it is dealing with Aboriginal communities. They speak, often with great optimism, of lessons they have learned from Aboriginal people. They understand how traditional top-down policy-making simply cannot work with First Nations. And they understand how a respect for community-based decision making requires renovation to the way policy analysis and program implementation is conducted. But they often feel constrained by departmental boundaries or corporate culture. Innovative approaches to the problems of Aboriginal communities require policy-makers to critically assess the ideological assumptions that make up bureaucratic culture – for example, ideas that perpetuate notions about the superiority of Western law or biomedicine.

The extension of state control through Western institutions takes many forms. The Indian Act, an antiquated piece of colonial legislation intimately understood by most Indian people, unknown to most Canadians, and unfathomable in its paternalism to most who have read it, continues to structure First Nation–government relationships and colour every aspect of reserve life. Bureaucratic rigidity and conservatism continue to hamper community-based attempts to reform even the most basic services delivered on reserve. I have tried to reveal some of the specific, and often insidious, effects of the continuing state intervention in Native community life. The 'democratic' elections of band councils, the suppression of traditional medicine and law, and funding arrangements that compartmentalize service delivery have been examined to suggest the ways in which state action continues to hamper a search for culturally appropriate solutions to community problems.

From preceding chapters it should be clear that governments must relinquish control over services so as to allow First Nations the freedom to experiment with innovative community-healing initiatives. Program enhancement in health, mental health, and justice services will greatly assist the community-healing process. Pilot projects in these fields should be encouraged and evaluated. If we accept the notion that cultural knowledge or the revitalization of traditional ways is essential to the process of community healing, then the funding of cultural initiatives – be they resource centres, powwows, traditional justice systems, or healing lodges – should be seen as central to the process of community development, rather than as a (frivolous) component of multicultural or ethnic programming.

The project of self-government is as complex and varied as the economic and cultural differences that exist between First Nations. Much work remains to be done by regional PTOs, tribal councils, and individual First Nations to determine how powers and jurisdictions will be shared. Tribal councils such as Mamaweswen have already invested considerable time and effort to lay the foundation for assuming control over a broad range of jurisdictions. At the same time devolution experiments are ongoing. First Nations in Manitoba are engaged in a ten-year process to eliminate the Department of Indian Affairs. Effort is also being expended to develop regional institutions – for example, Aboriginal educational institutions and health commissions. There is, then, much to be done in order to sort out the multi-level jurisdictions and powers that will support self-governing nations or tribal councils. Tribal councils have enormous potential as institutional vehicles for self-government. But considerable work remains to be done at the local level to develop trust and communication between First Nations. First Nations may insist on maintaining their authority – authority derived from the Indian Act – but ultimately new political arrangements will be required that link First Nations with regional and urban-based organizations if self-government is to be effectively administered. The work of negotiating new protocols necessary to ensure regional program delivery will be considerable, and will force First Nations to overcome mistrust, fear, and suspicion that often exist between small communities.

Aboriginal people have accomplished a great deal since the rejection of the White Paper more than twenty-five years ago. But much remains to be done to create and manage a new relationship between First Nations and the Canadian state. Non-Natives can provide support to the project of self-government. A slight majority of Canadians currently supports self-government. This tentative support needs to be translated into concerted political action, and this will emerge only with continued debate and dialogue about the true meaning of self-government. An excellent platform for these discussions now exists in the form of the RCAP reports. The Canadian public must recognize the complex work already occurring in Aboriginal communities, work aimed at developing community-based and culturally appropriate solutions to local problems. The reality of self-government is unthreatening once it is grounded in an understanding of the nature of Aboriginal communities and the legitimacy of Aboriginal cultural ways. A central premise of this book has been that the project of self-government is *ongoing*. Despite a lack of resources, despite a web of state regulation and the extension of bureaucratic control, First Nations are acting, through advocacy, through the courts, and often in direct opposition to government policy, to establish their control over new jurisdictions. But transitional, long-term thinking on the part of governments is needed to ensure the development of programs that are potentially more cost-effective, more culturally appropriate, and more efficient than those currently in existence.

As Charlotte Rich, a Davis Inlet elder, reminds us, change is like cleaning a caribou – you must do it slowly. The type of change necessary to ensure that self-government becomes a reality cannot be implemented with the scratch of a pen. Lasting reform must be generated from within communities, and built on the health and well-being of the next generation of Aboriginal children and families. Patience and perseverance are required – time heals. It takes time to discover the scars that have been left on the collective soul of communities by centuries of colonialism. It takes time for Aboriginal people to rediscover their culture and traditions and for individuals to restore authentic and vibrant social processes that can supplant the antiquated institutions of the state.

There is a sense of optimism that Aboriginal people are entering a critical age. Many Aboriginal people speak of the tangible signs that they are entering the seventh generation – a time when their children's dreams and visions can be fully realized and where reconciliation with mainstream society will occur. There exists a vision of a time when Aboriginal culture will be respected rather than denigrated, of a time when whites will turn to Native people for fundamental lessons – lessons that speak to human dignity, respect for human and animal life, and justice based on the need to heal rather than to punish. In all of this, there is a spiritual message, and though I suspect that I have expressed it inadequately, there is a spiritual awakening in Indian country that drives the processes of community healing and self-government.

This optimism is tinged by radicalism that the Canadian public has witnessed – at Oka and Ipperwash and through a series of minor protests, blockades, and office occupations that have occurred in recent years. Oka and Ipperwash remind us that some Aboriginal people clearly see the continuing effects of post-colonialism and are frustrated at the pace of change. But, by and large, these disruptions have been minor and temporary – at least when contrasted to the large-scale civil disobedience and violence associated with other social movements. The fact that the vast majority of Aboriginal people favour a cautious and measured approach to change should not give rise to complacency. There is a momentum to the self-government process that must be sustained. Aboriginal conservatism begins in First Nations, and is carried forward through the actions of Aboriginal political leaders who remain deeply committed to processes of consultation, consensus building, and tripartite discussion. Aboriginal patience is revealed in the quiet determination that accompanies First Nations as they proceed through years, and sometimes decades, of negotiations over land claims. And it is demonstrated in the final settlement of claims, which, by any evaluation, show that economic justice and self-sufficiency can be obtained without crippling the interests of mainstream Canadians.

This sense of optimism, pragmatic awareness, and a conservative approach to change is deeply embedded in Aboriginal communities and is evident in the dedication of people to long-term structural reform. There is little doubt that some First Nations could assume control over a wide range of jurisdictions tomorrow. But most Aboriginal communities recognize that much work needs to be done in preparation for self-government. The reality of most Aboriginal communities is this: people grappling with enormously complex social problems despite minimal resources, demonstrating incredible initiative, and gradually increasing their communities' capacity to plan, implement, and evaluate services in a wide range of jurisdictions. This conservative view of self-government *as process* is at odds with a vision of self-government that can be proclaimed overnight. Constitutional recognition for self-government is important and necessary; support for constitutional reform will be enhanced if Canadians understand self-government as a long-term process. Mainstream Canadians, and a great many Aboriginal people, remain suspicious about the implications of self-government and reject a rapid transfer of power to communities. Native leaders who utilize the political rhetoric to argue the benefits of self-government 'now' run the risk of being perceived as naïve optimists who have failed to learn the lesson of hidden government agendas throughout colonial history, or who are accused of turning a blind eye to the problems of their communities. It is a supreme irony that the rhetoric of self-government is now rejected by many Aboriginal people as a *government-driven* agenda for change that jeopardizes their treaty rights, and the long-standing fiduciary responsibilities of the Canadian state.

The unfinished dreams of Aboriginal people represent lost opportunities and lost lives. The dream is of many Nations within a Nation, of healthy communities and individuals who make a meaningful contribution to a new, more tolerant Canadian society. The dreams of Aboriginal people are easily articulated; they exist as a template for action. The crisis in Canadian politics is not one of dollars and cents, but one of vision and imagination. Aboriginal people are engaged in a painstaking process to improve the vision of the federal and provincial governments and to expand the circle of learning and respect. In as much as knowledge has the potential to bring people together rather than to divide, education is healing. What is required on the part of mainstream Canadians and their governments is greater understanding of how self-government might revitalize the country as a whole. Such a vision would demonstrate to the world that Canada is a leader in the field of indigenous rights. An apt starting-point would be support for the many initiatives that would increase the capacity for community healing. What Aboriginal people request of Canadians is long-term vision – something they often see is all too lacking in government, but is natural to a people who have endured centuries of colonial domination and are now beginning to fully assert themselves on the Canadian consciousness.

Notes

1: Self-Government: The Political Environment

1 This citation style indicates that a quotation is taken from the electronic transcripts of the Royal Commission on Aboriginal Peoples (1993a) CD-ROM database, released by Libraxis Inc., 221 Patterson Ave, Ottawa ON, Canada, K1S 1Y4; (613) 567–2484. The citation style includes the date of the public submission and enables the reader to locate the precise quotation through the database search engine/query program. Discussion papers or other published RCAP materials are identified separately in the bibliography and by author and date in the text.

2 For those readers unfamiliar with Native spiritual practices, smudging is the burning of sacred plants such as tobacco, sage, sweet grass, and cedar to spiritually cleanse or purify a person. Commonly the smoke is swept up by a person with the hands in a movement similar to washing oneself from a basin of water.

3 The North Shore Tribal Council First Nations are Whitefish Lake, Sagamok Anishnabek, Serpent River, Mississauga, Thessalon, Garden River, and Batchewana.

4 A brief note on terminology. Like Hedican (1995: 5–6), I use the general term Aboriginal and capitalize the term out of deference to Aboriginal practice, to indicate a unique status and unique identity. I use the word Indian when speaking of status Indians, that is, those people recognized under the Indian Act. This term, which has now fallen in disfavour, is still sometimes used by Aboriginal people, with radical or highly specific connotations; for example, as in the term 'Indian country' or 'Indian way,' and I retain these usages. Native is used as an alternative to Aboriginal and often as a stylistic device in contrast to the term non-Native. Finally, the terms Euro-Canadian or non-

Native refer to members of the predominant Western culture, and 'mainstream' Canadians refers to all non-Natives, including those of 'ethnic' backgrounds.

5 On the death of the Meech Lake Accord and its impact on constitutional expressions of Aboriginal rights, see RCAP (1996a: 212).

6 Richard Preston (personal communication) notes that one difference between guilt and shame is in the locus of action or belief: guilt is private and individuated; shame is public and socially sanctioned. At some level, therefore, this dichotomy may speak to the relative stress placed on individual versus collective rights and action.

7 Although each new poll brings questions that are worded differently, the general attitudes to self-government remain relatively consistent over time. See, for example, *The Globe and Mail*, 7 Dec. 1996, A4, for an August 1996 poll that reported that 40% of people believed self-government would improve living conditions on reserves, while 31% said it would bring little change. Here again, people living in Quebec and the Prairies had the most negative view of the impact of self-government.

8 See Simpson (1994: 220–5) for a more detailed analysis of public opinion polls, including the results of focus groups conducted across Canada by the Department of Indian Affairs and polls that revealed Aboriginal people to be against the stand taken by the Assembly of First Nations on the Charlottetown Accord.

9 Elected in 1990, the NDP government was generally seen as supportive of a wide range of Aboriginal initiatives and was the first provincial government to formally recognize First Nations' right to self-government through a political accord. It is generally accepted, however, that Aboriginal issues became less of a priority for the Rae government after Aboriginal leaders withdrew support for his constitutional initiative during the Charlottetown constitutional negotiations. None the less, a number of significant advances, most noticeably in health care, were made under the Rae government (see chapter 3).

10 See Hedican (1995: 204–15) for a description of a 'hateful little bit of literature' by Jacobson (1975), which emerged in the aftermath of the Anishnabe Park occupation. Hedican's discussion of racism is valuable because it is placed within the context of the politics of Aboriginal identity, including status Indians, non-status Natives, and Métis, which are the product of colonial policy.

11 Of course, the question of land and financial resources cannot be limited to the population of status Indians currently living on reserve. The RCAP projected a total Aboriginal population of 811,400, or 2.7% cent of the total population in Canada by 1996 (RCAP 1996a: 15).

12 See RCAP (1993d: 22). It appears that Francis is drawing on the RCAP figure of 10,313 sq. miles, which, as the RCAP notes, excludes areas of Northern Quebec and the Northwest Territories (including Nunavut), which are not subject to traditional treaties. That is, if we restrict the discussion to those 2,200 reserves designated as treaties, they comprise less than .05% of the Canadian land mass of 3.8 million square miles.

13 There are more than 1,000 references to problems associated with racism in the royal commission public hearings. Readers who wish to pursue further the issue of systemic racism might begin with the testimony of Theresa Holizki, chief commissioner of the Saskatchewan Human Rights Commission (Saskatoon SK. 92-10-28. PG 35) and Ronnie Leah, professor of sociology at the University of Lethbridge (Lethbridge AB. 93-05-24. PG 11).

14 The RCAP suggests a model of urban self-government that would see urban institutions as 'extensions of Aboriginal nation government' (1996b: 262–3). That is, urban institutions would be linked to groups of reserve-based nations, an interesting, if unrealistic, proposal given current tensions between on- and off-reserve groups. Urban Aboriginal communities are not the focus of this book. The size of urban populations make them equivalent to or larger than any First Nation in Canada. In Hamilton, for example, there are an estimated 10,000 to 12,000 Aboriginal people; in Toronto, between 40,000 and 80,000. While the development of urban Aboriginal institutions may be complex, I do not believe that there are any legal or philosophical obstacles that would prevent the recognition of self-government for Aboriginal people living off reserve.

15 For additional detail concerning the historical, philosophical, and legal foundation of Aboriginal rights, see Berger 1991; Nahanee 1993; Morse 1985; Ponting 1986; Boldt and Long 1985. For legal and constitutional reviews, including case law, see Slattery 1991, 1992; Borrows 1992; Pratt 1993, and the introduction to Kulchyski 1994.

16 See, for example, the recent Draft Declaration on the Rights of Indigenous Peoples by the Organization of American States (1995). The concept of intellectual property rights, which has important implications for social science research, is too complex to discuss here. Readers interested in this subject might begin with Greaves' sourcebook (1994); in particular, with articles by Pinel and Evans, and by Chapman.

17 The major formulation of resistance theory occurred without reference to the Canadian Aboriginal example, though recent analysis, for example of residential schools (Furniss 1995), has incorporated this idea. For the development and elaboration of the concept of resistance, see Comaroff 1985, J.C. Scott 1990, and Ortner 1995.

18 See also RCAP (1996b: 58–63) for analysis of contemporary treaty making or equivalent processes.

19 When considering land and resources it is also important to note that 62% cent of registered North American Indians live in what the RCAP defined as southern Canada, while the other 38% lived in the North (32% in the mid North and 6% in the far North). The reader should also consult the RCAP's analysis of the inadequacy of reserve land bases, particularly when compared to the size of reservations in the United States.

20 Elimination of the Indian Act or Indian Affairs bureaucracy should not be confused with self-government. Manitoba is in the midst of a ten-year experiment to devolve the responsibilities of the Indian Affairs department. The experiment began with an agreement signed by Ron Irwin, Minister of Indian Affairs, and Phil Fontaine, Manitoba Chiefs, on 7 December 1994, in Fort Garry Place, Manitoba. The ceremony was interrupted by the protest of one young Aboriginal demonstrator, who begged Fontaine not to sign the agreement (*Toronto Star*, 24 Apr. 1994).

21 The RCAP addresses this matter by arguing that claims by local communities numbering only a few hundred individuals would 'distort' the right of self-determination, 'which as a matter of international law, is vested in "peoples"' (RCAP 1996b: 177–8).

22 Certain bands, through historic peculiarities, or more commonly, because of their size, remain independent of regional political organizations. For example, Six Nations First Nation, with a registered membership of 17,603, and 8,500 people on reserve, is the largest reserve by population in Ontario, and remains independent of other political organizations (though it is linked to other Nations through traditional political alliances). The size of this band makes it larger than many tribal councils.

23 These are AIAI, the Association of Iroquois and Allied Indians, based in London, which represents Iroquois bands in southern Ontario; The Anishnabek Nation, also known as the Union of Ontario Indians, representing Ojibwa communities in southern, north-central, and northern Ontario; Treaty Three, which represents Ojibwa bands in northwestern Ontario (based in Kenora), and Nishnawbe-Aski Nation (NAN), based in Sioux Lookout and Thunder Bay, which represents Cree and Ojibwa bands in northeastern Ontario.

2: The Challenge of Community Healing

1 My discussion in this chapter draws on John O'Neil's excellent review 'Aboriginal Health Policy for the Next Century' (1993) for the Royal Commis-

sion on Aboriginal Peoples. See also the RCAP's (1993b) report on health and social issues. O'Neil (1993: n.1) notes that the term 'social health' first appeared in the literature on Aboriginal health in the work of Joan Feather (1991) to integrate 'ideas about health drawn from family and community medicine, mental health and Aboriginal ideas about holistic health and the medicine wheel.'

2 Dupuis (1993) notes that 'Aboriginal women suffer a dual handicap.' In 1991 the average salary of a full-time Canadian worker in the private sector was $38,198 (men $42,715 and women $31,538); the average salary of Aboriginal workers was $33,101 ($36,817 for men and $27,602 for women). In the public sector the average salary was $40,453 (men $44,734 and women $36,697) while the average salary of Aboriginal public servants was $36,227 (men $40,086 and women $33,848). The difference between the average salary of Aboriginal women and that of women generally was less marked in the public than in the private sector.

3 For additional information and analysis concerning Aboriginal education and economic well-being, see the following references, which have been culled from the RCAP CD-ROM database: Armstrong, Kennedy, and Oberle 1990; Banerjee et al 1991; Drost and Eryou 1991. For analysis of Native and non-Native labour market participation, see George and Kuhn 1993; Patrinos and Sekellariou 1992; and Peters and Rosenberg 1992. See also Brenda Tsioniaon La France (RCAP Discussion Paper No. 9) and the remarks of Joyce Goodstriker, superintendent of education, Blood Tribe, Ottawa, ON. 93-07-6 89. PG 154.

4 See the RCAP final reports for a major discussion of housing in relation to social policy (1996d: 365–421). For first-hand experience and testimony concerning the relationship between health and housing conditions the reader should consult the RCAP public hearings. See, for example, Tom Iron, Federation of Saskatchewan Indian Nations. (Wahpeton SK. 92-05-26 228. PG 143); see also Marg Beament (SK. 92-05-28 111. PG 109); Ronn Blinn (Watson Lake YT. 92-05-28 69. PG 53); Councillor Eric Large (Hobbema AB. 92-06-10 172. PG 232, 233); Marlene Poitras (Edmonton AB. -2 92-06-11 98. PG 309); Charlotte Wolfrey, (Rigolet) Housing (Makkovik NF. 92-06-15 219. PG 172); Harold Prince (Stoney Creek BC. 92-06-18 275. PG 147); Chief Stewart Paul (Tabilk NB. 92-11-02 11. PG 12); Philip Rich (Davis Inlet NF. 92-12-01 275. PG 99); Donna Roundhead (Sioux Lookout ON. 92-12-01 205. PG 243). For the effects of the National Housing Act on the financial burden of individuals seeking to build housing, see Tony Anderson, Torngat Regional Housing Association (Nain NF. 92-11-30 352. PG 254), and for an example of the housing problems faced by non-reserve Indians as a result of CMHC policies see Frank Sutherland (Orillia ON. 93–05–12 31. PG 58); Ken Harris,

Meensganist Housing Society (Prince Rupert BC. 93–05–26 211. PG 192); Mathew Stewart (Vancouver BC. 93-06-03 65. PG 399); and Sylvia Maracle (Toronto ON. 93-11-19 26. PG 352).

5 Inadequate housing – especially affordable housing for single mothers and low-income families – is a major problem faced by Aboriginal people in urban centres, where for years Aboriginal groups were not allowed funds under provincial cooperative initiatives (Warry and Moffat 1993).

6 Like many Canadians, I do not think Aboriginal reform should in any way replace or supplant commitments to international development. I mention this characterization because it is important to stress that Aboriginal communities perceive a need to emphasize the same kind of commitment to development as is frequently assumed in reference to the Third World.

7 See Warry and Moffat (1993). Even in Southern Ontario, Indian infants had rates of pneumonia that were more that 17.6 times greater than non-Native children (Evers and Rand 1982, 1983). The relatively recent (post – World War II) dietary shift among Natives from traditional to processed foods has resulted in an increased risk of a variety of health problems in children, including low birth weights, nearsightedness, iron deficiency, and obesity (T.K. Young 1979).

8 Cancer is one disease for which there is a lower incidence among Aboriginal people than in the mainstream Canadian public (Waldrum et al 1995: 4–18). But as the authors note, the survival rate for cancer patients is lower in Aboriginal people, possibly because of differences in diagnosis patterns and utilization of health services. See also Gillis, Irvine, and Tan (1991).

9 I return to the issue of Aboriginal suicide in chapter 4. Since the early 1970s the rates of Aboriginal suicide have dramatically climbed, and, over the past decade, have consistently remained two to three times the national average. Current statistics place the overall rate of status Indian suicide at 3.3 times the national average. The rate for Inuit is 3.9 times the national average. In the age category of 10–19, suicide rates during the period 1986–90 were 5.1 times the national average. For those under 25 years of age, the suicide rate is the highest of any racial group in the world (Canada 1992a: 18). Suicide rates are generally higher for males, while suicide attempts are more frequent in females. In the Sioux Lookout region, where 800 suicide attempts have been reported in a six-year period, the suicide rate is as much as seven times the national average.

10 Health promotion advocates suggest that more education about prenatal care is needed for Aboriginal women. Farkas et al (1989) suggest Aboriginal women may have different explanatory models of health during pregnancy, in which they view pregnancy as a natural event and not a medical risk.

11 These surveys can be questioned on methodological grounds, and I cite these figures, as reported, while acknowledging the difficulties of defining family violence for the purpose of surveys, and the difficulties of obtaining random samples among Aboriginal populations.

12 The reconstruction of pre-contact health and disease partly revolves around recent epidemiological studies of pre-contact populations, which have lowered the estimates of the numbers of Aboriginal people who lived in North America before contact (see Waldrum et al 1995; Herring 1992; Dobyns 1983).

13 In my experience, Aboriginal people seem to easily convey holistic analysis. They link what at first appearance are divergent or unrelated ideas, often on the basis of personal experience. For example, when he responds to a question about the meaning of 'community healing' it is not uncommon for a chief to start with the need for new forms of elections in offering a solution to patterns of alcohol abuse of interpersonal violence. These responses often seem to miss the intent of questions; they appear to be 'leaps of logic.' But on reflection and further elaboration, Native informants invariably trace critical causal links between various levels of action, and weave complex strings of explanation that bring history into the search for contemporary solutions. In this instance, the suggestion of a new type of council election speaks to the need to enhance a person's participation in political process and increase his or her sense of belonging to the community.

3: Vision and Illusion: Health-Care Planning and Community Control

1 A short-term evaluation of the initiative by Adrian Gibbons and Associates (1992) raised many specific concerns. Most of these revolve around the fact the policy does not allow for program evolution or enrichment. Scott (1993) notes, for example, that there are inadequate services for Fetal Alcohol Syndrome (FAS) and AIDS cases in the post-transfer scenario.

2 The expanded Health Board, involving all seven First Nations, was established in 1989. However, as Marlene Nose notes (personal communication 1995), the evolution of the board began in 1981 with the actions of three First Nations: Sagamok, Serpent River, and Mississauga. The experience of these three communities in planning and cooperating was important in sustaining the board's continued engagement in the transfer process.

3 For a review of the CHR program see Toulouse and Roberts (1988) and Assembly of First Nations (1988a). For the NNADAP program see Four Worlds (1990). Young and Smith (1992) review the literature on community participation in health policy and services. O'Neil (1986; 1990) analyses Inuit health and colonialism. On the topic of traditional health practice, including its

relationship to mainstream medical care, see O'Neil (1988) and Young (1988). The Health Transfer policy is outlined in Canada (1989b). Gregory et al (1992) document transfer in Gull Bay.

4 I use the term 'consultants' to refer to outsiders (external paid 'experts') as well as in the terms 'key consultants' and 'Aboriginal/Native consultants'; the latter are what anthropologists formerly referred to as key informants, that is, workers, elders, leaders, or other experts located in the community.

5 Because much of the survey focused on health perception, it cannot be used to compare NSTC health status to many of the health indicators cited in the previous chapter.

6 This discussion of health status draws on reports prepared by Doug Sider for the NSTC Health Board (NSTC 1995a, 1995b).

7 In the Ontario Health Survey (PD-37) the prevalence of alcohol problems was examined differently, through an alcoholism-screening questionnaire; but the OHS reported that only 10% (approximately) of Ontario Health Survey respondents over 16 years of age (males 14%, females 5%) were judged to have problems related to alcohol use.

8 O'Neil (1993: 37) notes that 'Canada is one of the few countries in the world where medical pluralism is not a taken for granted aspect of everyday life.' Acceptance of 'complementary' medicine has increased in recent years, but this progress has not been matched in other jurisdictions, for example, in legal pluralism (see chapter 5).

9 See Treat (1996) for a collection of articles written by Aboriginal people concerning Christian belief and its implications for cultural identity and revitalization.

10 The most powerful healers, either male or female, who possessed supernatural power and used this with good intention, are called *wabano*. The *wabano* are distinguished from specialists in ritual, *djiskid,* who held shaking tent ceremonies, and who acquired healing gifts and visions during the puberty fast, and from *mide,* who, according to consultants, could practice either good or bad medicine.

11 See Stephenson et al (1995) for a discussion of Aboriginal health, and health-care provision in British Columbia.

12 This is now the Canada Health and Social Transfer. See Kim Scott (1993) for a discussion of the need to reform funding strategies for Aboriginal people. She notes that CAP defined how the federal government shares the cost with provinces/territories and municipalities for the provision of social assistance and welfare services. EPF directed federal cost sharing of insurable health services, that is, medically necessary treatment, delivered by the provinces.

13 The strategy is to be formally evaluated in 1997. In 1996, after the completion

of the draft of this book, I, along with a number of colleagues, developed an evaluation design for the AHWS (Northwind: 1996). The information here is based on previous interviews and not on the consultation that led to the evaluation design.

14 The RCAP acknowledged the development of the Aboriginal Healing and Wellness Strategy as an example of how Aboriginal people can be involved in systems change. In fact, many aspects of the AHWS seem to have influenced the RCAP recommendations, including the call to develop a network of healing lodges, and recommendations 3.3.7 and 3.3.8, which emphasize integrated service delivery, and the involvement of Aboriginal organizations in regional planning and coordination of services (1996d: 242).

4: Mental Health: The Failure of Government Practice

1 There is little doubt that many forms of mental illness, including those that Western psychiatrists might diagnose as schizophrenia, depression, etc., exist in First Nations, and that front-line workers would benefit from training that would assist them in identifying these or other mental illnesses. These diagnoses, of course, are compounded by questions about the validity of diagnostic categories within a cross-cultural context. But here I am speaking of how Aboriginal people can reject theories of individual psychology in favour of more culturally appropriate explanations of spiritual, emotional, and psychological disease that are influenced by broader social relationships.

2 Reported rates of sexual abuse or family violence vary greatly according to the definition of abuse offered in the survey questions. Certainly, there has also been increased knowledge of these issues, which, presumably, has increased reporting rates. But the stigma associated with these behaviours would seem to me to suggest that actual rates may be even greater than those reported.

3 Unless otherwise noted, all quotations in this chapter are drawn from the 1995 consultation, many of which appear in Justice and Warry (1996). Because of issues of confidentiality, the names of consultants were not identified in that report, and I follow this protocol here.

4 Although certain drugs, for example, peyote, were used by some Aboriginal people in the United states, alcohol was not found in Native North America before contact with Europeans.

5 Many studies have highlighted the tragedy of Aboriginal suicide. For example, the *Report of the Advisory Commission on Indian and Inuit Health Consultation* drew specific attention to the incidence of violent and accidental death, pointed to the fact that the Aboriginal suicide rate had doubled since 1975, and acknowledged that, were an equivalent ratio of deaths to occur in the *non-Native*

population, this pattern would be 'viewed as a national disaster' (Canada 1980: 3). See also the *Report of the National Task Force on Suicide in Canada* (1987); *Indian Self-Government in Canada* (1983), also known as the Penner Report; and the Canadian Psychiatric Association (1985).

5: Restoring Justice: Conflict with the Law

1 My discussion is limited to criminal law, but I note that the ability to make laws in a range of jurisdictions is integral to the creation of self-governing nations. For example, First Nations have expressed their interest in having the power to make laws concerning resource use or citizenship.

2 For other testimony in the RCAP database concerning the problems faced by Aboriginal inmates and the need for correctional reform see Harvey Thunderchild (Sault Ste Marie ON. 92-06-11 218. PG 190), Alfreda Trudeau (92-06-11 220. PG 197), Brian Espaniel (Guelph CC. 92-06-25 246. PG 297), Wilson Plain (Sarnia ON. 93-05 154. PG 185), Sanford Cottrelle (Sudbury ON. 93-05-31 76. PG 92).

3 While employed by the Ontario Native Council on Justice in 1986, I conducted a small survey concerning legal-aid in Aboriginal communities. At the time, legal-aid certificates were rarely available at band offices, and the legal-aid 'means test' included many items such as boats and motors that, while considered luxuries in Southern communities, were necessities in the North. As a result of subsequent discussions with ONCJ staff, the legal-aid plan responded by making a number of changes and adjustments to its procedures.

4 Ryan (1995: see 21 (notes); 41) cautions us to interpret the status of women within the context of the times and correctly notes that the isolation of women rested on notions about their inherent procreative power; anthropologists' early descriptions of menstruation or menstrual blood as dangerous or 'contaminating,' therefore, reflect male bias and were inappropriate.

5 In an Alaskan case, two Tlingit teenagers convicted of assault and robbery were banished to a remote island for a year to 18 months by Alaskan elders in tribal court . But it soon became apparent that the offenders with the aid of friends, had left the island and that the traditional sentence would never be completed (*New York Times*, 4 Sept. 1994, 8).

6 Morrow (1992: 26) uses this term in a narrower sense for specific roles, such as court workers who link Aboriginal and western systems. But he notes that interface mechanisms do not need to be limited to these roles and that the 'common thread is the bridge they create between an Aboriginal Person and the criminal justice system.' My own use is meant to connote such mechanisms as systems of appeal, or agreements concerning hybrid offences, which would link plural systems on a political or jurisdictional basis.

7 Offences are divided into summary, indictable, and hybrid offences. Summary offences include minor infractions of the law, such as minor theft and property damage, and are punishable by fines or jail terms of up to six months. As Ross notes, these offences, in which the accused is not entitled to a jury trial, are often considered minor enough to be processed in Aboriginal communities. Hybrid offences are the largest category and, under the current system, it is the responsibility of crown attorneys to treat particular cases as either summary or indictable offences – according to the circumstances of the case, the previous record of the accused, the degree of physical or property damage, and so forth. Sexual assault and family violence also falls into this category. Ross notes the traditional suggestion of criminal justice personnel has been to allow only those offences deemed 'summary' to be heard in the community – but this option retains control of critical decision-making by the state, and leaves such minor offences to be processed in the community that the 'exercise seems pointless' to communities (1994: 4–5).

8 For reviews of pilot projects and programs across Canada see R. Ross 1996; Diablo and Mitchell 1993: 402–6; Loutit: 1993: 397–8; Stevens 1993: 385–9; Morrow 1992; Griffiths 1992; Harding and Forgay 1991.

9 Justice of the peace courts, or those relying on the use of elders in circle sentencing, have experienced several problems, including, for example, *perceived* bias on the part of elders who hear cases involving family members, lack of consistency in elder representation, poor liaison with, or unwillingness to utilize, health and human services, and a meting out of sentences that continue reliance on fines and probation rather than victim compensation or community service (see, for example, Obonsowin-Irwin: 1992a; 1992b). Elders may also resent or dislike being relied upon during the sentencing when they have little input into court proceedings, and when they are unable to work closely with youth in referral or the long-term prevention of crime.

10 Evaluations can be excessively onerous on programs that are in the early stages of development. From my limited knowledge of mainstream health- and human services, I would suggest that Aboriginal programs often attract a degree of government scrutiny that non-Native agencies would find intolerable. Thus, there remains fear and suspicion that the evaluation can be used as an instrument of state control – particularly if it is used to rationalize program cuts, or to force communities to adhere to external (non-Native) measures of success and failure. When evaluations measure success according to Aboriginal criteria, they are willingly embracedby First Nations.

11 Ross notes that provincial laws do cover such circumstances, but that Aboriginal people are often reluctant to apply provincial laws on reserve. He suggests that band by-laws might be devised to cover these situations, but many First Nations seem reluctant to use by-laws (which are approved at the discretion of

the Minister of Indian Affairs). Ross suggests that Aboriginal legal jurisdiction is needed before such community involvement occurs.

12 While it is easy to argue against borrowing on or against ideas from another culture, this statement rests on the assumption that Aboriginal law has more in common with other systems of tribal law than with Western or European law.

13 In discussing Aboriginal policing, Depew notes that more appropriate focuses for research and policy development have largely been obscured or ignored by government practitioners because of their emphasis on indigenisation and cross-cultural training, which 'reflects a legacy of ethnocentric colonial practices and state control' (1994a: i).

14 Spending on the justice system by governments in Canada has increased 34% over the past five years, to reach almost $10 billion in 1992–3 (*Globe and Mail* 24 Nov. 1994, A12). More than one-half of these costs ($5.7 billion) was for policing. The rise in costs, well beyond inflation, is an indicator that, despite Statistics Canada evidence that violent crimes are actually decreasing, the public is willing to support a variety of measures to ensure public order.

6: Visions of Community Healing

1 A copy of this report can be obtained by writing to Shared Visions of Community Healing, The North Shore Anishnabe Health Board, P.O. Box 28, 49 Indian Road, Cutler ON. P0P 1B0. Unless otherwise noted, quotations in this chapter are drawn from the 1995 consultation. Many of these quotations also appear in the 1996 report. Because of issues of confidentiality, the names of key consultants were not identified in that report, and I follow this same protocol here.

2 This observation in no way contradicts the suggestion, made in chapters 2 and 3, that feelings of individual or community control are central to perceptions of well-being. Rather, it is meant to imply that people cannot expect to control the overall direction or pace of change. Community planning does not occur according to a simple 'template' for action, but must take into account complex interpersonal and community dynamics.

3 See also the RCAP report *Gathering Strength*, which elaborates many issues involved in capacity building (1996b: 327–8)

4 This expression is associated with the video *The Honour of All: The Alkali Lake Story*. It is derived from the expression 'the hurt of one is the hurt of all, the honour of one is the honour of all.'

5 Wallace developed this concept with reference to the experience of key figures, such as prophets, who experienced dreams and visions as part of a

revitalization movement. His analysis was very much focused on the psychological states of exceptional individuals. My resurrection of the term here is meant to suggest that this term can express a more common and generalized experience than in Wallace's original analysis.

6 In fact, the percentages of Anishnabe speakers varies greatly across communities, so that in some communities, up to 40% of the 'middle generation' may have some fluency in their Native tongue.

7 This issue is similar to that put forward in the previous chapter concerning the rejection of 'neutral' legal authorities and the feasibility of developing mediation systems in kin-based communities.

7: The Nature of Change: Cleaning the Caribou

1 A report by David Crombie on the Intervenor Participation Project noted that 14 Aboriginal groups were given money, but never submitted reports to the commission. Ten per cent of the projects funded under this initiative were judged deficient by Crombie. Of the 142 groups funded under this $8 million initiative, many research reports were apparently filled with lists of grievances, but were short on practical solutions or detailed research findings (*Spectator*, n.d. 1994, A2; *Toronto Star*, 1 Oct. 1995, A16).

2 For examples of media coverage and editorials following the release of the commission's final reports, see the bibliographic entries listed chronologically under 'Newspapers and Magazine Articles' from 22 November 1996 to 26 February 1997.

3 For rebuttals to Gibson's inflammatory analysis see responses by Richter, Hall, and Deans under 'The future of aboriginal peoples' (*Globe and Mail*, 30 Nov. 1996, D9).

4 For non-Native and Native perspectives on the 'costs' of self-government the reader might consult the RCAP testimonies (1993a) beginning with: Yellowknife NT. 92-12-09 73. John Wittiman. PG 113; Timmins ON. 92-11-05 122. Don McKinnon. PG 91–6; Ottawa ON. 93-11-04 50. Gerald Morin. PG 842-3; Ottawa ON. 93-11-03 3. Ron George. PG 514.

5 See RCAP 1996f: 63, 67–9. The RCAP proposals call for a $300 million increase in funding for educational initiatives, $100 million for health care, $100 million for social services, and $25 million for justice services.

Bibliography

Aboriginal Family Healing Joint Steering Committee (Ontario) (AFHJSC). 1993. *For Generations to Come: The Time Is Now: A Strategy for Aboriginal Family Healing.*

Aboriginal Legal Services of Toronto. 1992. *Aboriginal Legal Services of Toronto: Community Council Project Outline.*

Adler, Peter S. 1995. The Future of Alternative Dispute Resolution: Reflections on ADR as a Social Movement. In S.E. Merry and N. Milner (eds). *The Possibility of Popular Justice: A Case Study of Community Mediation in the United States.* 89–122.

Alberta 1991. *Report of the Task Force on the Criminal Justice System and Its Impact on the Indian and Métis People of Alberta.* March 1991.

Andres, R. 1981. The apprehension of native children. *Ontario Indian.* January, 32–46.

Angus, Murray. 1991. Comprehensive Claims: One Step Forward, Two Steps Back. In D. Engelstad and J. Bird (eds). *Nation to Nation.* 67–77.

– 1992. *And the Last Shall Be First: Native Policy in an Era of Cutbacks.* Toronto: NC Press.

Armstrong, Harvey. 1978. Providing psychiatric care and consultation in remote Indian villages. *Hospital and Community Psychiatry* 29 (10): 678–80.

– 1993. Depression in Canadian Native Indians. In P. Cappeliez and R.J. Flynn (eds). *Depression and the Social Environment.* Montreal: McGill-Queen's University Press. 218–34.

Arno, Andrew. 1985. Structural communication and control communication: An interactionist perspective on legal and customary procedures for conflict management. *American Anthropologist* 87: 40–55.

Arnot, David M. 1994. Sentencing circles permit community healing. *National.* Canadian Bar Association. 14.

Asbury, K. 1986. *Disproportionate Involvement of Native People in the Canadian Justice System.* Toronto: Ontario Native Council on Justice.

Asch, Michael. 1984. *Home and Native Land.* Toronto: Methuen.
– 1988. *Kinship and the Drum Dance in a Northern Dene Community.* Boreal Institute for Northern Studies, Academic Printing and Publishing.
– 1993. Aboriginal Self-Government and Canadian Constitutional Identity: Building Reconciliation. In M. Levin (ed). *Ethnicity and Aboriginality.* 29–52.
Assembly of First Nations (AFN). 1987. *Indian Housing and Living Conditions.*
– 1988a. Community Health Representatives: Proposals for Enrichment and Expansion. Background Paper.
– 1988b. Initial Response to Task Force Report on Child and Family Services in Canada.
– 1991. A Critique of Federal Government Land Claims Policies. In F. Cassidy (ed). *Aboriginal Self-Determination.* 232–51.
– 1994. *Seizing the Agenda.* Discussion Paper, Confederacy of Nations Meeting. May 1994.
Auger, D., A. Doob, and P. Driben. 1992. Crime and control in three Nishnawbe-Aski Nation communities: An exploratory investigation. *Canadian Journal of Criminology* 34: 317–38.
Bagley, Chris. 1984. Child protection and the Native child: A case study. *Perception* 8 (1): 17–20.
– 1985. Child abuse by the child welfare system. *Journal of Child Care* 2 (3).
Banerjee, A.K., Alam Jahangir, and Paul De Civita. 1991. Wage Gap between Aboriginals and Non-Aboriginals in Canada: An Empirical Analysis. Paper Presented to the Annual Meeting of the Canadian Economics Association. Kingston. 2–4 June 1991.
Barnes, Gordon E. 1985. Canadian Indian health: A needs assessment project. *Canadian Journal of Native Studies* 5 (1): 44–60.
Bartlett, Kim (ed). 1988. A new ethic or an end to a way of life? *Animal's Agenda.* 7–23, 56–7.
Becker, Ernest. 1971. *The Lost Science of Man.* New York: Doubleday.
Berger, T. 1991. *A Long and Terrible Shadow.* Vancouver: Douglas and McIntyre.
Berkes, F. (ed). 1989. *Common Property Resources, Ecology and Community-Based Sustainable Development.* London: Belhaven Press.
Berkes, F., P.J. George, and R.J. Preston. 1991. *Co-managements: The Evolution of the Theory and Practice of Joint Administration of Living Resources.* Technology Assessment in Subarctic Ontario (TASO) second series, no. 1. McMaster University.
Berkes, F., P.J. George, R.J. Preston, A. Hughes, J. Turner, and B.D. Cummins. 1994. Wildlife harvesting and sustainable regional native economy in the Hudson and James Bay Lowland, Ontario. *Arctic* 47 (4): 350–60.
Berkhofer, Robert F., Jr. 1979. *The White Man's Indian.* New York: Vintage.

Berry, J.W. 1993. Psychological and Social Health of Aboriginal Peoples in Canada. Paper Presented at the Workshop on Children's Mental Health and Wellness in First Nations Communities. Victoria BC.

Boldt, M. 1993. *Surviving as Indians: The Challenge of Self-Government.* Toronto: University of Toronto Press.

Boldt, M., and J.A. Long. 1985a. *The Quest for Justice.* Toronto: University of Toronto Press.

– 1985b. Tribal Traditions and European-Western Political Ideologies. In M. Boldt and J.A. Long (eds). *The Quest for Justice.* 333–46.

Borrows, John J. 1992. A genealogy of law: Inherent sovereignty and First Nations self-government. *Osgoode Hall Law Journal* 30 (2): 291–353.

Borzecki, M., J.S. Wormith, and W.H. Black. 1988. An examination of differences between native and non-native psychiatric offenders on the MMPI. *Canadian Journal of Behavioural Science* 20(3): 287–301.

Braithwaite, John. 1989. *Crime, Shame and Reintegration.* Cambridge: Cambridge University Press.

Brant, Clare C. 1990. Native ethics and rules of behaviour. *Canadian Journal of Psychiatry* 35 (6): 534–9.

– 1993. Suicide in Canadian Aboriginal Peoples: Causes and Preventions. In RCAP 1993b.

Brascoupe, Simon. 1993. Strengthening Traditional Economies and Perspectives. Economic Round Tables. In RCAP 1993a.

Bray, D.L., and P.D. Anderson. 1989. Appraisal of the epidemiology of fetal alcohol syndrome among Canadian Native peoples. *Canadian Journal of Public Health* 80: 42–5.

Brodeur, J.P. 1991. *Justice for the Cree: Policing and Alternative Dispute Resolution.* James Bay QC: Grand Council of the Crees.

Brody, Hugh. 1981. *Maps and Dreams.* London: Penguin Books.

– 1987. *Living Arctic.* Vancouver: Douglas and McIntyre.

Brush, S., Indigenous knowledge of biological resources and intellectual property rights: The role of anthropology. *American Anthropologist* 95 (3): 653–89.

Canada. 1980. *Indian Conditions: A Survey.* Ottawa: Department of Indian Affairs and Northern Development.

– 1982a. *Indian Social Welfare.* Ottawa: Indian and Northern Affairs Canada.

– 1982b. *Indian Education Paper. Phase 1.* Ottawa: Ministry of Indian Affairs and Northern Development.

– 1983. *Indian Self-Government in Canada.* Report of the Special Committee on Indian Self-Government (Penner Report). Ottawa.

– 1984. *Canada's Native People: 1981 Census of Canada.* Ottawa: Supply and Services Canada.

– 1986. *Task Force on Indian Economic Development.* Summary Report to the Deputy Minister. Ottawa: Indian and Northern Affairs Canada.
– 1987a. *Indian Child and Family Services in Canada: Final Report.* Ottawa: Department of Indian and Northern Affairs.
– 1987b. *Adoption and the Indian Child.* Ottawa: Indian and Northern Affairs Canada.
– 1988. Department of Indian and Northern Affairs Communiqué 1–8810.
– 1989a. *The Canadian Aboriginal Economic Development Strategy.* Supply and Services Canada.
– 1989b. *Health Program Transfer Handbook.* Revised September. Program Transfer, Policy and Planning Directorate, Medical Services Branch, Health and Welfare Canada.
– 1990. *Indian Policing Policy Review.* Task Force Report. Ottawa: Department of Indian and Northern Affairs.
– 1991a. *Guidelines to Indian Self-Government Negotiations.* Ottawa: Department of Indian and Northern Affairs.
– 1991b. *Agenda for First Nations and Inuit Mental Health.* Report of the Steering Committee. Ottawa: Medical Services Branch, Health and Welfare Canada.
– 1991c. Aboriginal People and Justice Administration. Discussion Paper. Ottawa: Department of Justice.
– 1991d. *Health Status of Canadian Indians and Inuit, 1990.* Ottawa: Health and Welfare Canada. Supply and Services Canada.
– 1992a. Comprehensive Audit of the Department of Health. Report to the Legislative Assembly of the Northwest Territories. Ottawa: Auditor General of Canada.
– 1992b. *A Time for Action: Aboriginal and Northern Housing.* Fourth Report of the Standing Committee on Aboriginal Affairs, Larry Schneider, chairman.
– 1992c. *First Nations Policing Policy.* Solicitor General, Ministry Secretariat. Supply and Services Canada.
– 1992d. *First Nations Policing Tripartite Agreements.* Solicitor General, Ministry Secretariat. Aboriginal Policing Series no. 1992–10.
– 1993a. *Agreement between the Inuit of the Nunavut Settlement Area and Her Majesty the Queen in Right of Canada.* Ottawa: DIAND/Tungavik.
– 1993b. A Contemporary Proposal for Aboriginal Judicial Structure at X First Nation. Proposal/Memorandum of Understanding. Department of Indian Affairs and Northern Development.
– 1993c. *Evaluation of the Devolution of Technical Services.* Ottawa: Evaluation Directorate.
– 1993d. *Evolution from Direct Service Delivery to a Funding Agency.* Ottawa.
– 1993e. *Report of the Auditor General to the House of Commons for the Fiscal Year Ended March 1993.* Ottawa: Supply and Services Canada.

Canadian Psychiatric Association (CPA). 1985. *Suicide in the North American Indian: Causes and Prevention.* Edited Proceedings of the Canadian Psychiatric Association, Native Mental Health Section. Native Mental Health Association.

Cassidy, F. 1989. *Aboriginal Self-Government: Defining a Research Agenda,* second ed. Victoria and Montreal: University of Victoria and Institute for Research on Public Policy.

– (ed). 1991. *Aboriginal Self-Determination.* Institute for Research on Public Policy. Oolichan Books.

Castellano, Marlene Brant. 1982. Indian participation in health policy development: Implications for adult education. *Canadian Journal of Native Studies* 11 (1).

– 1986. Collective wisdom: Participatory research and Canada's native people. *IRDC Reports.* No. 3: 50–3.

– 1993. Aboriginal Organizations in Canada: Integrating Participatory Research. In Peter Park, Mary Brydon-Miller, Bud Hall, and Ted Jackson (eds). *Voices of Change: Participatory Research in the United States and Canada.* Westport CT: Bergin and Garvey.

Chapman, Audrey R. 1994. Human Rights Implications of Indigenous Peoples' Intellectual Property Rights. In T. Greaves (ed). *Intellectual Property Rights for Indigenous Peoples.*

Charles, G. 1991. Suicide intervention and prevention for northern Native youth. *Journal of Child and Youth Care* 6 (1): 11–17.

Churchill, W. 1994. *Indians Are Us? Culture and Genocide in Native North America.* between the lines.

Clairmont, Donald. 1992. *Native Justice Issues in Nova Scotia: Policing and Courts.* Halifax: Tripartite Forum on Native Justice.

– 1992. Alternative Justice Issues for Aboriginal Justice. Paper Prepared for the Aboriginal Justice Directorate. Ottawa: Department of Justice.

Clarke, G.S. 1987. *Developing Crime Prevention Activities in Native Communities.* Ottawa: Solicitor General of Canada.

– 1989. *The Mi'kmaq and Criminal Justice in Nova Scotia.* Halifax: Report of the Royal Commission on the Donald Marshall Jr Prosecution.

– 1990. *Aboriginal Customary Law Literature Review.* Report Prepared for the Public Inquiry into the Administration of Justice and Aboriginal People, Manitoba.

Clarke, Judith A. 1992. *On Their Own Terms: Health Perceptions of Urban Native People.* M.A. thesis, McMaster University.

Clifton, James A. (ed). 1990. *The Invented Indian.* New Brunswick NJ: Transaction Publishers.

Colorado, Pam. 1988. Bridging Native and Western science. *Convergence* 21 (2/3): 49–67.

Comaroff, Jean. 1985. *Body of Power, Spirit of Resistance.* Chicago: University of Chicago Press.

Condon, R. 1990. The rise of adolescence: Social change and life stage dilemmas in the central Canadian Arctic. *Human Organization* 49 (3): 266–79.

Connell, G., R. Flett, and P. Stewart. 1990. Implementing Primary Health Care through Community Control: The Experience of the Swampy Cree Tribal Council. In B. Postl et al (eds). *Circumpolar Health 90.*

Councillor, Randy. 1992. Okonagegayin: Using Traditional Therapies to Heal Chronic Solvent Abusers. Program Summary and Video.

Cowie, Ian. 1993. Presentation to the Royal Commission on Aboriginal Peoples (RCAP). Ottawa: Ian Cowie and Associates.

Cox, B. 1987. *Native People, Native Lands.* Ottawa: Carleton University Press.

Coyle, M. 1986. *Traditional Indian Justice in Ontario: A Role for the Present?* Toronto: Indian Commission of Ontario.

Crawford, James, Peter Hennessy, and Mary Fischer. 1988. Aboriginal Customary Laws: Proposals for Recognition. In Brad Morse and Gordon R. Woodman (eds). *Indigenous Law and the State.* Dordrecht: Foris Publications. 27–64.

Crnkovich, Mary. 1993. Report on the Sentencing Circle in Kangiqsujuag. Pauktuutit and the Department of Justice.

Cruikshank, Julia. 1991. *Life Lived like a Story.* Vancouver: University of British Columbia Press.

Darabont, Frank. 1994. *'The Shawshank Redemption': The Shooting Script.* New York: Newmarket Press.

Davies, Sue. 1992. Experiences with Circle Court. Unpublished Report. Ottawa: Department of Justice.

Dawson, Jennifer. 1995. *Here to Stay; Gone Tomorrow: Working as Service Provider in Moosonee and Moose Factory.* MA thesis. McMaster University.

Daybutch, Gloria. 1994. Mississauga First Nation Mental Health Proposal. Blind River ON: Mississauga First Nation.

Depew, Robert C. 1992. Policing native communities: Some principles and issues in organizational theory. *Canadian Journal of Criminology* 34: 461–78.

– 1994a. Aboriginal Policing: A Research Perspective. Report Prepared for the Royal Commission on Aboriginal Peoples (RCAP).

– 1994b. Popular Justice and Aboriginal Communities: Some Preliminary Considerations. Paper Prepared for the Aboriginal Justice Directorate. Ottawa: Department of Justice.

– 1994c. *First Nations Organizations: An Analytic Framework.* Report Prepared for the Policy and Strategic Direction Department of the Department of Indian Affairs and Northern Development.

Diablo, Winona, and Joyce King Mitchell. 1993. Court of Kahnawake. In RCAP 1993c. 402–6.

Dobyns, H.F. 1983. *Their Numbers Become Thinned: Native American Population Dynamics in Eastern North America.* Knoxville: University of Tennessee Press.

Driscoll-Englestad, Bernadette. 1995. *Silent Echoes: The Displacement and Reappearance of Copper Inuit Clothing.* Presentation to the American Anthropological Association, Washington DC. 18 Nov.

Drost, Helmar, and Tim Eryou. 1991. Education/Training and Labour Force Status: A Cross-Section Study of Canadian Natives. Paper Presented to the Annual Meeting of the Canadian Economics Association, Kingston ON. 2–4 June.

Dumont, James. 1993. Justice and Aboriginal People in Canada. In RCAP 1993c. 42–85.

Dupuis, Renée. 1993. Aboriginal Peoples and Employment Equity. Report to the Economic Round Table, Special Consultations. In RCAP 1993a.

Dyck, N. 1991. *What Is the Indian 'Problem'?: Tutelage and Resistance in Canadian Indian Administration.* Institute of Social and Economic Research. St John's: Memorial University of Newfoundland.

Dyck, N., and J. Waldrum. 1993. *Anthropology, Public Policy and Native Peoples in Canada.* Montreal: McGill-Queen's University Press.

Edouard, L., D. Gillis, and B. Habbick. 1991. Pregnancy outcome among Native Indians in Saskatchewan. *Canadian Medical Association Journal* 144 (12): 1623–5.

Educating Future Physicians for Ontario (EFPO). 1993. Some Views on Native Persons' Expectations of Physicians. EFPO Working Paper series 15. Component 1.

Elias, Peter Douglas. 1996. Worklessness and social pathologies in Aboriginal communities. *Human Organization* 55 (1): 13–24.

Engelstad, D., and J. Bird (eds). 1992. *Nation to Nation: Aboriginal Sovereignty and the Future of Canada.* Concord ON: Anansi Press.

Erasmus, George. 1986. Native Studies Review Comment. *Native Studies Review* 2 (2): 53–63.

Ervin, A. 1990. Some reflections on anthropological advocacy. *Proactive: Society of Applied Anthropology in Canada* 9 (2): 24–7.

Evers, S.E., and C.G. Rand. 1982. Morbidity in Canadian Indian and non-Indian children in the first year of life. *Canadian Medical Association Journal* 126: 249–52.

– 1983. Morbidity in Canadian Indian and non-Indian children in the second year. *Canadian Journal of Public Health* 74: 191–4.

Fanon, Franz. 1988. *Wretched of the Earth.* New York: Grove Press.

Farkas, C., C. Howe, I. Kalnins, R. Jewell, and S. Sorrell. 1989. Explanatory models of health during pregnancy: Native women and Non-Native health care providers in Toronto. *Native Studies Review* 5 (1): 79–95.

Favel-King, Alma. 1993. The Treaty Right to Health. In RCAP 1993b.

Federation of Saskatchewan Indian Nations, Government of Canada, Government of Saskatchewan (Joint Studies). 1985. Reflecting Indian Concerns and Values in the Justice System: Report from the Steering Committee.

Feit, Harvey. 1991a. Waswanipi Cree Management of Land and Wildlife: Cree Ethno-Ecology Revisited. In B.A. Cox (ed). *Native People, Native Lands.* 75–91.

– 1991b. Construction of Algonquian Hunting Territories: Private Property as Moral Lesson, Policy Advocacy, and Ethnographic Error. In G. Stocking (ed). *Colonial Situations: History of Anthropology.* Vol. 7. Madison: University of Wisconsin Press. 109–34.

Fiddler, Chief Thomas, and James R. Stevens. 1985. *Killing the Shamen.* Moonbeam ON: Penumbra Press.

Fiske, Jo-Anne. 1990–1. Native women in reserve politics: Strategies and struggles. *Journal of Legal Pluralism* 30–1: 121–37.

Flaherty, Martha (Pauktuutit Inuit Women's Association). 1995. The Repatriation of Cultural Knowledge in the North American Arctic. Remarks to Session on Challenges and Opportunities, American Anthropology Association, Washington DC. 18 Nov.

Four Worlds Development Project. 1984a. *A Wholistic Curriculum Can Contribute to Health.* Discussion Paper Seven. P. Lane, J. Bopp, and P. Bopp, Lethbridge AB: Four Worlds Development Project.

– 1984b. *Wholistic Educational Evaluation For Community Transformation.* Lethbridge AB: Four Worlds Development Project.

– 1986. *The Honour Of All.* Video. Produced by Phil Lane. Lethbridge AB: Four Worlds Development Project.

– 1990. Survival Secrets of NNADAP Workers. *Four Worlds Exchange* 2 (1): 24–39.

Furniss, Elizabeth. *Victims of Benevolence.* Vancouver: Arsenal Pulp Press.

Garden River First Nation. 1994. Garden River First Nation Healing Lodge Operation and Management Plan (Draft). Prepared by Darrell E. Boissoneau and Marlene C. Thunderchild.

Garro, L. 1988. Resort to traditional healers in a Manitoba Ojibwa community. *Arctic Medical Research* 47 (Suppl. 1): 317–20.

Gellner, E. 1993. What do we need now? Social anthropology and its new global context. *Times Literary Supplement.* 16 July 3–4.

George, Peter, and Peter Kuhn. 1993. *Expanding Employment in the Canadian Economy.* Revised version. Economic Round Table Discussion Paper. In RCAP 1993a.

George, Peter, Fikret Berkes, and Richard J. Preston. 1992. *Indigenous Land Use and Harvesting among the Cree in Western James Bay: A Historical and Contemporary Analysis.* Technology Assessment in Subarctic Ontario (TASO) second series, no. 5. McMaster University.

Gerber, L. 1979. The development of Canadian Indian communities: A two-dimensional typology reflecting strategies of adaptation to the modern world. *Canadian Journal of Sociology and Anthropology* 16 (4): 404–24.

Gfellner, B.M. 1991. A profile of Aboriginal youth in a community drug program. *Canadian Journal of Native Studies* 11 (1): 25–48.

Gfellner, B.M., and J.D. Hudleby. 1991. Family and peer predictors of substance use among Aboriginal and Non-Aboriginal adolescents. *Canadian Journal of Native Studies* 11 (2): 267–94.

Gibbons, Adrian, and Associates. 1992. Short-Term Evaluation of Indian Health Transfer Policy. Report Submitted to Medical Services Branch, Health and Welfare Canada.

Gibson, Nancy. 1988. Northern Medicine in Transition. In David Young (ed). *Health Care Issues in the Canadian North.* 108–17.

Gilchrist, Lewayne D., Steven P. Schinke, Joseph E. Trimble, and George T. Cvetkovich. 1987. Skills enhancement to prevent substance abuse among American Indian adolescents. *International Journal of the Addictions* 22 (9): 869–79.

Gill, Sam. 1990. Mother Earth: An American Myth. In James A. Clifton (ed). *The Invented Indian.* 129–44.

Gillis, D.C., J. Irvine, and L. Tan. 1991. Cancer Incidence and Survival of Saskatchewan Northeners and Registered Indians, 1967–1986. In B. Postl et al (eds). *Circumpolar Health 90.* 447–51.

Gilmore, A. 1990. Educating Native MDs: Always go back and serve your people in some larger way. *Canadian Medical Association Journal* 142 (2): 160–2.

Giokas, John. 1993. Accommodating the Concerns of Aboriginal Peoples within the Existing Justice System. In RCAP 1993c. 184–231.

Goddard, John. 1991. *Last Stand of the Lubicon Cree.* Vancouver: Douglas and McIntyre.

Graham, Robert (Chairman). 1988. Building Community Support for People: A Plan for Mental Health in Ontario.

Greaves, Tom (ed). 1994. *Intellectual Property Rights for Indigenous Peoples: A Sourcebook.* Oklahoma City: Society for Applied Anthropology.

Gregory, D. 1988. An Exploration of the Contact between Indian Healers/Traditional Healers on Indian Reserves and Health Care Centres in Manitoba. In David Young (ed). *Health Care Issues in the Canadian North.* 39–43.

Gregory, D., C. Russell, J. Hurd, J. Tyance, and J. Sloan. 1992. Canada's Indian Health Transfer Policy: The Gull Lake Band experience. *Human Organization* 51 (3): 214–22.

Griffiths, Curt Taylor (ed). 1992. *Self-Sufficiency in Northern Justice Issues.* Winnipeg: Northern Justice Society and Simon Fraser University.

Grinde, Donald A., and Bruce E. Johanson. 1995. *Ecocide of Native North America.* Sante Fe NM: Clear Light Publishers.

Gulewitsch, Victor. 1995. *Ipperwash Burial Ground Research: Complete and Brief History of the Ipperwash Provincial Park Chippewas of Kettle and Stoney Point.*

Haig-Brown, Celia. 1995. 'Not Vanishing': Implications of Residential School Research for Today's Communities. Paper Prepared for the American Anthropological Association, Washington DC. 1–27.

Hall, Bud. 1979. Knowledge as a commodity and participatory research. *Prospects* 9 (4): 393–408.

Hall, J., and A.J. Hanson. 1992. *A New Kind of Sharing: Why We Can't Ignore Global Environmental Change.* Ottawa: International Development Research Centre.

Hamilton, A.C., and M. Sinclair. 1991. *The Justice System and Aboriginal People.* Report of the Aboriginal Justice Inquiry of Manitoba. Winnipeg. Queen's Printer.

Hanvey, Louise. 1993. Working Paper on Health Status. Prepared for the Children and Youth Project, Premiers Council on Health, Well-Being and Social Justice.

Harding, Jim. 1991. Policing and Aboriginal justice. *Canadian Journal of Criminology.* 33 (July/October): 363–83.

Harding, Jim, and Beryl Forgay. 1991. *Breaking down the Walls: A Bibliography on the Pursuit of Aboriginal Justice.* Regina: Prairie Justice Research. Aboriginal Justice Series. Report no. 2. University of Regina. 1–108.

Harris, Michael. 1986. *Justice Denied.* Toronto: Macmillan Books.

Havemann, P., K. Couse, L. Foster, and R. Matonovich. 1985. *Law and Order for Indigenous People.* Regina: Prairie Justice Research. School of Human Justice. University of Regina.

Hawley, Donna Lea. 1986. *The Indian Act Annotated.* Second ed. Toronto: Carswell.

Hawton, Keith, and Jose Catalan. 1987. *Attempted Suicide: A Practical Guide to Its Nature and Management.* New York: Oxford Medical Publications.

Hazlehurst, Kayleen M. (ed). 1995. *Popular Justice and Community Regeneration.* Westport CT: Praeger.

– 1995. Indigenous Models for Community Reconstruction and Social Recovery. Introduction to Kayleen M. Hazlehurst (ed). *Popular Justice and Community Regeneration.* 3–20.

Hedican, E. 1995. *Applied Anthropology in Canada: Understanding Aboriginal Issues.* Toronto: University of Toronto Press.

Herring, Ann. 1992. Toward a reconsideration of disease and contact in the Americas. *Prairie Forum* 17 (2): 153–65.

Hill, Dawn J. 1995. Lubicon Lake Nation: Spirit of Resistance. Ph.D. thesis. McMaster University.

Hogg, Peter W., and Mary Ellen Turpel. 1995. Implementing Aboriginal self-government: Constitutional and jurisdictional issues. *Canadian Bar Review* 74 (2) 184–224.

Holman, J. 1990. Gap divides youth and elders. *Windspeaker* 8 (5): 12.

Hoover, J., and R. McDermott. 1989. Dental knowledge and behaviour in Native children living in northern Saskatchewan. *Canadian Journal of Public Health* 80: 150–2.

Hoover, J., R. McDermott, and T. Hartsfield. 1990. The Prevalence of smokeless tobacco: Use in Native children in northern Saskatchewan. *Canadian Journal of Public Health* 81: 351–2.

Hoyle, Marcia. 1992. Modelling Aboriginal Justice Systems in Canada. Paper Prepared for the Commission on Folk Law and Legal Pluralism. Wellington, N.Z., 27 August.

– 1994. Bringing Justice Home: Report of the Sagamok Anishnawbek Community Justice Research.

– 1995. A Fitting Remedy: Aboriginal Justice as Community Healing. In Kayleen M. Hazlehurst (ed). *Popular Justice and Community Regeneration.* 143–64.

Hylton, J. 1983. Locking up Indians in Saskatchewan: Some Recent Findings. In T. Fleming and L.A.Visano (eds). *Deviant Designations: Crime, Law and Deviance in Canada.* Toronto: Butterworths, 61–70.

– 1995. Social Policy and Canada's Aboriginal People: The Need for Fundamental Reforms. In Kayleen M. Hazlehurst (ed). *Popular Justice and Community Regeneration.* 3–20.

Indian Chiefs of Alberta. 1970. *Citizens Plus.* Edmonton: Indian Association of Alberta.

Indian and Inuit Nurses of Canada. 1990. No More Secrets: A Report on Child Sexual Abuse. Annual Assembly Report for 1990 on Child Sexual Abuse in Aboriginal Communities and Pauktuutit.

Jackson, Michael. 1988. Locking Up Natives in Canada. Report of the Canadian Bar Association Committee on Imprisonment and Release. University of British Columbia.

Jackson, Ted, Don McCaskill, and Budd L. Hall (eds.) 1982. Learning for self-determination: Community-based options for Native training and research. *Canadian Journal of Native Studies* 2 (1).

Jacobson, E.M. 1975. *Bended Elbow: Kenora Talks Back.* Kenora: Central Publications.

Jaimes, M. Annette. 1992. *The State of Native America.* Boston: South End Press.

Jamieson, K. 1986. Sex Discrimination and the Indian Act. In J.R. Ponting (ed). *Arduous Journey.* 112–36.

Jarvis, George K., and Menno Boldt. 1982. Death styles among Canada's Indians. *Social Science and Medicine* 16 (4), 1345–52.

Jilek, W. 1982. *Indian Healing.* Surrey, BC: Hancock House.

Johnson, Basil H. 1988. *Indian School Days.* Toronto: Key Porter Books.

Johnson, Joyce, and Fred Johnson. 1993. Alkali Lake Band. In RCAP 1993b.

Johnson, Judy. 1992. People Development Limited: A Review of Community Administered Non-Insured Health Benefits.

Johnson, Laura C., Barbara Muirhead, and Deborah Hierlihy. 1993. The Physical Environment as a Determinant of the Health and Well-Being of Children and Youth: A Review of the Literature. Paper Prepared for the Premiers Council on Health, Well-Being and Social Justice.

Johnson, Martha (ed). 1992. *Lore: Capturing Traditional Environmental Knowledge.* Hay River, NWT: Dene Cultural Institute and the International Development Research Centre.

Johnson, Patrick. 1983. *Native Children and the Child Welfare System.* Toronto: Canadian Council on Social Development. James Lorimer.

Jolly, Stan. 1983. *Our Children Our Hurting: Fact Sheet on the Disproportionate Involvement of Indian Young People in the Juvenile Justice and Child Welfare Systems of Ontario.* Toronto: Ontario Native Council on Justice.

– 1985. *Indian Children in Ontario's Juvenile Justice and Child Welfare Systems 1983–84.* Toronto: Ontario Native Council on Justice.

Jones, Rhys W. 1986. Practising Family Law for Indian and Native Clients: Child Protection Proceedings under the Child and Family Services Act, 1985. Annual Institute on Continuing Legal Education. Toronto: Canadian Bar Association.

Just, Peter. 1992. History, power, ideology and culture: Current directions in the anthropology of law. *Law and Society Review* 26 (2): 373–411.

Justice, Christopher, and Wayne Warry. 1996. *Shared Visions of Community Healing: A Discussion Paper for First Nations.* North Shore Tribal Council, Anishnawbe Health Board.

Kaufert, J., J.D. O'Neil, and W. Koolage. 1985. Cultural brokerage and advocacy in urban hospitals: The impact of Native language interpreters. *Santé/Culture/Health* 3 (2): 3–9.

Keating, Daniel P. 1993. Developmental Determinants of Health and Well-Being in Children and Youth. Working Paper Prepared for the Steering Committee on Children and Youth. Premiers Council on Health, Well-Being and Social Justice.

Keenan, David. 1993. Teslin Tlingit Justice Council. In RCAP 1993c. 397–8.

Kehoe, Alice B. 1990. Primitivists and Plastic Medicine Men. In James A. Clifton (ed). *The Invented Indian.* 193–210.

King, Paul R. n.d. Crisis Intervention. North Bay Psychiatric Hospital. Material Submitted to the Royal Commission on Aboriginal Peoples (RCAP).

Kirmayer, L.J. 1993. Suicide in Aboriginal Populations: Emerging Trends in

Research and Intervention. Report Prepared for the Royal Commission on Aboriginal Peoples (RCAP).

– 1994. Suicide among Canadian Aboriginal peoples. *Transcultural Psychiatric Research Review* 31 (1): 3–58.

Koenig, E. 1995. Toward a Historical Understanding of the Saugeen/Bruce Peninsula: Fish, Culture and Changing Landscapes. Paper Presented at the 'Leading Edge' Conference, Niagara Escarpment Commission. Collingwood ON.

Kulchyski, Peter (ed). 1994. *Unjust Relations: Aboriginal Rights in Canadian Courts.* Toronto: Oxford University Press.

Lajeunesse, Therese. 1991. Cross Cultural Issues in the Justice System: The Case of Aboriginal People in Canada. Manoa: University of Hawaii Program on Conflict Resolution.

Langford, C. 1992. Child welfare program misses most Natives. *Windspeaker* 10 (4): 1, 2.

LaPrairie, Carol. 1987. Native women and crime: A theoretical model. *Canadian Journal of Native Studies* 7: 121–37.

– 1992a. Dimensions of Aboriginal Over-Representation in Correctional Institutions and Implications for Crime Prevention. Aboriginal Peoples Collection. Corrections Branch, Solicitor General Canada, Ministry Secretariat.

– 1992b. *Exploring the Boundaries of Justice: Aboriginal Justice in the Yukon.* Report Prepared for the Department of Justice, Yukon Territorial Government, First Nations, Yukon Territory, and Justice Canada. Ottawa: Justice Canada.

– 1994a. Altering Course: New Directions in Criminal Justice. Sentencing Circles and Family Group Conferences. Draft discussion paper.

– 1994b. Community Justice or Just Communities: Aboriginal Communities in Search of Justice. Unpublished paper.

– 1994c. Project Evaluation Framework Discussion Paper: Aboriginal Justice Initiative. With the assistance of Robert Paiment and Deborah Whitehead.

– 1995. *Seen but Not Heard: Native People in the Inner City.* Aboriginal Justice Directorate. Department of Justice. Supply and Services Canada.

LaPrairie, Carol, Jean-Paul Brodeur, and Roger McDonnell. 1991. *Justice for the Cree: Final Report.* Cree Regional Authority, Grand Council of the Crees.

LaRocque, Emma. 1993. *Violence in Aboriginal Communities.* In RCAP 1993b.

Leland, J. 1976. *Firewater Myths.* New Brunswick, NJ: Rutgers Center of Alcohol Studies.

Lester, D. 1989. Locus of control, depression and suicidal ideation. *Perceptual and Motor Skills* 69: 1158.

– 1992. *Why People Kill Themselves.* Springfield IL: Charles C. Thomas.

Leung, Sophia, and James Carter. 1983. Cross cultural study of child abuse among

Chinese, Native Indians and Anglo-Canadian children. *Journal of Psychiatric Treatment and Evaluation* 5: 37–44.

Levin, M. 1993. *Ethnicity and Aboriginality: Case Studies in Ethnonationalism.* Toronto: University of Toronto Press.

Lilles, Heino, and Barry Stuart. 1992. The role of the community in sentencing. *Justice Report* (Canadian Bar Association). 8 (2), 1–5.

Linwood, M.E., G.F. Kasian, and J.D. Irvine. 1990. Child and youth accidents in northern Native communities. *Canadian Journal of Public Health* 81: 77–8.

Long, Kathleen Ann. 1986. Suicide intervention and prevention with Indian adolescent populations. *Issues in Mental Health Nursing* 8: 247–53.

Loutit, Reg. 1993. Attawapiskat First Nation Justice Project. In RCAP 1993c. 399–401.

Lowry, Kem. 1995. Evaluation of Community Justice Systems. In S.E. Merry and N. Milner (eds). *The Possibility of Popular Justice: A Case Study of Community Mediation in the United States.* 89–124.

Lyons, O. 1985. Traditional Native Philosophies relating to Aboriginal Rights. In M. Boldt and J.A. Long (eds). *The Quest for Justice.* 19–23.

Lytwyn, Victor P. 1995. Historical Research Report on Lake of the Woods Ojibway Fisheries. Historical and Geographical Consulting Services.

MacKay, R., and L. Myles. 1989. *Native Student Dropouts in Ontario Schools.* Toronto: Ontario Ministry of Education.

MacNeil, Robert. 1989. *Wordstruck.* New York: Penguin Books.

Manotsaywin Nanottojig. 1990. Za-Geh-Do-Win. Manotsaywin Nanottojig Family Violence Services Planning Project.

Manual, G., and M. Posluns. 1974. *The Fourth World: An Indian Reality.* Toronto: Collier-Macmillan.

Mao, Y., H. Morrison, R. Semenciw, and D. Wigle. 1986. Mortality on Canadian Indian reserves 1976–1983. *Canadian Journal of Public Health* 77: 263–8.

Mayfield, Margie, and Gayle Davies. 1984. An early intervention program for Native Indian infants and their families. *Canadian Journal of Public Health* 75: 450–3.

McCaskill, Don. 1981. Migration, adjustment, integration of Indians in Toronto, Winnipeg, Edmonton and Vancouver: A comparative analysis. *Culture* 1 (1).

– 1984. When cultures meet: Indians in Canada. *Bridges* 1 (5).

McCormick, James. 1988. To Wear a White Coat: Options for Traditional Healers in a Canadian Medical Future. In David Young (ed). *Health Care Issues in the Canadian North.* 8–14.

McDonald, J.M., T.A. O'Connell, D.B. Moore, and E. Bransbury. 1994. *Convening Family Conference: Training Manual.* Wagga Wagga, Australia: New South Wales Police Academy.

McDonnell, R. 1992a. *Justice for the Cree: Customary Beliefs and Practices.* James Bay, QC: Grand Council of the Crees.

– 1992b. Contextualizing the investigation of customary law in contemporary Native communities. *Canadian Journal of Criminology* 34: 299–316.

– 1993. *Prospects for Accountability among the Cree of James Bay.* James Bay QC: Grand Council of the Crees.

McGill AIDS Centre. 1992. Proceedings of the First Quebec Native AIDS Conference, Montreal.

McKenzie, H. 1991. Native Child Care in Canada: Background Paper. Political and Social Affairs Division, Research Branch, Library of Parliament, Ottawa.

McKinnon, A.L., J.W. Gartrell, L.A. Derksen, and G.K. Jarvis. 1991. Health knowledge of Native Indian youth in central Alberta. *Canadian Journal of Public Health* 82: 429–33.

McQuaig, Linda. 1995. *Shooting the Hippo: Death by Deficit and other Canadian Myths.* Toronto: Viking.

Merbs, C.F. 1992. A new world of infectious disease. *Yearbook of Physical Anthropology* 35: 3–42.

Merchant, Carolyn (ed). 1993. *Major Problems in American Environmental History.* Lexington MA: Heath.

Merry, S.E. 1995. Sorting out Popular Justice. In S.E. Merry and N. Milner (eds). *The Possibility of Popular Justice: A Case Study of Community Mediation in the United States.*

Merry, S.E., and N. Milner (eds). 1995. *The Possibility of Popular Justice: A Case Study of Community Mediation in the United States.* Ann Arbor: University of Michigan Press.

Merskey, H., C.C. Bant, A. Malla, E. Helmes, and V. Mohr. 1986. Symptom patterns of alcoholism in a northern Ontario population. *Canadian Journal of Psychiatry* 33: 46–51.

Metcalf, Ann. 1978. *Urban Indian Child Resource Centre.* Oakland CA.

Minore, B., M. Katt, P. Kinch, and M. Boone. 1991. Looking in, looking out: Coping with adolescent suicide in the Cree and Ojibway communities of northern Ontario. *Canadian Journal of Native Studies* 11 (1): 1–24.

Mississauga First Nation (MFN). 1992. Pre-Health Transfer Study. Community Health Plan.

– 1994. Human Resource and Management Development Project, Implementation Application.

Mitchell., A., and G. Aitken. 1993. Family Economic Circumstances and Child Health and Well-Being. Prepared for the Premiers Council on Health, Well-Being and Social Justice.

Moffatt, M. 1991. Nutritional deficiencies and Native infants. *Canadian Journal of Pediatrics.* Dec. 20–5.

Monture, P.A. 1989. A vicious circle: Child welfare and the First Nations. *Canadian Journal of Women and the Law* 3 (1): 1–17.

Monture-Okanee, Patricia A. 1993. Reclaiming Justice: Aboriginal Women and Justice Initiatives in the 1990s. In RCAP 1993c. *Aboriginal Peoples and the Justice System.*

Moore, D.B. 1992. Facing the Consequences. Paper Delivered to the Australian Institute of Criminology, National Conference on Juvenile Justice, Adelaide. Sept. 1–37.

Moore, Thomas. 1992. *Care of the Soul.* New York: Harper Collins.

Morgan, David L. 1988. *Focus Groups as Qualitative Research.* Qualitative Research Methods Series. 16. Newbury Park: Sage Publications.

Morrissette, P.J. 1991. The therapeutic dilemma with Canadian Native youth in residential care. *Child and Adolescent Social Work* 8 (2): 89–99.

Morrow, Doug. 1992. *Models for Native Community Involvement in the Delivery of Criminal Justice.* Ontario Native Council on Justice. 1–113.

Morse, Bradford. 1980. *Indian Tribal Courts in the United States: A Model for Canada?* Saskatoon: Native Law Centre, University of Saskatchewan.

– 1985. *Aboriginal People and the Law: Indian, Métis and Inuit Rights in Canada.* Ottawa: Carleton University Press.

Moskal, R.J. 1991. Effect of a comprehensive AIDS curriculum on knowledge and attitudinal changes in northern Canadian college students. *Canadian Journal of Counselling* 25 (3): 339–48.

Moyer, Sharon, and Lee Axon. 1993. *An Implementation Evaluation of the Native Community Council Project of the Aboriginal Legal Services of Toronto.* Ontario: Ministry of the Attorney General.

Muir, Bernice L. 1991. Health Status of Canadian Indians and Inuit 1990. Ottawa: Health and Welfare Canada.

Myers, Ted, L.M. Calzavara, R. Cockerill, V.W. Marshall, and S.L. Bullock, with the First Nations Steering Committee. 1993. *Ontario First Nations AIDS and Healthy Lifestyle Survey.* Ottawa: National AIDS Clearinghouse. Canadian Public Health Association.

Nahanee, T. 1993. Dancing with a Gorilla: Aboriginal Women, Justice and the Charter. In RCAP 1993c. 359–82.

Nandy, Ashis. 1983. *The Intimate Enemy: Loss and Recovery of Self under Colonialism.* Delhi: Oxford University Press.

Nelson, C.H., and M.L. Kelly. 1984. *Wichiwin,* Come along beside Me: Insights into Indian Helping. Paper Prepared for the Fifth International Congress of Child Abuse and Neglect, Montreal. 16–19 Sept. 35.

Newhouse, David R. 1993. Modern Aboriginal Economies: Capitalism with an Aboriginal Face. Paper Presented to the Royal Commission on Aboriginal Peoples (RCAP). 2 April. Revised 10 May.

Newspaper and Magazine Articles (Listed Chronologically):

8 in 10 native girls sexually abused, study finds. *Toronto Star.* 28 Jan. 1989, A1.

Sentencing hearing reflects native-style justice. David Roberts. *Globe and Mail.* 16 April 1993.

Native artists share sense of self. Susan Walker. *Toronto Star.* 18 April 1994, E4.

Manitoba takes first steps to axe Indian Act. Patrick Nagle. *Toronto Star.* 24 April 1994, F10.

Natives assail media for biased reports. Antonia Zerbisias. *Toronto Star.* 29 May 1994, A12.

Judge pushes for native justice. Sean Fine. *Globe and Mail.* 25 June 1994, A4.

Legal activist on and off the bench. Sean Fine. *Globe and Mail.* 25 June 1994, A1.

Give back our land. Dan Nolan. *Spectator.* 25 June 1994, B4.

Justice minister endorses separate system for Natives. *Spectator.* 15 July 1994, A13.

Natives eye land purchase for reserve. Wayne MacPherson. *Spectator.* 23 July 1994, B5.

Abusive schools at root of today's Native problems. Jack Aubry. *Spectator.* 9 Aug. 1994, A7.

Church defence slammed. Jack Aubry. *Spectator* 12 Aug. 1994, B6.

Tribal panel in Alaska exiles 2 teen-agers. *New York Times.* 4 Sept. 1994, P8.

Innu demand native justice centred on healing, not jails. *Toronto Star.* 11 Sept. 1994, A1, A5.

Self-government for natives takes a vital step. *Spectator.* 20 Sept. 1994, A7.

A postcard for the Innu. Ann Rauhala. *Globe and Mail.* 26 Sept. 1994, A2.

'Help stop gas-sniffing emergency,' Cree urge. Jim Rankin. *Toronto Star.* 4 Oct. 1994, A8.

Crees seek same choice as Quebeckers. *Globe and Mail.* 15 Oct. 1994, A1, A4.

Conservative leader has Natives upset. *Spectator.* 1 Nov. 1994, A14.

Aboriginal health program launched. Lisa Priest. *Toronto Star.* 2 Nov. 1994, A10.

Healing words. Shaun N. Herron. *Spectator.* 14 Nov. 1994, B5.

How a casino would bankrupt a whole area. John Fraser. *Toronto Star.* 27 Nov. 1994, A2.

Action needed. TB rates among Natives. *Spectator.* 30 Nov. 1994, A8.

Native groups conducted sloppy research, says report. *Spectator.* n.d. 1994, A2.

Canada edging to brink of debt crisis, conference told. Paul Loong. *Spectator.* 1 Dec. 1994, D10.

Justice spending soars. Alanna Mitchell. *Globe and Mail.* 24 Nov. 1994, A12.

The Globe plan: Balancing the budget. Andrew Coyne. *Globe and Mail.* 3 Dec. 1994, D1, D5.

Rock's unheralded new justice for youth. Doug Fischer. *Toronto Star.* 4 Dec. 1994, D4.

Indians vow to stay encamped in offices. Phinjo Gombu. *Toronto Star*. 26 Dec. 1994, A4.
New land plan divides Indians. *Toronto Star*. 26 Dec. 1994, A4.
Solving Native problems, the right way. Editorial. *Spectator*. 26 Dec. 1994, A10.
The truth is no one is owed anything they didn't earn. J.E. Somerville. Letter to the Editor. *Spectator*. 28 Dec. 1994, A10.
A commitment is a commitment, Prime Minister. Full-page ad by the Aboriginal and Treaty Rights Defence Fund. *Globe and Mail*. 30 Dec. 1994, A3.
Native tax guidelines fair, PM says. *Spectator*. 31 Dec. 1994, A11.
PQ policy on Natives linked to sovereignty. *Spectator*. 31 Dec. 1994, A11.
Give Natives own province, study says. Jack Aubry. *Spectator*. 19 Jan. 1995, A11.
$500 m Native debt alarms critics. *Spectator*. 24 Jan. 1995, A6.
Ottawa in no position to give debt lessons. *Spectator*. 25 Jan. 1995, A8.
Develop aboriginal system of justice. Jack Aubry. *Spectator*. 30 Jan. 1995a, B7.
Mayors hope new federal-provincial protocol will avoid land claims protests. Ed Rogers. *Spectator*. 30 Jan. 1995b, B4.
Millions wasted on land claims. *Spectator*. 30 Jan. 1995c.
Editorial. *Sault Star*. 31 Jan. 1995, A4.
Report on Native justice system disputed. *Spectator*. 31 Jan. 1995, A7.
Growing pains for Natives' role in the courts. Catherine Ford. *Spectator*. 4 Feb. 1995, A6.
Swift action needed to fight native suicides, report says. *Globe and Mail*. 10 Feb. 1995, A9.
B.C. wavers on Native concessions. Ross Howard. *Globe and Mail*. 11 Feb. 1995, A1.
Native communities: Working together. *Spectator*. 14 Feb. 1995, A10.
The spirits of Davis Inlet. Sharon Oosthoek. *Spectator*. 14 Feb. 1995, A10.
Canadian Forces soldiers walk a mile in Native moccasins. Peter Moon. *Globe and Mail*. 16 Feb. 1995, A8.
Health care deal with Natives falls through. *Spectator*. 17 Feb. 1995, A9.
Suicide study dangerous, panellist says. Rudy Platiel. *Globe and Mail*. 20 Feb. 1995, A3.
Banished to solitude. Tom Fennell. *Maclean's*. 12 June 1995, 18.
Time to get tough with the natives. Diane Francis. *Maclean's*. 10 July 1995, 11.
Non-Indians abusing Native faiths. *Spectator*. 13 July 1995, A13.
B.C. ends talks on land claim. Rudy Platiel. *Globe and Mail*. 15 July 1995, A4.
Chiefs snub proposal on self-rule. *Toronto Star*. 20 July 1995, A13.
Mercredi misstep. Editorial. *Toronto Star*. 20 July 1995, A22.
Ottawa allows trapnets in bid to end Micmac fish dispute. *Toronto Star*. 20 July 1995, A10.
Indians divided over benefits of blockades. *Globe and Mail*. 29 July 1995, A4.
Enforce the law, now. *Spectator*. 14 Sept. 1995, A9.

Saugeen Ojibwa sovereignty claim termed solid. *Globe and Mail.* 26 Sept. 1995, A10.

$58 million study questioned. Dan Smith. *Toronto Star.* 1 Oct. 1995, A16.

Mercredi blasts constitution bill. *Spectator.* 6 Dec. 1995, A6.

Nisga'a settlement a reason for celebration. Linda Goyette. *Spectator.* 17 Feb. 1996, A7.

PM's past suggests caution. Edward Greenspon and Rudy Platiel. *Globe and Mail.* 22 Nov. 1996, A1.

Vast changes sought to aid natives. Rudy Platiel. *Globe and Mail.* 22 Nov. 1996, A1.

Irwin seeks discussion of proposals for natives. Rudy Platiel. *Globe and Mail.* 23 Nov. 1996, A1.

Out of the past: The native commission. *Globe and Mail.* 23 Nov. 1996, D8.

Where the Aboriginal report takes a wrong turn. Gordon Gibson. *Globe and Mail.* 26 Nov. 1996, A19.

The future of aboriginal peoples. *Globe and Mail.* 30 Nov. 1996, D9.

Native self-government issue divides nation, poll says. Rudy Platiel. *Globe and Mail.* 7 Dec. 1996, A4.

Battle escalates over amendments to Indian Act. Rudy Platiel and Laura Eggertson. *Globe and Mail.* 13 Dec. 1996, A11.

Erasmus defends report on natives. Rudy Platiel. *Globe and Mail.* 26 Dec. 1996, A4.

Natives: Extra-funding idea unpopular. *Globe and Mail.* 15 Jan. 1997, A4.

First Nations chiefs try to save report. Rudy Platiel. *Globe and Mail.* 24 Feb. 1997, A4.

PM, Irwin no-shows at chiefs' conference. Jack Aubry. *Toronto Star.* 24 Feb. 1997, A12.

Aboriginal history is part Proust, part embellishment of the past. Jeffrey Simpson. *Globe and Mail.* 25 Feb. 1997, A14.

Mercredi wants protest day to shame Ottawa into talks. Rudy Platiel. *Globe and Mail.* 25 Feb. 1997, A6.

A view of life that harkens to a golden age for aboriginal peoples. Jeffrey Simpson. *Globe and Mail.* 26 Feb. 1997, A16.

Nicholson, Philip. 1987. *Economic Status of Native Women in Ontario.* Prepared for the Ontario Women's Directorate, Government of Ontario.

Nichter, Mark. 1995. Reconceptualizing the Household and Community: Contribution from Medical Anthropology. Paper Presented to the American Anthropological Association, 18 Nov. 1995, Washington DC.

North Shore Tribal Council, Mamaweswen. 1991. North Shore First Nations Government, Status Report. June.

– 1992a. Regional Health Plan. As submitted to Medical Services Branch, Health and Welfare Canada.

– 1992b. Reference Document. Health Transfer Project.

– 1993. Presentation by the North Shore Tribal Council. Chief Earl Commanda, Chief Jeannie Naponse, and Christopher Belleau. In RCAP 1993a.
– 1994a. Implementation Plan for Human Services Reform. Human Services System Development Project.
– 1994b. Long-Term Care Plan. Prepared by Peter Marks and Associates.
– 1995a. Analysis of Selected Health Issues Using the North Shore Tribal Council Community Needs Assessment.
– 1995b. Diabetes in the First Nations of the North Shore Tribal Council. Report based on North Shore Tribal Council Community Needs Assessment.
– 1995c. Pre–Health Transfer Negotiations.
Northwind Consultants. 1996. *A Framework for the Evaluation of the Aboriginal Healing and Wellness Strategy.* Prepared for the Evaluation Sub-Committee, Aboriginal Healing and Wellness Strategy. 90.
Obonsawin-Irwin Consulting Inc. 1992a. *An Evaluation of the Attawapiskat First Nation Justice Pilot Project.* Ontario: Ministry of the Attorney General.
– 1992b. *An Evaluation of the Sandy Lake First Nation Justice Pilot Project.* Ontario: Ministry of the Attorney General.
O'Neil, John D. 1986. The politics of health in the Fourth World: A northern Canadian example. *Human Organization* 45 (2): 119–28.
– 1988. Referrals to Traditional Healers: The Role of Medical Interpreters. In David Young (ed). *Health Care Issues in the Canadian North.*
– 1989. The cultural and political context of patient dissatisfaction in cross-cultural clinical encounters: A Canadian Inuit study. *Medical Anthropological Quarterly* 3 (4): 325–44.
– 1990. The Impact of Devolution on Health Services in the Baffin Region, NWT: A Case Study. In G. Dacks (ed). *Devolution and Constitutional Development in the Canadian North.* Ottawa: Carleton University Press.
– 1993. Aboriginal Health Policy for the Next Century: A Discussion Paper for the Royal Commission on Aboriginal Peoples National Round Table on Health Issues. Royal Commission on Aboriginal Peoples (RCAP), 1993b.
Ontario. 1987a. *Child and Family Services Act, 1984.* Ministry of the Attorney General.
– 1987b. Response to Indian and Native Services under the Child and Family Services Act, 1984: A Discussion Paper and Proposed Recommendations. Community Services Division. Children's Services Branch. Ministry of Community and Social Services.
– 1988. *Transitions: Report of the Social Assistance Review Committee.* Ministry of Community and Social Services.
– 1991. *Short-term Social Assistance Reforms for First Nations Communities.* First Nations Communities Project Team. Toronto: Queen's Printer.

– 1992a. First Nations Project Team Report. Principal Report on New Social Assistance Legislation for First Nations in Ontario. Toronto: Queen's Printer.

– 1992b. Health (Innovation) Strategies Fund: Project Summaries. Prepared for the Premiers Council on Health, Well-Being and Social Justice. January.

– 1992c. Ministry of Health Aboriginal Programs and Expenditures. Aboriginal Health Office. July.

– 1993. Self-Government and Land Claims Task Group. Ontario Native Affairs Secretariat.

– 1994. *New Directions: Aboriginal Health Policy for Ontario.* Ministry of Health. Toronto: Queen's Printer.

– 1996. *Aboriginal Healing and Wellness Strategy: Annual Report.*

Ontario Federation of Indian Friendship Centres (OFIFC). 1987. *Young Offenders Act Manual: A Native Perspective.* Toronto.

Ontario Métis and Aboriginal Association (OMMA). 1988. *A Process and Priority Agenda for Negotiations between Canada, Ontario and OMMA on Aboriginal Self-Government in Ontario.*

Ontario Native Women's Association, Ontario Federation of Indian Friendship Centres, and Ontario Métis and Non-Status Indian Association. 1983. *Remove the Child and the Circle Is Broken: A Response to the Proposed Children's Act Consultation Paper.* Toronto.

Organization of American States (OAS). 1995. Draft of the Inter-American Declaration on the Rights of Indigenous Peoples. Inter-American Commission on Human Rights. 18 September 1995.

Ortner, Sherry B. 1995. Resistance and the problems of ethnographic refusal. *Society for Comparative Study of Society and History* 10: 173–93.

Painter, Susan Lee. 1986. Research on the prevalence of child sexual abuse: New directions. *Canadian Journal of Behavioural Science* 18 (4): 323–39.

Patrinos, Harry A., and Chris N. Sekellariou. 1992. North American Indians in the Canadian labour market: A decomposition of wage differentials. *Economics of Education Review* 11: 257–66.

Pence, A., V. Kuehne, M. Greenwood-Church, M. Opekokew, and V. Mulligan. 1992. First Nations Early Childhood Care and Education: The Meadow Lake Tribal Council School of Child and Youth Care Curriculum Development Project. *Multiculturalism Magazine* 14 (2/3): 15–17.

Penner Report. *See* Canada. 1983.

Peters, E. 1992. Self-government for Aboriginal people in urban areas: A literature review and suggestions for research. *Canadian Journal of Native Studies* 12 (1): 51–74.

Peters, E., and Mark W. Rosenberg. 1992. *Indian Attachment to the Labour Force.* Ottawa: Indian and Northern Affairs Canada.

Phillips, Sondra B. 1985. Aboriginal Languages in Canada. Paper Prepared for the Secretary of State, Ottawa.

Pinel, Sandra Lee, and Michael J. Evans. 1994. Tribal Sovereignty and the Control of Knowledge. In Tom Greaves (ed). *Intellectual Property Rights for Indigenous Peoples.*

Plain, F. 1985. A Treatise on the Rights of the Aboriginal Peoples of the Continent of North America. In M. Boldt and A.J. Long (eds). *The Quest for Justice.* 31–40.

Plaut, Gunther W. 1993. Value Formation in Children. Working Paper Prepared for the Steering Committee on Children and Youth. Premiers Council on Health, Well-Being and Social Justice.

Ponting, J.R.1986. Institution-Building in an Indian Community: A Case Study of Kahnawake (Caughnawaga). In J.R. Ponting (ed). *Arduous Journey.*

– (ed). 1986. *Arduous Journey.* Toronto: McClelland and Stewart.

Postl, B. et al (eds). 1991. *Circumpolar Health 90: Proceedings of the Eighth International Congress on Circumpolar Health.* Winnipeg: University of Manitoba.

Potts. Gary. 1989. Last Ditch Defence of a Priceless Homeland. In B. Richardson (ed). *Drumbeat.* 203–28.

– 1992. The Land Is the Boss: How Stewardship Can Bring Us Together. In D. Engelstad and J. Bird (eds). *Nation to Nation: Aboriginal Sovereignty and the Future of Canada.* 35–8.

Prairie Justice Research. 1990. *Strategies to Reduce the Over-Incarceration of Canada's Aboriginal Peoples: A Research Consultation.* Regina: University of Regina. School of Human Justice.

Pratt, Alan. 1993. Aboriginal self-government and the Crown's fiduciary duty: Squaring the circle or completing the circle? *National Journal of Constitutional Law* 2: 163–93.

Preston, R. 1966. Edward Sapir's anthropology: Style, structure, and method. *American Anthropologist* 68 (5): 1105–27.

– 1995. Listening to What the People Say: Some Reflections on the Larger Context of Writing What I Found in Translation. Unpublished paper. McMaster University. 1–18.

Price, J. 1990. Ethical Advocacy versus Propaganda: Canada's Indian Support Groups. In James A. Clifton (ed). *The Invented Indian.*

Royal Commission on Aboriginal Peoples (RCAP). 1993a. *Public Hearings and Round Tables.* CD-ROM Folio Database. Ottawa: Libraxis.

– 1993b. *The Path to Healing: Report of the National Round Table on Aboriginal Health and Social Issues.* Ottawa. Canada Communications Group.

– 1993c. *Aboriginal Peoples and the Justice System: Report of the Round Table on Aboriginal Justice Issues.* Ottawa: Canada Communications Group.

– 1993d. *Public Hearings: Overview of the Second Round.* Prepared for the commis-

sion by Michael Cassidy, Ginger Group Consultants. Supply and Services Canada.
– 1993e. *Framing the Issues. Discussion Paper 1.* Supply and Services Canada.
– 1993f. *Focusing the Dialogue. Discussion Paper 2.* Supply and Services Canada.
– 1993g. *Suicide in Canadian Aboriginal Peoples: Prevention Strategies.* Second Suicide Prevention Special Consultation. Ottawa: Libraxis.
– 1994. *Public Hearings. Toward Reconciliation: Overview of the Fourth Round.* Supply and Services Canada.
– 1995. *Choosing Life: Special Report on Suicide among Aboriginal People.* Supply and Services Canada.
– 1996a. *Report of the Royal Commission on Aboriginal Peoples.* Vol. 1. *Looking Forward, Looking Back.* Supply and Services Canada.
– 1996b. *Report of the Royal Commission on Aboriginal Peoples.* Vol. 2. *Restructuring the Relationship: Part One.* Supply and Services Canada.
– 1996c. *Report of the Royal Commission on Aboriginal Peoples.* Vol. 2. *Restructuring The Relationship: Part Two.* Supply and Services Canada.
– 1996d. *Report of the Royal Commission on Aboriginal Peoples.* Vol. 3. *Gathering Strength.* Supply and Services Canada.
– 1996e. *Report of the Royal Commission on Aboriginal Peoples.* Vol. 4. *Perspectives and Realities.* Supply and Services Canada.
– 1996f. *Report of the Royal Commission on Aboriginal Peoples.* Vol. 5. *Renewal: A Twenty-Year Commitment.* Supply and Services Canada.
– 1996g. *Bridging the Cultural Divide: A Report on Aboriginal People and Criminal Justice in Canada.* Supply and Services Canada.
Reimer, Gwen. 1993. Community Participation in Research and Development: A Case Study from Pangnirtung, Northwest Territories. Ph.D. dissertation, McMaster University.
Richardson, B. 1989. *Drumbeat.* Assembly of First Nations. Toronto: Summerhill Press.
– 1993. *People of Terra Nullis.* Vancouver: Douglas and McIntyre.
Riddington, R. 1988. *Trail to Heaven.* Vancouver: Douglas and McIntyre.
Roberts, Simon. 1979. *Order and Dispute: An Introduction to Legal Anthropology.* London: Penguin Books.
Ross, A. 1983. Beatrice. *Canadian Woman Studies* 4 (4): 85–6.
Ross, H. 1988. Customary Care and the Economics of Child Rearing, Phase 1: The Shape of Customary Care. Paper Prepared for Payukotayno and Tikanagan Child and Family Services.
Ross, Marie. 1996. The Relationship between addiction and suicide in Aboriginal women. *Journal of the Society of Obstetricians and Gynaecologists of Canada.* 18 (3): 245–53.
Ross, Rupert. 1992. *Dancing with a Ghost.* Octopus Publishing Group.

– 1994. Managing the Merger: Justice-As-Healing in Aboriginal Communities. Draft Discussion Paper. Aboriginal Justice Directorate.

– 1996. *Returning to the Teachings: Exploring Aboriginal Justice.* Toronto: Penguin Books.

Ross, David P., and E. Richard Shillington. 1989. *The Fact Book on Poverty.* Ottawa: Canadian Council on Social Development.

Rudin, J., and D. Russell. 1993. *Native Alternative Dispute Resolution Systems: The Canadian Future in Light of the American Past.* Toronto: Ontario Native Council on Justice.

Rutledge, Donald. 1993. Education, Justice and Well-Being. Working Paper Prepared for the Steering Committee on Children and Youth. Premiers Council on Health, Well-Being and Social Justice.

Ryan, Joan. 1995. *Doing Things the Right Way: Dene Traditional Justice in Lac La Martre, N.W.T.* University of Calgary Press and Arctic Institute of North America.

Ryan, Joan, and Michael Robinson. 1990. Implementing participatory action research in the Canadian North: A case study of the Gwich'in language and culture project. *Culture* 10 (2): 57–71.

Saddle Lake Tribal Justice Centre. n.d. Proposed Tribal Justice System Statute. Alberta Law Foundation.

Sagamok Anishnawbek First Nation. 1994a. Community Development Planning Session Summary.

– 1994b. Naadmaada Research Project, Community Cultural Research. *The Way.* Unpublished manuscript.

Said, Edward. 1979. *Orientalism.* New York: Vintage.

Sampson, Fiona. 1992. *Aboriginal Children's Law.* Toronto: Ontario Native Council on Justice.

Sarsfield, P. 1988. Health Issues in Northern Canada. In David Young (ed). *Health Care Issues in the Canadian North.* 119–24.

Sawatsky, Len. 1992. Self-Determination and the Criminal Justice System. In D. Engelstad and J. Bird (eds). *Nation to Nation: Aboriginal Sovereignty and the Future of Canada.* 88-97.

Schinke, Steven P., and Robert F. Schilling. 1986. Prevention of drug and alcohol abuse in Amerindian youths. *Social Work Research and Abstracts* 22 (4): 18–19.

Schneider, L. 1992. A Time for Action: Aboriginal and Northern Housing. Fourth Report of the Standing Committee on Aboriginal Affairs. Ottawa.

Schuurman, Lisa. 1994. 'Fenced In': Horden Hall Residential School at Moose Factory. M.A. thesis, McMaster University.

Scott, E., W. McKay, and H. Bain. 1989. From Here to There: Steps along the Way: Achieving Health for All in the Sioux Lookout Zone. Scott-McKay-Bain Health Panel. Toronto.

Scott, James C. 1985. *Weapons of the Weak*. New Haven CT: Yale University Press.
– 1990. *Domination and the Arts of Resistance*. New Haven CT: Yale University Press.
Scott, J.K. 1991. Alice Modig and the talking circles. *Canadian Nurse*. June. 25–6.
Scott, Kim. 1993. Funding Policy for Indigenous Human Services. In RCAP 1993b.
Shields, Craig. 1993. Issues in Family Life and Family Support: A Background Report. Working Paper Prepared for the Steering Committee on Children and Youth. Premiers Council on Health, Well-Being and Social Justice.
Shkilnyk, Anastasia. 1985. *A Poison Stronger than Love*. New Haven CT: Yale University Press.
Silverman, R.O. 1992. *Aboriginal Peoples and Canadian Criminal Justice*. Toronto: Butterworths.
Simpson, Jeffrey. 1994. *Faultlines: Struggling for a Canadian Vision*. Toronto: Harper Collins.
Sioui, Georges E. 1994. *For an Amerindian Autohistory*. Trans. Sheila Fischman. Montreal: McGill-Queen's University Press.
Slattery, Brian. 1991. Aboriginal sovereignty and imperial claims. *Osgoode Hall Law Journal* 29 (4): 681–703.
– 1992. First Nations and the Constitution: A question of trust. *Canadian Bar Review* 7 (2): 261–93.
Smith, D. 1993. *The Seventh Fire*. Key Porter Books.
Smith, Melvin H. 1995. *Our Home or Native Land: What Government's Aboriginal Policy Is Doing to Canada*. Victoria BC: Crown Western.
Smith, S. 1992a. Crime rates plummet when sports camps visit (Northern Fly-In Sports Camp, Manitoba). *Windspeaker* 10 (9): 12.
– 1992b. Indian Affairs targets child welfare. *Windspeaker* 10 (3): 1, 2.
Speck, Dara Culhane. 1989. The Indian Health Transfer Policy: A step in the right direction or revenge of the hidden agenda? *Native Studies Review* 5 (1): 187–214.
SPR Associates. 1989. *An Evaluation of the Ontario Native (Criminal) Courtworker Program*. Don McCaskill, Ted Harvey, and Wayne Warry, for the Ontario Federation of Indian Friendship Centres, the Ministry of the Attorney General, and the Department of Justice Canada, 1–142.
Stenning, P. 1992. *Police Governance in First Nations in Ontario*. Report Prepared for the Negotiators of the Ontario First Nations Policing Agreement. Toronto: Solicitor General of Ontario.
Stephenson, Peter H., Susan J. Elliot, Leslie T. Foster, and Jill Harris (eds). 1995. *A Persistent Spirit: Towards Understanding Aboriginal Health in British Columbia*. Canadian Western Geographical Series, Vol. 31. Department of Geography, University of Victoria.

Stevens, Samuel. 1993. Northwest Territories Community Justice of the Peace Program. In RCAP 1993c. 385–9.

Stuart, C., and L. Gokiert. 1990. Child and youth care education for the culturally different student: A Native people's example. *Child and Youth Services* 13 (2): 253–61.

Taussig, M. 1993. Review comment to George Marcus (ed). *Perilous States.* Chicago: University of Chicago Press.

Taylor-Henley, S., and P. Hudson. 1992. Aboriginal self-government and social services: First Nations–provincial relationships. *Canadian Public Policy* 17 (1): 13–26.

Territorial Court of Yukon. 1992. Regina vs Philip Moses: Reasons for Sentencing. Circle Court Heard before Judge Barry Stuart.

Timpson, Joyce B. 1983. Indian mental health: Changes in the delivery of care in Northwestern Ontario. *Canadian Journal of Psychiatry* 29: 234–41.

Timpson, Joyce B., Susan McKay, Sally Kagegamic, Donna Roundhead, Carol Cohen, and Grace Matewapit. 1988. Depression in a Native Canadian in Northwestern Ontario: Sadness, grief or spiritual illness? *Canada's Mental Health.* June/September: 5–8.

Titely, R. 1989. *A Narrow Vision.* Toronto: University of Toronto Press.

Toulouse, Paul E., and E. Roberts. 1988. The role of Canadian Native health workers in achieving self-government. *Arctic Medical Research* 47 (Supp. 1): 66–9.

Treat, James (ed). 1996. *Native and Christian.* New York: Routledge.

Turpel, Mary Ellen. 1993a. Aboriginal Peoples and the Canadian Charter of Rights and Freedoms: Contradictions and Challenges. Chapter 5 in A.Q. Lodhi and R.A. McNeilly (eds). *Human Rights Issues and Trends.* Canadian Scholars Press. 51–67.

– 1993b. On the Question of Adapting the Canadian Criminal Justice System for Aboriginal Peoples: Don't Fence Me In. In RCAP 1993c, 161–83.

Union of Ontario Indians (UOI). 1987–8. *Native Community Care: Counselling and Development.* Curriculum Materials.

– 1993a. *Strengthening the Circle: A Case Management Program for Native Children, Youth and Family Mental Health.* Prepared by Wayne Warry.

– 1993b. *Strengthening the Circle. Facilitators' Manual.*

United Nations Working Group on Indigenous Populations. 1993–4. Draft Declaration as Agreed upon by the Members of the United Nations Working Group on Indigenous Populations at Its Eleventh Session. In *The Indigenous World 1993–1994.* International Working Group for Indigenous Affairs. 153–64.

Van Esterik, P. 1985. Confronting Advocacy Confronting Anthropology. In Robert Paine (ed). *Advocacy and Anthropology.* Institute of Social and Economic Research, Memorial University of Newfoundland. 59–77.

Van Velson, J. 1969. Procedural Informality, Reconciliation and False Comparisons. In M. Gluckman (ed). *Ideas and Procedures in African Customary Law.* London: Oxford University Press.

Van Willigen, John. 1986. *Applied Anthropology.* New York: Bergin and Garvey.

Vanast, Walter J. 1991. Hastening the day of extinction: Canada, Quebec, and the medical care of Ungava's Inuit, 1867–1967. *Etudes/Inuit/Studies* 15 (2): 55–85.

Waldram, J.B. 1993 Aboriginal spirituality: Symbolic healing in Canadian prisons. *Culture, Medicine and Psychiatry* 17: 345–62.

Waldram, J.B., P. Berringer, and W. Warry. 1992. Nasty, brutish and short: Anthropology and the Gitksan-Wet'suwet'en decision. *Canadian Journal of Native Studies* 12 (2): 309–16.

Waldram, J.B., D. Ann Herring, and T. Kue Young. 1995. *Aboriginal Health in Canada: Historical, Cultural, and Epidemiological Perspectives.* Toronto: University of Toronto Press.

Wallace, Anthony F. 1956a. Mazeway resynthesis: A biocultural theory of religious inspiration. *Transactions of the New York Academy of Sciences* 18: 626–38.

– 1956b. Revitalization movements: Some theoretical considerations for their comparative study. *American Anthropologist* 58: 264–81.

– 1969 (1972). *The Death and Rebirth of the Seneca.* New York: Random House (Vintage).

Wapachee, Chief George. 1993. Models of Community and Individual Enterprises: Income Security Program for Cree Hunters and Trappers. Paper Presented to Economic Round Table, 27 April. In RCAP 1993a.

Ward, J.A., and J. Fox. 1977. A suicide epidemic on an Indian reserve. *Canadian Psychiatric Association Journal* 22: 423–6.

Warry, W. 1986a. *Breaking the Cycle: A Report on the Native Inmate Liquor Offender Project.* Toronto: Ontario Native Council on Justice.

– 1986b. *The Native Inmate Liquor Offender: Program Manual.* Toronto: Ontario Native Council on Justice.

– 1987a. *Chuave Politics.* Political and Social Change monograph no. 4. Canberra: Research School of Pacific Studies.

– 1987b. *Notes on the Implementation and Evaluation of the NILO Pilot Projects.* Ontario Native Council on Justice.

– 1988. *Curriculum Plan: Social Competence and Deviant Behaviour.* Native Counselling and Community Care Program, the Union of Ontario Indians and the Association of Iroquois and Allied Indians.

– 1990. Doing unto others: Applied anthropology and Native self-determination. *Culture* 10: 61–73.

– 1991a. Alternative Justice Systems for Native Communities: Lessons from Papua New Guinea. Proceedings of the Commission on Folk Law and Legal Pluralism, Ottawa, 14–18 August 1990. Vol. 2: 841–58.

– 1991b. Ontario's First People. In Laura Johnson and Dick Barnhorst (eds). *Children, Families and Public Policy in the 90s.* Toronto: Thompson Educational Publishers. 207–30.
– 1992. The Eleventh thesis: Applied anthropology as praxis. *Human Organization* 51 (2): 1–13.
– 1993. Unfinished Dreams: Suicide, Self-Determination and Community Healing in Aboriginal Communities. Research Paper Prepared for the Royal Commission on Aboriginal Peoples. RCAP 1993.
Warry, W., and T. Moffat. 1993. The Health of Aboriginal Children. Paper Prepared for the Premiers Council on Health, Well-Being and Social Justice.
Wattie, Brenda. 1989. The Mental Health of Children in Aboriginal Communities. Paper Presented to the Conference on Children's Services in Ontario. November. Sparrow Lake, Ontario.
Weaver, Sally. 1984. Indian Self-Government: A Concept in Need of a Definition. In Leroy Little Bear, Menno Boldt, and J. Anthony Long (eds). *Pathways to Self-Determination.* Toronto: University of Toronto Press. 65–8.
– 1986a. Indian policy in the new Conservative government, Part 1: Nielsen Task Force of 1985. *Native Studies Review* 2 (1): 1–43.
– 1986b. Indian policy in the new Conservative government, Part 2: Nielsen Task Force in the context of recent policy initiatives. *Native Studies Review* 2 (2): 1–43.
Webber, Jeremy. 1993. Individuality, Equality and Difference: Justifications for a Parallel System of Aboriginal Justice. In RCAP 1993c. 133–60.
Weller, G., and P. Manga. 1988. The Feasibility of Developing an Integrated Health Care System in the North: The Case of Northwestern Ontario. In David Young (ed). *Health Care Issues in the Canadian North.* 140–50.
Wenzel, G. 1991. *Animal Rights: Human Rights.* Toronto: University of Toronto Press.
Westermeyer, J., and J. Neider. 1984. Predicting treatment outcome after ten years among American Indian alcoholics. *Alcoholism: Clinical and Experimental Research* 8 (2): 179–84.
Wharf, Brian. 1989. *Toward First Nation Control of Child Welfare: A Review of Emerging Developments in B.C.* Victoria: University of Victoria.
Willms, D.G., P. Lange, D. Bayfield, M. Beardy, E.A. Lindsay, D.C. Cole, and N. Arbuthnot Johnson. 1993. A lament by women for the people, the land [Nishnawbi-Aski Nation]: An experience of loss. *Canadian Journal of Public Health* 83 (5): 331–53.
Wilson, B. 1985. Aboriginal rights: The Non-status Indian perspective. In M. Boldt and J.A. Long (eds). *The Quest for Justice.* 62–8.
Yassie, Robert. 1993. Navaho Justice Experience – Yesterday and Today. In RCAP 1993c. 407–16.

Yates, Alayne. 1986. Current status and future directions of research on the American Indian child. *American Journal of Psychiatry* 144: (9): 1135–42.

York, Geoffrey. 1992. *The Dispossessed.* Toronto: Little, Brown.

York, Geoffrey, and Loreen Pindera. 1991. *People of the Pines.* Toronto: Little, Brown.

Young, David, and Leonard L. Smith. 1992. *The Involvement of Canadian Native Communities in Their Health Care Programs: A Review of the Literature since the 1970s.* Edmonton: Canadian Circumpolar Institute / Centre for the Cross-Cultural Study of Health and Healing, University of Alberta.

Young, T. Kue. 1979. Changing patterns of health and sickness among the Cree-Ojibwa of Northwestern Ontario. *Medical Anthropology* 3 (2): 192–220.

– 1983. Mortality pattern of isolated Indians in Northwestern Ontario: A ten-year review. *Public Health Reports* 98: 467–75.

– 1988. *Health Care and Culture Change: The Indian Experience in the Central Subarctic.* Toronto: University of Toronto Press.

Young, T.K., E.J. Szathmary, S. Evers, and B. Wheatley. 1990. Geographical distribution of diabetes among the Native population of Canada: A National survey. *Social Science Medicine* 31: 129–39.

Young, T.K., and G. Sevenhuysen. 1989. Obesity in northern Canadian Indians: Patterns, determinants, and consequences. *American Journal of Clinical Nutrition* 49: 786–93.

Zion, James W. 1993. Taking justice back: American Indian perspectives. In RCAP 1993a.

Index